M000281479

the

ROYAL ROUTE
TO HEAVEN
— *and* —
Blessings Out of Buffetings

ALAN REDPATH

CONTENTS

THE ROYAL ROUTE TO HEAVEN

PART I DISCIPLINE FOR THE JOURNEY

PART II DANGERS ON THE JOURNEY

Part III Dynamic for the Journey

CONTENTS

BLESSINGS OUT OF BUFFETINGS

the

ROYAL ROUTE
TO HEAVEN

FOREWORD

I always appreciate coming to a study in Scripture and knowing Alan Redpath will be one of my resources.

His insight and thought development never seem to come from a denominational predisposition. He is honest, impartial, and uncompromising in his perspective.

You can tell he has been before the Lord with his study.

I've read and reread his commentaries on First and Second Corinthians. For the amount of time you invest reading, you get great returns from Redpath.

The truths he develops are timeless. It's like he's watching the news in 2007 as he makes application. He makes the Word come alive. He always gets to the heart. The point of his sword is inescapable.

Lord, give us more Alan Redpaths.

Joe Focht
Senior Pastor
Calvary Chapel Philadelphia

PREFACE

The contents of this book represent the theme of messages preached from the pulpit of Moody Church over a period of several months. They do not claim to be in any sense a scholarly exposition of Paul's first letter to the Corinthian church. Such must be left to a far more gifted pen than mine. My only claim to justify their publication is the attempt to deal with what, in my judgment, is the priority need of the church today and to do so from a heart that has been deeply burdened with the urgency and relevance of the truths contained in these chapters.

If the reader turns to this book for greater understanding of the doctrines of the faith, he may well be disappointed. If, however, he turns with a hungry heart to which God has revealed the shallowness and ineffectiveness of the church in the world today, it will be my fervent hope he will find in these pages that which will be both food and fire.

We often hear it said that the church of today is at once unique in the wealth of its equipment and in the bankruptcy of its enduement. To recognize this is one thing. To take action about it is quite another, and this is something that can be personally painful and costly. Yet in the light of the judgment seat of Christ, how can we possibly allow things to go on as they are? Words could never express how grateful to God I would be if He could in some way use this volume to bring His people from the byways and blind alleys, along which Satan has driven so many, to commence the triumphant march along the royal route to heaven.

It would be lacking in courtesy were I not to bear testimony to the many hours of work on manuscripts that have been spent both by my beloved wife and Miss Arline Harris, to both of whom I owe a great debt of gratitude, and without whose consecrated efforts this book could never have been published.

Alan Redpath
Moody Memorial Church,
Chicago, Illinois

THE ROYAL ROUTE TO HEAVEN

There's a royal route to heaven—
Will you travel it today?
'Tis the path of full surrender
All along the homeward way.
It is yielding every moment
To the blessed Savior's will,
Seeking only for His glory,
And His purpose to fulfill.

There's a royal route to heaven—
'Tis the way the Savior trod.
'Tis the path of full surrender
And the deep, sweet peace of God.

There's a royal route to heaven—
They who travel it may know
Peace that passeth understanding
Which the Father doth bestow.
Dead to self and its desires,
Living unto Christ alone,
Finding joy and satisfaction
Which the world has never known.

There's a royal route to heaven—
Which will bring a rich reward
When the last long mile is covered
And we face our loving Lord.
Oh, how small will seem the trials
Of the steep and rugged way
When we stand in His blest presence
At the close of life's brief day.

—Avis B. Christiansen

PART I

DISCIPLINE FOR THE JOURNEY

CHAPTER ONE

RESOURCES FOR
THE JOURNEY

I CORINTHIANS I:I–9

The title *The Royal Route to Heaven* implies that there may be other roads leading to the same destination. We find that to be true before we journey far in this first epistle to the young church at Corinth. There is, of course, only one starting point in the Christian life: Calvary, where the sinner meets his Savior and is ransomed, healed, restored, and forgiven. But beyond that starting point may occur many deviations from the plan of God; in this letter the apostle Paul warns us of some of them.

It is possible for a Christian to live on a carnal level instead of on a spiritual level. It is possible to walk after the flesh even though we are converted to walk in the Spirit. It is possible to be saved, but to be saved as by fire: one day to stand before the judgment seat of Christ stripped of everything but our soul's salvation. On the other hand, there is a royal route to heaven, and the word "royal" implies sovereignty. In the Christian life, it means placing the crown where it rightly belongs: on the Savior's brow. That is the main burden of these messages.

I am not interested in getting to heaven by the skin of my teeth, are you? My one desire is to get there by the grace of God, after a useful life in which the purpose of the Lord in saving my soul has been fulfilled.

This Corinthian letter exposes the tragedy of low-level Christian living, and reveals the glory of a journey made under the sovereignty of Jesus Christ. Before we launch into a detailed study, here is a telescopic view of the route we are going to follow.

The city of Corinth was a Roman colony on Grecian soil, the seat of Roman government for the area, and a center of Greek commerce. A proud and wealthy city, it has been called the "Vanity Fair" of the Roman Empire. Indeed, the word "Corinthian" came to be a synonym for loose living. These Greeks were notorious for their shallowness. They loved to argue just for the sake of argument; they were very proud of their knowledge — in fact, they thought they knew everything!

In such a place Paul had planted the seed of the gospel. Arriving there after a shattering experience at Athens, he later declared, "I determined not to know any thing among you, save Jesus Christ, and him crucified" (2:2). He stayed in Corinth eighteen months preaching the gospel (Acts 18:1–18), then he visited there again on his third missionary journey (Acts 20:2–3). At that time he became deeply burdened for these converts, and subsequent letters brought him distressing news of sin in the Corinthian church (1:11).

Now here is a psychological point I would like to underline: in spite of the sin in their midst, these people had the audacity to write and ask theological questions of Paul. When people come for spiritual advice, I find they very rarely mention the real root of the problem. Instead, they will ask a variety of theological questions. But it is not long, if you know anything of the art of diagnosis, before you discover that behind the whole thing there is, more often than not, tragedy. That is exactly what happened with the church at Corinth.

Therefore Paul did not hurry to answer their questions. Not until chapter 7 did he say, "Now concerning the matters about which you wrote" (RSV). In the first six chapters he deals with the situation that existed in Corinth. He goes right to the root of the trouble first, before he answers their theological questions.

To analyze this letter briefly, we find that the first eleven chapters deal with carnality. He exposes the tragedy of their living in sin and worldliness, and applies the positive remedy of the cross of Jesus Christ. Then, as if he has had enough of it, he says, "Now, concerning spiritual gifts" (12:1), and he lifts us up to the tremendous heights of the gospel of resurrection and life. The last five chapters of this epistle deal with spirituality, and are constructive. For every aspect of carnality, Paul prescribes the dynamic remedy of the full message of the gospel.

There is a great deal of preaching today that does not follow Paul's example here: preaching the gospel of forgiveness of sins which is not accompanied by preaching on deliverance from s-i-n. That was the whole trouble with the church at Corinth: they knew all about the forgiveness of sins; there was nothing wrong with their theology, but a great deal wrong with their practice. They did not understand the gospel of deliverance from s-i-n, and that is the thrust of Paul's letter to them.

After this brief glimpse of the background, we now commence a more detailed study. We watch how this great missionary preacher approaches a church that is living on such a low level. He might have been indignant; he might have lashed out at them, but we find he doesn't do that. Paul adopts the tactics of the Master Himself, tactics which the Lord would have us all practice in such a situation, I'm sure. He lifts up the believers by reminding them of the glory of their salvation and of the great privileges that are theirs in Christ.

Will you notice with me, therefore, as we come to grips with this epistle, how Paul reminds them of their relationship to God? Then he reviews their equipment for the journey and their resources as Christians traveling this road. He begins by emphasizing his authority: "Paul, called to be an apostle of Jesus Christ through the will of God" (1:1). Although they do not recognize the school from which he came, he reminds them that he is speaking as an apostle, a "sent one," because he is in the will of God.

Then he addresses them as "the church of God which is at Corinth" (1:2). The Greek word *ecclesia* (translated "church") means "called ones," and they were the "called-out of God" in Corinth. They were not to cringe in fear before ungodly people, but to live as those called into the only position of authority any Christians can have in a pagan world: a position of dignity and power in Jesus Christ. He Himself said, "I will give unto thee the keys of the kingdom of heaven: and whatsoever thou shalt bind on earth shall be bound in heaven: and whatsoever thou shalt loose on earth shall be loosed in heaven" (Matthew 16:19).

In the next phrase Paul writes, "to them that are sanctified in Christ Jesus, called saints," not "called *to be* saints," as we have the verb inserted in the Authorized Version. This is what they are in the sight of God, His separated ones, "called saints." In the remaining portion of verse 2 he opens it up to include every one of us: "with all that in every place call upon the name of Jesus Christ our Lord, both theirs and ours."

Here they were, God's called-out people in Corinth, and here we are also, given a flaming message to proclaim, the good news of redemption in Christ Jesus. Here is the gospel for a city with all its corruption and licentiousness, vice and ignorance—a gospel that is completely adequate for every situation when it is intelligently preached and intelligently understood. This letter is addressed not just to a few people in Corinth, a city that is now in ruins, but to the church of Jesus Christ in any city of the world in any era of history, even the times in which we live. We are God's separated, called-out ones to a position of authority, that is to say, a position in which we are supposed to know what we believe, to live it and proclaim it. That is the only way through which others can find the living Christ. We may be called, also, as was the church at Corinth, to live in a city notorious for its corruption and licentiousness, but that is a sphere in which the church, by contrast, should shine at its brightest.

"Called out"—that is our relationship to God and His message. To those who are in that wonderful position the Lord gives resources for the journey that are "abundantly above." You find Paul listing them for us, beginning in verse 3: "Grace be unto you, and peace, from God our Father, and from the Lord Jesus Christ. I thank my God always on your behalf, for the grace of God which is given you by Jesus Christ." Here the Holy Spirit points out to us that double spiritual power which, if we understand and appropriate it, will be adequate for everything that we can ever meet in life. What is it? "Grace and peace" (1:3).

If I asked you to define the word "grace," perhaps you would say, "It is the undeserved lovingkindness of God which has met us in our sin and need." Yes, grace is that, but it is far more than that. It comes, as Paul says here, from God our Father through the Lord Jesus Christ: God the Father is the source and Jesus Christ is the channel through whom it comes. Grace, therefore, is His life of purity and holiness; His death that was sufficient to pay the price for our sins; and His present ministry by which He imparts the Holy Spirit today, enabling us to die to sin and live in His power.

It seems to me that "grace" in the New Testament is that which brings into our lives everything that delights the heart of God. There is grace to make me like the Master, grace to give me triumph when otherwise I would fail, grace to make me patient where I would be impatient, grace to enable me to glorify the Lord Jesus in every situation. Are you concerned about pleasing God today? Let me remind you that He has already placed within you that possibility: His life, His character, His Spirit.

The second word, "peace," does not imply laziness or inactivity. It is movement without friction, creating perfect harmony. It also means balance and unity which result from every part of your life being centered upon doing the will of God. These two inner powers God has given to each one of His children. If we are Christians, therefore, and have begun to travel this royal route to heaven, we have some tremendous potentials.

Not only have we been given grace and peace, but other wealth, also. "That in every thing ye are enriched by him, in all utterance, and in all knowledge" says the apostle in verse 5. Here we take a backward look to the moment of our conversion, when we were *enriched*. When we came to Jesus Christ, He imparted to our life spiritual wealth that is going to be revealed "in all utterance and in all knowledge." We have a message to proclaim, for God has given us His gospel to preach, His Word to live by, His life to live out—"all utterance." He has given to us the Holy Spirit, the great Discerner of truth, by whose wisdom and strength we can understand and appropriate the grace of God and the riches of our Lord Jesus Christ—"all knowledge."

We should pause here to remind ourselves that these promises are to all the church of Jesus Christ. This is the purpose of our salvation; here is the vantage ground that God has gained when He saved you and me. His convincing argument to the world is the Christian who is possessed and indwelt by the Spirit of God. It is only through your life and mine that God can do things in our neighborhoods that He could not accomplish otherwise. That is His way of working, the way in which His sovereign purpose is fulfilled—through a people to whom He has made Himself known, a people who have enlightenment from the Word of God, a people whose very lives demonstrate that the God in whom they believe is alive because He dwells within them.

That possibility should be a very solemn, challenging thought to our hearts: to know that God has a beachhead in us, that He intends to do something with our lives that He would not accomplish apart from His Spirit dwelling with each one of us. Therefore, regardless of the amount of theory or intellectual understanding you may be acquiring, the conclusive argument for His gospel of redemption is your life and mine in the place where God has put us.

Then let me ask you to notice the tremendous privilege that is ours as Christians, which is defined in the ninth verse: "God is faithful, by whom ye were called unto the fellowship of his Son Jesus Christ our Lord."

You will recall a verse near the end of this letter, where Paul writes, "Therefore, my beloved brethren, be ye steadfast, unmovable, always abounding in the work of the Lord, forasmuch as ye know that your labour is not in vain in the Lord" (15:58). Apart from greetings, that is the end of his letter, and it seems as if that verse goes right back to this one in the first chapter: "God is faithful ... *therefore* be ye steadfast, unmovable." How can we be steadfast? Because God is faithful, and He has called us into the fellowship of His Son. This is the priceless privilege of the Christian life.

The Greek word for "fellowship" here is *koinonia*, which means having everything in common. It is the thought of communion together, of mutual understanding. We who have been enriched, made wealthy by the grace of God so that our lives may reveal Christ to others, experience this tremendous privilege of having everything in common with our Lord. We are in partnership with Him, if you like.

A partnership is a business relationship, but it is also a family tie. A husband or wife may refer to the other one in their marriage as their "partner," because they have all things in common. At least, that is God's intention; His plan is the sharing of all interests. We have the same thing in our Lord Jesus Christ. Your interests are His: your mind and its development, your body and its sanctity, purity and holiness, your spirit and its graciousness, tenderness and love. Your concern is to be His glory, the wonder of His person, the majesty and greatness of His power. Your constant ambition should be not only to learn about doctrine, but to know Him. His interests are in your development, your progress, your growth. Your interests are to be in the glory of the sovereignty of Christ.

There should be not only mutual interests, but mutual devotion. How wonderful to know that all the resources of Christ are yours! "In him dwelleth all the fulness of the Godhead bodily. And ye are complete in him" (Colossians 2:9–10). What a breath-taking verse that is! All your resources are His: your personality, your possessions, your abilities, whatever they are. That is the completeness of communion: all He has belongs to you, and all you have (which is so little at best) belongs to Him. That is the response He is seeking from His children.

As we set out on this royal route to heaven, we have the resources of grace and peace; we are enriched in all utterance and in all knowledge; and we are given this great and precious privilege of partnership with Christ. All He has is at your disposal now, and His desire is that all you have should be at His disposal now and always. Are you in that living, vital relationship with the Lord Jesus today?

CHAPTER TWO

DIRECTION
DECIDES DESTINY

1 CORINTHIANS 1:10–18

In 1 Corinthians 1:18 the revised versions render more correctly the Greek verbs: they indicate continuous action in the present. "For the preaching of the cross is to them that *are perishing* foolishness; but unto us that *are being saved*, it is the power of God." Here we have two contrasting experiences of life: "being saved," and "perishing." Paul highlights them for us, showing us that neither of them is static, that both suggest movement, a journey along some road. The category to which each one of us belongs is quite clearly defined by our attitude toward the message of the cross: "…to them that are perishing, foolishness; but unto us that are being saved, it is the power of God."

In its context, we find this tremendous statement set against a church situation which was full of strife, envy, and a divisive spirit. "I am of Paul," said some. "And I of Apollos," said others, or "And I of Cephas." Still others were saying, "I don't belong to any of them. I am not a denominationalist: I am of Christ" (1:12).

To that Corinthian church, split by this party spirit and demonstrating all the evidences of immaturity, Paul has taken a stand: "I determined not to know any thing among you, save Jesus Christ, and him crucified" (2:2). In this significant epistle you will find that Paul constantly brings his hearers back to the cross. He is convinced that the answer in each controversy and to every failure, as well as all hope for the future, is "the word of the cross."

First, we consider these two conditions which Paul describes for us here: perishing and being saved. To comprehend the meaning of that dreadful word, "perishing," we need first to fully understand the meaning of the words "being saved."

These days the word "salvation" is rather like a well-worn coin, which is being passed from hand to hand until it is almost unrecognizable. In many instances it has been reduced to a convenient little formula, and if you fit the formula you are all right. But in the New Testament sense, the word "salvation" has both a negative and a positive implication. Negatively, it means being saved from danger, being made secure; positively, it is emancipation from sin: sanctification. It is deliverance from guilt and the forgiveness of all our sins by virtue of the blood of Jesus Christ our Lord shed for us on Calvary.

Joy abounds in a forgiven sinner as he realizes the blessedness of his experience. He is very glad to be able to announce to everybody, "I have been saved!" But it is not long before such a man begins to recognize that the sins from which he has been forgiven are only the symptoms of a disease that goes far deeper. Soon he begins to cry out to God, "Is there no deliverance from this fire still burning in my life, this untamed passion in my soul?" He prays from the depths of his heart in the words of the psalmist, "Create in me a clean heart, O God!" (Psalm 51:10).

Can his prayer remain unanswered? Is the man forgiven from his past sins to continue to live unsatisfied, defeated, impure? Let me remind you that the pardoned man does not change his circumstances, neither his home conditions nor his job. He does not run away from his past situation in life—if he attempts to do so, he cuts the very nerve of the refining process that would make him a saint. But in his life he begins to discover that the demands upon him as a Christian are absolutely overwhelming; they are impossible for him to meet by himself. There comes from his heart a deep cry, "O God, give me power—power over myself, power over my sin, power over what I am by nature." He is a forgiven sinner, but he is a defeated man.

Am I exposing a basic need in your life? Are you conscious of feeling that you are only half delivered? You know you have forgiveness from sins, but there is a cry in your heart, "Is there no answer to the problem of what I am?"

In the New Testament sense of the word, "salvation" is not merely a negative thing, the forgiveness of sins. That which leaves a man stumbling and defeated, impure and unholy, is an incomplete and imperfect redemption. Praise God, salvation is more than this! When the Lord saves a man He does not bar the gate through which sins enter and attack him, but He opens the gate through which Holy Spirit power can come in to make him holy. When God saves a soul, He does not simply blot out the memory of past sin—it is that, thank God. Nor does He simply see that man with a righteousness that Christ imputes to him—it is that, thank God, but it is not only that! Salvation is positive: taking a man who has been twisted and bent by the disease of which sins are the symptoms and causing him to glory in complete deliverance.

Now let us look at the second word, "perishing." It means entire failure to be what God intends a man to be: the disease of sin running its course unchecked. It indicates an increasing distance from God, a gradual sinking into depravity, a withdrawal of the only source of real happiness and power. It is the drift downward in spite of all the efforts made to pull oneself up.

Each one of us is in one or the other of these categories: either we are being delivered from the disease of self and sin, or we are becoming more sinful and more selfish and more depraved in spite of all our self-effort.

But notice, in the second place, that both "being saved," and "perishing" describe a continuing process. Life is pictured for us here as something that is moving and active. In the New Testament we have the great idea of salvation considered from at least three different points of view. Sometimes it is spoken of as having been accomplished in the past, "Ye have been saved." That describes the initial act of faith in the blood of Jesus Christ as Savior. Again it is spoken of as in the present, "Ye are being saved," as in verse 18. Sometimes it is relegated to the future, "Now is our salvation nearer than when we believed" (Romans 13:11). But there are many passages which describe salvation as a continuous experience, running through life, such as "By one offering he hath perfected forever them that are [being] sanctified" (Hebrews 10:14).

One thing that will characterize the life of every genuine believer in the Lord Jesus, truly born of the Spirit of God, is growth, development. He will not talk about having arrived; he does not say he has had a tremendous second experience of sanctification; he would not boast in his holiness, nor exalt his own experience, but there are evidences of his growth in his behavior. As he is more and more filled with the Spirit, he grows more gracious, more gentle, more Christlike, and as we stand back and watch his life, we see God working a miracle. As the clay in the hand of the potter, so the man's life is being molded, shaped, and conformed to the image of the Lord Jesus.

May I say kindly, yet firmly, that unfortunately many professing Christians show no evidence of such growth at all. In fact, do I exaggerate if I dare to say that it is the majority of them? They may have been saved, perhaps, for twenty years, but they are still as mean, hot-tempered, selfish, jealous, unkind, impure, and worldly as ever. There are no marks of maturity, no evidences of becoming more like the Lord Jesus.

The moment we accept forgiveness through the blood of the Lord Jesus we are obligated by bearing His name to stand for righteousness, purity, and holiness. Our business in life is to seek to win somebody else for Jesus; the redemptive ministry of the love of God should be expressed through our lives in service to others. That is the mark of the real thing. How desperately we all need power to stand for the right, power to speak for the Lord Jesus, power to live for Him day by day.

Just as "being saved" is a constant process, so is "perishing." It is becoming more and more interested in worldly things, accepting defeat and compromise without blushing. How many who have professed to be Christians for a long time find it so much easier now to submit to things that are selfish, mean, and worldly!

Paul describes salvation as a process that is going on constantly. Therefore, it is not only registering a decision for Jesus that evidences your destiny; it is the direction of your character. Perhaps that decision has even brought you into Christian training or some form of ministry, but if it is not accompanied by direction of character, there is room to question whether or not it is authentic. The Bible tells you to examine yourself, whether you be in the faith (2 Corinthians 13:5).

May the Holy Spirit challenge your heart with this New Testament description of real salvation! What has been the trend of your character in the past twelve months? Your body comes to church, maybe to teach a Sunday school class. You listen to sermon after sermon, but deep down in your own soul, is there progress into the Lord or regress into sin? Do you have increased hunger for truth, for holiness, for righteousness, for the Lord Himself? Or is there carelessness and worldliness and superficiality, an easy slipping into habits that you never dreamed you would allow a year ago?

We make constant progress along one road or the other, but what is the determining factor? What guides our direction and governs our destiny? It is the "preaching of the cross." Now let us be careful that we understand what that phrase means. It does not mean the act of preaching, itself. We have here the Greek word *logos*, the same word that is in the first chapter of the Gospel of John: "In the beginning was the Word, and the Word was with God, and the Word was God ... and the Word was made flesh..."(John 1:1, 14). It is "the *word* of the cross."

When we speak, so often we express just a dream, a wish, a desire. When God speaks, He speaks with authority and conviction; "the word of the cross," which God proclaims, is power and action on a divine scale.

I heard an eminent professor of theology say to students in his seminary class, "Gentlemen, I ask you to remember that you are called upon to know something of the foolishness of preaching, not the preaching of foolishness." In my heart I retorted, "He is wrong! The word of the cross is absolute foolishness." It says so in my text: to those who are perishing, the word of the cross is foolishness. It stands in contradiction to all the philosophy, education, and knowledge of this world, for the preaching of the cross puts the sentence of death upon them all. It is the word of absolute power, but it is also the word of absolute weakness.

With the shoes off our feet, and with heads bowed reverently, let us go up a green hill outside a city wall and hear the word of the cross: "Father, forgive them; for they know not what they do" (Luke 23:34). Here is a cry of unutterable anguish from the heart of our Redeemer, coming through pain and suffering, but the prayer was heard!

"Today shalt thou be with me in paradise" (Luke 23:43). A dying Man, crucified and helpless, turns to a fellow sufferer and speaks the word of victory, and the word was heard!

"Woman, behold thy son. [Son,] Behold thy mother" (John 19:26–27). Heartbreak and loneliness, a sword going into the soul of Mary, but the concern of her Son in the hour of His death introduces her to a new and wonderful relationship.

"My God, why hast thou forsaken me?" (Matthew 27:46). Alone in the darkness, utterly cut off from God, He is introducing a countless multitude to glory; this is victory through isolation.

"I thirst!" (John 19:28). Out of the agony of lips that are parched there flow rivers of living water to men and women like you and me.

"It is finished!" (John 19:30). Obedient unto the very death of the cross, Jesus Christ fully accepted all the will of God. He has been forsaken by friend and foe, but now it is all finished, the price is paid, the last drop of the cup is drunk. The outcome — resurrection!

What is the word of the cross in your life and mine? It is power through weakness, life through death, resurrection through crucifixion. What does that involve in terms of personal experience? How can you make contact with that word of the cross? It is only when you get to the end of every attempt to do anything without Jesus Christ, when you lay aside your ambitions, crucify your prejudices, die to your so-called intellectual approach, and humble your pride that you can look up into His lovely face and say, "Lord Jesus, I live; yet not I ..." (Galatians 2:20).

It may sound easy to say, but it is mighty hard to face! We have to get to the place where we can say to Him, "O Lord, I yield to Thee. I am willing to be nothing. I recognize that this self in me with all its pride, its haughtiness, its self-righteousness and self-importance is only worthy of crucifixion." At the moment we agree with His knowledge of ourselves, then we come into contact with His throne and begin to touch omnipotence and receive power.

If you need to get rid of impure thoughts, burn the books and pictures that incite such thoughts. If you would break the habit of drink, throw it all out of your house. If you want to touch the power of the cross, cut off every friendship that is leading you into sin; stop every habit that is pulling you down. Look into the Lord's face and say, "Lord, I know this thing is sin. I am going to get rid of it today, and I will never allow it again."

Which direction are you going? Deep down in your heart is the direction downward? You may be a Sunday school teacher or a Christian worker of long standing, and you want desperately to touch the place of omnipotence and stop the drift. Outwardly you are one person, but inwardly you are quite another. Outwardly you are perhaps theologically correct and sound, but inwardly far away from God. Now you want to look up into the face of the Lord Jesus and tell Him that you agree with His verdict upon self, your utter weakness and bankruptcy.

It is time to take action. Are you prepared to break that unworthy friendship? Are you prepared to finish with that habit, leaving no possible line of retreat? Are you prepared to go to your room and clear out those books and trashy magazines that only incite you to sin? "There-fore ... let us cleanse ourselves from all filthiness of the flesh and spirit, perfecting holiness in the fear of God" (2 Corinthians 7:1).

> Cleanse me from my sin, Lord;
> Put Thy power within, Lord;
> Take me as I am, Lord, and make me all Thine own.
> Keep me day by day, Lord;
> Underneath Thy sway, Lord;
> Make my heart Thy palace and Thy royal throne.
>
> *— R. Hudson Pope*

CHAPTER THREE

Down Peacock's Feathers!

1 Corinthians 1:19–31

The heading given to this chapter is not original. It is the title of a book written by an Episcopalian minister, a commentary on a prayer in the Church of England prayer book called "The General Confession," which begins, "Almighty and most merciful Father, we have erred and strayed from Thy ways like lost sheep." In the most amazing language, this prayer gives expression to the bankruptcy and helplessness of man's best—all that we can ever be apart from the grace of God and the redemption that is in Jesus Christ our Lord.

Such is the major theme of Paul's message to the church at Corinth: down with pride of intellect, down with self-confidence—"He that glorieth, let him glory in the Lord" (1 Corinthians 1:31).

This letter is addressed, as the second verse of this chapter tells us, to "the church (*ecclesia*) of God which is at Corinth." They would have known what he meant by "the *ecclesia* of Corinth," because that was the title given to the civic authority of that day, those called out from among the population of Corinth to administer the affairs of the city. "The *ecclesia* of God," by analogy, is the called-out of God, the church which has been redeemed in Jesus Christ our Lord, in order that through them the will of God may be made known and the authority of heaven be brought to bear upon the world.

Corinth was known for its divisions and party spirit, for its philosophy, and at the same time for its sinfulness. Boasting of its culture, the city was bankrupt in its morality. And the greatest tragedy was that the spirit of Corinth was invading the church. This little group of believers, instead of attacking the city in the name of the Lord, was being infiltrated by the worldliness of Corinth. Instead of representing the authority of Christ there, they were being overwhelmed by the pagan city and their testimony was becoming completely devitalized. Instead of bringing to bear upon that city the transforming power of the gospel, the Christians were succumbing to the sin around them.

Speaking to this church that was being conquered by the spirit of the age in which it lived, Paul emphasizes the dynamic transforming power of the word of the cross. Right through this chapter he contrasts two things: wisdom and foolishness, the wisdom of men and the foolishness of God, then the foolishness of men and the wisdom of God. "The wisdom of words," in verse 17 is set against "the preaching of the cross" or "the word of the cross" in verse 18.

The wisdom of words was the thing that had seduced this church. Earlier in this chapter we noticed how the party spirit had crept into the church, bringing divisions and arguments. Paul turned upon them and asked three piercing questions: "'Was Paul crucified for you?' 'Is Christ divided?' 'Were you baptized in the name of Paul?'" He didn't answer them; they were intended only to point out how ridiculous was their spirit of division, which had eaten into the testimony and power of the church.

The remedy for the situation, Paul insists, lies not in philosophy, but in the revelation of the Son of God by the Holy Spirit in their lives. The moment a Christian, or a church, departs from the principle of revelation and goes into high criticism or intellectual understanding of the Bible, all spiritual authority is lost.

This is very relevant to the days in which we live and to the land in which we live. Instead of attacking a city in the name of the Lord, the very spirit of the city gets into the life of the church. The local church becomes full of party strife and division, and believers become materialistic. The Bible is approached on the basis of "What I cannot understand I will discard." If we submit the Word of God to our own intellect and refuse to believe in the possibility of absolute authoritative revelation, the church loses its power and authority. And if it loses its ability to say, "Thus saith the Lord," it has no answer to the problems of our times.

If the church in our day is to invade a city for God, then it must get back to a place of absolute dependence upon the wisdom of God. But what is the wisdom of God? The translation in the margin of the American Standard Version (the revision of 1901) is, "Christ Jesus, who was made unto us wisdom from God, both righteousness and sanctification and redemption" (1:30). The wisdom of God, therefore, seems to sum up the whole thing; it is given to establish righteousness and to produce sanctification and holiness.

Notice Paul's scornful words in verses 27 and 28: "God hath chosen the foolish things of the world." Yes, the wisdom of God is utter foolishness to the worldly philosopher, to the self-opinionated, clever person. "God has chosen the things that are base and despised." Certainly righteousness was despised in a city like Corinth. "God hath chosen the things that are not to bring to nought the things that are"—the things that are not: redemption, deliverance from all that separates us from the presence of God; sanctification, being made into the likeness of Jesus Christ. Against all their cleverness and ability, their philosophy and education, their helplessness to do anything about the sinfulness of the city in which they lived, God puts His wisdom, which is the message of Calvary: His righteousness, His sanctification, His redemption.

For us today there is this tremendous contrast. On the one hand we have the opportunity of seeking to meet the need of the day by human intellect and education. On the other hand, we have access to the wisdom of God, which leaves men with absolutely nothing to glory in, for "he that glorieth, let him glory in the Lord." There faces all of us this choice, these two principles, and the tragedy today is that very largely the church has chosen its own wisdom and lost its power.

We must look a little more closely at what is meant by this definition of God's wisdom: righteousness, sanctification, and redemption. What is this word, "righteousness"? Here is the wisdom of God, for it means that somehow God is able to take hold of a life that is twisted and broken, sinful and defeated, immoral and down-and-out, and to make it conform to the standard of His Son. He is able to make the crooked life straight; He is able to make a broken life whole. The life that is marred, sinful, impure, unholy, by the miracle of His grace He can remake into the image of Christ.

The righteousness of God is not just a dry doctrine, but the act that brought a holy God down from the throne of heaven to the manger at Bethlehem and then to the cross of Calvary, in order that He might rescue us and bring us to Himself, cleanse us from sin and make us whole. To use a theological phrase, it means Christ *imputed* to me. That is, the moment I cease from my own effort and trust the living Christ for salvation, from that moment God sees me as in the righteousness of Christ Himself. When I am prepared to come into Calvary as a guilty, sinful man, knowing that there is nothing I can do, and that I am utterly dependent on God's grace for forgiveness—at that moment He makes me right.

However, that is not the last word of Christian experience, but the first. Just as you formed habits that led you to failure and sin until now, when you accept God's righteousness you will begin to form habits that lead you into the holiness of His image and into His purpose for your life. That is Christian living, and it is no easy thing.

There is no short cut, and therefore we have the second word, "sanctification." This is the wisdom of God which means not only that Christ is imputed to me, but that the life of Jesus is *imparted* to me. I recognize that I am separated for God's will and service, and therefore I must be yielded to Him for whatever He may want me to do. This growth into the likeness of the Lord is slow. I know that is true, not because I look at other people, but because I have to live with myself seven days a week.

But perhaps it need not be as slow as it is. Two Christian men were talking together, and the first one said, "I am so glad that God knows our frame, and He remembers that we are but dust."

"Yes," replied his friend, "but do you really think we ought to be as dusty as we sometimes are?"

That was a good answer! That is why our progress in Christ is often so slow. We remain in the dust when we have no business to be there. We allow Satan to keep us down when we ought to be growing in the likeness of the Lord Jesus.

I would interject a thought here. There is nobody in all God's universe who is more orthodox than Satan—he knows all the truth, every bit of it. And you too can know the truth like that, and still not be a believer. The test of genuine faith in Christ is that there is submission to Him and growth into His likeness. The evidence that you are saved is that you begin to look with the eyes of Christ, you begin to love with the heart of Christ, you begin to think with the mind of Christ. Because the living Christ is in you, His character begins to express itself through you.

The third word is "redemption," a word that occurs only eleven times in the New Testament. On each occasion it is used in reference to that tremendous day when we will find ourselves in the very presence of our Lord, when we are fully redeemed. There is a sense in which a man is redeemed the moment he is forgiven, but there is a great deal yet to be done in the man. "Now are we the sons of God," says the apostle John, "and it doth not yet appear what we shall be: but we know that, when he shall appear, we shall be like him; for we shall see him as he is" (1 John 3:2). Redemption is the completion and fulfillment of all the purposes of God. Surely that is the wisdom of God. There is no other answer to the world's need except the wisdom of God that can make a man right and pure, and one day will take him, in the very image of the Lord Jesus, into the presence of the Father, spotless and faultless. What other hope is there than that?

What had all the intellect at Corinth done to meet the situations of human need? What had they accomplished? "Where is the wise?" asks Paul. "Where is the scribe? Where is the disputer of this world?" (1:20).

It is an amazing and tragic thing that when emphasis on philosophy, intellect, and ability seeps into the life of the Christian church and into our Christian service, we discover ourselves with no authority, no spiritual power, nothing that we can do to bring blessing to a soul. But when the living Christ comes into my life, somehow the desert of my heart begins to blossom. The man who has been paralyzed by sin, helpless and down in the dust, is taken hold of by the Spirit of God, and is made anew. That is the wisdom of God and the power of God.

The righteousness of God puts a man back in the center of God's will. The sanctification that God brings to a man makes him grow day by day in the likeness of the Lord. The redemption of God one day will lift him faultless into the very presence of God. That is the message of the cross.

Perhaps somebody has been thinking, "Now does this mean that I just scrap my brains altogether? Are we supposed to become robots that never do any thinking for ourselves?" Of course it doesn't! It just means that if you want an enlightened mind upon the Word of God, you have to live a crucified life; that's the principle.

During the last century we have talked about the spread of modernism and neo-orthodoxy as if those things were new. But they are as old as the New Testament. The moment a man begins to put his confidence in his own mind, in his ability to understand the Word of God, in his personal criticism of the Scriptures, he is finished as far as divine revelation is concerned. But if he is prepared to come to the cross, if he is prepared to take the place of death with Christ, if he is prepared to glory in the Lord and not in himself, that man will have an enlightened mind upon the Word of God that can challenge any philosopher. God gives the illumination of His Spirit into the life that is crucified with Christ at Calvary.

Are we supposed to ignore the problems that confront us? No, but half a dozen men on their knees for sixty minutes, waiting upon the Lord with the absolute conviction that they have no answer, that their human ideas and programs are ineffective and bankrupt—they will accomplish more than fifty men around a table discussing their problems for a whole year.

Where God can find a little group of crucified men, upon those men He will give the enlightenment of His Spirit upon every problem that might threaten to overwhelm them. That is not only true in Christian work, it is true in your home life, in bringing up your children—to every practical problem of life, the answer is the wisdom of God. "He that glorieth, let him glory in the Lord," says Paul.

You have two alternatives before you. One is the philosophy of men, depending upon human intellect, human ability, pushing your way through, determined at any cost to get to the goal you set before yourself. Or you can take your achievements, intellect, talents, and put them all in one scale—and in the other, the wisdom of God, in which a man glories not in himself but in the Savior. You must choose the principle on which you will guide your life, on which you will study and work, on which you will serve the Lord. May we each say, "Not I, but Christ" (Galatians 2:20).

CHAPTER FOUR

STANDING IN THE POWER OF GOD

1 CORINTHIANS 2:1–10

The statement, "I determined not to know any thing among you, save Jesus Christ, and him crucified" (2:2), should be for us all, not a record of achievement but, humbly before God, the desire of our hearts in our ministry for Him. That is the way the course of the ship of the church (or the life) must be set to catch the breeze of the Spirit of God from heaven.

That brings me right to the very heart of the message of this portion of Scripture. Paul is addressing himself to a situation which, humanly speaking, is far too big for him — a situation in which many a preacher has found himself ever since. He sees in Corinth what I would call, in the first place, a mission to be fulfilled: "That your faith should not stand in the wisdom of men, but in the power of God" (2:5).

In a city like Corinth, so full of human pride and sin, Paul knows perfectly well that the little group of Christians cannot face the challenge of presenting Christ if their faith is based only on intellectual assent. Their faith must stand on the rock of revelation rather than on the sands of human philosophy. Nothing but the miracle of the grace of God revealed in lives transformed by the Spirit of God can ever convict a Corinth. If these young Christians lack reality, they will crumble under the pressure and be sucked into the quicksand of sin around them. Corinth is far too clever for them, and far too sinful; therefore their faith must stand in the power of God and not in the wisdom of men.

This is Paul's concern for the young church, the mission that as preacher, servant, and ambassador of the cross, he knows must be fulfilled, or else the outcome will be disaster. Somehow the little band of believers must confront that great city with the reality of their faith, proving that their message is something that God has communicated to them from heaven itself.

That is equally true today. Whether or not we realize it, if you and I are even to survive as Christian people (putting it on the lowest level), let alone live triumphantly in Christ, a theoretical presentation is totally inadequate. The world we live in is too clever and sinful for that and if we have nothing more, we will be sucked under by the whirlpool of philosophies and "isms," the tides of sin and vice.

"We have this treasure in earthen vesssels," says Paul, "that the excellency of the power may be of God, and not of us" (2 Corinthians 4:7). These earthen vessels are helpless and weak in themselves and in the battle of life we must stand "By the word of truth, by the power of God, by the armour of righteousness on the right hand and on the left" (2 Corinthians 6:7). In other words, we must recognize our own weakness, even glory in it, that the power of Christ may rest upon us.

Oh, that our world may feel the impact of faith—your faith and mine—that stands in the power of God! So that in whatever circumstances of testing you may live, others will see in you the miracle of standing not only in the power of God, but also in the authority of God. As you live, surrounded by every possible evil influence that would contrive to pull you down in this wicked age, you have a mission that must be fulfilled, to stand in the power of God. It is dependent upon your acceptance of the verdict of Calvary, of the bankruptcy of self and the futility of anything untouched by the power of God the Holy Spirit.

How can our mission be fulfilled, then? By the message we have to proclaim: "I determined not to know any thing among you, save Jesus Christ, and him crucified" (2:2). The emphasis Paul intends is this, I think: "not to know anything among *you* save Jesus Christ, and him crucified." That is his theme for Corinth, and that should be the theme of all preaching today. It must be the message of your life in your circumstances, the principle of your life if you are to stand in the power of God.

I would remind you that Paul had come to Corinth, as he says himself, in weakness, in fear, and in much trembling. He had come to the European continent for the first time and his reception had not been very pleasant. He was imprisoned at Philippi, smuggled out of Thessalonica, driven out of Berea, and when he reached Athens and started to argue with them on the basis of their agnosticism, he accomplished very little. He was pressed in spirit as he came to Corinth, and God Himself had to encourage him: "Be not afraid, but speak, and hold not thy peace: For I am with thee, and no man shall set on thee to hurt thee: for I have much people in this city" (Acts 18:9–10).

Knowing the strength of Corinthian wisdom and the character of that city, the depths of its sin and the tremendous boast of its intellect, he determined that he would not argue or debate with anybody, but present the crucified, risen Lord in the conviction that what Jesus said was absolutely true, "And I, if I be lifted up from the earth, will draw all men unto me" (John 12:32). So the man must get out of the picture, the personality of the preacher become obscured, and the Lord be at the center of all. "For we preach not ourselves, but Christ Jesus the Lord; and ourselves your servants for Jesus' sake" (2 Corinthians 4:5). The Lord gets the glory, and the result is absolutely convincing: "My speech and my preaching was not with enticing words of man's wisdom, but in demonstration of the Spirit and of power" (2:4).

The principle here is as true today as it was then. First there must be a life willing to efface itself, to retreat from its imagined cleverness and wisdom, from its own efforts to stand against the pressure. There rests upon such a life the anointing of the Spirit of God, with this tremendous result that faith shall stand, not in the wisdom of man, but in the power of God.

When Paul says, "I am determined not to know any thing among you, save Jesus Christ, and him crucified," quite obviously he is excluding other things. What were they? "The Jews require a sign and the Greeks seek after wisdom: But we preach Christ crucified" (1:22–23). Slowly but surely today—and I say this with a deep conviction of heart—God is driving the church into a corner from which there is no escape. There are various alternatives which we have tried in place of this message—I am not speaking of the message that Christ died for our sins, but that of our death to sin in Jesus, the message of a crucified life. The poor, cheap, noisy substitutes which the church has tried in place of that message are being exposed for the paltry, futile things they really are. Along with all the so-called progress there is the most alarming spiritual decline. The church has never had better machinery, neither has the church ever been so helplessly ineffective in meeting the problems of the day.

One by one the gadgets are dropping out of our hands when we are recognizing their spiritual ineffectiveness. God is stripping from us every false hope and making us face reality. He is teaching us these days that nothing less than the outpouring of the Holy Spirit in revival can ever meet the need. God is trying to tell us that our currently popular version of Christianity—comfortable, humorous, superficially interesting, worldly-wise—is exposed for the irreverent presentation that it is of the Gospel of Christ.

When revival comes, we shall find our lives revolutionized and our values turned upside down. Do you know why revival tarries? Because God does not take our praying seriously when we behave the way we do in public. When our confidence is in gimmicks, programs, schemes, and planning, and we have not learned to seek first the Lord in the power of God the Holy Spirit, in brokenness at Calvary, we inevitably go on being defeated and losing the battle. May the Lord drive us into that corner, so that we will fall before Him and say, "Lord, I would know nothing except Christ and Him crucified."

One might equally well say, "I am determined to know everything in Christ and Him crucified." This is not excluding something, but including everything that really counts, for the message of the cross includes everything to meet the need of the human heart. Of course, it does not meet the demands of an entertainment-crazy generation that is seeking for a sign, but a preacher is commissioned to give people, not what they want, but what they need. No man has any business to be in a pulpit to entertain; he is there to present Calvary in all its fullness of hope and glory.

When Jesus Christ was asked for a sign to prove His authority, He replied by saying, "An evil and adulterous generation seeketh after a sign; and there shall no sign be given to it, but the sign of the prophet Jonas" (Matthew 12:39). As Jonah was three days in the fish, so the Son of Man would be three days in the heart of the earth.

Dare we say the message of Calvary is not good enough today? It goes straight to the bottom of your need and mine. It brushes aside the superficial; it exposes sin for what it really is. And when a man or woman, fellow or girl, is prepared to accept the verdict of Calvary upon pride, self-sufficiency, and intellect, and to come trusting and resting entirely upon the cross, there falls upon his or her life the anointing of the Spirit of God. Their testimony then is not in their own faith and wisdom; they do not have to meet men on the basis of human philosophy, but stand in the power of God and with the anointing of the Spirit.

When you are prepared to meet Jesus at Calvary He will drive you into a tight corner. Has He put you on the spot? Has He put you into some desperate experience? You try to wriggle and squirm to get out of it, but the Lord is relentlessly holding you there until you learn that your wisdom is useless and your philosophy has no answer, and that you are helpless to stand against the current of temptation until you learn to cling to Him.

Once you are determined to know nothing in this particular situation (whatever it may be) but Christ and Him crucified, then you are also saying, "By the grace of God, in Christ and Him crucified I have everything."

"That's all very well," you may be saying to me, "but I'm afraid of putting it into practice. Suppose I let go and let God, what then?"

Then there is a mystery to be revealed. "Eye hath not seen, nor ear heard, neither have entered into the heart of man, the things which God hath prepared for them that love him," says Paul. "But God hath revealed them unto us by his Spirit" (2:9–10).

The preaching of the cross, the living out of this Christian life day by day, is not unintelligent: "we speak wisdom among them that are perfect [i.e., full-grown or enlightened]: yet not the wisdom of this world ... but ... the wisdom of God in a mystery" (2:6–7). The Christian is not a fool, although the world may frequently think he is. He has an enlightened mind, and he is speaking wisdom to those who can understand, "speaking the wisdom of God in a mystery."

What is a mystery? Is it something you cannot understand? No, in Scripture a mystery is something that once was hidden but now is revealed: "God hath revealed them unto us by his Spirit" (2:10). When the Lord Jesus comes to dwell in your life, your eyes are opened, your ears are unstopped, and you begin to understand some of the things that God has prepared for you. What are they? Jesus said, "I go to prepare a place for you ... I will come again, and receive you unto myself; that where I am, there ye may be also" (John 14:2–3). Hope of heaven, and the resources of heaven down here, also: "The mystery which hath been hid from ages and from generations, but now is made manifest to his saints: To whom God would make known what is the riches of the glory of this mystery among the Gentiles; which is Christ in you, the hope of glory" (Colossians 1:26–27).

Persecuted, harassed, distressed Christian, God has not left you to fight the battle alone. "I will not leave you comfortless [orphans]," said the Lord. "...The Holy Ghost, whom the Father will send you in my name, he shall teach you all things. ... Peace I leave with you, my peace I give unto you" (John 14:18, 26–27). Peace, hope, heaven—these are some of the things that God has prepared for them that love Him, things He has revealed unto us by the Spirit that "searcheth all things, yea, the deep things of God."

Wonderful truth—the Christian has the life of God in him! He has access to the One in whom, says the Word, "dwelleth all the fullness of the Godhead" (Colossian 2:9); the One "in whom are hid all the treasures of wisdom and knowledge" (Colossians 2:3), for all that is in Jesus, and He is in you. That is the mystery which the Holy Spirit reveals to the life that has confessed its bankruptcy and is shut up to the mercy of God.

In the light of what has been said, which course are you going to follow? Are you so operating in your sphere of Christian service that you may expect revival? With your confidence in Him, are you living your life, conducting your program, and thinking about your problems in such a way that you may expect the Holy Spirit to come in power at any moment? Or, secretly, is your confidence in the flesh and in the machinery of human effort? In what do you glory? Where do you place your trust?

Let us be realistic. Are you prepared to change gears? Do you recognize your bankruptcy? Are you willing to place no confidence in the flesh, to step out of the place of frustration and despair, anxiety and futility, into the place where the Holy Spirit can come with anointing and with power? Then look up to Him and say, "Now, Lord, it's up to You."

There must be no false gods, nor misplaced confidence in something or someone, no secret boast that says, "I can pull it off; I can see it through." No compromise, no unconfessed sin, no theoretical faith, no unsurrendered life, no critical spirit, no unbroken heart, no worldliness, no self can be allowed—*nothing*! For "I determined not to know any thing among you, save Jesus Christ, and him crucified."

CHAPTER FIVE

WHICH CLASS ARE YOU TRAVELING?

I CORINTHIANS 2:11–3:6

There is a unique factor in the Christian gospel which makes all talk about comparative religions utterly beside the point, in my opinion. The life of the Founder of our faith inhabits the personality of every person who trusts Him for salvation; every child of God has living within him God the Holy [Spirit]—not an influence, but the Third Person of the Trinity.

"If any man have not the Spirit of Christ, he is none of his," said Paul in Romans 8:9. And in 1 Corinthians 6:19, "Know ye not that your body is the temple of the Holy Spirit?" Therefore every Christian—no matter how weak and feeble, how poor and helpless, perhaps with a sense of utter inability and frustration—whatever his own personal feeling may be, is indwelt by the Third Person of the Trinity. The Holy Spirit has come into our lives so that we might develop character; the "fruit of the Spirit" in Galatians 5:22 is character-fruit, the reproduction of the character of Jesus Christ.

We ought to hang our heads in shame as we ask ourselves, "Why is it that so little of His life is produced in us and so much of ourselves still remains?" The answer to that question is in the verses we are to study here.

Paul introduces us to two different kinds of Christian life. He says in 3:1, "I, brethren, could not speak unto you as unto spiritual, but as unto carnal, even as unto babes in Christ." Please notice the word "brethren";

he is writing to those who are born again of the Spirit of God and who are within the Christian church. Here are two different classes of people, both of them Christian, both of them born of the Spirit of God, but one of them is designated "carnal," and the other, "spiritual."

I would remind you that Paul describes yet another kind of person in 2:14, the "natural man." Of him Paul says that he "receiveth not the things of the Spirit of God; for they are foolishness unto him." This, of course, is the unbeliever, perhaps the charming pagan, the intellectual agnostic, or the nice religious sort of well-educated person, but still the "natural man." Because he is "natural," he does not understand the things of the Spirit of God, having never been born into the family of God.

Now the tragedy is that many who profess to be Christians react so often on the level of the "natural man." You have heard Christian people say something like this: "You know, Mrs. X said something utterly untrue about me—it was only natural that I should be angry." "Only natural"—exactly! And unfortunately there are those born of the Spirit of God who, in terms of daily life and reactions, are still living in the natural realm. Though latent within every child of God is the possibility of reproducing the character of Jesus Christ, the fact is that this is not always accomplished. Why? Because too many Christians continue to live on the carnal level.

In the first place, a carnal Christian is living a life of perpetual conflict and repeated defeat: "For ye are yet carnal: for whereas there is among you envying, and strife, and divisions, are ye not carnal, and walk as men?" (3:3). The fellowship of the Corinthian church was split by envy, strife, and divisions—Paul calls it "carnality." But what a group of Christians are in their fellowship is simply the reflection of what they are individually. Therefore, here is a statement of the condition of a Christian life that is lived on a carnal plane.

Remember the language of Paul back in Romans? "What I would, that do I not; but what I hate, that do I" (Romans 7:15), and later on in the same chapter: "...when I would do good, evil is present with me. For I delight in the law of God after the inward man: But I see another law in my members, warring against the law of my mind, and bringing me into captivity to the law of sin which is in my members" (Romans 7:21–23).

That whole chapter is a portrait of the carnal Christian. Within him there is a constant conflict, a moment by moment battle between two natures, the one spiritual and the other carnal. He is forgiven, he is born again, he is living as a child of God within the fellowship of the Christian church, but he is desperately unhappy. Occasionally the Spirit of God gets the victory, but the perpetual habit of his life is downward, away from God into sin and failure. Although indwelt by the Holy Spirit, he is mastered by the flesh.

Does that describe you today? Is your experience perpetual conflict and repeated defeat? You may be rejoicing in the forgiveness of sins, but you find no power over the principle of sin in your life. Therefore you are often torn by envy, strife, and division; there is no song of joy on your lips, no spring in your step, no light in your eyes, no radiance on your face. The carnal Christian has left the world he used to live in and entered into a new experience, a new area of fellowship, but he cannot enjoy it because he is defeated: constantly fighting and constantly going down.

Another mark of the carnal Christian is that he is living a life of protracted infancy and retarded growth. Paul calls these Corinthians "babes in Christ," saying, "I have fed you with milk, and not with meat: for hitherto ye were not able to bear it, neither yet now are ye able" (3:1–2).

It is a very wonderful experience when a baby comes into a home, but it is a tragedy if the child does not grow. What are the characteristics of a baby? In the first place, he is absolutely dependent upon other people. He cannot walk; he has to be helped up. He cannot feed himself; another has to feed him. And he is only happy, really, when he is the center of interest.

So it is with the carnal Christian. He is always leaning on other people, always seeking this preacher and that leader for spiritual counsel. He cannot walk by himself; he always has to be propped up. You get him going for a little while and you think, "Praise the Lord, he has got through at last!" But before long he is down again, because he is dependent upon human friends and Christian fellowship to see him through.

He cannot feed himself, either. His minister is a kind of spiritual milk bottle that feeds him on Sunday, but that is all he gets. He has not learned to feed himself upon the Word of God, and therefore he does not grow spiritually. Of course, if he is the center of interest, then he is happy, but he is very sensitive and touchy, quickly angry if he is criticized. He constantly displays the marks of protracted infancy and retarded growth.

A third mark of the carnal Christian is that he is living a life of fruitlessness and worldliness. "Every branch in me that beareth not fruit, he taketh away" says the Lord in John 15:2, "and every branch that beareth fruit, he purgeth it, that it may bring forth more fruit."

I am not speaking of outward success, but the genuine New Testament fruit in terms of character and Christlikeness. The carnal Christian is one who spends too much time with his television and neglects his Bible. He is more interested in novels than in the Word of God. You do not find him very often at a church prayer meeting; nor is he in the heart of the fellowship of the church. He is not reliable; he will sometimes work at a job in the church, but will very easily quit and someone has to take his place at the last minute. Quite obviously his heart is still mostly in the world, and there is an atmosphere of worldliness about him. The carnal Christian is a child of God, born again and on his way to heaven, but he is traveling third class.

Do you find yourself looking into a mirror? This is not my description, but that of the Word of God. The carnal Christian may believe what he ought to believe, may even have been trained in doctrine; he may know his Bible in some measure, theoretically, at least. But his life is constant conflict and defeat, infancy and retarded growth, fruitlessness and worldliness. It is possible to live all your life like that: the Holy Spirit within you grieved, quenched, and powerless to do anything through you because you live on a carnal level.

Then what are the marks of a spiritual Christian? What does Paul say about him? "He that is spiritual judgeth all things, yet he himself is judged of no man" (2:15). In other words, you cannot explain him. I would suggest, in the first place, that he is living a life of perpetual conflict but repeated victory. Did I say conflict? Yes, I did; there is no place in the Christian life free from inner conflict, not until we get to heaven.

But there is a sense in which the conflict of a spiritual Christian is fought on a higher plane than that of the carnal Christian. "For we wrestle not against flesh and blood, but ... against spiritual wickedness in high places" (Ephesians 6:12). The spiritual Christian—the man who is going on with God and who is determined to be as pure and godly as a man saved by grace can be—that man is the focal point of the attacks of the devil. He knows never a moment's release from the heat of the battle. But in the midst of the conflict, the spiritual Christian knows a deep and absolute peace in his heart, "the peace of God, which passeth all understanding" (Philippians 4:7). Throughout the constant temptation and battle, he is trusting, resting, and conquering in the Lord Jesus Christ.

It is not that such a man does not commit sin, but that he does not practice the habit of sin. It is not that he does not slip, but rather that it is always possible for him not to do so. He is sometimes very conscious of failure, but the trend of his life is not downward, but upward; the habit of his life is victory and not defeat. The spiritual Christian can say with Paul, "In all these things we are more than conquerors through him that loved us" (Romans 8:37), and "Thanks be unto God which always causeth us to triumph in Christ" (2 Corinthians 2:14).

Another mark of the spiritual Christian is a life of progressive growth and radiant Christlikeness. It would be wrong for me to suggest that the Christian who is living on a spiritual plane is the kind of person who goes about saying, "Well, now I have arrived." This man knows that he can glory in nothing save in the cross of Jesus Christ our Lord. But as you watch, as you observe him day by day, you see evidences of growth in holiness and purity, in temperance and grace, in meekness and gentleness—likeness to the Lord Jesus. There is the fruit of the Spirit instead of the working of the flesh.

In the midst of the testings of life, deep down in his heart there is peace; he is drawing upon infinite resources that are sufficient to strengthen and keep him, to enable him to walk with God. Day by day, as he reacts to troubles, misunderstanding, and heartaches, his actions all glorify the Lord Jesus.

A third mark of the spiritual Christian in the Word of God is that he is bringing forth permanent fruit. "I have chosen you, and ordained you, that ye should bring forth fruit, and that your fruit should remain," said the Lord Jesus in John 15:16. There is something about the spiritual Christian that is constantly revealing faithfulness. There is character that is being formed; it is not simply what he says, but that back of what he says there is a life that is real. Just as the carnal Christian reveals worldliness, so the spiritual Christian reveals a life of separation to the Word of God and devotion to the Master.

Are you a believer, knowing you have received forgiveness of sins? Then in which class are you traveling along the road to heaven? Are you a carnal or a spiritual Christian? Is it perpetual conflict and repeated defeat in your life or is it perpetual conflict and repeated victory? Is it protracted infancy and retarded growth, or is it development in Christlikeness of life and character? Is it a life of pathetic fruitlessness, or is it a life filled with permanent fruit for the glory of God?

If this mirror of God's Word reveals that you are traveling "third class," then how do you move into "first class"? How can you move into the life that is spiritual?

May I give you a simple threefold statement of principle by which, if you are prepared to follow it, you may begin to live your life on another level; you may move from carnality and defeat into spiritual victory and power? This is not something that happens as the years go by, something into which you grow automatically. This crisis is as real and definite as was the moment of your conversion, when you passed out from "condemnation" into "no condemnation," out from guilt into forgiveness, out of alienation from God into adoption as His child.

In the first place, it is the crisis of cleansing: "If we walk in the light, as he is in the light, we have fellowship one with another, and the blood of Jesus Christ his Son [keeps on cleansing] us from all sin. ... If we confess ours sins, he is faithful and just to forgive us our sins, and to cleanse us from all unrighteousness" (1 John 1:7, 9).

The trouble with the carnal Christian is that he is unclean. God demands that we face this fact; things that are allowed to continue in our lives which are contrary to the nature of the Spirit of God: worldliness, faithlessness, lack of growth are marks of uncleanness.

He is "the Spirit of truth" (John 14:17). When a Christian continues acting a lie or professing to be something he is not, God demands that such sin be dealt with.

He is "the Spirit of faith" (2 Corinthians 4:13). The Christian who is not trusting in God to deliver him from the root principle of sin goes on being a carnal Christian. God demands complete trust and commitment.

He is "the Spirit of grace" (Hebrews 10:29). Do you allow bitterness in your life? Are you harboring resentment against another child of God? Then you are continuing that which is not of Christ, but of the enemy.

He is "the Spirit of holiness" (Romans 1:4). Do you allow in your life that which is unholy? "Know ye not that your body is the temple of the Holy Ghost?" (6:19). What sort of traffic has been going on in the temple of your life?

He is "the Spirit of glory" (1 Peter 4:14). Are you allowing worldly affections and desires to go on, unchecked? Are you living for His glory, or are these things, the hangover of unconverted days, still part and parcel of your life? It will take a crisis to deal with them. You cannot deal with them one by one; they are far too many: by the time you deal with one little sin here, one big sin there, another one breaks out somewhere else.

Perhaps the Spirit of God has been speaking to you about these things. Confess them to Him and trust Him for cleansing, for when the Holy Spirit convicts of uncleanness, then the blood of Jesus is applied.

The next condition of moving into "first class" is surrender, the surrender of your body: "I beseech you, therefore, brethren … that ye present your bodies a living sacrifice" (Romans 12:1). If you would move by a definite crisis experience out of the wilderness into the land of blessing, there must be confession that leads to cleansing, surrender that brings power upon the life, faith that secures the anointing of the Spirit of God.

Surrender says, "I present my body." Faith says, "Christ now lives in me." Surrender says, "Lord, what wilt Thou have me do?" Faith says, "I can do all things through Christ, which strengthens me." Surrender crowns Christ as Lord of my life. Faith appropriates Jesus to *be* my Life. Therefore surrender is one step, but faith and appropriation is the other.

I ask you again, in which class are you traveling to heaven? The Lord can enable you to take the step of faith that appropriates Jesus Christ to be your life and lifts you from the class of carnality to that of spirituality, in which it is no more you, but Christ in you, the hope of glory.

CHAPTER SIX

THE CHRISTIAN'S CHARACTER

1 CORINTHIANS 3:7–23

Paul's letter to the church at Corinth deals with the carnality which revealed itself in many different ways. They had written to him asking certain questions about church government, but not exposing their real need—typical, so often, of people who seek counsel. In the first few chapters of this letter Paul is making them face the reality of the sin in their lives so that he might point them forward to spiritual attainment that they might grow into fullness of blessing in Christ.

What, then, is his line of emphasis in such a situation? We do not find it to be a word of anger nor denunciation. Rather, he shows these believers what they are in the sight of God, pointing out to them the purpose for which Jesus died, rose again, and ascended into heaven: that they might become a people worthy of His name.

In the midst of all their strife and failure, he reminds them of what they really are: "Ye are God's husbandry; ye are God's building" (3:9); "Ye are the temple of God" (3:16); "ye are Christ's, and Christ is God's" (3:23). They were God's possession, so why should they live on such a low level? The problem, so often, in the life of a Christian is to achieve his true character, to outgrow "babyhood" and move into the spiritual maturity in which God intended him to live.

One of the marks of carnality in the Corinthian church was their worship of leadership, personified in Paul and Apollos: "I am of Paul," and "I am of Apollos." It was a church divided by loyalty to people.

Speaking of himself and of Apollos, and of the others who were subjects of hero worship in this church, Paul says, "We are [but] labourers together with God." In other words, "Why bring us into the situation? We are only God's messenger boys; we simply do what He tells us to do and don't ask any questions. That is what *we* are, but *ye* are God's husbandry."

In the margin we read, "ye are God's tillage"—God's field, if you like. "I have planted, Apollos watered," says Paul, "but God gave the increase. So then neither is he that planteth any thing, neither he that watereth; but God that giveth the increase" (3:6–7). In that field there must be plowing and sowing and watering before there is a harvest. Paul and Apollos had planted the seed and watered it, but they could not make it grow; only God could do that.

We are reminded, of course, of the parable of the sower in the gospel of Matthew. A man went out to sow the seed, which was the Word of God, and some fell by the wayside and the fowls came quickly and devoured it. Other seed fell on a stony ground where there was not much soil, so that it sprang up quickly and was scorched. Other seed fell among thorns and thistles, and although it grew for a little while, it soon became choked out. And still other seed fell on good ground and brought forth fruit.

After speaking this parable, the Lord Jesus took His disciples, who alone could understand Him, and explained it to them. He said that the seed which fell by the wayside is like the man who does not understand the Word which has been given to him, so he does not heed it, and the fowls of the air snatch it away—it never comes into his life and character. Then there is seed that has been sown in rocky ground, and it has sprung up quickly because it has no depth of soil. This is the man who receives the Word joyfully for a while, but because he is superficial and shallow, the Word has never taken lodging; it has been scorched by the trials of the day, and the man has never grown. The third category is the seed which was sown among thistles and thorns, the cares of this world and the deceitfulness of riches which choked the Word. But there is yet another, the man who receives the seed into good ground. His heart is prepared and hungry for it; he has taken it all in gladly. It has been planted, watered, and there is fruit: thirtyfold, sixtyfold, and a hundredfold.

Now to bring my illustration back into the context of this chapter: Paul says to the Corinthian church, "Ye are God's husbandry." All he has done is to plant the Word and water it, but the life-giving principle is not from the one who plants, nor from the one who waters, but in the seed. It will grow according to the way in which it is sown and the way in which you receive it.

The seed may be received carelessly and heedlessly. It may be choked by the pressure of worldly cares, or ambition, or riches. It may be received on dry, hard ground, where it cannot take root, and quickly disappears. Or it can come into a heart that is wide open for all that is of God in Jesus Christ: the seed is fallen into good ground and brings forth fruit abundantly.

Twenty-five per cent of the seed in the parable brought forth fruit; the rest was wasted. I wonder if that is not a fair average. There are some in whose lives the seed has been planted, but it has not been understood; the principle of life in Jesus Christ seems vague and unreal: the Word is snatched away and forgotten. There are others who have received it gladly, with much emotion and many tears; the Word has sprung up quickly, but because there is no root, the plant has been scorched, and they are not growing, for they have not grasped the principle of it.

Others have listened amid the pressure of many cares and responsibilities. How hard it has been to sort it all out, to shake free from the things that pull in many directions! The Word has been received with a hungry heart, but the deceitfulness of this world's goods has choked it. However, there are some who have received the Word with open hearts; they have been like a plant watered by the rain, growing under the sun and bringing forth much fruit.

Whatever our state, we are God's field, and He is looking for the harvest. One day the great Husbandman is coming to take the harvest of our lives. Everything depends upon how we have received the seed—not upon the preacher, nor any man who has planted or watered.

Another mark of carnality in the church was their lack of growth: Paul calls them "babes in Christ. I have fed you with milk, and not with meat ... for ye are yet carnal." He reminds them, however, that even in that protracted spiritual infancy, "Ye are God's building." All he had done was to lay a foundation. "As a wise masterbuilder, I have laid the foundation, and another buildeth thereon. But let every man take heed how he buildeth thereupon" (3:10).

But what a foundation he laid! It was strong and thorough and deep. We read in Acts 18 where even the chief ruler of the synagogue in

Corinth was converted. The foundation is foursquare, "For other foundation can no man lay than that is laid, which is Jesus Christ" (3:11).

"Upon that foundation take heed how you build," he says. You can choose to build upon this foundation gold, silver, and precious stones, or wood, hay, and stubble, then, one day, "Every man's work shall be made manifest: for the day shall declare it, because it shall be revealed by fire; and the fire shall try every man's work of what sort it is. If any man's work abide which he hath built thereupon, he shall receive a reward. If any man's work shall be burned he shall suffer loss: but he himself shall be saved; yet so as by fire" (3:13–15).

I would remind you that something more has gone into the building of your life even in the last week; it is inevitable that the building is going up. The Lord Himself has laid the foundation, if we are His children; He is the rock upon which we stand, and upon that solid rock we are building. But what kind of materials are we using? During the days just past, have you put in some bricks? Have you put in the window of prayer? Is there the gold of a pure testimony, the silver of a life that is radiant for the Lord Jesus, the precious stone of victory over temptation? Is there submission to the will of God in the time of suffering? Is there surrender to the cross which we would not have taken of our own choosing? Is there progress along the path of the Master's choice, a forsaking of what seems to us more attractive? If we have chosen His will, in our life the building is going up to the glory of God with gold, silver, and precious stones.

But in another life there has been much feverish activity, pressure in business and at home, or even in Christian work, and that life has become prayerless. There has been too much to do, too many things to cope with. There has been futility, irresponsibility, defeat, powerlessness—the building has gone up, but it is just wood, hay, and stubble.

One day every man's work is going to be put through the fire at the judgment seat of Christ. The Lord, who shall judge us in that day, is the One whose eyes, John tells us in the Book of Revelation, are as a flame of fire. The building which we are putting up, the building of our character, is going to pass under His scrutiny, and if any man's work shall abide in that day then, says the record, he shall receive a reward. But if the eyes of our Lord, which are as a flame of fire, shall find only wood, hay, and stubble, it shall all be burned. That man shall suffer loss, although he himself shall be saved, but as by fire. Take heed how you build!

Paul approaches the subject of their carnality from yet another angle: "Know ye not that ye are the temple of God, and that the Spirit of God dwelleth in you? If any man defile the temple of God, him shall God destroy; for the temple of God is holy, which temple ye are" (3:16–17).

Two different Greek words are translated in our New Testament by the English word "temple." One means the building itself, the other means the sanctuary, the Holy of Holies where the glory of God dwells — that is the word here. We are God's sanctuary, the place of His holy, awesome presence.

Paul goes on to say, "If any man defile the temple … him shall God destroy." But the word "destroy" does not mean to annihilate, it means to spoil or mar: "if any man spoils (corrupts) the temple, him will God corrupt or defile." If we defile the sanctuary of God then it is not very long before our whole life becomes corrupt, worldly, indifferent to the things of God. One of the evidences of carnality in the Corinthian church was jealousy — envy, strife, and division. The whole testimony was being spoiled; the holy place, which should have been filled with the glory of the indwelling Christ, was marred by all kinds of carnality. The temple was being defiled, and therefore the church had become corrupt and worldly.

You too are God's sanctuary; your body is the temple of the Holy Spirit. You are not simply the structure in which He lives, you are the dwelling place of the Shekinah glory. God wants to reveal Himself there, controlling and guiding your life, shining through it with His radiance and power.

Remember the Old Testament tabernacle with its outer court where the public walked, the inner court which was the holy place of service, and the Holiest of all, the sanctuary of the presence of Jehovah. We are not to live our lives in the outer court, which is public property. We are not to live only in the busy rush of Christian service that is the inner court, the holy place. We are introduced into the Holiest of all by the blood of the Lord Jesus — we are the sanctuary of God. Therefore we should walk as holy men and women, with dignity and reverence and worship.

Paul has one more thing to say to this church, and this is the most precious of all: "Therefore let no man glory in men. For all things are yours; whether Paul, or Apollos, or Cephas, [for what they are worth, they are yours] or the world…" (3:21–22) that is yours, too.

I love to go out into the country and remember that this is my Father's world, and because it is His, it is mine. I may never own legal title to an inch of it, but it is all mine in the Lord Jesus. "Or life, or death, or things present, or things to come; all are yours," Paul says. Yes, even death is yours, because Jesus Christ has taken the sting out of it; it is now a defeated enemy.

Everything is working together for good to them that love God, and best of all, even though you are still living in carnality, just remember; "ye are Christ's; and Christ is God's" (3:23). You are an heir of God and a joint-heir with Christ; you have an inheritance in Him, and the Lord Jesus has also an inheritance in you: "They shall be mine, in that day when I make up my jewels [i.e., special treasure]" (Malachi 3:17).

Paul counteracts carnality by pointing out the kind of people we are intended to be. Have we received the Word and borne fruit? We are God's husbandry, and He is looking for a harvest. You are God's building, according to Paul, and you are responsible for what you put into the building. Have you been putting in the bricks of prayer and testimony and faithfulness?

You may be thinking, "But you don't know the pressure of my life: how many hours I have to study, how many problems I have to cope with, how many people I have to try to satisfy." But if you say you have no time to see to the spiritual building of your life, then I say to you in the name of the Lord, you are just too busy! For you will never have more time than you have right now. There will never be less pressure; indeed, if I may venture to say so, the more you go on with the Lord, the greater the pressure will become.

You are the sanctuary of God; you are intended to reveal the glory of the Lord. Most of all, you belong to Him, every bit of you! How could we ever live on the low level of carnality when we have such a Savior as He!

CHAPTER SEVEN

The Road
to Fame

1 Corinthians 4:1–21

It would be well to remind ourselves of the great thrust of Paul's letter to the church at Corinth, lest we get lost and cannot see the wood for the trees. They had written to him about certain matters which affected church administration and policy, in which things they were concerned to be very exact and orthodox. They had not, however, said a word about the real state of affairs, that within their church there was sin that was unmentionable and Christian living that was carnal in the extreme.

Paul knew how they boasted of their learning and philosophy, and that their religion was more a matter of head knowledge than heart understanding. They were concerned about correctness and niceties, but deep down there was desperate need and much sin. To this condition Paul addresses himself in this letter, and the crux of what he had to say to them is in the twentieth verse of the chapter 4: "For the kingdom of God is not in word, but in power."

Just before that, he tells them they are living in a kingdom of their own vain imagination. They were so proud, and they imagined that they had all the answers! "Who maketh thee to differ from another?" he asks. "What hast thou that thou didst not receive? Now if thou didst receive it, why dost thou glory, as if thou hast not received it? Now ye are full, now ye are [enriched], ye have reigned as kings without us: and I would to God ye did reign, that we also might reign with you" (4:7–8).

The amazing sarcasm of those verses ought not to be missed. "You think you are authoritative; you think you are in the place of kingship and control, but look at the condition you are in! You are all talk and intellect; your religion is just theory without reality. The kingdom of God," Paul declares, "is not in word [it is not just philosophy and dogma], but in power, the one thing you haven't got!"

The whole trouble with them was—and I don't use a modern phrase but the words Paul used—"You are just puffed up [gas bags]!" (4:18a, 19). "It is reported commonly that there is fornication among you, and such fornication as is not so much as named among the Gentiles," Paul says, "And ye [in the face of that] are puffed up" (5:1–2). What an incredible situation existed in that church! They were so proud of what they thought they had, so sophisticated, and yet in the one important thing they were destitute: Holy Spirit power and authority.

Although we study this situation way back in the New Testament era, is it really very far from us, today? These are times when we are eager for education, talent, wisdom, philosophy—the church today strives after these things. We all need, rightly, to know all we can about truth—I would not decry the search for knowledge and understanding, the necessity for discipline and training for the ministry. There is a great need for proper preparation, because the Lord should have the best of all we possess. However, I wonder if sometimes competence is a covering for our lack of the transforming power of God the Holy Spirit. If we do not have that, what is the value of all these other things?

Paul builds up his argument by telling them, "in every thing ye are enriched by Christ," and in Him they have "all utterance, and … all knowledge" (1:5). The kind of knowledge and understanding that will give authority, wisdom, and power is not to be found simply in education, but in the Lord Himself. For that reason, Paul continues, when I came to you, it was "not with the wisdom of words, lest the cross of Christ should be made of none effect" (1:17).

He came not with excellency of speech, but determined to know nothing among them but Jesus Christ and Him crucified; therefore his preaching was a demonstration of the spirit and of power. He turned his back on an intellectual approach to the situation because there is no philosophical argument that can meet the need of a church like that, where sin is permitted to exist unrebuked.

On the other hand, the wisdom of God is not something foolish, outmoded by civilization and education. "We speak the wisdom of God in a mystery" (2:7). The message of the cross, in all its fullness, is the message of God's wisdom and authority. Then Paul went on to remind them that in spite of all their appalling failure, they were intended to be God's husbandry, His field from which He looked for a harvest. They were His building, erected upon the foundation which is Jesus Christ. They were His sanctuary, from which the glory of the Lord should shine.

Most of all, they were God's own purchased possession—that was Paul's answer to their situation, pointing them to the path he, himself, has chosen, the royal route to heaven.

Two roads are clearly offered to each of us in life. One is the road of the self-life that seeks after intellectual entertainment and wins the applause of men, but ends in corruption, failure, and defeat. The other road leads a man by the way of the cross, the path of unpopularity, making him a spectacle to the world, often criticized and derided, even persecuted, certainly thought of as out-of-date and old-fashioned. That is the road Paul chose. Which path are you and I traveling today?

We find here the principle of all ministry, the background for all Christian living, the thing that distinguishes the man who knows God and walks with Him from the man who is just theorizing about religion and accumulating philosophy, but whose heart is empty and hopeless. Paul says, in effect, "I want you to think of me as no more than a minister of Christ and a steward of the mysteries of God," and "Moreover it is required in stewards, that a man be found faithful" (4:2).

The word "minister" here literally means "an under-rower." It pictures the great ships of Paul's time, which were manned by galley slaves, two rows of men under the last of their overseer—and those on the lower deck were the most despised of all. They were the "under-rowers," and Paul affirms he is no more than that. It is the same word the Lord Jesus used when He said to Pilate, "If my kingdom were of this world, then would my servants [under-rowers] fight" (John 18:36). It occurs again when Paul and Barnabas set out on their missionary journey and took Mark with them as their "minister," their "under-rower" (Acts 13:5).

Paul was glad to count himself a slave of the Lord Jesus Christ, completely submitted to His authority, happy in the Master's service. A one-time leading member of the Sanhedrin, the man who boasted of his religion and intellect, a proud Pharisee among Pharisees, now he delights to say, "I am nothing—simply a slave of my Lord Jesus Christ."

Paul says, moreover, he is also a steward of the mysteries of God. That is our English word "housekeeper," or "manager," someone who gets in the supplies to dispense to the family. A happy slave of Jesus Christ—that is his relationship to the Lord; a steward of the mysteries of God—that is his responsibility in view of this relationship. What he had received of the Lord Jesus, that he delivered to the church. He was content to be a channel through whom God's power and authority and Word could go out in blessing to the world.

The first step along the road to fame, therefore, is for a man to turn his back deliberately upon all self-ambition and self-confidence, submitting to the sovereignty of Jesus Christ in his life. When he has done that, he is entrusted with the flaming message from heaven. Because his relationship with God is that of a bond-slave, his relationship to the people is that of God's messenger speaking in demonstration of the Spirit and of power.

The second step on the road to fame is that we face judgment as we go through life. It is not something relegated only to the future; judgment comes daily from three different quarters.

Notice in the text: "But with me it is a very small thing that I should be judged of you, or of man's judgment: yea, I judge not mine own self. For I know nothing by myself [and I think I am correct in saying the translation here would be "I know nothing against myself"]; yet am I not hereby justified: but he that judgeth me is the Lord" (4:3–4). Paul had come under the scrutiny of people who were wondering if he would lead them off into extremes! Isn't it amazing how people are far more scared of holiness than they are of sin? But he was not concerned with what they thought about him; he was not responsible to them. He even declares that he is not judging himself, because he could not find anything in his life of which he was aware that was against him: there was no known sin that he was committing. The one thing he says he is concerned about is the scrutiny of the Lord, who knows all our hearts, our desires, our every thought and motive.

"Therefore judge nothing before the time, until the Lord come, who both will bring to light the hidden things of darkness, and will make manifest the counsels of the hearts: and then shall every man have praise of God" (4:5). One day God will make manifest "the hidden things of darkness," not necessarily the evil things, but our inner motives: why it was we turned from our own ability and philosophy of life and chose this path of the cross. He knows why, and one day every man shall receive—and mark the next word—not blame or condemnation, but *praise* of God!

The man who has chosen the path of the crucified life, the path of unpopularity, must expect misunderstanding down here. But his concern is not for the judgment of the world, only that day by day the Lord has His eyes upon him. The road to fame and glory is, first of all, submitting to the sovereignty of Christ, and then being a channel through whom the message of the living Word of God burns like a fire.

Paul's experience is a costly one, and perhaps we can follow him thus far, seeking to stand for the same message and preach the same full truth of salvation which can save a man from inbred corruption as well as from the sins of daily life. But do we want to go with him all the way? For in the course of his path he says, "We are made a spectacle ... We are fools for Christ's sake" (4:9–10a). "But you think yourselves wise," he continues, again with a touch of scorn, I think. "We are weak, but you think yourselves strong. You are honorable to other people and are popular along the way you have taken, and it is accounted a good thing to be in that line," he says, in effect; "but we are despised" (4:10b).

"Even unto this present hour we both hunger, and thirst, and are naked, and are buffeted, and have no certain dwellingplace; ... being reviled, we bless; being persecuted, we suffer it: Being defamed, we intreat: we are made as the filth of the world, and are the offscouring of all things unto this day" (4:11–13). Here Paul and I have parted company. Why? Because, though deep down in my heart I can face you and say that to the best of my knowledge I want this life which glories not in the flesh but only in the Lord—and maybe you could say "Amen" to that—there is something in all of us that wants both.

We want a middle road, a little bit of praise and popularity, a little bit of recognition and thanks, a little bit of the applause of men. At the same time we want the anointing of the Spirit and the authority of God; we want the power without the cost. So Paul has said "Good-bye" to some of us and gone ahead, because for him to tread that path for the Lord Jesus has meant he became a gazing-stock to the world; in short, it meant crucifixion.

The royal route that leads to glory is the route the Master trod. He, being defamed, prayed, "Father, forgive them." Being reviled, He reviled not again; being persecuted, He submitted without a murmur. Everything that Paul faced, Jesus had faced before him. Everything that Paul went through, Christ had gone through, only more. He endured to the very end, down to the last drop of His blood on the cross outside Jerusalem, to redeem man from his boasting and confidence, from his self-importance and human pride.

The road that leads to heaven is the route of faithfulness to God; it is the way of crucifixion with Christ. Therefore, Paul said, "I will come to you shortly ... and will know, not the speech of them which are puffed up, but the power. For the kingdom of God is not in word, but in power" (4:19–20). One thing he knew: when he came to that church to speak with them face to face, he would know wherein lay their power.

You may be going out to the mission field soon to blaze a trail for God, or you may teach a Sunday school class week by week, or you may minister the Word of God in a church. Whatever your service for the Lord, you can only meet the needs of the people around you in the power of God the Holy Spirit! It is only as men and women have hearts aflame for Jesus and are channels of the power of God that they are going to meet the needs of the age in which we live.

Up to the limit of the light that God has given us, are we walking the royal route to heaven today? Being approved by Him is really all that matters. If you are crucified with Christ, then when you work in the office before unconverted people, or you visit a home where people are unsaved, or you teach your Bible class, or you stand in a pulpit, you will know the power of the Lord, which can break into the hearts of corrupt men and overcome sin in His name. Have you begun by submitting to the sovereignty of Jesus Christ in your life? If you have, then you are beginning to prove His power in the place of your own ineffectiveness.

CHAPTER EIGHT

WATCH
YOUR STEP!

1 CORINTHIANS 5:1–13

The variety of subjects with which Paul deals in this letter makes it very profitable for meditation and study. We come to grips now with the root of the trouble in the church at Corinth, the sin that ruined its testimony and made their pride in worldly wisdom and human philosophy so blatantly out of place. Here we deal with no easy subject, but a very important one, a thing which is all too often the crippling factor in Christian testimony today, yet over which there is deliverance in the Lord Jesus, and in Him alone. It is not just something in Greece many years ago, but in America today. I ask you, therefore, sympathetically and prayerfully, with an open mind, to follow as we seek the profitable lesson in this portion of God's Word.

In the first place, I would like to look with you at this disaster which has to be faced. "It is reported commonly that there is fornication among you, and such fornication as is not so much as named among the Gentiles, that one should have his father's wife. And ye are puffed up, and have not rather mourned, that he that hath done this deed might be taken away from among you" (5:1–2).

The church at Corinth, so obsessed by its wisdom and philosophy, had become completely careless of the moral implications of the gospel. Their price of human intellect had tragically failed to prevent a moral breakdown; these Christians were paralyzed, absolutely powerless. On the other hand, the wisdom of God, the word of the cross, the message of the full gospel, devastatingly exposed their sin and possessed mighty power to save from it. All through this Corinthian letter these two things are contrasted.

Paul now brings this group of believers face to face with the disaster that has taken place in their fellowship. The message of the cross, with its implications in Christian behavior, was being ignored. Therefore, Paul says, "it is commonly reported," or "it is everywhere noised abroad," that a certain situation exists. This is not the gossip of a few people—it is the talk of the city! I need not dwell on the particular case except to state quite bluntly that it was a matter of the perversion of one of the most sacred things in human personality—the perversion of sex. It was of so serious a nature that no case so flagrant could be found even among the unconverted people in Corinth.

Now the whole point was this: not simply a breakdown in the life of one individual, but the wide influence that sin was having upon the life of the church that tolerated it. This group of people had been separated to Christ through the word of the cross, called into fellowship with the Lord Jesus, and their testimony was the channel by which God could reach the whole city. Yet the purpose for which they existed was in danger of total collapse because of sin in their midst.

"And ye are puffed up," Paul accuses them, "you are haughty and proud, so occupied with your discussions and theological arguments that you are closing your eyes to this terrible thing that is going on right in the very center of your church life." There was no possibility that they were ignorant of it, because it was known everywhere. Maybe they were proud of their tolerance and blind to the fact that their testimony was being ruined, that the church had become a laughingstock to the people outside. Their only real weapon, God the Holy Spirit, was grieved, quenched, withdrawn. So occupied were they with window-dressing, discussions and arguments, that they were insensitive to sin. They did not mourn about it; they did not weep over it; they did not feel the shame and agony of it.

Is this something so remote as a group of Christian people in Corinth nineteen hundred years ago? Who can tell how paralyzed is the witness of the church in these days of moral laxity because of this kind of thing? The alarming horror of juvenile crime has, as one of its biggest factors, sex perversion. This evil stems from the self-indulgent age in which we live; from the kind of thing that people watch on television and hear on the radio; from the kind of printed trash available on almost every corner; from the lack of parental control; and most of all, from the lack of the presence and power of God the Holy Spirit in Christian living.

Occupied so much with our correctness of doctrine, we are in grave danger of failing to recognize that this evil thing is not only outside the camp, but inside. There are people who have decided for Christ and claim to be converted—they have come to Him to seek forgiveness and cleansing from this very thing. Oh, that I might speak with utter tenderness and candor about such a subject as this, and not with an attitude of censorious judgment! There are people who have carried such sin over into Christian life without having victory and deliverance. They are in the Christian church and are taking leadership in Christian activity, and therefore sex perversion is found within the holy fellowship of the church of God.

In the second place, there is a duty to be performed: "I verily, as absent in body, but present in spirit, have judged already, as though I were present, concerning him that hath so done this deed. In the name of our Lord Jesus Christ, when ye are gathered together, and my spirit, with the power of our Lord Jesus Christ, ... to deliver such an one unto Satan for the destruction of the flesh" (5:3–5).

Paul made up his mind what must be done. The guilty man, who brought this sin of his own life into the setting of Christian fellowship, must be put outside. It interprets what the Lord Jesus said in Matthew 18:15–17: if your brother sins, you are not to condone it. You are not to say that it has nothing to do with you, because you are a fellow member of the body. Because he is within the Christian group, the whole fellowship is affected by it. Go, therefore, and see this man alone, and if he hears you, you have won him. It he won't hear you, take two or three others; if he won't hear them, take it to the church, which then must act. If he refuses to listen, to repent, to confess, then there is only one course left: he must be dealt with as a heathen and a publican. Thus saith the Lord, and thus saith Paul: "Deliver such an one unto Satan for the destruction of the flesh."

We must be sure we understand what that means. Some who expound this verse say that this man had to be put outside, and then he would suffer some awful physical disease in order that he might be brought to his senses. I do not think it means that at all.

Paul did not say "the destruction of the body," he said, "the destruction of the flesh." It was the flesh which had mastered this man. Paul makes a distinction between the Christian who is carnal and the one who is spiritual. The man who, though indwelt by the Spirit, is still under the control of the flesh, is utterly carnal, yielding to all the principles of the old nature, which was supposed to be on the other side of the cross. Now, this man in the Corinthian church is to be given over to Satan until that principle of yieldedness to the flesh is ended, until this principle of the self-life is finished.

Hand him over to Satan, Paul says, before whose authority he has been surrendering. Cut him off from Christian fellowship; remove him from any false feeling of security within the Christian church; expose him to the dreadfulness and loneliness and awfulness of the sin of which he is guilty. Let the world see that sin cannot be tolerated within the holy fellowship of God's people. Put him out for the destruction of carnality, until he loathes the very thought of the thing which he is practicing.

This is the duty to be performed, but is this man to be left excommunicated and abandoned? No, indeed! This guilty man is a sinner for whom Jesus died. There is a deliverance to be secured. Notice the second part of this verse, which I omitted above: "To deliver such an one ... for the destruction of the flesh, *that the spirit may be saved in the day of the Lord Jesus*" (5:5).

When Paul gave these instructions, I am sure he did it with the love of the Savior in his heart. Indeed, when he refers to this again in his second letter, he says it was "out of much affliction and anguish of heart I wrote unto you with many tears" (2 Corinthians 2:4). The man must sample the awfulness of his sin; be cut off, if you like, from the imaginary halo of church membership that might enable him to go on in sin and think he was getting away with it. Let him be satiated with it until, like the prodigal, he begins to be in want and cries out, "I will arise and go to my Father!"

How far from God can a Christian go? How deep in sin can a man sink after he is born of the Spirit? Only a backslider who has tasted the bitter fruit of an experience like this can ever know. But someone may say, "Is it not a dangerous doctrine to suggest that a man can live like this and yet be saved?" Oh, no!

I remind you that the medicine Paul prescribed for this man and for this church proved effective. Look at the second letter: "Sufficient to such a man is this punishment, which was inflicted of many. So that contrariwise ye ought rather to forgive him, and comfort him, lest perhaps such a one should be swallowed up with overmuch sorrow. Wherefore I beseech you that ye would confirm your love toward him" (2 Corinthians 2:6–8).

And a few chapters later: "For behold this selfsame thing, that ye sorrowed after a godly sort, what carefulness it wrought in you, yea, what clearing of yourselves, yea, what indignation, yea, what fear, yea, what vehement desire, yea, what zeal, yea, what revenge! In all things ye have approved your-selves to be clear in this matter" (2 Corinthians 7:11). The man was forgiven and restored; the church repented with godly sorrow and was blessed. This is always the outcome of dealing with sin in the life of a genuine Christian.

The only security we have is in the Lord Jesus Himself, and He will not let us go. Even though He has to chastise, perhaps allow a man to drink the fruit of his sin until he is nauseated with it — if that medicine does not succeed in bringing the man back to God, it only proves that he was never saved in the first place. No true Christian can go on sinning and be happy in it. Yet if he is refusing to judge himself, then in order that deliverance might be secured, he has to be given over to the power of Satan until this principle of yieldedness to the flesh is overcome. You see, that action sorts out the genuine from the spurious; it shows the reality of conversion as against a mere profession in the Savior.

But Paul also points out that there is a distinction to be observed: "I wrote unto you in an epistle not to company with fornicators: Yet not altogether with the fornicators of this world, or with the covetous, or extortioners, or with idolaters; for then must ye needs go out of the world. But now I have written unto you not to keep company, if any man that is called a brother be a fornicator, or covetous, or an idolater, or a railer, or a drunkard, or an extortioner; with such a one no not to eat" (5:9–11). Judgment, says Paul, must begin at the house of God.

The attitude of the Christian toward the unsaved should never be one of judgment because of his sins. There are many who, perhaps by heredity or environment, perhaps by reason of their own passions, are victims of this dreadful business — but we are not to hold up our hands in holy horror. We must go after such people with the flame of Calvary love and with the message of deliverance, never shocked or deterred by the depths of sin that we find revealed. We have only to look within our own hearts to see the potential of it there, but for God's grace. Ours is the privilege of proclaiming deliverance even from a perversion of this character.

Here is an example which I would put simply and bluntly. Consider a man who is homosexual, and the poor fellow is absolutely beaten and defeated. One day the gospel is preached to him, and there is no difficulty persuading him that he is a sinner. He is pointed to the way of the cross, the way of forgiveness and cleansing, and he gladly receives it. Then he is brought into the church, accepted for membership on the basis of his profession of faith in Jesus Christ.

Before long he is given Christian work to do and opportunities for testimony. Everything goes well for a while, until Satan attacks and he is down again, tripped up by the same thing that conquered him before he was saved. In the love of Christ and for the sake of the purity of the fellowship, this man has to be brought to understand that, when he comes to Jesus Christ, he accepts responsibility for the standards of Christian living, and he must live worthy of his high calling. He cannot be allowed to continue in Christian leadership, or even in the fellowship of the church, until the sin has been confessed and repented of, and he is right with God. If he refuses to face that himself, the church must face it for him for his sake and for theirs.

Why? Because there is a dynamic to be restored: "Purge out therefore the old leaven, that ye may be a new lump, as ye are unleavened. For even Christ our passover is sacrificed for us: therefore let us keep the feast, not with old leaven, neither with the leaven of malice and wickedness; but with the unleavened bread of sincerity and truth" (5:7–8).

Paul's final answer to every problem is the cross. Look at this wretched sin in the light of the blood that has been shed. See what carnality has done to the church and to the individual, in spite of his profession. It hasn't been altogether his fault: he was given Christian leadership, and perhaps was unwisely put in the limelight. But there has been no judgment of sin in his life, no repentance, no confession. Such a member causes the church to be absolutely paralyzed in its witness, takes away the power, removes the authority of the Holy Spirit. Any unholy fellowship is always defeated. To tolerate sin is going to ruin the church, says Paul; the extent to which sin is permitted is the measure in which appetite for the Word will depart. The Christian who is pure is powerful, but the man who is compromising is spiritually impotent.

"But remember," says Paul, "Christ is sacrificed for us. Therefore purge out the old leaven." The Passover was eaten with the unleavened bread of purity, the symbol of deliverance. Then he tells how: be what you are, "a new lump, as ye are unleavened." Take up your position on the resurrection side of the cross and claim your heritage.

The dynamic that has gone out of the church fellowship must be restored. Don't let such things go on a moment longer—the futility of our testimony, the powerlessness of our service must be dealt with. Do you recognize the disaster?

Poor struggling soul, gripped by the bondage of this sort of thing, I beg of you that you would just cling today to your place in Jesus Christ and remember you are on resurrection ground. "Now ye are clean," says the Lord Jesus, "through the word which I have spoken unto you. Abide in me" (John 15:3–4). Do you believe that? Though this bondage of sin has gone on so long in your life the power of the blood goes further and can cleanse you from all sin. There is no power of Satan to grip this human body, either by temperament or heredity or by your own choice, that can outreach the grace of God which can save you from slavery to sin.

Then feed on Him: "Therefore let us keep the feast, not with old leaven, neither with the leaven of malice and wickedness; but with the unleavened bread of sincerity and truth." If you would seek to be on the royal route to heaven, claim His life by obedience which submits to His control, by surrender which brings His love and His power into your heart and life.

CHAPTER NINE

THINGS GOD EXPECTS
YOU TO KNOW — I

1 CORINTHIANS 6:1–11

As you glance at the whole scope of this sixth chapter of First Corinthians, you will see that over and over Paul addresses this church with the challenge, "Know ye not? — Don't you know?" I cannot escape the conclusion that it is almost with a touch of sarcasm that he writes, in effect, "You who profess to be so clever and intellectual, can it be that you are ignorant of these basic facts?"

Paul asks them six questions that fall into two divisions. Notice the first three: "Do ye not know that saints shall judge the world?" (6:2). "Know ye not that we shall judge angels?" (6:3). "Know ye not that the unrighteous shall not inherit the kingdom of God?" (6:9). In other words, "Remember what you are."

Look at the next three; "Know ye not that your bodies are the members of Christ?" (6:15). "Know ye not that he which is joined to an harlot is one body ... but he that is joined to the Lord is one spirit?" (6:16–17). "Know ye not that your body is the temple of the Holy Ghost? ... Ye are bought with a price" (6:19–20). In other words, "Remember to whom you belong."

All the way through this epistle Paul adopts the principle that the mightiest drawing power to lift a man out of carnality, worldliness, and sinfulness is the cross of Christ. We need to remember how we have been redeemed, what we are in the sight of God, and to whom we belong, our Lord Jesus Christ. I believe that to be the most effective weapon in the hands of any preacher. Paul does not condemn this church, though he speaks to it in mighty straight language. He simply reminds them that they are not their own; they have been bought with a price.

The argument of these first eleven verses is rooted in a particular condition that existed in the Corinthian church, but which is to be found potentially in almost every fellowship today. Paul begins with a rebuke for their trivial disputes, then he asks them to see these things in the light of their true dignity as children of God and their great destiny as Christians. In view of that, he issues a recall to triumphant discipleship.

Let us look at the first of these things, the rebuke for trivial disputes within the church: "Dare any of you, having a matter against another, go to law before the unjust, and not before the saints?" (6:1). Here Paul is addressing himself again to the carnality of the church at Corinth. He had said previously, "Are ye not carnal, and walk as men? For there is among you envying, and strife, and divisions" (3:3). Now he directs his attention to these divisions among them, and to what was even worse: instead of settling them privately, they had presumed to ask for settlement in a pagan court. "Brother goeth to law with brother, and that before the unbelievers" (6:6).

"Surely there is one man among you who has enough sense to settle the thing privately among yourselves," he implies. "If you cannot find anybody to do it, then instead of parading your dissentions and carnality before an ungodly world, let God vindicate the right, or rather allow yourselves to be defrauded than bring scorn upon your testimony" (6:5, 7).

Of course, that does not mean that a Christian must never go to law. There may be circumstances when it is necessary. But disputes and divisions among brethren should be settled within the church and not outside it. Here is the extent to which strife goes, the damage it causes when we forget who we are, and parade our disputes in front of the world.

These conditions are not confined to New Testament times; I think they may be found in church life today. They are tragically emphasized when envy and strife, bickering about points of creed and dogma, are deliberately publicized to an unbelieving world. One of the greatest tragedies on many mission fields is the way in which sectarianism at home is extended abroad and threatens to ruin Christian witness, insisting upon agreement on every point of the Bible before we can have mutual fellowship, for instance. In fundamentalism today, such divisions frequently are paraded before the general public, to the confusion of the whole Christian testimony. Of course, it usually begins when one Christian has a quarrel with another, and it is not settled privately, but becomes public. No wonder people are amazed and repulsed by a church which is supposed to be united in Christ but which constantly demonstrates its disunity. These things ought to make us bow our heads in shame. Clearly revealed unity and love have great power to draw the unbeliever. How contrary is internal strife to the command of the Lord Jesus: "By this shall all men know that ye are my disciples, if ye have love one to another" (John 13:35).

Here, then, is the basis upon which Paul is building his argument. This church, which is squabbling publicly about practically nothing, is at the same time ignoring glaring moral breakdown within its fellowship. How does Paul, by the Holy Sprit, address himself to this situation? By a reminder of the true dignity of the child of God: "Do ye not know that the saints shall judge the world? and if the world shall be judged by you, are ye unworthy to judge the smallest matters? Know ye not that we shall judge angels? how much more things that pertain to this life?" (6:2–3).

These Christians had become shortsighted, occupied with their own strife and trouble. Paul asks them now to lift their eyes, to look beyond the present, to think of that day when they will be associated with the Lord Jesus Christ in the judgment of the world and of angels. For one day the tables are going to be turned. The world, which has despised the Christian faith, is going to be judged by those whom it has, in this life, condemned as foolish.

Listen to the words of the Lord Jesus in Matthew 19:28: "I say unto you, That ye which have followed me, in the regeneration when the Son of man shall sit in the throne of his glory, ye also shall sit upon twelve thrones, judging the twelve tribes of Israel." Listen again to the language of Jude 14 and 15: "Behold, the Lord cometh with ten thousands of his saints, to execute judgment upon all, and to convince all that are ungodly among them of all their ungodly deeds which they have ungodly committed, and of all their hard speeches which ungodly sinners have spoken against him." Listen to Paul writing again in 2 Timothy 2:12, "If we suffer, we shall also reign with him."

On that great day of final judgment, far beyond the time when the church will be caught up by the Lord Jesus to be with Him, beyond even the millennial reign of Christ, the church, ransomed and glorified, is going to participate in the overthrow of everything that is ungodly and unrighteous. We are going to be counted worthy of judging the world, and not only the world, but angels! "God spared not the angels that sinned, but cast them down to hell, and delivered them into chains of darkness, to be reserved unto judgment" (2 Peter 2:4).

What a day! The world against which we have fought to maintain our stand for Christ, the world that has called us narrow, bigoted, out-of-date, escapists from reality, the world with its ungodliness, its immorality, its sin, its utter rejection of the authority of God—one day the children of God are going to sit in judgment upon that world! And the devil, who has flung temptation at us from every direction, who has done everything in his power to discourage, to deter, to frighten, and to make us doubt, who has flung one fiery dart after another to hinder our progress to glory, to cause us to fail and to sin—one day we are going to share in the judgment of Satan!

"This is to be your ultimate destiny, "says Paul in effect. "Why, then, are you spending your time quarreling about inconsequential things? Surely you are capable of settling your petty disputes! If you are not, how do you think you are going to be worthy of the dignity that is yours as a Christian? Remember what you are!"

Then he pulls them back again, as much as to say, "Now you may think that is very much up in the clouds. That overwhelming thought may be too much for you to grasp, for it concerns eternity. But what about this life, here and now? I want to turn you from your carnality to the kind of life that you have been saved to live." He recalled them to triumphant discipleship: "Know ye not that the unrighteous shall not inherit the kingdom of God? Be not deceived: neither fornicators, nor idolaters, nor adulterers, nor effeminate, nor abusers of themselves with mankind, Nor thieves, nor covetous, nor drunkards, nor revilers, nor extortioners, shall inherit the kingdom of God" (6:9–10).

What an awful, ugly list! Some of these things are unfit for public mention. We dealt with them in part in our last study—the collapse of sex relationships, the disintegration of human personality, the descent to bestiality instead of an ascent to a life that is worthy of a child of God.

As I read again in the presence of God this list of ten unmentionable sins, I had no trouble with nine of them. I could bow before the Lord and say, "Yes, Lord, surely none that is guilty of this could ever enter the kingdom of God."

There was one word, however, that puzzled me, one right in the middle of the list: "effeminate." Why should such a word as that find its way into this list, among the things that make entrance into the kingdom of Heaven an impossibility? As I looked into it a little more carefully, I found that it touches the very root of the problem in the church at Corinth. It took the strength out of their discipleship, the tang out of their testimony.

The word means "flabby"; "soft" would be the literal translation of the Greek. It is found only in two other places in the New Testament. When God sent the forerunner of Christ, John the Baptist, He chose a man of the wildernesses, whose clothing was rough and whose food was locusts and wild honey—a strange, austere figure. Later, some people asked the Lord if such a man could be authentic. He had not come through the recognized religious channels of his time.

Jesus turned upon them and said, "But what went ye out for to see? A man clothed in soft raiment?" (Luke 7:25). That is the word. What did they expect to find, an indulgent man? Did they expect someone spineless, whose doctrine was but cold, dry bones like the other religious leader of the time? "What sort of man did you expect? Who else would be able to move a day like that for Me?" asks the Master.

This exposes the whole trouble with the church at Corinth: they were just soft. They were tolerant of sin, squabbling among themselves, bogged down by carnality. There was no vision among them, no Holy Spirit dynamic. They had no conviction of their calling, no sense of discipleship, and Paul sought to recall them to this.

How can we escape saying in our hearts, "This would be me, but for the grace of God"? How does a church lose Holy Spirit power? Why does it become tolerant of sin? How can a Christian excuse himself for his obvious carnality? Simply because we are soft; evangelicals, yes, but frequently with more jelly than evangel!

Our visions gone, our burden for souls lost, the self-indulgent church just settles down comfortably alongside things that ought to be destroyed.

Paul's object is to recall the Corinthian believers to triumphant discipleship; "And such were some of you: but ye are washed, but ye are sanctified, but ye are justified in the name of the Lord Jesus, and by the Spirit of our God" (6:11). Paul is making them look themselves squarely in the face: "such were some of you, but…" I think that is a thrilling verse; there is a sharp distinction in it, a clear line of demarcation, they were all this: idolaters, fornicators, soft, and all the rest of the ugliness, "but ye are washed, but ye are sanctified, but ye are justified…"

Altogether, one distinct, tremendous transaction with God: ye are washed: "Now ye are clean through the word which I have spoken unto you" (John 15:3). Ye are sanctified: "Through sanctification of the Spirit, unto obedience and sprinkling of the blood of Jesus Christ" (1 Peter 1:2). Ye are justified: "Being justified freely by his grace through the redemption that is in Christa Jesus" (Romans 3:24). This is what you are, says Paul to these believers who are flabby and tolerant of sin. He reminds them that they have been washed by the Word, set apart by the Holy Spirit, and declared righteous by the blood of Jesus Christ before the God of heaven.

The man who is made righteous in the sight of God has to be made holy by the grace of God. It is impossible to live like the devil's children and hope to go to heaven with God's children. Here they were: defeated, idolatrous, effeminate—and such were some of you. But here they are now: washed, sanctified, justified. How can they walk in their former sins?

With so many professed Christians it is sometimes hard to discover where their Christianity ends and the world begins in their lives. There is no clear line of demarcation; they love being coddled and they do not like being challenged. But the business of the church is not to coddle the saints, but to challenge them to win others for Jesus Christ. "Remember who you are," says Paul.

Oh, the tragedy of carnality: people occupied with petty quarrels that ruin Christian testimony, when they are destined one day to judge the world and angels! We are intended in this life to live in the glory of Christ and by His power in us. This is what we are by the grace of God and in the sight of God. Therefore, in the power of the Spirit, we should be what we are, so that one day we will be fit to take part in the judgment of the world and of angels.

CHAPTER TEN

THINGS GOD EXPECTS
YOU TO KNOW — II

1 CORINTHIANS 6:12–20

These chapters of Paul's letter require very careful and prayerful treatment in public ministry. But I believe they concern matters of importance to the whole Christian church and to each one of our lives today. Paul addresses himself straightforwardly to the sin which lay at the root of the situation in the Corinthian church and gives the supreme answer to it. Victory and deliverance are yet possible. He is always seeking to point people away from their failure, to get them to look up to the Lord; Paul's answer to every situation is Calvary.

He has already dealt with the individual who was personally responsible, telling the church what they must do: deliver him to Satan for the destruction of the flesh and the saving of the soul in the day of our Lord Jesus Christ. Then he goes on to rebuke them for their petty disputes and calls upon them to remember what they are as Christians: washed, sanctified, justified. Now we hear him saying, "Remember to whom you belong," and telling us to bring that relationship between the soul and the Savior to bear upon every matter of life.

The whole theme of this portion of Scripture is the Christian's attitude toward his body. His moral standards must be recognizably different from others, and he must be able not only to explain why they are necessary but also how they can be maintained.

The apostle who writes this letter under the inspiration of the Holy Sprit is the one who, perhaps above all others, proclaims salvation in the

Lord Jesus Christ by faith alone. "For by grace are ye saved through faith; and that not of yourselves ... not of works, lest any man should boast" (Ephesians 2:8–9). This is Paul's great gospel, that a man comes to know Jesus Christ only on simple faith in the atonement for him at Calvary.

Yet the apostle Paul also relentlessly declares that no one can claim salvation and go on practicing sin like an unbeliever. If the outer life of a child of God is not made pure, it is evidence that the inward heart has never been renewed. The faith that does not produce holiness is not New Testament faith; it is not saving faith, for "without [holiness] no man shall see the Lord" (Hebrews 12:14).

With that background in mind, let us turn to what Paul has to say concerning our relationship to our body and think of it carefully, prayerfully, and soberly in the presence of God. First of all, Paul lays down some principles of Christian liberty: "All things are lawful unto me, but all things are not expedient: all things are lawful for me, but I will not be brought under the power of any" (6:12). That was a master stroke on Paul's part, for that was exactly what everyone in Corinth said: "All things are lawful" was their attitude on the matter of sex relationships.

That is also what the twentieth century is saying: "Have your fling! Go to the registrar, if you like, to get a little legal authority to practice what you have already been doing." There are to be no inhibitions, no frustrations because, we are told, these things are not sin. "Express yourself! Away with the prohibitions that come from an outmoded method of life and thinking!" That is what Corinth said, and the spirit of the city had got into the church. Who can say that the spirit of what is practiced today has not penetrated our churches? Has not this very thing eaten into the vital testimony of professing Christianity today?

"All things are lawful unto me," writes Paul, "and there is not a single faculty or appetite of the body which is not for me to use lawfully." But because we are Christians there are two things we must bear in mind as we exercise our liberty.

The first is this: "All things are not expedient." That word means "bearing together," "helping together." Paul is saying, therefore, that he no longer lives to himself; as a Christian he is one of a fellowship, and he can only use the appetites of the body so long as he is not hurting another. He is governed by the effect upon other people, not upon himself.

Not only that, says Paul, but "I will not be brought under the power [authority] of any." If through the unrestrained use of the body he is mastered by these things, then he is denying the right of Jesus Christ to the sovereignty of his life.

Notice his simple illustration here: "Meats for the belly, and the belly for meats: but God shall destroy both it and them. Now the body is not for fornication, but for the Lord; and the Lord for the body. And God hath both raised up the Lord, and will also raise up us by his own power" (6:13–14). We need food for our physical appetite, but a day is coming when God is going to destroy both. That does not mean the body will be destroyed. That will mark the end of its physical desires and physical limitations, the end of its demand for physical satisfaction. Although this thing in which we live may be put in a grave, one day it will be raised and transformed into the likeness of the Lord Jesus Christ. The body is not finished when it is put into a coffin; it is to be brought into the very presence of God. This body is for the Lord, for His use and not for mine.

That gives us a new slant on the problem of sex, an attitude peculiarly Christian, rooted in the fact of the resurrection of Jesus Christ as the "firstfruits of them that sleep." It is based on the reality of eternity; we were not created only to live down here. Our body is God's, and we cannot play fast and loose with it, because it is for His use. We have Christian liberty, but only in consideration of others and in carefulness with regard to the damage we might do. Our liberty is only within the fellowship of God's people and under the authority of the Lord Jesus. The body is not to be played with; it is for Him.

Here, very briefly, is the principle for Christian living. Now, in what sense is the body for the Lord? It is not only that it is going to be transformed into His likeness, but that we will be held responsible before the judgment seat of Christ, as Paul himself tells us, for the deeds done in this body. That will put discipline and restraint into life. It will mean that certain habits must stop because I am a Christian. Certain practices that the world may consider "the thing to do" are going to have no part in my life, because I am a Christian.

When we look further into this chapter, I think we will see why — it is the prevention of license. Notice again one of Paul's great questions: "Know ye not that your bodies are the members of Christ? Shall I then take the members of Christ, and make them the members of an harlot? God forbid. What? Know ye not that he which is joined to an harlot is one body? For two, saith he, shall be one flesh. But he that is joined unto the Lord is one spirit" (6:15–17).

May I ask you to follow me very carefully here. We who have been redeemed by His precious blood are His body here on earth, the channels through which He works. Our Lord, instead of being subject to the time and space limitations of one physical body, as when He was here on earth, now acts through the bodies of His people in whom He lives. "He that is joined unto the Lord is one spirit," says Paul. Wherever He can find a body surrendered to Him, a man or woman who will receive Him as their Lord and Sovereign, then they become His means of revealing Himself to the world around them. "Ye are members of Christ."

You will always find in Scripture that God works through a human body. That is why it was said of the Lord Jesus, "Lo, I come to do thy will, O God ... by the which will we are sanctified through the offering of the body of Jesus Christ once for all" (Hebrews 10:9–10). It was in a body that man sinned; it is in a body that we sin. It was in a body that Jesus came to earth; it was in a body that He lived triumphantly and overcame where we have been overcome. It was in a body that He died and rose again, and now by His Spirit He comes to live within the body of His people.

Satan always works through a body, also. The only way he can thwart God's purposes is to get a body surrendered to his use, available for his diabolic power and ugly purposes.

This is the question of choice in a Christian's life: shall he take that which is a member of Christ and give it to some unworthy use? Shall he take his body, the means through which God's will is to be done, and yield it to the immoral, sinful purposes of Satan? What will happen if he does? He becomes one body if he is joined to that which is sinful. But if he is joined to the Lord, he is one spirit. That means that in every physical faculty the human frame is under the control of the Lord's Spirit. That Spirit enabled Jesus Christ to live day by day in a human body and never deviate from the will of God, never yield to all the tremendous temptations of the devil.

If we are joined to Christ, we are therefore enabled by His grace to control the body. But if we join ourselves to that which is immoral, we become one flesh with that which we love, and therefore we become part of judgment, condemnation, and punishment, the inevitable result of such action.

Here is the issue from the moment of our birth until the moment when we meet God face to face: either the Spirit of God is to triumph and the life of the flesh die out, or that which is of sin and of the flesh will control us that the Spirit of God ceases to speak. That tremendously solemn alternative faces everyone. Everything is lawful for the child of God, but only under the authority of the Lord Jesus Christ. What He permits, I will do; what He refuses, I will reject. What His Word tells me is right, I will accept; what His Word tells me is wrong, I will refuse. This is the battleground where you and I fight every day.

However, lest I seem to place burdens upon you that are impossible to carry, there is something else Paul tells us, the answer to "how."

I repeat, Paul always brings his hearers back to the cross, back to the place where Jesus died for them. He is never afraid to reveal the ugliness of sin for what it is; he exposes it and drags it to the very foot of Calvary that it may be dealt with there: "What? Know ye not that your body is the temple of the Holy Ghost which is in you, which ye have of God, and ye are not your own? For ye are bought with a price: therefore glorify God in your body, and in your spirit, which are God's" (6:19–20).

Here is Paul's plea for loyalty, and it is sufficient to make a man stand when otherwise he would fall. In making his greatest argument for holiness and purity, for power to keep the body in subjection, Paul points back again to the place where "ye were not redeemed with corruptible things, as silver and gold, … but with the precious blood of Christ, as of a lamb without blemish and without spot" (1 Peter 1:18–19).

An infinite price, the price of His precious blood, suggests infinite pain. I can never enlarge upon the physical point of our Lord Jesus, great as that must have been. But I don't believe that was by any means the depth of the horror of the cross. The pain of Christ was expressed in His cry, "My God, why hast thou forsaken me?" It was in being made sin for me: coming all the way down the shame and agony of the cross, enduring the judgment of a holy God on the sin that was mine, paying the price I could never pay.

You who have been playing fast and loose with your body, you who have been letting the standard down and not caring, you who have allowed the spirit of the age to catch you: remember you have been bought with a price. Therefore it follows that you are not your own. The greatest tyrant in life is self: the demand for freedom from restraint, a "me first" attitude, touchiness and loneliness. But the Bible says we are not our own, and what a real comfort that is!

Again I say, if you refuse to acknowledge that, you have no right to claim salvation. If you refuse the implication of His claim upon you, then what business have you to hide in the shelter of John 3:16? You cannot have the grace of God without the government of God. Real deliverance demands real holiness. The price of His precious blood demands a practical surrender of all your body. You cannot have free salvation unless, as you accept it gladly from the risen Savior, you acknowledge, "I am no longer my own; I am bought with a price."

Then if that is true, let me say this quietly but firmly: you have no right to injure God's property. "If any man defile the temple of God, him will God destroy." You have no right to drunkenness, immorality, uncleanness. You have no right to indulgence or laziness. You have no right to lack of control in any appetite. Furthermore, you have no right to let yourself lie waste. If you belong to the Lord, then you should be going to work for Him. You have no right to any reservations, no right to self-government. When Satan comes with all his insinuations, you must tell him that you are not your own. Every power and faculty, all the time, is altogether God's.

Paul concludes his argument by saying, "Therefore glorify God in your body." How can you? By chastity, discipline, temperance in the way you eat and drink and sleep: whatever you do, do all to the glory of God. The feet that led you into sin should now take you to the house of God and to the place of prayer. The eyes that once looked upon things that aroused lust should now be turned upon your wonderful Savior. The ears that listened to doubtful stories should now be eager to hear the Word of God. The hands that once squandered your money should now labor in the cause of the Lord Jesus Christ. The tongue that talked so loosely and glibly should now be singing His praises and telling others of His love.

Your body is the sanctuary of the Holy Spirit. Is everything in the temple singing "Glory to God!" today? I could not conclude more appropriately than to remind you of the great words of Paul in the conclusion of his letter to the church at Rome: "I beseech you therefore, brethren, by the mercies of God, that ye present your bodies a living sacrifice, holy, acceptable unto God, which is your reasonable service" (Romans 12:1).

PART II

DANGERS ON THE JOURNEY

CHAPTER ELEVEN

The Secret of a Happy Marriage

1 Corinthians 7:1–22

Here Paul begins to answer the questions the people at Corinth had written to him. He has devoted six chapters to dealing with the carnal conditions of the church there. He has laid down principles of actions by which to settle these things, and in every instance he has pointed them back again to the cross of Calvary.

They asked him four specific questions. Certain problems of marriage are dealt with in this chapter, and the following three chapters concern the meat sacrificed to idols. Then Paul has something to say about the place of women in the church, and finally, in chapter 11, he discusses the observance of the Lord's Supper. At the conclusion of that he says (I imagine with a sense of relief), "Now concerning spiritual things..." as if to deal with these matters had been a troublesome necessity. All the time he had been anxious to get to spiritual things.

In this passage on marriage some things that have a local background, and apply particularly to the situation at Corinth. But there are also some principles given here which are desperately needed in days like these.

There is language here which is found nowhere else in all the New Testament. For instance, Paul says, "I speak this by permission and not of commandment" (7:6); "And unto the married I command, yet not I, but the Lord" (7:10); "But to the rest speak I, not the Lord" (7:12); "Now concerning virgins I have no commandment of the Lord: yet

I give my judgment" (7:25); "She is happier if she so abide, after my judgment: and I think also that I have the Spirit of God" (7:40).

He is clearly drawing a distinction between specific instruction which he has received from the Lord by the Holy Spirit and his own judgment in cases where he has received no such instructions. In other words, he is using his own judgment supported by what he believes to be the authority of the Holy Spirit. That does not invalidate this teaching in any way. It does, however, recognize that in matters concerning marriage there is no law so inclusive as to apply to every situation. Each case will call for the careful exercise of human judgment under the direction and authority of the Holy Spirit.

As a matter of act, Paul is using here the office of a scribe, who interpreted and applied the law. The Lord Jesus said concerning such men: "Every scribe which is instructed unto the kingdom of heaven is like unto a man which is an householder, which bringeth forth out of his treasure things new and old" (Matthew 13:52).

That is exactly what Paul is doing in this chapter. Remember, please, that he is doing it in the context of the situation at Corinth. For instance, the Gentiles of that time saw no evil whatever in multiplied wives; polygamy was the practice. And the Jews saw no evil in putting away their wives in certain circumstances. After they had returned from captivity in Babylon, many of them took wives of the people of the land, and Ezra commanded that they should put away their foreign wives. Some of the Jews who were converted to the Christian faith thought perhaps they should follow the same principle. Should they put away their unbelieving partner in marriage?

There is much local background, but there are also tremendous principles laid down here for the most sacred relationship in life. Let me ask you to notice, therefore, that Paul speaks first of marriage in its purity. He makes no attempt here to state the Christian doctrine of marriage in all its wonderful fullness; he does that in Ephesians and Colossians, comparing marriage to the relationship between the Lord Jesus Christ and His church.

At first sight, you would almost think Paul is advocating celibacy and undervaluing marriage. But in the context of the Corinthian church he is saying no such thing: their question was, in essence: "In view of all the immorality, impurity and unhappiness that is rampant in these days, isn't it safer to stay outside the marriage relationship altogether?"

Paul replies that it is good for a man not to be married, but he does not say it is better. In other words, celibacy is proper and good so long as such a person who is unmarried keeps himself pure; "But if they cannot contain, let them marry: for it is better to marry than to burn" (7:9). For the sake of the Kingdom of Heaven and for the cause of the Christian faith, celibacy may be the high and holy calling of God to a man or to a woman.

The Lord Jesus had something very wonderful to say about this: "His disciples say unto him, If the case of the man be so with his wife, it is not good to marry. But he said unto them, All men cannot receive this saying, save they to whom it is given. For there are some eunuchs, which were so born from their mother's womb: and there are some eunuchs, which were made eunuchs of men: and there be eunuchs, which have made themselves eunuchs for the kingdom of heaven's sake. He that is able to receive it, let him receive it" (Matthew 19:10–12). Then in the next verse the Lord said, "Suffer little children, and forbid them not, to come unto me: for of such is the kingdom of heaven." How wonderfully the Lord links together the glory of men or women who, for the sake of the kingdom, have kept themselves single, and in the next moment He honors marriage and children.

As to marriage itself, Paul insists on monogamy: "Let every man have his own wife, and let every woman have her own husband" (7:2). That is basic to the Christian faith. In that relationship, Paul tells us, there are sacred responsibilities where the conjugal rights of husband and wife are to be respected and honored. Christian marriage is not to be used as an excuse for lust and license, the satisfying of the flesh. He recognizes the intimacy of such a precious partnership when it is centered in the Lord Jesus Christ.

At the heart of these verses we find that in this relationship of Christian marriage there should be love, discipline, and mutual respect, the one for the other. There is a recognized admission of the rights of the wife and husband in the sexual relationship. Deep down at the bottom of it all, there are two lives united together in the Lord. This is what Paul has to say about the purity of the marriage tie.

In concluding his argument, Paul says that a man should abide in the calling to which God has called him (7:20). If a man, for the sake of the Kingdom of Heaven, determines that he will stand alone, and he believes that to be the calling of God, the evidence that he is not being peculiar or sanctimonious is that he will be given power from God to keep himself pure. But if he cannot do that, let him marry; let him not take a pious position and say, "For the gospel's sake, I am remaining single" and then live in sin. But marriage is not for license or self-indulgence. It is a holy, sacred relationship between man and woman which has to be kept disciplined in love, with mutual honor and respect, in the power of Christ.

Let me ask you again to consider with me, not only marriage in its purity but — oh, how important — marriage in its permanency: "And unto the married I command, yet not I, but the Lord, Let not the wife depart from her husband: but and if she depart, let her remain unmarried or be reconciled to her husband: and let not the husband put away his wife" (7:10–11). In other words, Paul says there is to be no separation; or if there must be a separation, then there must be no remarriage.

Now this, of course, confirms the teaching of our Lord. When the Pharisees came to Him about this, they quoted the law of Moses as the basis of their authority: Moses suffered a bill of divorcement to be written in certain cases. The Lord replied that Moses did that because of their weakness and unbelief, but in the beginning it was not so. "God made them male and female, and for this cause shall a man leave his father and mother, and shall cleave to his wife: and they twain shall be one flesh ... what therefore God hath joined together, let not man put asunder" (Matthew 19:4–8).

This relationship, which antedates both Christianity and the law of Moses, goes right back to the very beginning of creation as God's purpose for a man and a woman. There was to be only one exception to its permanency: infidelity within the marriage itself. The Lord Himself tells us that the very act of adultery breaks the sanctity of the tie (Matthew 5:32). Therefore there is only one ground for divorce.

I want to have respect for others who may think differently, but, in my judgment, the Bible teaches that the guilty party can never be remarried. Some of my brethren in the ministry (whose convictions I respect deeply, as I trust that they will respect mine) will not remarry either party. They say there is no such thing as divorce under any circumstances whatsoever. In the light of the teaching of the Lord and also of Paul, and in the light of the circumstances of each case, I am happy to grant Christian marriage to the innocent party when a marriage has broken down through the adultery of the other party—and concerning which I am satisfied that he or she *is* the innocent party.

There may be circumstances, as verse 11 indicates, when the behavior of one party makes living together an impossibility. So often people come to my study and talk to me about these things, saying, for instance: "I just cannot go on any longer! My husband comes home drunk and beats me up. ... How much longer must I live with that man?" Then I reply, "I think it would be well if you left him today."

Does that shock you? I have authority for it: "If she depart, let her remain unmarried, or be reconciled to her husband: and let not the husband put away his wife" (7:11). There is no reason I can see why a woman should continue to live with a man who has become a drunken sot and whose behavior is making the home a hell on earth; but that is not divorce. Let the innocent person depart, but let her remain unmarried. And let her motive in leaving (as we have already studied in 1 Corinthians 5:5) be to deliver him to the devil for the destruction of the principle of the flesh and the saving of the soul.

God knows it will be with many a tear and heartache, if she has to take up her roots and leave the man who has treated her so badly. But her whole desire should be for the deliverance of her husband and for his salvation, that the home might yet be restored in the love of Christ. Just think of the confusion were such a person, having left her husband, to remarry, if perhaps years later the man is saved on skid row. He has the right to come back to the woman who has left him and ask her to take him back again. Although in certain circumstances it may be right for one party of a marriage to leave the other, that does not alter the great truth of the Word of God concerning the permanence of the marriage tie.

May I point out just one more thing in the latter part of the chapter: marriage in its power. What comfort these words bring to some who are suffering the awful heartbreak of an unequal yoke! And that is the issue here.

It is possible for a Christian so to forget his responsibilities to God and the commands of His Word that in a moment of excitement her or she is carried away and becomes linked to an unsaved person. That is, however, no ground for divorce. His part, rather, is to do everything he can to win his partner for the Lord Jesus, that, in spite of his sin and disobedience, God may have mercy upon him and extend that mercy to the person to whom he is married. Again, if one party to the marriage is converted after the wedding, both of them being unbelievers when they were married, what mutual understanding and love is necessary! "The woman which hath an husband that believeth not, and if he be pleased to dwell with her, let her not leave him" (7:13).

Perhaps you have just been saved, and you are the first one in your family to become a Christian, your partner being still unconverted. Be careful how you treat him (or her), won't you? Don't nag at him; don't drive religion down his throat and give him a miserable time because you are saved and he isn't. Be patient and tolerant, although the change in your life may make him absolutely furious with you. If you long to see your loved one converted, then be grateful to God for His mercy in your own soul, and pray with all your heart that you may so live in patient love with your husband (or wife) that the very difference in your life may attract him or her to the Lord Jesus.

A colleague of mine in the ministry had just that experience. When his wife was converted, he thought that was just one more burden to an already energy-consuming business career. His wife had gone off her head religiously! Then he discovered within a matter of a few months that she had become so much more patient and gentle, kind and loving. He said to himself, "She has something that I must have," and he found the Savior too.

That's the way! Thank God for His mercy, and pray that your life-partner may share it. Be infinitely patient and forbearing, but raise the Christian standard high, even though in so doing it makes your husband or wife angrier than ever. If since your conversion God has spoken to you about drinking, gambling, dancing, shows, or other things, and you feel that you cannot now go to these places, your unsaved mate may say in disgust, "If you don't come with me, I'll go out with another woman (or man)." Then you know the sword in your own soul, but the only way to see him saved is to be true to the Lord, no matter what it costs.

Stay together, says Paul in verse 14, because by your conversion the whole family has been brought onto praying ground; "For the unbelieving husband is sanctified by the wife, and the unbelieving wife is sanctified by the husband: else were your children unclean; but now they are holy." As a child of God, you are His vantage point to reach them, and it is not God's will that one of them should perish. I believe that if one party is saved after marriage, that person has every right to claim the salvation of the whole household, even though it takes years.

But if, in spite of everything, the unbeliever goes, then you must let him go. If he does depart, you have no right to be remarried, unless in his departure he himself commits adultery. But if the unbelieving partner of a marriage leaves because he or she cannot stand the testimony of the other, then let him (or her) go, even though it breaks your heart. But you have no right to be remarried; yours is the right to pray that even in his departure he might be brought to know the Lord Jesus, "For what knowest thou, O wife, whether thou shalt save thy husband? or how knowest thou, O man, whether thou shalt save thy wife?" (7:16). If you hold on and pray and believe, you may see God answer prayer exceedingly abundantly above all you can ask or think!

What is the principle behind the power in marriage? It is summed up in the last little phrase in verse 24, "Let every man, wherein he is called, therein abide with God." This reinforces what is said in verse 20: "Let every man abide in the same calling wherein he was called." If God calls a man or woman to remain single, he will give grace for it. If God calls to the married life, and that involves hardship, or maybe a divided home, or even suffering, He will give grace for that too.

The one whose family life is an example to others is to be respected. The one who remains for the Kingdom's sake is to be respected. The one who suffers the cruel misunderstanding of an unbelieving partner is to be respected, also. In every instance we are to abide in our calling: submitting to the will of God, depending upon the grace of God, making every effort to bring glory to God, striving to be approved by Him, always bearing in mind that one day we shall all stand before the judgment seat of Christ.

CHAPTER TWELVE

Happy, Though Unmarried

1 Corinthians 7:23–40

Some very delicate and difficult problems had been submitted to Paul for his decision and judgment by the church at Corinth. Among them was the whole subject of marriage from the Christian standpoint. Several related questions were treated in the earlier part of this seventh chapter, and now we come to the problems of those who are not married. Paul looks at this from two different aspects: First, those who are daughters of Christian parents, and then those who have lost a partner and are left in a state of widowhood.

The apostle puts a boundary line around what he has to say about this topic: "Now concerning virgins I have no commandment of the Lord" (7:25). We can search the four Gospels thoroughly without finding any teaching from the Lord Jesus concerning the unmarried state except, of course, by implication.

"The wife is bound by the law as long as her husband liveth; but if her husband be dead, she is at liberty to be married to whom she will; only in the Lord. But she is happier if she so abide, after my judgment." Will you please notice that Paul does not say "as long as the man liveth?" He may have died as a *husband*, although the man is still alive, when he has been unfaithful in the marriage relationship and leaves his partner. If the marriage is broken by the tragedy of adultery, then the one who is left is entitled to Christian marriage. Our Lord taught that perfectly clearly in Matthew 19. Paul concludes the above advice by saying, "I think also that I have the Spirit of God" (7:39–40).

I want to underline something very significant: here Paul distinguishes carefully between "thus saith the Lord," and that which comes by the exercise of his own judgment. However, that qualification does not render what he has to say any less authoritative. He speaks "as one that hath obtained mercy of the Lord to be faithful" (7:25). He gives his judgment from a mind that has been enlightened by the Holy Spirit and taught from the Word of God.

In both instances, in the case of the virgin (the unmarried daughter), and of the widow or the widower bereft of a life-partner, he comes to the same conclusion: "He that giveth her in marriage doeth well; but he that giveth her not in marriage doeth better" (7:38). "She is happier if she so abide, after my judgment" (7:40).

That is quite startling, especially in these days when apparently the unmarried condition is to be avoided at any cost. Some people most unadvisedly put some kind of slight upon those who are single. How could a man speaking under the direction of the Spirit of God come to the conclusion that under certain circumstances it would be better to remain single? That is our question: how to be happy, through unmarried.

As I studied this chapter, it seemed to me that Paul presents a plan to be adopted: "Art thou bound unto a wife? Seek not to be loosed. Art thou loosed from a wife? Seek not a wife" (7:27). Two words that stand out here are these: "seek not." For instance, consider how dangerous it would be to fall in love with someone whose idea of loyalty to Christ is certainly not the same as your own. Here is the carefully conceived plan of a man who knows how to maintain the situation under the control of the Spirit of God: Paul says, "seek not a wife."

That stands in refreshing contrast to the frenzied search for a life-partner which is conducted by many people today. When one witnesses the frantic efforts made by some to find a mate, one can only trust that the person who is victim of such an assault has retained enough emotional stability to be able to conduct a strategic withdrawal immediately, before he or she becomes deeply involved in the situation. Much wreckage has been caused by the tactics of a person who seeks a life-partner at any price.

Paul has already given us this principle when he says, "All things are lawful unto me, but all things are not expedient: all things are lawful for me, but I will not be brought under the power of any" (6:12). Here is a man who is really living in victory; he has control over himself by the power of the Spirit of God. In some instances, as in the thirty-sixth and thirty-seventh verses of this chapter, he recognizes that marriage may be necessary: "Nevertheless he that standeth stedfast in his heart, having no necessity, but hath power over his own will, and hath so decreed in his heart that he will keep his virgin, doeth well." Marriage is perfectly lawful; marriage, in some instances, may be necessary; but, Paul says, that is not the issue.

He is able to disassociate himself from the situation and keep a cool head: the real point is, "Is it expedient?" Is it right for the individual in the light of what Paul describes as "the present distress" (7:26)? Now I take that statement to mean not simply the local conditions that existed in Corinth; I rather think Paul meant the tremendous pressures that were being brought to bear upon this little group of believers by the spiritual forces of wickedness. If that was true then, certainly it is equally true today.

Here is the plan that a fellow or a girl who is unmarried should adopt: *seek not.* You do not come for training at a Bible Institute or a Seminary in order to find a wife or a husband. You do not live in order that somehow or other, at any price, you may be married. You must ask yourself if this is something that is going to be expedient in the light of the pressures that are going to come, and in the light of what you believe to be God's will for your life. Know what it means to stand in control of your affections and emotions. This is no easy thing; it requires intense spiritual discipline. If it is difficult, you may ask, why should this plan be adopted?

Paul goes on to show us that there is a purpose to be achieved: "I would have you without carefulness. He that is unmarried careth for the things that belong to the Lord, how he may please the Lord: But he that is married careth for the things that are of the world, how he may please his wife" (7:32–33).

"I would have you without carefulness. …" He says, "that ye may attend upon the Lord without distraction" (7:32, 35b). Here are two great purposes to be achieved in a man's life. They are possible whether you are married or unmarried, but, in Paul's judgment, easier to achieve if you are single. If a man or a woman enters into the relationship of matrimony, this may result in the interests of each other crowding out the interests of the Lord.

I have known a man called to the mission field, for instance, who married a girl with no call, and years afterward have seen him sinking into the quicksands of life. The blessing of God has departed long since; he had missed God's best. I have seen a girl, too, dedicated to the Lord, but afraid of going through life alone. She entered into matrimony out of God's will, and it was not very long before her home and family and immediate circumstances crowded out loyalty to the Lord Jesus Christ.

Don't tell me such a person is happy! He has to look back upon the day he made a choice from which there is no escape, and knows he is living in God's second best. By involving himself in a relationship out of the will of God, he has become full of carefulness; his interests are in the things of the world and not in the things of the Lord.

However, that need not always be the case. There is not question, obviously, but that marriage in the Lord can be a tremendous blessing, a great and wonderful experience. "But and if thou marry," says Paul, "thou hast not sinned" (7:28). There is no necessity for marriage to put the Lord Jesus in second place. But if it is marriage out of God's will, and it is going to lead to distracting care, then it is better, as Paul says, to remain single.

"Without carefulness... without distraction." I would lovingly put those two words into the thinking and conscience of those who are single. There is a tremendous potential of blessing in serving the Lord with freedom and concentration. In any event, Paul says, if you are going to marry, you are going to have trouble (7:28). No matter how saintly people are and how far they are on together in the Christian life, when they begin to live together, problems are bound to come. It is not on the great sorrows or trials that marriage flounders, but rather upon the irritations of everyday difficulties: a crying child, a late breakfast, a short temper, an unsympathetic mother-in-law—this kind of thing can cause a marriage to become shaky, unless right at the very heart of it is the Lord Jesus Himself.

As we think about attending upon the Lord "without carefulness," our minds go immediately to that familiar story where the Lord Jesus spoke to two sisters and said to one of them, "Martha, thou art careful and troubled about many things," and to the other, "Mary hath chosen that good part, which shall not be taken away from her" (Luke 10:41–42).

It is possible, both in the married and in the unmarried state to live without carefulness and without distraction. It is that which makes married life so wonderful and the unmarried state so full of potential blessing.

One other thing I would get out of this passage, perhaps the most important of all: there is a principle to be accepted. You will notice how Paul brings in eternity here: "This I say, brethren, the time is short: it remaineth, that both they that have wives be as though they had none; And they that weep, as though they wept not; and they that rejoice, as though they rejoiced not; and they that buy, as thought they possessed not; And they that use this world, as not abusing it: for the fashion of this world passeth away" (7:29–31).

As Paul gives his judgment on this question of being married or unmarried, he shows us the principle upon which a man or woman may make their decision: the times are troubled; the Lord is coming soon; the opportunity for service is brief. Life is short, at best, and it can end quickly and unexpectedly. Therefore these relationships of life should be treated as though they did not exist, in the light of the urgency of these days. He speaks of marriage, of sorrow and joy, of business life, of the world itself, how to use it and how not to use it. Because of the pressures upon us and the spiritual evil confronting us, these things must take second place — almost be regarded as non-existent.

Now Paul is not implying that we should be callous or unkind; that would be totally contrary to all the teaching of the New Testament concerning our relationship with one another. But he does bring the reality of eternity right into everyday life, so that we may live in the ordinary realm with the recognized presence of the Lord Jesus and in the light of heaven.

What does that involve? It means that on the questions of being married, everything is to be governed by our relationship to the Lord Himself. For those who are married, there will often be times when the comfort of the home and joy of each other's presence has to be denied, has to take second place for the sake of the Lord, His work and His service.

Sometimes sorrow threatens to take us away from our duty, our loyalty to the King of kings, our service for the Lord. It must not be allowed to do that; if in the time of heartbreak and sorrow we are tempted to give in, these things have to be regarded as though they did not exist. We must press on in the love of God and for the sake of the Lord Jesus.

Sometimes thrilling circumstances make us full of happiness, but if joy conflicts with our duty to the Master, then it has to be swept to one side. Nothing must be allowed to make us neglect or delay, or to be anything less than our best in His service. If business threatens to interfere with the Christian life, says the apostle, you cannot help going on buying—but be sure that you hold the things you buy very loosely, and that your interest and affections are not centered on them, but on the things of God.

The principle to be observed, as you seek to apply these things to your own life and come to a decision on important matters, is in the two words we have considered already: "seek not," linked with another command of the Lord Jesus: "Seek ye first the kingdom of God, and his righteousness; and all these things shall be added unto you" (Matthew 6:33).

In other words, if in your life you put God first, and His call, even if it seems at the moment it would tear your heart in pieces, if it means denying some human love, turning your back upon some fascinating possibility, then everything that is in the good and acceptable and perfect will of God for you will be added to you.

If only people today, young and old alike, facing these tremendously intimate and personal problems, would follow that principle, seeking first His Kingdom, how wonderful it would be to watch how the Lord, as He is put first, frequently brings into their lives the partner of His choice. He gives to them the persons He has waiting for them as He sees that they are determined above everything else to serve Him without carefulness and without distraction.

Finally, a word of loving concern and warning. You have seen what the apostle has to say concerning this situation of marriage or singleness, and I have sought to show you that all this should lie within the sphere of the sovereignty of the Lord Jesus. My word of warning is this: to step into any relationship outside the government of the Lord, that is to say, outside His permissive will, is not only to involve yourself in tragedy, but perhaps to bring sorrow into the lives of a generation yet to be born. For a person who enters into marriage out of the will of God and brings children into the world may cause their whole lives to know the blight of unhappiness and misery, because their parents were married out of the will of God.

What a tremendous thing it is to be able, by the grace of God and by the power of His Spirit, to do what Paul did, to stand in victory, in control of his emotions, making the decision he knows to be God's will, that which is expedient in the light of all the pressures upon him. Then whether you are to go through life single or married, you are going to live without carefulness and attend upon the Lord without distraction. May that be your happy portion and mine until our Lord Jesus comes!

CHAPTER THIRTEEN

SETTING AN EXAMPLE

1 CORINTHIANS 8:1–13

One of the loveliest things about being a Christian, I think, is the fellowship into which we are introduced with others who know and love the save Savior. It crosses over boundaries of race, class, and background, and draws us together in the precious recognition that we are one in Christ. There is a fellowship about which the unbelieving world knows nothing, a relationship based upon our spiritual union in the body of Jesus Christ, into which all who love Him are placed at the moment of their new birth.

What a tragedy it is when we reveal our low level of Christian experience by allowing divergence of opinion to break fellowship, or by our example cause another Christian to stumble! But it is a wonderful thing when our fellowship in Christ is experienced and expressed so that the desire of our Lord is fulfilled: "By this shall all men know that ye are my disciples, if ye have love one to another" (John 13:35).

I believe that the greatest soul-winning help in the whole world is unity among believers. Likewise the greatest hindrance to soul-winning is division in the Christian church. Therefore our fellowship in the Lord carries with it a tremendous responsibility. A very important yet most neglected aspect of Christian teaching today is the duty we owe our brother and sister in Christ. This is the theme of the chapter now under consideration, in which Paul answers the second question with which the Corinthian church has confronted him.

Let us be clear about the meaning of the question they are raising: he begins, "Now as touching things offered unto idols" (8:1). This subject may seem to have no possible connection with our lives today. However, as we see this in its true light, we begin to realize that it has immense significance for us. Paul devotes no less than three chapters to his answer, applying it to different aspects of Christian living. It brings into clearer view the whole question of the influence of this young church on the great city of Corinth. Indeed, what should be the influence of any Christian group in a pagan community?

From the context, we find that certain portions of the animals that were offered as sacrifices to idols were put on public sale in the market place. Even in Old Testament times, some parts of the animals sacrificed were retained as food for the priests, and the rest consumed by fire as an offering to God. In Corinth, this kind of mean was very common — the parts of the carcasses not offered in the heathen temples were put on sale at cut-rate prices, and human nature, being the same then as now, was always out for a bargain. Therefore the question arising in the minds of these Christians was this: Does the purchase and use of this mean, part of which has been offered to idols, involve us in compromise with idol worship? The fact that they ask the question of Paul certainly shows that they are uncertain and divided about it.

The immediate situation is purely local, but it is not as local as Corinth, nor as ancient as Paul's day, in its application to your life and mine. Each of us faces the same sort of situation six days a week, in one way or another.

Take, for instance, the Christian and his relationship to movies. Some of them, of course, are obviously rotten and filthy, even in the way they are advertised, so that they are no place for the child of God at all. But not all are like that: some are excellent, others are educational, and some have other kinds of value. Therefore, some will argue, is it not all right for a Christian to practice discrimination, to attend only the ones he knows will do no harm? Or if you have television in your home, you know that some things that are shown are bad from beginning to end, but other things are quite good and of educational value. Therefore, surely you can choose what you will watch — that won't do any harm, will it? This is the argument we often hear in favor of the policy of selectivity.

What about the matter of social drinking? Of course it is wrong to drink too much; nobody is going to argue about that. But just one drink in business circumstances, at a luncheon with executives: "Well, you know, it will help in putting over the deal. And it doesn't do me any harm, I know when to stop." So say some Christians. If we set definite limits and know where to draw the line, why isn't an occasional drink permissible for a believer?

Looking at this truth from the opposite angle, the Christian may say, "I believe certain things about my bible. I have been brought up in a particular school of doctrine and theology, and I accept certain kinds of interpretations. Therefore I must have no fellowship at all with anyone who does not think exactly as I do."

One could quote many things that would portray the same principle: meat offered to idols. The immediate situation has no connection at all, but the principle is relevant to our lives today. This is the question raised.

Then what is the issue involved? Let us look in the first verse: "We know that we all have knowledge." Here is Paul's immediate answer to the question; he says that because we are Christians we all have knowledge. Now he does not suggest that because we are believers in Christ we know everything. He means that, since we have entered into that relationship to Jesus Christ our Lord when we were born again, the Spirit of God within us has shone a floodlight of revelations upon questions like this.

"Concerning therefore the eating of those things that are offered in sacrifice unto idols, we know that an idol is nothing ... to us there is but one God, the Father, of whom are all things, and we in him; on Lord Jesus Christ, by whom are all things, and we by him (8:4, 6). Because we are Christians, our eyes have been opened by the Holy Spirit and we know that an idol is not real. There is only one God, our Father, and Jesus Christ our Lord. There cannot be contamination from something that does not exist. In that respect, there can be no harm in eating this meat—we are perfectly free to do it. Of course we are, if that is the only factor involved.

But wait a minute! To make a decision about what is right in these cases based upon what you know because you are a Christian and the Holy Spirit has revealed to you the Word of truth—to make a decision on that alone is dangerous. As a Christian you do not live to yourself, nor do you live only for the Lord. There are others involved in the situation.

"Knowledge puffeth up," says Paul in verse 1, and he goes on to say, "if any man think that he knoweth anything, he knoweth nothing yet as he ought to know" (8:2). The key that originally opened the door for us to the Holy Spirit's teaching was a broken and contrite heart, when we came to the Lord in repentance and faith. And that is the only kind of life upon which any truth has shone from heaven about anything. A man may think he knows the truth because his intellect has been taught, but he really knows about the things of God only when the Holy Spirit reveals them to his heart. Things he could never have known by study or research becomes clear, for the Scripture says that God has revealed them to babes and hid them from the wise and prudent.

In other words, the danger is that when God has shown us truth, even through the experience of a broken heart, we might become spiritually proud and conceited. We can say, "Whereas once I was blind, now I see." We can become humble, yet proud of being humble. That kind of pride can lead to spiritual conceit and dogmatism, which is usually accompanied by contempt for anyone who thinks differently.

If I make a decision, therefore, about what I can or cannot do, based merely upon what I know, I shall go wrong, because there is someone else involved. What about my Christian friend? What about the example I set before the unbeliever? What about my fellowship with other Christians?

The unpleasant side of a movie may not affect a Christian; it has not appeal because he is dead to it all in Christ. He has victory over it and is "free from the law, O happy condition!" The Holy Spirit has shown him this, therefore that which used to attract him has no further claim. He very carefully selects and enjoys the film that is instructional or educational. In the light of his relationship to Christ and on that basis alone, he decides. He knows how to discriminate in the use of his television set. When something comes on that he knows he should not see, he turns it off. He quickly recognizes something that this conscience rejects because he has been instructed by the Lord and enlightened by the Spirit.

Similarly, in the matter of social drinking, he says he can take a drink occasionally because he knows when to stop. In Christ, he has victory over it and power over his own will. He can take a drink and it does not affect him. This type of Christian is saying that because God has met and saved him, and has filled him with His Spirit and given him victory in Christ, these things make no appeal now, and therefore he is perfectly free. But he has never begun to think about other people.

Let us look at the principle at stake here: "Howbeit there is not in every man that knowledge: for some with conscience of the idol unto this hour eat it as a thing offered unto an idol; and their conscience being weak is defiled. … But take heed lest by any means this liberty of yours become a stumblingblock to them that are weak" (8:7, 9).

Paul says that knowledge puffs a man up, making him spiritually conceited and proud. Eventually he comes to the bursting-point, for anything that is constantly inflated explodes in the end. "But love edifies [builds up]" (8:1). If a man has knowledge only, then he is incapable of judging aright. But if in his life the knowledge of what God has taught him is mastered by his love for his fellow Christian and a deep concern for those who do not know the Lord, then that love leads him to think of others.

The unbelievers watching these Christians at Corinth do not know that an idol is nothing to them at all. They worship idols, and do not understand that the Christian is indifferent to them, that they make no appeal, that to him the idols are not real. To the pagan they are very real, an important part of his life. If he watches Christians buying food offered to idols, in his eyes they are acknowledging the reality of that sacrifice and of the gods to whom the meat has been offered.

The believers, therefore, have to act not only on the basis of the knowledge that they have, but upon the basis of the love of God shed abroad in their hearts by the Holy Spirit. The Christian must recognize that by his example he may be putting a stumblingblock in the way of a weaker brother, or keeping some person from Christ, and that is a sin against the Lord Himself: "But when ye sin so against the brethren, and wound their weak conscience, ye sin against Christ" (8:12).

In other words, knowledge and spiritual understanding alone may lead us astray, so that we become smug and sanctimonious and spiritually proud. To do things which may not be wrong for us, which may not be harmful, but which may cause others to stumble or to be offended, making their path to the Lord Jesus the more difficult, is to sin against the Lord Himself.

You may think you can go to that movie alone or watch that show on television, and it may not hinder you at all. You may think you can take your drink and it does not harm you, but there may be a business associate watching you who is on the verge of confessing Christ. Perhaps he is spiritually troubled and concerned, and in his path to the cross you have put a stumblingblock because you are doing something which is causing him to be offended. Love, therefore, must master the Christian's knowledge, and some of the things he may feel he is perfectly entitled to do he will renounce for the sake of others.

Here then is the principle. It is not that you see no harm in doing this or that, but rather that you cannot afford to do it because of what it might do to someone else. You may say you can go to the movies and it will not affect you at all, but what about your friend to whom it has a base appeal? He does not know that it has no effect upon you, and he is watching your example. You can choose your television programs, but how do you know where to draw the line? How do you make this decision, bearing in mind another who is more easily affected by that kind of thing than you are? Are you a stumblinglock in his way to the Lord?

You know when to stop in the matter of social drinking, but does the colleague who attends the same function with you? As he watches you indulging, even though only in a limited way, does he say, "If he can do it, so can I"? Is he not likely to conclude that a Christian is not so very different from other people after all?

Are you cutting off from your fellowship the man who does not agree theologically with you in everything you say? Are you going to regard him as accursed, or show him the love of God in your heart and through your life? You owe him a ministry that only a Spirit-filled Christian can bring, the love of the Lord Jesus Christ.

Out of this answer of Paul to the Corinthian church on the matter of sacrifice to idols emerges a tremendously significant aspect of the Christian life. What sort of example are you setting as a child of God in your immediate circle of friends? Is the Lord asking you to forego something that you consider perfectly harmless for the sake of some-one who is watching your life critically? If you were to face that one thing in your life, it might remove a block in the way of someone. One step to the cross would be made easier for another because the Lord Jesus is revealed in your life more clearly now that you are taking a stand.

Christian fellowship is a lovely gift, but it carries great responsibili-ties. Being all one in Christ is precious, but we have to make our every decision not only in regard to our relationship to the Lord Jesus, but also in regard to our relationship to our brother and sister in Christ. Have you thought about that in terms of your entertainment, of what you eat and drink, of where you go and what you watch?

Jesus Christ said, "Greater love hath no man than this, that a man lay down his life for his friends" (John 15:13). He Himself had an even greater love, for He laid down His life for His enemies at Calvary. But that is the principle upon which you are called to live as a child of God in the light of the cross, to lay down your life for your friends, to forfeit things that you may consider to be perfectly legitimate in order that your friends may find the way to Jesus more easily. That is just what will happen. If you lay down your life as a mat for other people to walk on, there will be plenty who will come around and say, "You are too narrow!" There are others who will insist that you are compromising by your fellowship with others who do not agree on some points of doctrine. But the master principle is not what you know by revelation, but how you love by the impartation of the Holy Spirit. It doesn't matter what others think if you can look into the face of your lovely Lord and hear Him say, "Well done!"

As you go out into your daily life, remember others are watching: not only your Lord in heaven, but the person by your desk, in your home, on your street, in the hospital, or at your school. God is asking you to make your decisions about what you do or what you don't do, not only in the light of what He has taught you, but in the light of how it is going to affect the approach of others to Calvary.

Perhaps I should add that as far as I personally am concerned, there is no room in my life at all for the movies, television, social drinking or anything else of that character. But my reason for abstention is not based upon a legalistic argument which only serves to create a vacuum in the life of the one submitting to it, but rather upon love to the Lord Jesus Christ which involves total consecration of time, money and everything I am to Him, and also upon my concern for my brethren in Christ, and especially for the young convert, before whom I would ever seek to be an example for His sake.

CHAPTER FOURTEEN

THE GENUINE ARTICLE

1 CORINTHIANS 9:1–27

It would seem strange that Paul has to defend his authority at a place like Corinth. As he wrote earlier, "I have planted, Apollos watered; but God gave the increase" (3:6). Here he reminds them again, "Are not ye my work in the Lord?" (9:1). Is it possible that they are the seal of his apostleship and yet they question his authority?

But the evidence of spiritual authority is not success — that is where we go wrong. We judge a Christian by his success, and that is not the basis of heaven's judgment upon any of us; the issue is much deeper than that. It is not enough that Paul had founded the church at Corinth: "You should be adequate evidence; why should I have to say more than that?" He is prepared to face them and give clear reasons for the spiritual unction that rested upon his life and testimony: "My answer to them that do examine me is this" (9:3), he says, and throughout the chapter he proceeds to give his credentials.

"To examine" means to make a searching scrutiny. It is the same word used of Pontius Pilate in his "examination" of Christ. Every Christian must expect the same treatment. We will be examined by people who do not accept the reality of our gospel; we live in the glare of the searchlight. We have no right to expect to be hidden from the world, and that world is going to judge Christianity by those who represent it. The believer will be submitted to a careful scrutiny day and night by his colleagues and friends concerning the quality of his Christian life.

Of course, there are situations in which it is altogether wrong for a Christian to vindicate himself, to stand up for his rights. But that is not the issue here. If a man is to stand the test as a child of God—not merely as a minister, but as a Christian anywhere—he must be able to produce credentials to indicate that he is genuine. I believe the world is tired of religion that is a sham. People want to see in the hearts and lives of those who profess Christ the characteristics of the genuine article. Unless these marks are upon our testimony, others will not desire our Lord. Therefore we must ask ourselves if there is something in our life that gives indisputable answer to those who raise a query concerning this Christian gospel of ours.

We are not to be judged by our success nor by the number of conversions produced by our ministry. We are not to be judged by our creed or doctrine, for people are not primarily interested in what we believe. We are not to be judged by our orthodoxy nor by the particular associations which we may keep in the fellowship of the Christian church. There is one thing by which a Christian is going to stand or fall, and that is his reality with God. Are the marks of Holy Spirit unction about him in his daily walk? Is there a clear and authentic ring to his testimony so that, although people may not agree with what he says or how he lives, they cannot dispute the fact that the man is close to God?

This was Paul's argument, and he produces here three clear statements to defend his apostleship. In considering them we must ask ourselves if there is the same stamp of genuineness about each one of us.

In the first place, every Christian has a right to certain things in life. He has a right to food; he has a right to love, to a family, to a home; he has a right to decent pay; he has a right to recreation and physical activity. He has as much right to these things as anyone else. But Paul is saying that one mark of Christian discipleship is that he has completely renounced his right to these things.

"Have we not power to eat and drink?" (9:4). Of course he had a right to normal rations. "Have we not power to lead about a sister, a wife, as well as other apostles?"—especially Peter (9:5). They all thought very highly of that disciple in Corinth, for some had said, "I am of Peter." He was married; has not Paul the right to be married, also? Has he not the right to romance, to a home and family life?

"Have not we power to forbear working?" (9:6). Of course he has a right to normal recreation. He has the right to care for his body, to have physical exercise, to take time off and to enjoy it. "They which preach the gospel should live of the gospel" (9:14). Had he not the right to expect that as he preached, he was paid for it? Was he not entitled to normal remuneration, just as anybody else?

Then in verse 15 he makes a tremendous statement: "But I have used none of these things." The Lord Jesus was dearer to Paul that anything else, and he could stand before them and say that he had renounced every one of his rights. The test of apostleship is one that many of us will find very difficult to attain.

Many of our missionary family, however, have denied themselves the right to a normal life. Of every one of them it can be said that they have a right to an adequate salary, to a Christian home, to good food, to reasonable recreation. But each of them can say, "I have used none of these things for the sake of the gospel." We could go to any part of the world and find examples of those who come within this test of apostleship today.

Many of us are in the place where we are because we believe we are in the will of God, but are we there at the loss of even one meal for the sake of Jesus? Has your Christian testimony cost you anything? You have a right to good food, of course, but have you even denied yourself one meal that something extra might be given to the Lord, or that extra time might be spent in prayer and the Word? That is the practical meaning of fasting.

You are entitled to human love, a wife or husband, a home and children. Perhaps there was a time in you life when you knew God was calling you in one direction and you were involved in a legitimate romance with someone who would call you in another, and at the cost of breaking your heart you let your love go for the sake of the gospel. You were perfectly entitled to that romance, because the other person was a Christian, but he or she was not called to do the thing to which you were called, and you renounced that which was your right for Jesus' sake.

You have a right to adequate pay, but as an evidence of the reality of your Christian testimony you are working for about a third of what you could be earning—because you are in Christian work. Thank God in your heart that whenever people raise the question about your Christian life, you bear the mark of authenticity because you have said "no" to things that are normal and right for the sake of your Lord; you have renounced your claims.

"What things were gain to me, those I counted loss for Christ," was the testimony of Paul thirty years after this Corinthian letter, when he was writing to the church at Philippi. He was able to say that the experience was still true of him: "Yea doubtless, and I count all things but loss for the excellency of the knowledge of Christ Jesus my Lord" (Philippians 3:7–8).

Paul vindicates his apostleship by pointing out things that were absolutely legitimate, but to which he has said "no" for the Lord's sake. Within the scope of that test, what counts is not my doctrine or my orthodoxy, or my connections, but that my heart and life bear the brand of the cross: it has cost me something to follow Jesus.

But there is something else, for Paul says, "Though I preach the gospel, I have nothing to glory of: for necessity is laid upon me; yea woe is unto me, if I preach not the gospel!" (9:16). He is able to face those who question his authority with the fact that he has maintained a testimony. This is an obligation which is laid upon every one of us.

Have we maintained a clear testimony through the years of our life as a Christian? Has it been kept true and clear? Is our ministry being maintained? Is our testimony above question? If that were made a condition of church membership, I wonder how we would fare. It certainly is made a test of fellowship with the Lord Jesus. Woe is me if I testify not to the Savior of the world! There will be lost communion and fellowship with Christ, lost opportunities, a fruitless life.

Paul had maintained his testimony, and this is how he did it: "Unto the Jews I became a Jew" (9:20–22). He observed their law; he put himself voluntarily under their obligations in order that he might win them for Christ.

To the Gentiles he became as one of them in their freedom, yet he never forgot that he was the Lord's bond-slave and therefore under His authority. Paul did not compromise his position in the sight of heaven, but he went right alongside those men in their need and sin to win them for Jesus.

To the weak he became as one weak. He refused to use his liberty as a Christian in any way that might become a stumblingblock or lead another astray. "I am made all things to all men, that I might by all means save some" (9:22). He maintained his ministry by going anywhere and everywhere, no matter what the situation and surroundings were, to reach people with the message. He crossed over boundaries of prejudice in race and religion to win men and women for Jesus Christ.

I do not wish to be uncharitable, but isn't it sad that in so many instances Christian people move in their own little watertight compartments and never launch out into somebody else's situation at all? They are locked in; their circle never touches the circles of unbelievers. They move only in their little circle of Christian fellowship; very seldom do they take the plunge outside in order to win another for Christ. I believe perhaps the greatest need of all in our evangelical circles today is that we might have the boldness in Christ to cross some of the barriers that exist to win others for Him. "Woe is unto me if I preach not the gospel!" says Paul.

But there is another acid test that Paul applies here. He exposes something in his life about which we would know nothing unless he told us. There is an enemy he has been wrestling with: "I therefore so run, not as uncertainly; so fight I, not as one that beateth the air: But I keep under my body, and bring it into subjection: lest that by any means, when I have preached to others I myself should be a castaway" (9:26–27).

J. B. Phillips, in his *Letters to Young Churches*, paraphrases it like this: "I am no shadow-boxer, I really fight! I am my body's sternest master, for fear that when I have preached to others I should myself be disqualified."

I do not think for moment that Paul was concerned that he should be lost, but he was desperately concerned that God might remove his testimony and take him from his place of opportunity and witness because deep down in his heart he had been failing to contend with the enemy. Perhaps this is the greatest battle any child of God has to face.

In connection with this whole issue of preaching a so-called "gospel of works," I would say that the only faith that matters is a faith that is expressed in the action of your body. The faith that has qualified a man for heaven gets into his feet, his hands, his mind, his tongue — in other words, it is expressed in the physical. If his faith in Jesus Christ does not begin to make his whole body move in the will of God, there is no evidence that it is saving faith at all. It is how a Christian uses his body that proclaims his eternal destiny. That is why Paul says these tremendous things, "I buffet my body; I keep it in subjection." Like any athlete daily keeps himself in training behind the scenes to win an earthly crown, he keeps his body down.

Do you qualify for apostleship under this test? In that body of yours that has not yet been redeemed, what is happening? Are you, as the apostle said of himself, keeping your body in subjection? It is possible for a child of God to be indwelt by the Holy Sprit, yet to be mastered by the flesh. It is possible for appetites and indulgence, all the claims of the body, to rule the life of the child of God.

As other people examine our lives, do they see that you, as a Christen, have left behind certain things to which you are entitled for Jesus' sake? Do they see you as one who is maintaining an unblemished testimony? You have not let down the standards, and you are taking the gospel message out to an ungodly world. But do they see, above all, a man (or woman) who is triumphing in his own personal walk because he is not allowing the flesh with its appetites and intemperance to dominate his life, a man living under the control of the Spirit of God? These are the authentic marks of Christian experience.

But even the apostle Paul could never have expressed those thing in his life were it not that within him was the indwelling life of the risen Lord Jesus which enabled him to do so. It is true that Paul renounced his rights, but what about the Savior? The Lord Jesus counted it not a thing to be grasped after to be equal with God, but laid aside every right He had and came down all the way to the cross. It is true Paul maintained his ministry but what about the Lord? He set His face steadfastly toward Jerusalem and refused to be diverted from a ministry that cost Him his life. It is true Paul engaged the enemy at close quarters and kept his body in subjection, but what about the Lord Jesus? In the wilderness and in the garden, on the dusty road and on the cross, in every detail and at every moment, He answered every accusation of the enemy by quoting from the Word of God, and stood against every temptation that would take Him for God's will until He defeated Satan at Calvary, and from the open tomb.

Perhaps you have been saying to yourself, "I don't know whether I can pass the tests—I'm not sure if I've renounced anything for Jesus. I'm not sure about my ministry; I don't know about this battle with the enemy." But the Holy Spirit within you, my friend, will give you unction to maintain you ministry and testimony; He will give you courage to combat Satan at close quarters and defeat the enemy of your soul.

CHAPTER FIFTEEN

OVERCOMING PITFALLS IN THE WAY

1 CORINTHIANS 10:1–14

In our last study Paul was defending his apostleship against those who refused to recognize his authority. He had spoken very firmly to the church at Corinth, for his ministry and whole apostolic authority were under question. Above everything, he had told them something that they would never have known other wise: "I keep under my body, and bring it into subjection: lest that by any means, when I have preached to others, I myself should be a castaway" (9:27).

As Paul said that, he was exposing the soul of a Christian, for it was something that went on in the inner part of his life. Not that he feared to lose his relationship with the Lord, but he was concerned lest he should lose his apostleship. He feared that somehow the sense of unction might in some strange, irrevocable manner be taken from him, the sense of divine authority, the knowledge that God was speaking to him, the consciousness of Holy Spirit power in his testimony. If that went from him, he knew that he would have nothing left, for this was the evidence of his approval before God and his authority before men.

This holy fear ought to posses not only the apostle but every Christian, the fear that somehow we might so live and so grieve the Spirit that we become like Samson, who went out in imagined strength and knew not that the Spirit of the Lord had departed from him. It is possible that evidence of real power and supernatural authority may be lost.

This is something that every Sunday school teacher ought to dread, every mother who has the care of little children, every man witnessing for Christ in the business world. It is something that every child of God ought to fear. If we lost our "thus saith the Lord," our unquestionable mark of integrity, our Holy Spirit life and liberty, what have we left?

You may have natural ability, great personal charm, and much education, but if as a child of God you lose that thing which Paul dreaded to lose—that sense of heavenly authority about his life—you have nothing left that can bring a soul near to Jesus. We can never lose His presence, for He is near and ever will be until He takes us to heaven; but we may stumble and fall, so slip in our Christian life that we lost His power and unction.

The Sunday school teacher will speak to the same little group of children, but there is no spiritual effectiveness to her teaching. The businessman may witness to others of Christ, but it is all just talk. The mother may lead her little family in prayer, but she has lost the power that grips their hearts to win them for Jesus. To lose that is to become a sounding brass or a tinkling cymbal. This is what Paul meant when he climaxed his whole warning by saying, "let him that thinketh he standeth take heed lest he fall." On this royal route to heaven there is many a pitfall, and the devil's great objective is to cause the child of God to stumble, to be tripped up so that he loses the power of the Holy Spirit in his witness. When he has lost that, Satan knows, if we do not, that he is helpless.

To illustrate this great truth, Paul draws upon an Old Testament story, the experience of his own nation; "All these things happened unto them for ensamples... [to us] upon whom the ends of the world are come" (10:11). These things happened that they might be a warning and example to us who live in an age which is rapidly folding up, the sunset age, when the night will soon be upon us and no man can work. As Paul goes back to the Old Testament illustrations, he points out the great privileges of God's people, and yet the tragedy of their failure and collapse on the journey.

Great are our privileges, and therefore great are our responsibilities, and all the more tragic it is indeed when the child of God loses the authority of the spirit. What peril we are in when we begin to trust in our privileges, in our Christian home, in our Christian fellowship, without recognizing that they bring us tremendous responsibilities which we must accept or become castaways.

Will you notice that as Paul introduces this theme, he underlines the great sweep of God's love for His people. The first four verses show what immense privileges were those of the people of God. Notice the frequent repetition of the word "all": they were all under the cloud; they all passed through the sea; they were all baptized into Moses; they did all eat the same spiritual meat; they did all drink the same spiritual drink. Every one of them, the feeble, the strong, the sick, the weak—every one of them was brought through. They all experience the wonderful guidance and protection of God under the cloud. They all knew the deliverance of God from Egypt through the Red Sea.

"They were all baptized into Moses," which is a quaint way of saying that God's purpose for His people saw that they should be united and disciplined, linked together under the leadership of one man. They were made into an entity, and community, and ultimately into a great nation.

"They did all eat the same food, and they all drank the same drink"; they were all sustained by the same supernatural power which gave them manna every morning and water from the rock. And there was not one casualty; they owed everything to the supernatural power of their God, Jehovah. There was not a thing that they could do for themselves—everything about that journey was humanely impossible—it was all of Him.

What a picture that is of the privileges of the child of God today: no matter how weak and ineffective, how poor and isolated and useless we may feel, all of us are under His guiding hand. We have all been delivered out of the bondage of sin by the blood shed at Calvary. We have all been baptized into our Moses, into the body of Christ. All of us have been sustained by manna from heaven and by the river of life from the throne of God. You notice Paul says in his Old Testament illustration, "that Rock was Christ."

These tremendous ties bind us one to another in Jesus; the deepest things in our lives we share together. We are not left to be an unruly mob of individuals, unguided and unprotected. We have had the cleansing of His blood, the forgiveness of our sins. We have experienced baptism into the fellowship of the body of Christ. We have known what it is to feed upon His word, and to drink of the living water from heaven. We are all being sustained by the grace of God, and we have done nothing to deserve it at all.

Then the question coming to mind at once is this, "If that is so, how can such a people ever fail?" But the fact is, the greater the height, the greater the fall. Therefore Paul goes on to point out the seriousness of their failure; "But with many of them God was not well pleased" (10:5).

With many of them? How many? I would say that is about the classic understatement of the Bible, if I may dare say such a thing concerning the Word of God. Nearly three million came out of Egypt. With how many of them was God not pleased? With all except two! Only two who came out of Egypt entered into the land of blessing; only two of that generation went right through with the purpose of God — Caleb and Joshua.

The others were "overthrown" in the wilderness. That same word is used in that graphic incident in the life of Jesus Christ when He entered into the Temple and saw the people exchanging money and selling sacrifices. He took a whip and overthrew the tables of the money-changers, scattering them all over the court of the Temple.

That is what happened to the people of God; they were scattered, overthrown. They were to have been a united people, but soon they were scattered and disintegrated. Why shouldn't that privileged people have kept together and gone right through to the Promised Land? Paul leaves us not in doubt: he shows us four things that spell out tragedy, not only to the people in Moses' time, but in the lives of believers today.

The first of them is lust. We must not confine that word to the narrow meaning that is put upon it these days in a moral sense. The full story is in Numbers 11: the desire of those people en route to the land of blessing was for something out of the will of God. He provided for them all the food they needed, but they wanted more — something different, a change of diet. They asked for something which was perfectly legitimate, but which was not provided for them in the plan of God. He knew what was best for them, but they demanded their way, and God gave them what they wanted.

What a tremendous statement that is in the Psalms where David, recounting the history of God's people, says, "He gave them their request; but sent leanness into their soul" (Psalm 106:15).

In the beginning of human history, when Eve saw that the tree was good for food, and a tree to be desired to make one wise, she took, and ate, and gave to her husband. That is always true: the first thing that takes men away from God is a desire for something other than what

God has planned for them. And desire leads to participation, because no one ever sins all alone; he tries to involve someone else. That which started the whole trouble in the world is the thing which has disintegrated Christian fellowship ever since.

God always meets a man on the level of his desire. If we hunger and thirst after righteousness, God will fill us with the fruit of it. He satisfies the longing soul and fills the hungry with good things. But if we desire something out of the will of God, He will give us that, too. If we persist in refusing God's plan and demand something that is out of His will, then he gives us what we want but, terrifying truth, He also sends leanness to our souls. The mark of spiritual authority vanishes, the ring of integrity departs; the one thing that distinguishes a Christian, a man of God, from other people, leaves us.

Paul says that Israel disintegrated with idolatry: "Neither be ye idolaters, as were some of them" (10:7a). The story is in Exodus 32. When Moses had been a long time on the mountaintop with God the people became restless. Aaron, who had been left in charge, eventually received their gold and jewelry, melted, it, and fashioned a calf. When Moses came down and questioned him about this, Aaron said, in effect, "All I did was take the people's gold and jewelry—when I flung it all into the furnace, out came this calf!" (Exodus 32:24).

I don't believe it operated like that! Aaron deliberately set up something in the place of God, pretending it was unintentional, that it really happened by accident. But it was idolatry; he knew what was going to come out of the furnace. And the people worshiped it, they "sat down to eat and drink, and rose up to play" (10:7b). In other words, they substituted play time for prayer time, indulgence for reality; they took the sacrifice out of their religion and made it comfortable and easy.

The third word I find here is "fornication": "Neither let us commit fornication, as some of them committed, and fell in one day three and twenty thousand" (10:8). That story is in Numbers 25, where we find wrong relationship, and unequal yoke with ungodly people. Their standards, which had gradually been lowered, ceased to exist altogether, and they made marriages (and worse than marriages) with ungodly people, the people of Moab. They became guilty of illicit relationships which are utterly contrary to God's will, but which are related in God's word, that it may be faithful in exposing the human heart as it really is.

The last word is "unbelief": "Neither let us tempt Christ ... Neither murmur ye..." (10:9, 10). The story is from Numbers 21. The people had become weary of the journey, they had become sour on the whole project of going to the Promised Land.

How often we find Christians living in sourness instead of radiance, without hunger for God's Word, lacking desire for the royal route to heaven! Let us humble ourselves before Him and be honest. We have wrestled against the will of God and desire things out of His plan. All too often we have put something in His place, as well. We have allowed strong relationships. We have complained and grumbled about the journey, that it was too hard.

Now the result is that the evidences of God's power have departed altogether, and that is why others are not being won for Jesus Christ. That is why the Sunday school class seems to be so unruly and unresponsive. That is why our immediate circle seems to be so unreached by our testimony.

Oh, the privileges we have thrown away! The responsibilities we have failed to accept! Is that true of your life today? But the downward process can be stopped; the tide can be turned. There can come again the authority which once you knew, the power which you once had.

How? Because there is a secret of deliverance in the Lord Jesus: "There hath no temptation taken you but such as is so common to man; but God is faithful, who will not suffer you to be tempted above that ye are able; but will with the temptation also make a way to escape, that ye may be able to bear it. Wherefore, my dearly beloved, flee from idolatry" (10:13–14).

In this journey on which we are all fellow travelers through the wilderness of this life, we may have fallen into pitfalls; we may have been tripped up. God does not say He will remove the pitfall nor that He will not permit you to fall. But what He does say is that it need not happen. The man who falls into temptation knows that it need not have happened. Just a moment's desire for something out of God's will, and he has slipped; he knows it could have been stopped, if only ... if only what?

God will not remove from you the temptation that is common to all. But he tells you that you are not unique; if today you feel beaten and baffled, utterly at the end of your rope, God is still faithful in everything. He has not pets! All the Israelites came out of Egypt under the cloud; they were all protected and sustained.

Temptation will always be graded to the fiber of your life. God will not allow it to go on a moment longer, nor to be more severe than you can take, for He knows your needs. Why did He suffer the manners of His people in the wilderness? So that He might prove them and humble them, that He might show them the sin in their hearts, that they might see their helplessness and learn to depend completely upon Him.

That is why He allows things to happen to you, that He might show you how absolutely corrupt, sinful, and hopeless you are in yourself, that you might know that in your flesh dwells no good thing. Temptation will be sent along the particular line that God knows you need in order that He might draw you to Himself, but the way of escape is guaranteed. "He will with the temptation *also* make a way to escape."

Check it in your own life and experience — every time temptation comes, there has been a way out, hasn't there? Every time Satan has hit, there has been a way through the temptation, if you had chosen it. Not before it or after it, but alongside it, right with the fiery dart that comes into your life, at that very moment there is a way of victory.

Sometimes the only way of escape is to run for your life. "Wherefore ... flee from idolatry." Where do we run? Into the arms of Jesus, the only place of safety. That is not cowardice; sometimes it is evidence of strength and spiritual maturity, the sight that you are growing in grace. It is in the presence of Christ that authority and unction are restored. When there is renewed power and grace, from your life will flow again the rivers of living water in blessing to others.

CHAPTER SIXTEEN

RULES FOR
THE ROAD

I CORINTHIANS 10:15–33

We have now traveled many miles on the royal route to heaven, and should have learned many lessons. This journey involves a Christian in many problems. It certainly is not easy; it is narrow and dangerous, and we are prone to slip and stumble. The man who would walk this way is much watched by others, much criticized and misunderstood. But in his heart is a conviction that nothing can ever shake: on this royal route to heaven he is walking with God.

In the course of a life that is lived like this, inevitably there are questions arising as to what to do in this situation or that. I wonder if any of us have gone through one day without having been faced with some kind of problem: a decision when to do this or that, whether to act this way or that way, how to react in a certain situation, what choice to make, what company to keep.

It is not easy to know how we should walk on the royal route to heaven, and therefore God has provided rules of the road. You cannot go along any highway without regulations, and there are rules for Christian living which, if you break them, result in disgrace to your own life, disaster in the lives of others, and dishonor to the name of the Lord.

In our portion for study Paul gives us three rules of the road. The point at issue would seem to be something very remote from our sphere of living today. Paul dealt with it in some measure in chapter 8, and now he brings to the climax what he has to say concerning meat offered to idols.

Here is the case of a believer who has been asked out to dinner with unsaved friends, and he accepts the invitation. I am so glad Paul underlines the fact that we are permitted to do so; it is tragic that so many Christian people just dare not to go into an unbeliever's home in case they get contaminated. Now Paul says, "If any of them that believe not bid you to a feast, and ye be disposed to go" (10:27a), then go and enjoy yourself.

The life of the people of Corinth was so mixed up with idolatry that it was difficult for a Christian to know where to draw the line. Paul maintains that a believer may go and eat and enjoy it, and when meat is put before him he is to "eat, asking no questions for conscience sake" (10:27b). In other words, he is not to ask where it came from, for that would be rude. But if the host intimates that this was meat offered to idols, then he should not touch it. If the host mentions it to his guest, quite clearly he attaches some importance to it. Therefore the Christian must not be identified with him in idol-worship, and must abstain from eating the meat. If nothing is said about it, and the guest knows nothing about the origin of the meat, then he is not to start trouble by asking; he is free from any possible compromise. That is the point at issue.

Isn't that far removed from us? Not so far as you think! This introduces us at once to the first rule of the road: "Let no man seek his own, but every man another's wealth" (10:24). In other words, live sacrificially for other people. You are saved not only that you might serve the Lord but that you might live before other people so that nothing you do, in your actions or reactions will cause offense.

You will be able to go into the homes of non-Christian people and eat with them, converse with them; you will move among them in a natural manner, but never for one moment will you lower your standard of Christian living. You will do nothing that will put any kind of hindrance in the way of another, nothing that will be a stumblingblock to him. Your first concern is the spiritual wealth of that person. It may be a social date or it may be a formal occasion, but deep down in your heart your one purpose is that you might enrich that man spiritually. You are on the King's business, and He grants no vacations. This is the first rule of the road.

I would pause a moment to underline something: it is clear from the teaching of the apostle here that the Christian as an individual, or the Christian fellowship as a group, is not called upon to live in some watertight compartment, inoculated against possible contamination through contact with unconverted people. Father, we are to move among them, talk with them, live with them—but always maintain the standard of Christian living. Principles must never be lowered; stumblingblocks must never be put in the way of an unbeliever. The one objective on every occasion is not a social contact; rather, the great concern of the child of God is the spiritual enrichment of his friend. The Christian's mission in this world is not primarily seeking to make himself more holy, but through contact with an unbelieving world to do everything in his power to win others to Jesus Christ.

Now, of course, if we accept this as the rule of the road, it will cause us to break through many barriers, leap over many walls, and enter many different circles. The Christian is called upon to launch out into uncharted areas among ungodly people and never to fear. He is to go there because God is sending him that he might reach others for Christ, and this situation may be fraught with great peril. How is he going to associate with them and not lower his Christian principles and standards? How is he going to mix with unconverted people and yet himself stand true?

The second rule of the road takes us back a few verses: "The cup of blessing which we blessed, is it not the communion of the blood of Christ? The bread which we break, is it not the communion of the body of Christ? For we being many are one bread, and one body: for we are all partakers of that one bread" (10:16–17).

If you apply the first rule of the road, and begin to break through into the circles of ungodly people and associate with them, immediately you will face the problem of maintaining your testimony. What is to be the guiding factor in your behavior?

We have seen previously how time and time again Paul takes us back to the cross, and he does it again here: "The communion of the blood of Christ … the communion of the body of Christ." To observe the first rule of the road would be disastrous unless we constantly recognize that we start out from Calvary. We must remember that in our new life our fellowship is not with the world and its ungodly people, but with the Lord Jesus in His death and resurrection.

This teaching is particularly important for those in training for the ministry and the mission field, but every Christian needs to understand it. Paul is saying to the Corinthian believers that they have a table, a special fellowship and sustenance: "Behold Israel after the flesh: are not they which eat of the sacrifices as partakers of the altar? ... But I say, that the things which the Gentiles sacrifice, they sacrifice to devils, and not to God: and I would not that ye should have fellowship with devils. ... Ye cannot be partakers of the Lord's table and of the table of devils" (10:18–21).

This may sound as if it contradicts what Paul has already said, but it does not. He draws here an important distinction to which Christian people today have apparently shut their eyes: our fellowship is at Calvary, but our contact must be with the world. Our fellowship is with the Lord Jesus, but our friendship is for those who do not know the Savior. Our fellowship is in the blood shed on the cross, in the body of Jesus broken for us, but in His name we become all things to all men that by all means we might win some. The love of Christ constrains us and we should be willing to go anywhere, if only in so doing we might win a soul for Jesus.

In others words, Paul distinguishes between our associations and our fellowship, between our contacts and our communion. Some people do not understand that. If a Christian moves in ungodly circles, has a meal with an unsaved person, goes to the house of unbelieving friends, or has social contact with them, immediately the world says (or worse still, his Christian friends say), "he is lowering the standard, he is having fellowship with unbelievers." He is doing nothing of the kind! His fellowship will stay at Calvary and his heart in tune with God while for the sake of the Lord Jesus he moves into contact with ungodly people that he might win them for Him.

The second rule of the road, therefore, is to live in separation to God. This is something that only you and I as individual Christians can discern when we are right before God. If I move in ungodly circles and discover that my heart is going out to the things they enjoy, if I realize that I am faltering in my devotion to the Lord Jesus, if I am beginning to hanker after the things of the world, then this rule of the road comes with shattering authority to tell me that I must stop. It is impossible to belong to Christ and live in the enemy's camp. Absolute separation to God is demanded, but remember that separation is not isolation.

Separation can include an openhearted outreach in the name of a crucified, risen Savior. As the child of God moves among others, speaks to others, is in contact with others who do not think as he does, deep down in his heart his fellowship is with the Lord, and in that situation he is kept by the power of God, although others may accuse him of compromise if he associates with idolaters and unbelievers. But if someone doesn't go to them, how are such people ever to be won for the Lord?

The second rule of the road is to be applied in both directions. You must watch your behavior as you make contact with the world, the unbelievers, the people who don't think as you do. Be careful all the time that your fellowship and communion with the Lord is being kept. You must be certain that your heart is right with God, that you are clear and transparent in your relationship with Him, then in all your contacts you are conscious of His everlasting arms around you, and you know He is keeping you by His power. But if that is not true, then you must retrace your steps and get back to Calvary; you must break any possibility of *fellowship* with unbelievers. Will you watch that danger?

On the other hand, you must watch the danger of being so wrapped up in contemplation of the Lord Jesus that you never dare venture out of your "reserved compartment" to seek out souls in His name.

The third rule of the road is to be found in the closing part of the chapter, which is really the climax of the whole argument: "Whether therefore ye eat, or drink, or whatsoever ye do, do all to the glory of God" (10:31). We are not to do some things for the glory of ourselves, to make a name or a reputation. We must maintain a singleminded purpose for the glory of the Savior.

The child of God who is observing these three rules: sacrificial living for others, separation unto God, singlemindedness of purpose for the glory of the Lord, as he faces many questions almost every day of his life, before making a decision, he will ask himself three things.

First, "Is it a stumblingblock to other people?" For if it is, we must cut it out, because of our concern for their welfare. Then, "Can I ask the blessing of the Lord Jesus Christ of this action that I take?" If we cannot expect Him to bless us in it, then we will not do it, for the blessing of the Lord makes us rich and adds no sorrow—we dare not lie for a moment without the sense of His fellowship. After that, we ask ourselves, "Can I do this thing for the glory of God?" If not, then we cannot do it at all. In other words, all this talk today about participating in everything, just taking it a little gently, is not for the Christian who seeks to please His Lord. A Christian is to live boldly, but with a life that maintains absolutely clear-cut principles.

There are simple rules, but to break them brings disaster to yourself, disgrace to your testimony, and dishonor to the Lord. Keep them, and you will experience the liberty of the child of God, free from the condemnation of the law, but, as Paul says in the last chapter (9:21), under the law to Christ. Oh, the blessedness of submission to His sovereignty! May that be your portion now and forever.

CHAPTER SEVENTEEN

GUIDANCE FOR
THE HOME

1 CORINTHIANS 11:1–16

We come to another very interesting subject which the Corinthian church has raised with Paul, because of the conditions of their time, concerning the behavior and attitude of women in the church fellowship. Once again Paul exposes the fact that their question is not touching the root of the issue, and he takes the opportunity of answering them by lifting the question up from the detail to the principle: the beauty and glory of a Christian home.

There are women who have so misunderstood this portion of the Scriptures that they will not even bow before a meal at home without wearing some sort of head covering. But that is neither the real meaning nor the significance of this passage, which brings us to a consideration of the ideal balance in the Christian home.

One thing that places this nation in great peril is the breakdown of its homes, even Christian homes, and the collapse of the sanctity of marriage. Paul has some things to say about this as he reveals the principle, and against that background he explains the detail about which they had written to him.

He begins by saying, "Be ye followers of me, even as I also am of Christ" (11:1). This is a tremendous claim for a preacher to make, but Paul states that the Lord Jesus Christ is now his standard. Everything that he has to say he first received from the Lord; therefore he can safely say, "Be ye followers of me." He goes on to put in a word of praise:

"I praise you, brethren, that ye remember me in all things, and keep the ordinances" (11:2). Whenever Paul could find opportunity to be grateful to others in spite of their imperfections, he was careful to give that word of thanks.

After that very tactful opening of what is, of course, a delicate subject, he draws them away from the question of a woman's behavior to a great principle he wants to bring to their attention; "But I would have you know, that the head of every man is Christ; and the head of the woman is the man; and the head of Christ is God" (11:3). Many people love the middle part of that verse and others dislike it, but no one can understand what it really means unless we see it as the jewel in the lovely setting of the other two relationships. The fact brought to our attention is that the head of the woman is the man in the Christian home. But how do you explain, and how do you carry out the relationship? You do so only when you understand the other two.

"The head of Christ is God," says Paul. Here we enter on holy ground, into a realm of mystery which we cannot fully understand. Yet we can know this much from the lips of our Lord Himself: "I and my Father are one" (John 10:30). Christ is equal with God in character and in deity. He also said, "I am not alone, because the Father is with me" (John 16:32). Christ and the Father were one in cooperation, in service, in ministry. The Lord Jesus said again, "My Father is greater than I" (John 14:28b). Here is the submission which He voluntarily took upon Himself when he humbled Himself and stopped to the death of the cross for us.

Jesus Christ claimed equality with God but offered submission to God. He was claiming to be one with God, and yet delighting in the fact that He was submitting to God. Here submission is in the context of absolute fellowship, complete equality, utter understanding. Here is oneness of character, oneness of service, oneness of purpose, oneness of life. Yet he was subject to His Father for the purpose of redemption.

The second relationship in this verse is that Christ is the head of man. This is true in what I would call the generic sense of the word. That is to say, when God made the human race it was His intention that there should be the same principle of headship as there is between Christ and God. There was to be an equality of life and a communion of nature, for God made man in His own image. There was to be unity of life, identity of character, complete cooperation, but at the same time there was to be a voluntary submission that the purpose of God might be fulfilled and that the glory of God might be revealed.

That voluntary submission was not given by man, however, instead, there was an act of rebellion, and the identity was lost, the likeness ruined, the purpose spoiled. But the whole message of God's grace is that His likeness is recovered through Jesus Christ: His shed blood, His empty tomb, and the outpouring of the Holy Spirit. That which was lost in the fall of creation has been restored in redemption.

If we are born of the Spirit of God and are members of the body of Christ, there is identity of character for we are partakers of His nature. There is to be unity of cooperation in His service and submission to the authority of Jesus Christ. Here is the relationship between Christ and man. It is a glorious thing to be the child of God, to share the character of the Lord through His redemptive purpose, and to have the experience of voluntary submission to His authority.

Against that background is set forth the glory of the relationship between man and woman that makes marriage so wonderful and the Christian home so precious. It is in the light of the relationship between God and Christ and between Christ and man that Paul puts into the forefront the relationship between man and women. It is to be exactly the same in God's purpose as the other two relationships.

When God made woman, he took her from the man, but not from the head in case she should dominate him, nor from the feet in case he should trample upon her. God took her from his side, close to his heart, that she might be his companion, his comfort, his love. That is how God made woman, and He said to her, "Thy desire shall be to thy husband, and he shall rule over thee" (Genesis 3:16).

Paul, writing to the Ephesians, insists upon this authority, also: "Husbands, love your wives, even as Christ also loved the church, and gave himself for it. ... Wives, submit yourselves unto your own husbands, as unto the Lord" (Ephesians 5:22, 25). The rule of the family is that, just as Jesus Christ voluntarily submitted Himself to the Father, so the husband is to submit himself to Christ. As the woman is to be man's companion, so she is to submit to an authority which is exercised in love as expressed at the cross. And I do not know a woman in all the world who will not give glad submission to an authority like that.

The marriage relationship is something sacramental. When you think of authority in the home you should think of the cross, where

Jesus has brought us into submission to Himself. That is where we learn how much He cares for us, and where we are brought in humility before His feet. That is how He secures our love and our surrender — "even as Christ loved the church and gave himself for it." A man who cannot exercise authority like that had better remain unmarried. A man who can rule only by stamping his foot had better remain single. But a man who knows how to govern his house by the love of the Lord, through sacrificial submission to the Lord, is the man who is going to make a perfect husband. The woman and man who cannot submit to an authority like that had better remain single.

Dr. Campbell Morgan tells how he asked a friend of his, a lady who was a spinster, "Why do you remain single?" She replied, "Because I have never met a man who can master me." You smile at that, but she knew something of the principle of marriage. Such a person had better remain single, for she is much happier working things out for herself.

Even Christian homes are many times unhappy and broken because authority, if it is exercised at all, is not exercised in submission to the one or to the other in the light of the cross. Some homes, though fundamental in terminology, are desperately lacking in Christian love and discipline. Marriage has been kept going for appearances' sake, but there is no real love or discipline, no acceptance of authority. In some homes, the wife dare not accept the authority of her husband, because he has never met God in Jesus Christ at Calvary. When a husband exercises his authority away from the will of God, without submission to the Lord in his own life, the result can be tragedy for all.

Here is the basis of the loveliness of a Christian home. God is the head of Christ: He is equal in fellowship, in character, in service, but submitted to the will of God. And Christ is the head of man: we are one in character and in purpose, but submitted to the will of God in Christ. Man is the head of woman, and yet one, because the woman is taken from the man: one in life, in companionship, in character, for God's purpose to be fulfilled, submissive in the will of God. Here then is the permanent principle, the lesson of the Christian home.

But in the light of those relationships, Paul now brings to the foreground a detail following the principle: "Every man praying or prophesying, having his head covered, dishonoureth his head. But every woman that prayeth or prophesieth with her head uncovered dishonoureth her head; for that is even all one as if we were shaven" (11:4–5).

Notice that the man who prays and prophesies covered dishonors his head—not the twelve inches above his neck, but God. Christ is honored, for He is the head of man. On the other hand, the woman who prays and prophesies uncovered dishonors her head, not the inches above her neck, but the man, for the man is the head of the woman.

Praying, a man is speaking to God on behalf of others. Prophesying, he is speaking to others on behalf of God. Paul says if he does that uncovered, he is dishonoring God. If I preached with my hat on, you would think me very irreverent. But why is it irreverent?

Paul, himself a Jew, is writing to many that are Jews, and what he says here cuts completely across the understanding of the Jews. Why does the Jew keep his hat on when he worships God? Because of a misconception of his own history. "Not as Moses, which put a veil over his face, that the children of Israel could not steadfastly look to the end of that which is abolished: but their minds were blinded: for until this day remaineth the same veil untaken away in the reading of the old testament; which veil is done away in Christ. … Nevertheless when it shall turn to the Lord, the veil shall be taken away. Now the Lord is that Spirit: and where the Spirit of the Lord is, there is liberty. But we all with open face beholding as in a glass the glory of the Lord, are changed into the same image from glory to glory, even as by the Spirit of the Lord" (2 Corinthians 3:13–18).

The Jews say that Moses veiled his face when he came down from the mountain because the people would not be able to gaze upon the glory. But Paul says Moses did it because he knew the glory was fading, and he did not want the people to see that. But the veil is done away in Christ; in Him is no fading glory, because He is the same yesterday, today, and forever.

Made in the image of God, but losing that image, man is recreated in Jesus Christ and shines with something of His glory that shall never fail, and therefore the veil is unnecessary. The Christian man worships uncovered in the house of God that he might reflect something of the glory of the Head. Brethren, this means to say that others should see on your face that glory which never fades. The fact that you can worship Him uncovered is a reminder that you have been recreated in Jesus Christ after His own likeness, and the glory that will never fade is yours. It is wonderful to see a man grow old with the glory on his face, one who has been through the battles of life with his Lord along the royal route to heaven. He is not able now to serve actively in the church as once he did, but the glory is on him! There is no fading glory for the Christian.

But if that is true of the man, what about the woman? When she prays and prophesies (and I dare mention that Paul assumes that she does—remember the prophet Joel said, "your sons and your daughters shall prophesy"), if she does it uncovered, says Paul, she dishonors her head, the man. Why?

The women in Corinth who went through the street unveiled were the prostitutes. Now Christian women were saying, "We are all one in Christ; all things are lawful, so we do not need to bother about this covering." Paul says, "Yes, you do! For if you go through Corinth uncovered you will be identified with that kind of woman, and therefore you are dishonoring your husband." We need not quarrel about the detail here: "But if any man seem to be contentious," Paul says, "we have no such custom, neither the churches of God" (11:16).

If you would live day by day in submission to the Word of God, particularly in these days when anyone talking of holiness may be laughed at, I want to suggest to you that true reverence will affect your clothes, and the church will cease to be a sort of dress parade. We meet in the presence of the living Christ, whose glory can never fade, and we behold Him with open face. Paul goes on to say that a woman's hair is a glory to her, and therefore when she meets in the presence of the Lord and the fellowship of believers, there should be no competition with the glory of the Lord.

"For this cause ought the woman to have power on her head because of the angels" (11:10). That word "power" means a covering, authority. This is a reminder that even the angels cover their faces as they worship Jehovah, and they want to look down and see a Christian woman worshiping God also in reverence. It is for you individually to apply the details, but this passage suggests that we should worship the Lord in such a way that the glory is all His.

"Neither is the man without the woman, neither the woman without the man, in the Lord" (11:11). We are nothing without Him, and yet as the woman is from the man by creation, evens so is the man also from the woman by human birth, but all things are of God, and in Jesus Christ the man and the woman are together in love that is submissive for the glory of the Lord Jesus.

CHAPTER EIGHTEEN

Pause for Fellowship

1 Corinthians 11:17–34

Up to this point Paul's ministry has been very largely corrective. He has exposed the sins and failures of the church and has sought to answer their problems: some delicate, some difficult, some very personal. Now he takes us a step further, because on the royal route to heaven there are moments when we need to get away from the difficulties and conflicts in order that we might be refreshed in green pastures and beside still waters, and might have time for reflection.

It is significant that at this particular point in the letter Paul introduces what he has to say about the Lord's Supper. It is as if to say we are to forget for a while the things that test us and draw aside together to meditate upon our Lord. This is our purpose here, a time of fellowship with Jesus, a pause for reflection upon the cross, upon His resurrection, upon the meaning of the table of communion.

It was the practice in the early church to meet together for what they called "love feasts" in their homes. This was simply a time of social fellowship which they followed with the breaking of bread.

There is the suggestion of this custom almost immediately after the resurrection. Walking on the road to Emmaus were two of His disciples, and the Lord drew near and walked with them. They invited Him to stay for a while in their home and He went in with them. They entertained Him as their guest at the table, but at the end of the meal He became Host, and He was known to them in the breaking of bread

(Luke 24:13–32). We find a similar thing in Acts 2:46, where we are told that the early disciples continued steadfastly every day in the breaking of bread and in feasting with gladness and singleness of heart. Such was the practice of the early church.

The trouble was that in Corinth it had gone too far, and the Lord's table had become abused because of the surfeit of eating and drinking. The remembrance of the Lord's death had become a travesty on its solemn significance, and Paul has a word of rebuke concerning their behavior. "When ye come together therefore into one place, this is not to eat the Lord's supper. ... What? Have ye not houses to eat and to drink in? Or despise ye the church of God, and shame them that have not? What shall I say to you? Shall I praise you in this? I praise you not" (11:20, 22). "And if any man hunger, let him eat at home; that ye come not together unto condemnation" (11:34). This abuse of the Lord's table could not enter our observance today, yet it does remind us that when we break bread together, we must be careful how we come to His table, how we ought to worship Him.

Paul begins to talk about the first observance of the Lord's Supper: "I have received of the Lord that which also I have delivered unto you: That the Lord Jesus the same night in which he was betrayed took bread" (11:23).

May I pause here to point out a great principle for every preacher: this was not something that Paul got secondhand; it came to him straight from the heart of God. I picture a man meeting the risen Lord on the road to Damascus, going into the desert in Arabia, spending three years in Tarsus before Barnabas brought him to Antioch and into missionary work. It was in those years of solitude and preparation he received of the Lord that which henceforth he was to preach in public. Nothing that you say in the name of the Lord will ever be effective in the life of another unless it comes direct from His heart to yours.

What, therefore, has Paul to tell us in this chapter about the sacred feast of the Lord's table? In the first place, he introduces it to us as a remembrance of the past: "and when he had given thanks, he brake it, and said, 'Take, eat; this is my body, which is broken for you; this do in remembrance of me'" (11:24).

In the margin of many Bibles you will find, "This do for the remembrance of me." When we meet around the Lord's table in the company of His people, we are doing not only what the Lord commanded us to do, but what He has asked us to do in case we forget Him. As a Friend he asks for the fellowship of His friends, as a love asks for the communion of the one who loves Him. It is the One who has given something for us at Calvary asking each of us to remember His death, to put that at the very center of our Christian experience. It is He who loved us even unto death calling us out from the busyness, and often the barrenness, of all our pressure and work, that we might wait upon Him in the stillness of our hearts, and worship Him. He points us back, not to His life or example, but to that which is at the very heart of the Christian gospel: the atonement of the cross, the finished work of Calvary and the open tomb.

Perhaps the thing that Paul is asking us to think about most of all is that when Jesus took bread, the symbol of His broken body, and gave it to His disciples, He did not murmur or complain, He did not just endure it, but He gave things. At the moment when all the powers of hell were being arrayed against the Lord Jesus, and He was going out into Gethsemane and up the hill to Calvary, He gave thanks, because from the very beginning it was said of Him. "I delight to do thy will, O God!"

The communion table is a memorial of the past, a reminder of the cross and of the centrality of its message, a recognition that there the Lord Jesus was thankful for the tremendous privilege that was His in dying for sinners like you and me. Amazing grace! Therefore our central thought should be worship to Him.

This takes away from the Lord's table any magic, any suggestion that when we break the bread and drink the wine we are partaking of the body and blood of the Lord. The Lord Jesus was in a human body when He took the bread, and He gave it as the symbol of His body. The removal of everything that could be superstitious about this act of worship emphasizes the glorious truth that we meet around His table to remember the one who loved us and gave Himself for us.

But Paul tells us it is to be not only a remembrance, but it is to be an expression of love for the living Christ: "As often as ye eat this bread, and drink this cup, ye do [proclaim] the Lord's death till he come" (11:26). The word is really "preach," here: "Ye do preach the Lord's death." There is one moment of your life above all others when you are preaching a sermon—that is when you meet around the Lord's table. You are preaching to the powers of darkness, "proclaiming the Lord's death" which has vanquished them. Also, to the Lord in heaven who looks down and sees your heart, you are witnessing your trust in His atoning work. When we meet around His table, we are feasting upon Him as He is received into our hearts by faith; as our heads are bowed in worship around His table we are sharing in fellowship with the living Lord, and are telling Him what He means to us.

The true life-giving principle in a Christian is that every faculty we possess is feasting upon Jesus Christ. My soul is feeding upon Him with thanksgiving that He loved me and died for me, that He protects and guides me, and that one day He will take me safely home. As I meditate upon these things my soul is refreshed, my heart begins to take comfort and courage, and my mind accepts the Word of God and begins to meditate upon it and to rejoice in it.

My heart feeds upon His love, His care, His thoughtfulness, His faithfulness, and responds, with thanksgiving and adoration. My will feeds on His commands, and I begin to recognize that His Word is to be obeyed; I bow before the sovereign will of God. My soul hopes in the fulfillment of His promises that have never yet failed throughout history.

Therefore, as we break bread together, every part of our lives—our hearts, our minds, our souls, our wills—are all feasting upon the Lord, and He is at the very center of all.

I wonder how much of all that the Lord has seen in your life as you feast upon Him? 'He that eateth me...' said Jesus, "shall live by me." Where is the hunger of your heart satisfied, its thirst quenched? Is it in the loveliness of your dear Savior? As you break bread and bow your heart before Him, what sort of sermon are you preaching? What does the Lord see? What does Satan see? Here is an expression of our love that demands far more than the busyness of our lives; it takes the devotion and surrender and worship from our hearts.

Paul has something else to say to us about the Lord's table, that it is a place of tremendous hope: "ye do proclaim the Lord's death ... till he come." I think it is very significant that reference to the Lord's table is to be found in only four books in the new Testament, whereas the coming again of the Lord Jesus is in twenty-three books out of twenty-seven. Of the four in which there is no reference to His second coming, three of them have only one chapter, and the other is the Epistle to the Galatians.

With great emphasis the Word of God sets forth the hope of the Christian church: any moment, any day, the clouds may part and Jesus, our Savior, may come again. As we break bread together and remember the Lord's death, we are doing it "Until he come." Isn't it wonderful to remember that there will be a day when there will be no more need to do that any more? We meet around the Lord's table only "until he come," until the day when there will be no more sin, or regret, or sorrow, or struggle. There will be more weakness, no more discouragement, nor more ignorance, nor empty places at our family table—we will all be together with Jesus.

The Lord Jesus went out from the Last Supper with His disciples to die for them. The disciples went out, one to betray Him, others to be prayerless and forgetful, all to desert Him. Often we have broken bread together around the Lord's table, and them we have gone out to do just what those disciples did—we have denied Him.

Paul adds a warning: "Wherefore whosoever shall eat this bread, and drink this cup of the Lord, unworthily, shall be guilty of the body and blood of the Lord" (11:27). He does not say "if we are unworthy,' for we could never be worthy; our worthiness is in Christ. Has that statement every puzzled you? I wonder if perhaps it has even kept you away from the Lord's table. Notice the next verse: "But let a man examine himself, and so let him eat of that bread, and drink of that cup. For he that eateth and drinketh unworthily, eateth and drinketh damnation to himself, not discerning the Lord's body" (11:28–29).

First, when I meet around the Lord's table I am to remember the Lord's body. I believe in this sense the word suggests to us not simply His body that hung on the cross, but the body of Jesus Christ in the world today, His church. I am to discern that I am part of this, and if in my life I am in any way sinning against the body of Jesus Christ, I am grieving the Lord, and am therefore eating unworthily.

Secondly, I eat and drink unworthily, and am guilty of the body and blood of the Lord, if I come to His table without examining myself. "For this cause many are weak and sickly among you, and many sleep" (11:30). That is, of course, many have even died. "For if we would judge ourselves, we should not be judged. But when we are judged, we are chastened of the Lord, that we should not be condemned with the world" (11:31–32).

I believe in faith healing, though I prefer to call it divine healing, but I do not believe that at any moment I may demand physical healing for a person, and these verses substantiate my position. I do not believe that you can go to any sick person, pray over him, and demand that he should immediately be restored. It may be that he is laid aside in the chastening of God because he has failed to examine himself. To demand healing may be to resist the very discipline of God upon the man's soul. Now I would be careful to add that all sickness is not the judgment of God in that sense. But in this instance, it is the chastening of God, because whom the Lord loves He corrects, and it is through the means of illness so often that a man is brought out into strength and renewed testimony of the glory of the Lord Jesus.

Paul is insistently warning us that if we keep coming to the Lord's table without self-examination and heart-searching regarding our sins, there will come a day when God will judge us and chasten us. He does not put a barrier around the Lord's table to keep us from it, but a warning that would drive us to the Lord in confession, in repentance, in meltedness of heart. "Let a man examine himself, and [not 'let him stay away'] so let him *eat*."

Are you a member of the body of Christ? When you break bread, what does it mean to you? The only thing that properly keeps you from the Lord's table is that you have never come as a sinner to the cross and received His forgiving mercy. Today you may come to Jesus, and as you begin to feast upon the living Lord you will find strength for every day's need and all the problems of life. You will rekindle the hope that burns so brightly in our hearts that one day we shall see Him face to face. It is a wonderful thing to be a member of His body!

CHAPTER NINETEEN

EQUIPMENT FOR
THE ROAD

1 CORINTHIANS 12:1–12

In the course of any journey that takes thought and preparation, it is good from time to time to stop and take stock of our position. As we look back over the distance we have come on our royal route to heaven, we see some of the pitfalls from which we have been delivered. Then we look at what lies ahead, and ask ourselves whether or not we really have the equipment that will see us through to the end of the road.

As we look back over the ground we have covered, one thing impresses itself upon my mind above every other: there is no situation in life, no part of the journey, but that the answer is to be found at Calvary. Every problem of a church fellowship, every departure from personal morality, every difficulty of the journey is settled there. Paul takes us back to the cross of Christ constantly in this letter.

As we turn to survey the route we have yet to follow, Paul begins to speak about spiritual gifts. The thing that matters now is whether or not we have the needed equipment for the rest of the journey. Are we quite confident that we are fitted out for the royal route to heaven, and that our equipment is adequate to take us through until we meet Jesus face to face? These two things are vitally connected. The difficulties and burdens of the past and the ruggedness of the road ahead are not separate.

The problem of the Corinthian church was a three-fold one. What is the remedy for their divisions and carnality? The unifying life of the

Spirit of God: that is Paul's answer in chapters 12 and 14. What is the cure for their basic immorality and sin? The unfailing love of God that knows no limit to its endurance and will stand when everything else is falling: Paul gives that answer in chapter 13. What is the solution for their difficulties: problems of church administration and of life in general? The ultimate answer to that is the resurrection day when "this corruptible shall put on incorruption." One day their problems will all be ended, their burdens lifted, and they will be ushered into the presence of the King. Paul reminds them of that hope in chapter 15. The pattern of the letter is unified and complete.

As we turn to this portion for our study, notice that Paul speaks here about spiritual gifts, not spiritual graces. There is a big difference between the two. The graces of the Spirit of God are found in Galatians 5:22–23: "The fruit of the Spirit is love, joy, peace, longsuffering, gentleness, goodness, faith, meekness, temperance." There are for myself, that my character may be formed into the likeness of Jesus Christ. Paul isn't talking about them here, he is talking about gifts, which are for my service and for the benefit, not of myself, but of other people. Let us be clear about this point: you can have all the graces, but you cannot have all the gifts. Paul concludes chapter 12 by saying, "Covet earnestly the best gifts." The great thing is to recognize the gifts that have been given to us and to use them for the glory of God, finding out day by day how better to develop and strengthen them for the Savior's honor.

We are each different in temperament and personality; the members of the church of Jesus Christ are so varied in type, race, social background and much else, but each of us goes to the same source for our gifts: "now there are diversities of gifts, but the same spirit. And there are differences of administrations, but the same Lord. And there are diversities of operations, but it is the same God which worketh all in all" (12:4–6).

The same God our heavenly Father, who knows what is best for each one of His children, is in charge, as it were, of all the gifts that He would give to the church. The same Lord Jesus our Savior, the Head of the church which is His body, desires that all His children should be so endowed that they might be not only equipped individually for the journey but that they might be a mutual blessing, profit and help the one to the other. He knows how to distribute the gifts, and He "dividing to every man [according] as he will" (12:11). In other words, it is His sovereign right to withhold or bestow them. The same Holy Spirit, the great

Executive of the Godhead, the third Person of the Trinity, who lies in your heart and mine, knows how to take the gift that has been received from the Lord and make it useful for His service.

We have absolutely nothing for the road except we receive it from Father, Son, and Holy Spirit. In other words, we are saved by grace, and by grace alone. It was by God's grace and by the shed blood that we came to know our Savior, and we are kept and equipped for the rest of the journey by grace alone. It is not man's natural gifts that God uses, but the gifts of the Spirit which He imparts. Until we have received the gift of His Spirit for service, we have nothing to offer which can be a help or a blessing to anyone.

Do we really recognize that we have absolutely nothing at all unless we receive it from Him? That is what the Lord Jesus said: "I am the vine, ye are the branches; He that abideth in me, and I in him, the same bringeth forth much fruit; for without me ye can do nothing" (John 15:5). What a wonderful sense of unity and dependence that gives us! What a very precious thing it makes of Christian fellowship when we recognize that whatever we contribute to the service of the King of kings, we must all get from the same source! We are not alone on the road; there are many other travelers — in fact, all who have been washed in His precious blood, and all who are sharing the gift of life in Jesus Christ.

In the second place, Paul speaks about the diversities of ministry, and he brings to our attention several different gifts of the spirit. H says there are differences of gifts, of administration, and of operation. Now in this particular portion of the chapter we will think only of the first of these; he expands the discussion in the second part of the chapter and returns to it again in chapter 14.

I cannot help being impressed by the significance of the order in which Paul lists some of these gifts of the Spirit. The one that comes first is wisdom, and the last is the gift of tongues.

First, the gift of wisdom. You may begin to say, "I have some of that, for it is something I can attain." No, it isn't! For this letter began by saying, "God hath chosen the foolish things of the world to confound the wise," so you haven't any wisdom at all. When you come to know Jesus Christ as Savior and Lord, you have only the foolishness of sin and worldliness and you know nothing in God's realm. One of the gifts of the Holy Spirit that God gives to His children is wisdom; understanding and discernment.

Next is the gift of knowledge, of understanding the Book—not cleverness, but the gift of conviction, of that absolute assurance which comes from having enlightenment from God. Then he speaks of the gift of faith. Even faith is not something acquired naturally. To believe God is a gift, to trust in Him even though you do not fully understand Him. It is a gift that will take you through all kinds of emergencies and problems.

Healing is a gift, and I believe without any shadow of doubt God has given it to some—the ability to command disease to be removed from a human body in the name of the Lord. But I believe that for every ten who practice the gift, probably only one has it in the sovereignty of God. There is no gift so trafficked with and commercialized today as this one. It is something nobody can demand in every situation, for sickness is sometimes in God's will, and may be His discipline or His chastening. Nevertheless, healing is a divine gift. There are those also, I believe, who have the gift of healing a broken heart. Do you have that gift of comfort, that ministry of refreshment that brings restoration to a heart that is broken, to a life that is at the end of its rope? What a precious healing ministry that is!

"To another the working of miracles"—that is the ability to do something supernatural. The Lord Jesus said to His disciples, "He that believeth on me, the works that I do shall he do also; and greater works than these shall he do; because I go unto my Father" (John 14:12). This is also the gift of being able to overcome where once you were beaten, to triumph were once you only knew failure.

Then Paul speaks of the gift of prophecy. If I understand that word correctly in its biblical usage, it is not so much foretelling the future as forthtelling the present: seeing the world in which we live in the light of the Word of God, and bringing the Scriptures to bear upon any generation with absolute, heavenly authority, as "thus saith the Lord." It is the gift of the man who, in the name of the Lord and in the power of the Spirit, is able to speak with authority from the Book to the day in which he lives.

"To another discerning of spirits"—that is detecting between the false and the true. The spirit of discernment enables you to know what is wrong and what is right, which is the spirit of error and which the spirit of truth.

"To another divers kinds of tongues; to another the interpretation of tongues" (12:10b). This, the last in order of the gifts, although perhaps least in importance, nevertheless is a gift of the Spirit. Unquestionably it is to be used for the purpose of praise and adoration of the Lord Jesus, but always by interpretation.

No one, I repeat, has all the gifts. Because you have one of them, you are not entitled to become a spiritual aristocrat because somebody else does not have your gift. Don't demand that, in order for another person to be spiritual, he must heal, or he must speak in an unknown tongue. Be careful when you criticize those who may not have your gift — he has his own, which you may not have, because nobody has all of them. However, God gives to each of His children one or more, not that we may have spiritual pride, not to make us think we are clever, or good, or favored, but for the benefit of others.

There are certain things that you cannot do, but other Christians can, certain gifts of the Spirit that your brother has that you may need in order to get through life to the gates of heaven. All together the church, as it marches along the royal route to heaven in the fellowship of the Holy Spirit, is equipped as a body in victory. Observe closely that victory is in the group and not in isolation. One of the most damaging things that is done today in the name of fundamentalism is to grieve the Holy Sprit and divide the body. For victory, the body must work together in harmony and fellowship and love, under the authority of the Holy Spirit. I need your gift to see me through and you need mine: all of us need each of us, for we have mutual dependence as a body. God forbid that any of us should do one thing, or say one thing, that would harm the Lord's body, the church, by ruining another's gift or destroying the fellowship.

You may ask me, "How do I get these gifts of the Spirit?" that is an important question, because some people masquerade with gifts that are simply pretense. Many profess to have the gift of healing or of tongues, this gift or that, and the public is exploited by it. How can you know the sign of reality? How do you know what gifts you possess? What are the evidences of them?

Paul gives the answer to us very clearly: "Wherefore I give you to understand,... and that no man can say that Jesus is the Lord, but by the Holy Ghost" (12:3). The first part of that verse could be paraphrased, "No man speaking by the Spirit of God is indifferent to the Lord Jesus Christ." The man who speaks by the Spirit will put the Lord Jesus in His rightful place, on the throne. I can speak the words, "Jesus is Lord," and so can you. Anybody can say it, because no one can check our vocabulary. But no man can say with authority and absolute certainty that Jesus Christ is Lord, and back it up by the evidence of his life, but by the Holy Spirit.

To understand this, let us review our picture once again. The company of the redeemed is on the road to heaven; every day brings us nearer the end of the journey, when we will see our Lord face to face. We have been washed in His blood, and we share together the indwelling Holy Spirit. We have the same Father in heaven who knows what is best for His children. Our Lord Jesus Christ is at God's right hand; He is our Head and we His body. Each of us is necessary to Him and to each other, as the Holy Spirit He has given to us, on His behalf, administers the gifts He bestows.

Therefore, how do I know if I have them in reality? By the submission of my heart to Jesus Christ as Lord. When He is sovereign in my life, I am not going to ask for the gift of another out of envy. God bless him if it is really and make him a giant! I am glad of his fellowship, but don't let him start calling me carnal because I do not have his gift. The only gifts I would ask for are the gift of speaking with a tongue controlled from heaven and the gift of healing and comforting a broken heart.

If I am submitted to the dictatorship of the Holy Spirit, then it is for Him in His sovereignty to give me a gift; I gladly accept the wisdom, the knowledge, the understanding, the miracles, the discernment—whatever the gift may be. I will thank Him for it and for the friends who have gifts that I do not have. I will rejoice that God has caused my path to cross theirs, that in the church alongside me there are folks who know the Lord in a different way from myself, some who have the wonderful gift of refreshing those who are discouraged, and who help me along the way.

What a precious thing is Christian fellowship in the body of Christ! If you are walking today in the company of God's people, you find strength and comfort from gifts they have that you do not possess. The secret of reality is a blessed submission all along the road to the authority of the Holy Spirit, who will give you all you need to be a blessing to others.

CHAPTER TWENTY

TEAMWORK
ALONG THE WAY

I CORINTHIANS 12:13–31

The passage under consideration is one of the most significant in the Bible dealing with the great theme of the Christian church. It speaks to us about the character of the church, which is its form; the purpose of the church, which is its function; and the relationship of the church, which is its fellowship.

The sad plight of the church today is obvious evidence that the true character of the church is misunderstood, or some of us would not behave as we do. We would treasure it instead of tearing it apart; we would love all men with the love of Christ, and our testimony would right with a new note of passionate concern. If we are ever to see the answer to our prayers for heaven-sent revival, the dead church must begin to live, the wounded church must be made whole, the indifferent church must be rekindled with the flame of Calvary love.

This means, first of all, recognition of our real unity: "now ye are the body of Christ, and members in particular" (12:27). Paul uses the human body as an illustration of our mutual relationship: "For as the body is one, and hath many members, and all the members of that one body, being many, are one body; so also is Christ" (12:12). Paul is pointing out here some obvious lessons; the fact of our unity, our fellowship in diversity, and the fallacy of expecting identity.

To understand the significance of these things we need to go beneath the surface. "The body of Christ"—what does that suggest?

Surely not, in the first place, the spiritual union between believers, but the human physical body in which Jesus Christ lived, walked, talked, worked, and died, in which there was incarnated expression of the whole purpose of God in saving mankind from sin. His physical body was an essential preparation for the fact and function of the spiritual body which is His church. Indeed, the church would never have existed if it had not been redeemed first of all through the sacrifice of the physical body of our Lord Jesus.

When God came down to this earth in human form, miraculously conceived in the womb of the Virgin Mary, He came to reveal to us the whole principle upon which we should live our lives. The physical body of Jesus Christ expressed perfectly what God intends should be perpetuation through the spiritual body of Christ, the church of which you and I are part.

That physical body involved Jesus Christ in three things. First, complete identification: this was seen in His delight to do the father's will, His submission to the limitations of His human form, His obedience unto death, even the death on the cross. It was seen also in His oneness with us; "the children are partakers of flesh and blood, he also himself likewise took part of the same" (Hebrews 2:14), because He was "in all points tempted like as we are, yet without sin" (Hebrews 4:15).

In the second place, we see His identification with the need and condition of the human race; He prayed for our identification with Him, "as thou, Father, art in me, and I in thee, that they also may be one in us: that the world may believe that thou has sent me" (John 17:21).

His identification was with a view to total penetration. His coming was an attack on all fronts; it was total warfare, a full-scale invasion from heaven upon every aspect and expression of sin. It penetrated every level of life: social, political, ecclesiastical, moral. He healed the sick, raised the dead, cleansed the leper, restored the sinner, comforted the sorrowing and the weak, scorned the Pharisee, scorched the hypocrite. Crucified in weakness, He was raised by the power of God, and He left behind Him in this poor, prodigal world an indelible impact. There was no part of human life that escaped the penetration for the redemptive purpose of God in Jesus Christ.

But total penetration of this sinful world involved Him in no assimilation to sin itself. He was so close to us, but He was so separate from us. None came so close, but none was ever so different. Holy, harmless, undefiled, yet separate from sinners; touching sin at every point, yet never being contaminated. Healing, blessing, restoring, comforting—touching sin at every point, yet never catching the infection. As He moved in every circle of life, He never assimilated any of the sin, but imparted to everything He touched the very breath of heaven, the very life of eternity itself.

One day His physical body was laid in a tomb. The world crucified Him, rejecting the whole principle of life for which He stood. "We will not have this man to reign over us," was their cry. They were not willing to have this complete identification—they wouldn't stand for total penetration with no assimilation. This kind of thing was too costly for them. But God raised Him from the dead, and He ascended into heaven; by His own blood and His outpoured love He won for all of us the right of access to God's throne.

At Pentecost, the resurrected body of the Lord Jesus in heaven was united, as the Head, to the spiritual body being formed on earth, in order that the principles that involved Him might involve us, and what He had begun in His physical body might be perpetuated in us until He comes again to complete our redemption. I know that we can never add a word, nor a thought, nor a deed, to the finished work of Calvary. That which purchased our redemption was indeed a finished work, but the Lord Jesus in the human body was not ending something, He was beginning a great campaign which He Himself, in the limitations of a human body, could never complete, the task of world redemption.

These principles He made clear as He lived them out, and He gave them back, together with the Holy Spirit power to fulfill them, to a little group of disciples, that they themselves might live in complete identification with God, in total penetration of the world, but with no assimilation of sin.

Therefore, as Paul says, we are the body of Christ, and our bodies are the temples of the Holy Spirit. As the body of Christ on earth, we are here to fulfill in our lives and through our testimony that which Christ, in His physical life, began. We are here that in and through our bodies, by the power of His indwelling life, the redemption He purchased might be brought to complete fruition and total victory. All this lies behind the surface truth here, and throws a flood of light through Paul's teaching concerning the great function and character of the Christian church.

In the light of that background, let us consider the fact of our unity; "by one Spirit are we all baptized into one body … and have been all made to drink into one Spirit" (12:13).

Here is the mystery, the glory of the church of Jesus Christ. If we have been saved by God's grace, washed in the blood of Christ, at that moment we were baptized by the Holy Spirit into the body of the Lord Jesus and, therefore, we drink of the same fountain of life, are sustained by the same power, comforted by the same Shepherd, directed by the same Commander-in-chief, and kept by the mighty hand of the same wonderful God. This is complete identification.

No matter how great the disparity may be between Christ and people—race, gifts, talents, ability, whether a man be a prince or a throne or a beggar in the streets—if anyone is alive in Christ he has been made one by the same quickening Spirit and he is partaker of the same divine nature.

We are very conscious of certain ties that bind us one to another, such as the tie of national origin. Swede meets Swede, Englishman meets Englishman, German meets German, and immediately they discover an affinity. But what about this greater tie, our baptism by the Holy Spirit into the church, the body of Jesus Christ? What does *that* mean to us?

Just as among people there are different complexions, different features, and we are all different, so is the body of Christ. You see that difference in some points of doctrine. Some people are Calvinists, and other are Arminians. There will be differences in points of government and discipline, but there is not one person in the body of Christ today who has not felt himself a lost, guilty soul, and who has not known true repentance toward God and faith in Jesus Christ crucified and risen. This is the church: a company of men and women who have met God as sinners at Calvary, and have been formed into the body of Jesus Christ. No one is a genuine Christian unless he has been through that. We are not a mass of individual units, but a body completely identified with Him in His death and resurrection, completely united in our spiritual life, in our ministry of redemption, in the whole purpose for which we are left here.

But, alas, we are unrecognizable—the body of Christ is split from head to foot, torn asunder by this view and that view, because so many of us have accepted only superficially the whole principle of baptism by the Spirit into His body. There has been a refusal to accept the principle of the cross and death to the capital "I". But in the mind of the Lord Jesus Christ we have complete identification—with Him in death and resurrection and with the human race in its need—and are united together by faith and repentance, baptized by the same indwelling Spirit into the same new nature.

There is in this body not only complete identification, but the fellowship of diversity; "When one member suffer, all the members suffer with [him]. When one member [is] honored, all the members rejoice" (12:26).

The body of Jesus Christ was for total penetration at every point, into every aspect of life, for the glory of God and for the redemption of men. This is His purpose for His spiritual body, the church. In every relationship of life: religious, ecclesiastical, political, social, moral, there should be felt the impact of a group of people who are so absolutely one that their witness is irresistible. If this is to be accomplished, there must be a recognition of our absolute fellowship in our diversity. Therefore, as Paul points out, there is not one member of the body who can say of another, "Because I am not the eye, I am not of the body" (12:16).

There is a vast difference, of course, between the various members of the body, and yet when one member suffers, all suffer. If you are walking along a country road and a thorn gets into your foot, what happens? Your nerves send out the signal and the whole body becomes active: your back bends and your hands reach out to remove the thorn: your eyes may begin to water and your voice begin to complain—the whole body has felt the impact of that wound.

Fellowship in diversity is caring one for another, illustrated in the covering and protection which we give to the weaker parts of our physical body in order that the life of the whole body may be preserved. When every member of the body is functioning happily in its appointed place, caring each for the other to preserve the life and health of the body as a whole, then the body is prepared for total penetration into every aspect of life.

Alas, the world never feels that penetration at all if we as the body of Christ do not know the meaning of our fellowship in diversity. We become jealous of the gifts of other people, and instead of covering the weaker members for the protection of the whole, we are all too ready to expose them. We criticize, we judge, we condemn, and very often young believers have been disillusioned by the lack of Christian love and care that they have found in the church from which they expected so much.

So often it seems that the flame of love has practically died out within the Christian church! Millions around us go to Christless graves while the church quarrels and bickers, while the body of Christ is torn apart and becomes totally ineffective. The church has forgotten the secret of her absolute fellowship in the midst of so much diversity.

On the other hand, there is the fallacy of identity: "The eye cannot say unto the hand, I have no need of thee: nor again the head to the feet, I have no need of you" (12:21). Picture for a moment what a body would look like if it were all ear or all eye. What a monstrosity! Of course, it could not live, as it would not have the other organs necessary for life and breathing. "God hath tempered the body together" (12:24) so that it should function in the will of God by being perfectly healthy. The impossibility of all being alike, and of all doing the same thing, is shown in verse 28, for God has given—and this is an incomplete list, I hope, for there are not pastors or evangelists here—"first apostles, secondarily prophets, thirdly teachers, after that miracles, then gifts of healings, helps, governments, diversities of tongues." But each of us can get in that little word "helps." We can all do that. All these are necessary in order that the body may function as a healthy whole and that there should be no assimilation of evil. You cannot keep disease out of an unhealthy body, but if the body is strong, and each members function as it ought, then there is resistance to disease.

The church is to function as a healthy body, with every member happy in the will of God. There is not self-deprecation (12:15); neither is there to be depreciation of others (12:21). Here is the whole body without disability, functioning according to the plan of God, its members completely loyal the one to the other.

We are living in an evil age, when morals are lax and even many Christian homes are caught up into the unhappy, sinful state of society. Yet the church of Jesus Christ should be a body which penetrates everywhere and assimilates nothing. Today there is little penetration but plenty of assimilation in the body of Christ.

A scientist lectured recently to the Chicago Medical Association and said this, "Consider the average 150-pound body of an individual from its chemical aspect. It contains lime enough to white wash a fair-sized chicken-coop, salt enough to fill a small shaker, iron enough to make a ten penny nail, plus water. The total value of the ingredients is 98 cents, or about 60 cents per hundred-weight on the hoof."

That is all we are worth to a scientist! But that is not all the truth about the body: we are fearfully and wonderfully made, and we are worth infinitely more than that to God. We were created that we might be taken up into the mystery, to be formed as the body of Christ, members one of another, an agency through which God's whole program of world evangelization will be fulfilled, and one day to be the jewels in his crown. That demands a recognition of the fact of our unity, of our identification with Christ at the cross as well as complete identification with the needs of man. It means that you as a Christian are not here simply to participate in a church program or to enjoy church services. It means that you are here for total penetration for Jesus, at any price, bringing the good news of His love into every area of life in which you move.

This is only possible as we recognize that within the church we have fellowship in our diversity, as we learn to love and to care for our brethren who are different, always recognizing the utter futility of identity. Are we here in the name of the Lord that there may be total penetration without any assimilation, that God may preserve us blameless and one day present us faultless before His throne? Are you living on that principle today?

PART III

DYNAMIC FOR THE JOURNEY

CHAPTER TWENTY-ONE

LOVE IS
THE WAY

1 CORINTHIANS 13:1–3

As we travel this royal route to heaven, we have already found many difficulties in the church which have been answered by the message of the cross. The conflict will be renewed before we come, so to speak, to the journey's end, but in this chapter everything is fragrant. It is like waking up to a spring morning full of sunshine and warmth after the coldness and darkness of winter. We will not hurry over this chapter, but savor its refreshment to our hearts. I trust you will get a wonderful spiritual suntan as you look into the face of our Lord Jesus Christ and absorb the glow of His love.

Three chapters here have to do with spiritual gifts: chapter 12 tells of God's rich endowment of gifts to His people; chapter 13 tells of God's energy imparted to our lives, which makes it possible for us to use the gifts to His glory; chapter 14 gives God's instructions for the exercise of the gifts. Between the endowment of the gifts and the exercise of the gifts there is the great chapter on love, showing us that the only way to safeguard and rightly use our spiritual gifts is by administering them in the love of God.

When Paul came to this particular point in dictating this letter, I somehow feel his face lit up with glory. Surely the first twelve chapters must have caused him pain as he wrote to this church concerning their low spiritual state. As he himself said, they "come behind in no gift" (1:7), but they were tragically lacking in this quality of love. I think it must have been a precious release to him to put in this wonderful potion. The love of God is the answer to all the problems, not only in Corinth, but in our cities and church today.

It is significant that it was Paul the theologian who brought to us this great passage, and not John, the disciple of love. Those two men differed widely in their gifts and ministry, but they were united in this one thing, the greatest any Christian can possess, the grace of love. In fact, Paul tells us quite plainly that if we have no love, we have nothing; but if we have love, though we may lack much else, then we have what matters most.

First, we need to understand the significance of this word, which the Authorized (King James) Version translates by our English word "charity." The revised versions change it to "love," and rightly so. The former word suggests something very different today from what it did in 1611, having now the meaning of benevolence or tolerance, and that is a totally inadequate meaning of the Greek word which is used in this chapter.

There are three Greek words translated by the English word "love." One of them is found only in the Septuagint (Greek Version) in Proverbs and the prophecies of Hosea and Ezekiel. It does not occur in the New Testament at all. It is a word that suggests sensual desire, and it has very unpleasant associations. Perhaps that is why the Holy Spirit keeps it out of the New Testament altogether.

From the second word, the Greek noun *philia*, we have derived, for instance, "philosophy" and "Philadelphia." It means friendship, a natural affection for other people, the love you might have for your friends and relatives. This is a word we find occasionally in the New Testament.

The third Greek noun, used throughout this chapter and used most frequently in the New Testament, is *agape*, from which we get our English "agony." It meant the actual absorption of every part of our being in one great passion. It is used most often in relation to God: "God so loved [verb, *agapaō*] the world, that he gave his only begotten Son" (John 3:16). This word has little to do with mere emotion; it indicates love which deliberately, by and act of will, chooses its object, and through thick or thin, regardless of the attractiveness of the object concerned, goes on loving continually, eternally.

It is a word that speaks of complete self-denial. To love in this way means never thinking of ourselves at all; the self-life does not enter into the picture. It is always used when the will is involved rather than the emotions. That is why, in regard to the Christian's attitude to his enemy, this is the word the Lord used: "thou shalt love [not *phileō*, 'like,' but *agapaō*, 'agonize over'] thine enemies."

This word is the only one in the Bible (and what an honor!) that is used to describe God without any qualification or explanation: God is *agape*. When we sing that lovely hymn of George Matheson's "O Love, that will not let me go!" We are not singing about an abstract thing. Or again, when we sing Charles Wesley's hymn, "O Love Divine, how sweet thou art!" we are assaying that God is Love.

Every description of love in this chapter is applicable to the Lord Jesus Christ. Jesus suffers long, and is kind. Jesus envies not; Jesus vaunts not Himself, is not puffed up, does not behave Himself unseemly. Jesus seeks not His own, is not easily provoked, takes not account of evil, rejoices not in unrighteousness, but rejoices with the truth. Jesus bears all things, believes all things, hopes all things, endures all things. Jesus never fails.

Love is the one thing, therefore, that is completely indestructible; while other things pass away, love lasts. It is not dependent on anything outside of itself; it is not affected by the worthiness or unworthiness of the one it loves. When we become New Testament Christians, that *agape* is born in us, and if these studies are to mean anything, by the time we are through you and I will have to be able to say, "I suffer long and am kind…" If that love really grips your heart, your Christian experience will be utterly revolutionized.

The distinction between the two Greek words is brought out in the conversion between the risen Lord and Peter by the lake shore that morning after His resurrection; it is recorded in John 21.

> "Simon, son of Jonas, lovest (*agapaō*) thou me more than these?"
> "Yes, Lord, thou knowest that I like you (*phileō*)."
> "Simon, son of Jonas, lovest (*agapaō*) thou me?
> "Yes, Lord, thou knowest I have an affection (*phileō*) for thee."
> "Simon, son of Jonas, are you sure that you have an affection (*phileō*) for me?"

And Peter was grieved because the Lord asked him a third time — not because of the repetition, but because the third time He came down to the lower word. Peter cried out, "Lord, thou knowest all things; thou knowest I have an affection for thee!" I know what that poor man felt, and so do you. He was so ashamed because of his denial of Christ that he could not even bring himself to use that tremendous word, agapaō. Of course he couldn't—not until Pentecost, that day when the Holy Spirit came from heaven and shed abroad the love of God in his heart.

I feel it is almost a desecration to tear this chapter apart by outlining it, but for the sake of those who like some system in Bible study, here are the divisions we will be using. In the first place, in verses 1 through 3, there is what I am calling the pre-eminence of love, that is, its value; in verses 4 through 7 there is the prerogative of love, that is, its virtue. And in the closing part of the chapter, in verses 8 through 13, there is the permanence of love, that is, its victory. In the first three verses we see a life without love, and in the following verses, love as the strength of a man's life and character. In the closing part of the chapter we see a life with love as its goal and ambition.

We find, first, the picture of an individual who is blessed with gifts and talents to an amazing degree, and yet without love his life is empty and worthless. Here the searchlight of heaven is turned upon a man or woman who has strong power of emotion, tremendous power of intellect, and the most amazing powers of will, but lacking love (*agape*), he has absolutely nothing. Notice the threefold repetition of the phrase: "but have not love."

In the first verse I find this principle: love must be sovereign in the heart. "Though I speak with the tongues of men and of angels, and have not love, I am become as sounding brass, or a tinkling cymbal." Paul has been talking about the gift of tongues, the highest expression of emotion, praise and worship. Here he supposes himself to be in possession of this gift to such a degree that he speaks not only with the tongues of men, but with the tongues of angels, as well. Even if he can do this, and has no love, it is all valueless. In other words, the silver-tongued orator who is a loveless man is just a big noise: a clanging cymbal or noisy gong.

The power behind your tongue, your speech, is not determined by the extent of your vocabulary but by the depth of your heart by how much you love. What use is eloquence without love? The tongue possesses power to do devastating damage. Its hiss can be as full of venom and spite as a poisonous serpent. It is often the last thing that God gets hold of in the Christian's life. But when *agape* comes to a man's life he does not need words, he has a new medium of expression, for love is universal in every language.

As I was preparing this message, outside in the street a police car passed by with its siren screeching. Then downstairs in the church auditorium there was the sound of the organ. What a vivid contrast it was! The siren was a voice without love, while the music was a voice of worship and love.

I have heard preachers whose oratory has left me breathless and made me go away saying, "Wasn't that magnificent! His command of language was absolutely tremendous." Oratory may command admiration, but only love can reach the heart. That is why Jesus said the most important commandment of all is "Thou shalt love (agapaō) the Lord thy God with all they heart ... and thy neighbor as thyself." Here is love sovereign in a man's emotions and revealed in his speech.

Then we find in the second verse that love must be sovereign in our intellect: "And though I have the gift of prophecy, and understand all mysteries, and all knowledge; and though I have all faith so that I could remove mountains, and have not love, I am nothing."

There are four things here that belong to our intellect as distinct from our emotions or our will. The first is prophecy, the power to declare the things of God, and power to interpret life, the power to bring the word of heaven to bear upon earth, the power to bring eternity into time. Mysteries—I take that to mean the discernment of spiritual things, understanding God's secrets. Knowledge is intelligence in the truth, and understanding of Scripture. And faith means that firmness of belief which will take a man through difficulties and problems and testing, because he trusts God.

You may possess all these, says Paul, but without love you are nothing. There are men in the Bible who illustrate this. For instance, Balaam was a prophet, but he had not love, and therefore he betrayed his prophetic office. Caiaphas, the High Priest, had discernment, for he knew that one must be slain for the nation, but he was without love, and he became a leader among those who crucified the Lord of glory. Judas Iscariot had knowledge, all that he could acquire at the master's feet in three years, but he had not love, and he betrayed the Lord.

Prophecy, mystery, knowledge, faith—all these are gifts; love is not a gift, but a grace, and it is the primary proof of a genuine new birth. In Galatians 5:22, the first fruit of the Spirit mentioned is love *(agape)*. The first thing that happens to a man when he is born again is the melting of his heart in love.

Apart from this divine love, the gifts of the Spirit may be exercised in selfishness. A man with faith but no love can embitter the lives of other people because in him is the possibility of dreadful cruelty. A man with a faith that can move mountains right out of his path, if he has not love, will throw them right into the path of somebody else. People with many gifts and much power may become celebrated theologians, renowned missionaries, great authors or scholars or teachers of the Word. But if something less than the *agape* of God in Jesus Christ is the animating power behind their lives, then the Bible says they are nothing.

There is one other thing here: love must be sovereign in a man's will. "If I bestow all my goods to feed the poor, and if I give my body to be burned, and have not love it profiteth me nothing" (13:3).

Love is to dominate not only my emotions and my intellect, but my will. These are the three principle faculties of a human being, and they must be kept in harmony. If we are going to be sane and well balanced under the pressure of days like these, the love of God must be in control to keep our intellect, our emotions, and our will in balance.

Paul takes two extreme examples here. If a man distributes everything he has to feed the poor, or even surrenders himself to the flames — in other words, he goes to the limit of absolute sacrifice — yet has not love, it is all worthless. You might say that he would never do that unless he loved. What about the heathen cutting himself to death to make peace with his God? That is not love, but fear. What about almsgiving to the point of penury? That is not done out of love, but from hope of a reward in the hereafter. These are attempts to make an atonement, and in the same way even a Christian may make a supreme sacrifice for the wrong motive.

I would say this carefully, but I believe the trouble with many of us is that although we will fight and die for our faith, we reject altogether the principle of living in the spirit of love. It is pointless to die for a wrong motive. I recall with a sense of fear in my soul the words of the risen Lord to the church at Ephesus; "I know thy works, and thy labour, and thy patience, and how thou canst not bear [evil men] ... and for my name's sake hast laboured, and hast not fainted. Nevertheless I have somewhat against thee, because thou hast left thy first love (*agape*)" (Revelation 2:2–4). What a solemn, terrifying picture of busyness, patience, discernment, toil, endurance, but absolutely without the one thing that matters — love!

Notice, finally the five "ifs" in these verses. You will find it "though" in the Authorized Version, but the meaning is "if," as in the revised versions. "*If* I speak with the tongues of men... *if* I have the gift of prophecy... *if* I have all faith... *if* I bestow all my goods... *if* I give my body to be burned..." Notice, also, the four *alls*: "and understand *all* mysteries, and *all* knowledge... and if I have *all* faith... if I bestow *all* my goods..."

If such an individual ever lived on the face of this earth who did all that, I tell you, without *agape*, he is nothing. Of course he isn't! Why? Because God is love, and without love, he is without God.

You may have all these gifts and all these things, but without the Lord Jesus in your life, what is the use of it? You are not something or somebody, but you are absolutely nobody, worthless for time and for eternity. What have you got that is going to be currency in that day when you pass from this earthly scene and meet God face to face? Your gifts, your abilities, your knowledge, your sacrifice, your faith — but "he that hath not the Son of God hath not life." The one thing that matters is Jesus Christ and His love, His passion, in your heart. Do you possess that now?

CHAPTER TWENTY-TWO

THE LOVE
LIFE

1 CORINTHIANS 13:4–7

On the royal route to heaven in 1 Corinthians, we have come to the love chapter—the greatest thing ever written on that subject. We are pausing here so that the atmosphere and spirit of love may encompass our lives, that the warmth and glow of love may flood our hearts and minds. I am quite certain there is nothing we need more than a refreshing of the love of God in our lives.

In the first of this chapter there are two contrasting pictures. In the opening three verses we see a man who has a lot of gifts, but no love. In the next four verses we see a man who has a lot of love, but apparently no gifts. In some measure the church at Corinth fitted into the first of these, but it found no place in the second at all, for it was completely without love.

In the second picture there is no reference to any gifts, and yet as we read these wonderful words we feel the impact of this life of love, this Christlikeness of character. While gifts without love are absolutely worthless, yet love, apparently without any gifts, is a quality which will stand the test of time and eternity.

This picture of love is a photograph of the Lord Jesus Christ in His inner character. And in His church, His body, He wants to have many reprints. We are looking at the Original, Himself; He looks at us, for what He is in this world so are we to be. He is looking for the perfect reproduction of His life of love in us. To love like this is to be like the Lord, and our unlikeness to Christ is proportionate to our failure to love. Christians are those born again by the Holy Spirit, in whom the Savior has become incarnate again, for we are partakers of a new nature—His Character, which is love.

This description of love shows it in sharp contrast to everything the Corinthian church was, and also of what we have ever been.

Love is very patient, but we are impatient. Love is very kind, but we are discontented and unkind. Love knows no jealousy, but we are always envious of others who have more than we do, or we think they do. Love makes no parade, but we are so proud. Love gives itself no airs and is never rude, but we are ill-mannered. Love is never selfish, but we are self-centered. Love is never irritated, but we become short-tempered so easily. Love is never resentful, but we look for slights and cherish wrongs. Love is never glad when others go wrong, but we take a secret delight in the failures of other people. Love is gladdened by goodness, always slow to expose and eager to believe the best, but we are so censorious.

Sin and Satan have robbed us of all likeness to God's character, but here is an outline of what the grace of God and the power of the indwelling Holy Spirit has come to do in our lives. In verses 4 to 6 are listed the qualities of character with which love has nothing to do, the things about which it is passive and negative. The power of love holds as life in restraint, that it may not do evil. In verse 7, love is active and positive: believing, bearing, hoping, enduring. Here is love sending out, constraining. Love holds us back from what we would be by ourselves; love forces us on to that which, humanly speaking, we are helpless to accomplish.

There are fourteen descriptions of what I might call "the ingredients of love" in these few verses. In each we see Jesus Christ and recognize His purpose that each of us should be like Him in His character of love.

1. *Love suffers long.* That is the first quality love displays. In other words, having been wronged, love is patient and silent. It refuses to give way to anger, though it could rightfully be resentful when it had been unjustly treated. Though love suffers wound and injury, it does not strike back. The Lord Jesus, when he was reviled, reviled not again. How about you?

2. *Love is kind.* To endure wrong could be just a triumph of obstinacy, but to be kind to the person who has done the wrong is a triumph

of grace. The love of God is not only patient but kind. The Lord Jesus showed the greatest kindness to Judas Iscariot, who betrayed Him. Even to our friends, how loveless and how unkind we have been. The greatest thing that you can ever do this side of heaven—and perhaps we have not much longer to do it—is to be kind to God's children. Love not only takes the injury, but shows positive grace and kindness to the person responsible for it. Are we like that?

3. *Love envies not.* It does not begrudge the greater privileges and gifts of others, or seek out gain for itself. Only love can see all the inequalities of life and remain content with its own place. Where there is no love, there will inevitably be envy. This was the seed of the first murder in human history, and it has been a seed of murder ever since. Envy appears even in the hearts of Christians, and is a vice so unlovely, so grievous to the Lord, so hard to overcome. But love is perfectly content with the will of God. The Lord Jesus went about doing good and never desired good to be done to Himself. Are you eaten up with envy, jealous of other's gifts, opportunities, abilities, possessions, position in life?

4. *Love vaunteth not itself.* As Moffatt puts it, "Love makes no parade." It does not show off or boast or brag; it is not proud or conceited. Love never seeks to win the praise and applause of others. When a man begins to boast, he is advertising his emptiness and his ignorance. There is no swagger about love, it is too big for that. The Lord Jesus never "showed off." His greatness was revealed not merely in what He displayed but in the things He suppressed. He laid aside His glory and humble Himself for the sake of others. How about you? Are you boastful, conceited, proud?

5. *Love is not puffed up.* It is never arrogant, but humble. It is never self-satisfied or contemptuous of others. "Love gives itself no airs," is the way Moffatt translates it. The person who is self-satisfied is always contemptuous of others. The Lord Jesus never showed vanity or conceit or contempt of others. Do you?

6. *Love does not behave itself unseemly.* It is not rude or ill-mannered, but always courteous. This is the love of God shown in the little, everyday things of life: the good manners of a child of God. There is so much blundering goodness, uncouth religion, unlovely testimony, unattractive Christian witness, because of lack of love. The Lord Jesus always said and did the right thing in the right way at the right time. Yet there is such a lack of real Christian goodness and courtesy in our everyday lives. How about you?

7. *Love seeks not her own.* That is to say, love is not selfish, but self-forgetful. Love does not grasp for its own rights, but find its joy in serving others. How often we seek our own advancement and interests, sometimes at the expense of other people, entirely unconcerned for their welfare, their blessing and growth.

8. *Love is not easily provoked.* That is a shattering statement! It simply means that love is not bad-tempered. Actually, there is not sin that so disrupts a home, so spoils a Christian family, so ruins children in their upbringing, as sheer bad temper. It is often excused as something that people cannot help, but it demonstrates a lack of love. Of course, love can be angry with sin, but love is never irritable or touchy. The Lord Jesus hated sin, but He was never angry at wrong done to Himself. He was never vindictive, and never did he retaliate. Do you find yourself temperamental, thin-skinned, easily offended, quick to be resentful? Love is not easily provoked.

9. *Love thinks no evil.* Love will always keep a record of the many kindnesses it receives, and be thankful for them, but love will not keep a record of wrongs it has suffered with a view to getting even. It does not cherish in its memory a list of injustices; love has an amazing power to forget. The Lord Jesus Christ came to blot out our transgressions and to remember them against us no more forever. For when the blood of Jesus Christ was shed for the remission of my sins, and God sees the blood and my faith in my Lord's atoning sacrifice, He not only forgives, but He forgets. Has that ability been imparted to your life? Or do you build up a list of wrongs done to you and bide your time for retaliation? It is said of Abraham Lincoln that he never forgot a kindness, but he had not room in his mind for the memory of a wrong. How about you?

10. *Love rejoices not in iniquity, but rejoices in the truth.* I like Moffatt's paraphrase, "love is never glad when others go wrong; love is gladdened by goodness." In others words, love does not delight in exposing the weakness of other people. It will weep over sin and be brokenhearted over failure; it will condemn the sin, but love will always yearn to cover and protect the man who has fallen.

How the Lord Jesus yearned over sinners! He often sought to protect them from the injustice of others. For instance, in His interview with the woman taken in adultery, as recorded in John 8, He did not condone her sin, but He protected and forgave her, the sinner. This is a very searching test of character. Are you heartbroken at the misfortune or breakdown of other people? Or do you have a tendency to gloat over them secretly and delight to gossip about them? Love does not do that, for at the cross mercy and truth met; there Jesus condemned sin but pardoned the sinner.

11. *Love bears all things.* Love suffers wrong without retaliation; that is the negative aspect of the statement. But love gets under the load of life and bears it to the limit, and that is positive. Love patiently endures what it has to suffer, and is not shaken by ingratitude; it is proof against hardship and reproach. The Lord Jesus patiently bore all the wrong and injustice, and prayed on the cross, "Father, forgive them, for them know not what they do." The same time, He put His shoulder under the load of sin and bore the crushing burdens of others. How about you?

12. *Love believes all things.* Not that love is easily deceived—I do not think it means that at all, or that love is blind. Puppy love maybe, but not the love of God. Rather, it means that love is not basically suspicious. It takes the kindest view of others in every circumstance, as long as it possibly can. Love will consider the motives and make every allowance for failure. And when a man has fallen, love will think about the battle that he must have fought, and the struggle that he must have had before he went down.

The Lord Jesus never misjudged anybody, because He did not judge by outward appearances. He had an amazing way of looking at an outcast and seeing in him an infinite capacity for regeneration. "Wilt thou be made whole?" he asked the worst case at the pool of Bethesda. He became the Friend of sinners. We are apt to view every action with suspicion and become cynical toward those who are down, but love is not suspicious.

13. *Love hopes all things.* When love is disappointed in the one in whom it trusted, it will yet hope for better things, although others may long since have ceased to do so. Love never despairs of anybody. Of course, it does not try to persuade itself that a thief is honest or that the criminal is innocent, but I know that God is not willing that one should perish. The Lord Jesus never gives up hope of anyone! When other people have given up hope for us and when we have become absolutely hopeless about ourselves, the Lord is never discouraged. Christ, because He is love, never gives in to dismay or gives up to despair. I am so glad I have a God like that, for when others give up on us it is wonderful to know there is a God in heaven who goes on hoping and planning for our good.

14. *Love endures all things.* This is perhaps the most wonderful thing of all: love cannot be conquered. It bears, believes, hopes, and then endures. In other words, when the person in whom you have trusted has let you down, love never gives in. It holds its ground in the day of defeat and still endures. Such love took Jesus to Calvary. How He endured the contradiction of sinners against Himself! "Hereby perceive we the love of God, because he laid down his life for us: and we ought to lay down our lives of the brethren" (1 John 3: 16).

This has been a photograph of Jesus Christ, and perhaps you have felt Him looking into your own heart and asking about the reproduction of His love in your life. If you would learn to live like this, first you must receive that love into your heart: you must come to Jesus, take Him as your Lord and yield to Him. How wonderful it is to know that Christ loved you so completely and perfectly! Open your cold, dead heart to welcome Him in, and then go out to love others as He did.

It is not a question of admitting to a truth, but admitting God into your life, and He is the God of all truth. It is not being orthodox, merely, but of becoming dynamic in the power of the love of Jesus. It is not trying to produce these qualities by self-improvement; it is submission to the Holy Spirit, who sheds abroad the love of God in our heats day by day.

Does this photograph find you out? Does it show your life to be the reverse of everything that Jesus is? If so, I can tell you that grace can triumph, and make you just like this as you yield yourself to Him.

CHAPTER TWENTY-THREE

THE PERMANENCE OF LOVE

1 CORINTHIANS 13:8

In our two previous meditations upon this wonderful chapter of God's Word, we have seen in the first three verses the supremacy of love, in the next four verses the qualities of love, and now we come to what I have called the permanence of love, or, if you prefer, the power of love.

"Love never faileth." Now "never" is a long time, but love reaches to the uttermost. The greatest thing about love is that it lasts. You ask why? The answer is very simple: God is love. That love of God is shed abroad in our hearts by the Holy Spirit, so that the evidence of genuine Christian experience is not what we say we believe, but how much we love. This love is not only a quality of life but also a responsibility which we owe to fellow believers. The apostle John reminds us, "Every one that loveth him that begat loveth him also that is begotten of him" (1 John 5:1).

The three words, "Love never faileth," are not only the heart of this chapter, they are the heart of the whole message of God to the church at Corinth. We begin, therefore, with a brief consideration of the contrast that love should bring.

Here in the wicked city of Corinth is a church supposedly indwelt by the life of Jesus Christ. It is to be governed by His will and to reveal His love. But the city is mastered by materialism by antagonism to the things of God, and by resistance to the Spirit of God; self-centered, self-willed, and utterly callous to the things of eternity. There should be a great contrast, therefore, which marks out clearly where every inhabitant of that city stands in his relationship to heaven. Even though in everyday life they are rubbing shoulders constantly in business, in social life, in commerce, there is to be one factor which demonstrates unmistakably who is a Christian and who is not.

The church is called into fellowship with Jesus Christ (1:9); all His resources belong to them, and all their resources belong to Him. This is a partnership which, with dual commitment, is intended to be irresistible and completely victorious. It carries responsibility for all others: "I am debtor both to the Greeks and to the barbarians," declares Paul in his letter to the church at Rome. To make Christ known in Corinth is the obligation of this church, and to make Him known in Corinth is the obligation of this church, and to make Him known by this weapon of love is to insure their victory.

Salvation and obligation have always been inseparable. This contrast is true in the world in which we live today, and you can put the name of your own city or town in the place of Corinth. It is not your belief but your love that distinguishes your relationship to heaven in your particular surroundings.

But the church at Corinth had been failing in its task because its convictions concerning the gospel were shallow and inadequate. Not that there was anything wrong with their doctrine, but there was a great deal wrong with their behavior. A carnal church, a divided church, a worldly church, an indulgent church, a compromising church, can never effectively proclaim a spiritual message.

The trouble, of course, is very simply diagnosed. It is just that the spirit of Corinth—its luxury, indiscipline, cleverness, philosophy, all of these things—had crept into the life of the church. Party spirit, moral laxity, selfishness, and indulgence were sapping the vitality of this little group of believers until they were nearly overcome by the sin of the city around them.

Paul dealt with this, you recall, first by correction (1–11), and then by instructive teaching (12–13). He made it perfectly plain that what happened in Corinth need never have happened at all. It happened because the church was feebly trying to resist the avalanche of corruption by carnal methods: eloquence, wisdom, philosophy. All the time the church was ignoring its only source of victory and power, the law of love imparted by the Holy Spirit. When a church or a Christian begins to function on that higher ground, they live on a plane that puts them beyond all competition.

Once again, all this is manifestly true of the Christian church today. Our convictions concerning the gospel have too often been shallow and inadequate, especially in terms of our responsibility to others. It is not that our beliefs are wrong, but that somehow they do not seem to have affected our behavior. Indulgence breeds selfishness, indiscipline breeds shallowness, worldliness breeds compromise, materialism breeds spiritual laziness. All these things today threaten to engulf the whole Christian church until we lose the reality of our testimony to this generation. The intended contrast between the Christian and the unbeliever is absolutely unrecognized.

Where, therefore, is the conquest of the church? What can put us on a level where no one can compete? The answer to the need of the church today, I believe, is not a new visitation of God from heaven, but that Christians will begin to live in accordance with the principles laid down in the Word of God, especially the love of God imparted by the Holy Spirit when we were born again.

A love that never fails—that is the quality that is to characterize every child of God in every circumstance, seven days a week. The total Christian impact is made by a fellowship of Christian people mastered by the cross of Christ, imbued with the passionate love of the Lord, and therefore impelled by a principle that never fails.

This very remarkable word which we find translated "faileth" in our English New Testament has several significant meanings. Let me give you a few so that you may see the power of the thing that God puts into our lives.

The first meaning would be "love never falls to the ground," like the petals of a flower begin to fall, because there is decay in them. Love never does that, because there is not trace of decay in love. "Love never loses its strength," as does a traveler who sets out on a long, weary journey and grows tired, because love is inexhaustible. "Love never leaves its place," because love is immovable. As you look out on a starlit night, the stars sometimes seem to fall, but love never loses its place. "Love never drops out of line," like a poor, exhausted soldier on the march might do, because love is absolutely tireless. All its comrades may fall on the march, but love doggedly, patiently perseveres, because it can never fail.

As Phillips puts it: love "can outlast anything. It is, in fact, the one thing that still stands when all else has fallen" (13:8). Such love has its origin in heaven and its perfect expression in Jesus Christ our Lord, who "having loved his own which were in the world, he loved them unto the end" (John 13:1).

This is the love of God from which nothing can separate the Christian, and this is the quality of life by which you and I are to be distinguished from everyone around us. Throughout all time and eternity we will be realizing more fully than ever the breadth, length, depth and height of the love of God which passes knowledge. Disappointments, disillusionments, and defeats can never rob it of its power, for love is of God.

To what extent has this love gripped us? There are some strange substitutes for love which master many people. A colleague of mine in the ministry had a hectic phone call from a young lady who said to him, "Pastor, what shall I do? There is a man who loves me so much he says that if I don't marry him he will shoot himself. What shall I do?"

"Nothing," my friend replied, "Let him shoot himself."

Such a threat is not love; it is pure selfishness, desire, lust, whatever ugly word you might like to call it. Real love is self-communication. "God so loved the world that He gave..."Love is communication of everything I have, also, for Him.

In 1951, twenty-four leaders of the China Inland Mission Overseas Missionary Fellowship met together in Manila at a moment of great crisis. Their personnel had come out from China intact, but what was to be the next move? One of those who was present told me, "It was a baffling experience. There was no awareness of the presence of God. There was no sense of the divine direction; we felt completely at a loss as to what to do."

One day, by invitation there came into that conference the last surviving daughter of General Booth, the Marechale. As she sat around the table with them, listening to their conversation, she suddenly interrupted: "Gentlemen, how do you spell 'love'?"

There was an embarrassing silence, and someone was on the verge of saying, "Well, l-o-v-e, of course," when the Marechale very gently shook her head and answered their unspoken thoughts. "No, gentlemen. Will you allow me to spell 'love' for you? It is spelled s-a-c-r-i-f-i-c-e."

Into that strategic conference came the melting and moving power of the Spirit of God, and for the past eight years that missionary society, reborn out of the flame of that moment, has undertaken one of the greatest efforts of missionary history in Southeast Asia.

"Though I speak with the tongues of men and of angels, and have not *sacrifice*, I have nothing."

Some people say that in certain churches there is no sense of worship. Maybe they are right, but what do you think can make a sense of worship in a congregation? It is not aesthetic beauty; it is not a building; it is not a psychological atmosphere. It is a congregation who has given themselves to God, and in whose lives there is love and sacrifice to the limit—then that church is just lit up with the glory of the indwelling Christ.

To be very practical, and to bring this right down to earth in our lives—if this is something that we would experience, here are some suggestions.

First, live in simplicity; hold the things of this world lightly.

Second, recover mobility. As a church we must move out today for God, and not be hindered by the machinery of organization or the lethargy of custom.

Third, determine priorities. What comes first in the life of a church, a board of administration or a prayer meeting? What matters most to us, a committee, a service, a bit of work, or travail in prayer?

Fourth, share responsibilities. Not everyone can do the work, but we are each given the measure of grace according to our gifts.

Fifth, limit activities. It is no mark of spirituality to be out at a meeting every night of the week. Busyness can be barrenness.

Sixth, exploit opportunities. Where you are right now, in your job, in your situation—there, attack for Jesus.

What are the consequences of all this? At the Judgment, love is the ultimate test with which we are going to be faced. In Matthew 25 our Lord was speaking about the time when all nations are to be gathered together before Him for judgment, and He Himself separates the sheep and the goats. What is the determining factor? What is the thing that puts them on one side or another for all eternity? It is love!

"I was hungry, and ye gave me meat; I was thirsty, and ye gave me drink: I was a stranger, and ye took me in: naked, and ye clothed me; I was sick and ye visited me: I was in prison, and ye came unto me."

"Lord, when did we do all this?"

"Inasmuch as ye have done it to one of the least of these my brethren, ye have done it unto me."

If I fail right here it is strong evidence that I may not have known Jesus Christ at all. No matter what I have claimed to believe, no matter what doctrine of faith I have supported, no matter what position I may have taken to defend the truth, if I have failed in love, I am not fitted for the presence of God. For it simply means that I have never been near enough to the heart of Jesus to feel His love and compassion.

Not that it does not matter what you believe; it matters a great deal that you should accept the Word of God from beginning to end as basic in your life. But the great test is: How much do you love? Love brings heaven near to others. Love lifts the fallen and comforts the sorrowing. Love challenges corrupt moral standards. Love faces broken homes and leads back to the new Testament standards of life.

How much do you *love*?

CHAPTER TWENTY-FOUR

The Victory of Love

1 Corinthians 13:9–13

The last section of this chapter Paul begins with a great declaration, "love never faileth." Then he ends with an injunction, because the first three words of chapter 14 really belong to chapter 13: "Follow after love." In between that declaration and that injunction he puts a contrast and a comparison. Love is contrasted with gifts, and love is compared with other virtues. Then his great argument is brought to a triumphant note of victory: "the greatest of these is love."

In the last chapter I did not attempt an exposition of these verses, but that is what I want to do now. Let us look, first, at love contrasted with gifts.

The Corinthian church, you remember, was very proud of its gifts. The word "talents," which is quite popular today in some circles, would certainly have been popular with the church at Corinth. They were a very talented people; they had many gifts and much in which to take pride. But Paul is attempting to deflate their pride and put everything into right perspective.

He takes three of their most cherished gifts, prophecies, tongues, and knowledge, and contrasts them with love. He has already begun this chapter by pointing out that if you have all these gifts, and have not love, you are nothing. Now he considers them again, these things of which we are so ready to boast: "But whether there be prophecies, they shall fail; whether there be tongues, they shall cease; whether there be knowledge, it shall vanish away" (13:8).

In passing, please notice an important distinction: "For we know in part, and we prophesy in part," says Paul, "But when that which is perfect is come, then that which is in part shall be done away" (13:9–10). They will not cease, but they will be transformed. Tongues, on the other hand, will cease altogether. Prophecy and knowledge will be replaced by perfection: "Then shall I know even as also I am known" (13:12).

We need to be very careful before we boast of our knowledge. My father handed down to me an encyclopedia when I was a boy and told me, "This is the last word in everything you ought to know." That was true then, but the encyclopedia is not worth the paper is written on now as far as its information is concerned.

Knowledge is only in part now, but one day it is going to give way to perfection. Surely when Paul speaks about "when that which is perfect is come," he can mean only "when Jesus is come." The marks of imperfection are upon everything in this life except love. That goes on forever, and has on it the hallmark of eternity. Everything else is passing and transitory.

Paul uses a personal illustration here: "When I was a child, I spake as a child, I understood as a child, I thought as a child: but when I became a man, I put away childish things" (13:11). A person who is a man in years, but a child in mind, is a monstrosity. It is wonderful to listen to the chatter of a little child, but if you hear a man chattering like that, it is tragic! Every man, however, is still in essence a child; he has taken all the elements of childhood into manhood, but they have been developed and transformed; he has put away childish ways of speaking and habits of life and thought. So all spiritual gifts belong to childhood, and no one will go through into glory with them. At best, the greatest of mature Christians is but a child this side of eternity. But when Jesus comes and our maturity is reached, these gifts will become unnecessary.

As childhood is based on growing into manhood, so spiritual life here is based upon spiritual life in eternity. We begin our eternal life now. When I partially know something and I partially attain, I am moving toward the goal of that spiritual life which has its fullness and perfection in glory. Make heaven your goal, make maturity your aim, make Christ your object—but be very careful how you boast of your attainments. As childhood is absorbed into manhood, so one day our incomplete understanding of the things of God will be absorbed into perfect knowledge.

It is going to be wonderful to get to heaven! It will as completely transcend our deepest experience of Jesus Christ in this life as the midday sun transcends dawn. *Now* everything is only a dim reflection. I like that lovely translation of verse 12 by Moffatt, "At present we only see the baffling reflection in a mirror, but then it will be face to face."

We have sometimes been baffled by the reflections we have seen. Nature reflects the glory of God, but we cannot understand the earthquakes and volcanoes that destroy so many lives. And history reflects the government of God. As we trace its course, we know that all through the ages God has been ruling in the affairs of men, but we cannot understand war and suffering and the horrors of strife between nations.

The Bible reflects the grace of God. But many circumstances come into our lives which we cannot understand, and we ask God why things happen to us as they do.

These things are just baffling reflections in a mirror, but then there will be no dullness of understanding, no more bewilderment. Then we shall look back upon a hundred and one circumstances that we have fought against, prayed against, complained about, and we will find that all things, after all, have worked together in a pattern for good—though we did not really believe it. Then there will be no sin to cloud our vision; there will be no interruption in our communion with God.

Everything here is imperfect, except love. It is love alone which is going to last, while all the talents, the gifts, the knowledge, the prophecy, the preaching about which we have been so proud, will all be done away. Love never fails; it goes on forever, in contrast with gifts, which pass away.

But I want to hurry on to the lovelier pastures in this chapter, because we find love compared with virtues: "And now abideth faith, hope, [love], these three; but the greatest of these is [love]" (13:13).

How often these three words, "faith," "hope," and "love," are found together in the New Testament. For example, "Being justified by faith … we rejoice in hope … because the love of God is shed abroad in our hearts" (Romans 5:1–5). Then in the opening verses of Colossians: "we heard of your faith in Christ Jesus, and of the love which ye have to all the saints, For the hope which is laid up for you in heaven" (Colossians 1:4–5). And again in 1 Thessalonians 1:3, "your work of faith, and labour of love, and patience of hope." These three virtues are put alongside each other and compared; you cannot magnify love by minimizing faith and hope.

What is faith? Faith is trust that rests upon evidence and leads to action. That is the only kind of saving faith I find in the Bible. The whole fabric of life, social, commercial, and political, is based upon this principle. Our civilization could not exist without a measure of faith. But in terms of spiritual things, it is the foundation of our relationship with God. Only by faith do we become His children: "But as many as received him, to them gave he power to become the sons of God" (John 1:12). Unless I have faith, I am not His child, "for he that cometh to God must believe that he is, and that he is a rewarder of them that diligently seek him" (Hebrews 11:6).

What is hope? Hope is confidence in the future. I marvel at the tenacity of some people's hope in themselves and in the world, their attitude of, "Well, somehow it's going to work out all right in the end." From one tragedy and disappointment and heartbreak after another they pick themselves up and go on hoping, because they know if they stop, life will crash and everything will become dust and ashes, because their hope does not reach beyond the grave. The child of God has a hope laid up for him in heaven: "But if we hope for that we see not, then do we with patience wait for it" (Romans 8:25). Christian hope is not a vague guess, but an absolute, confident assurance.

Both faith and hope are related to love. You cannot separate them. Faith possesses the past by laying hold upon Calvary and making it real in my life. Hope claims the future, and looks beyond into glory. Love dominates my life right now—this is Christian living. Faith says, "Jesus Christ came to save me;" hope says, "He is coming again to take me to be with Him"; love says, "He abides in my heart today."

What is faith without hope and love? Just a cold, intellectual conviction with no saving power at all. What is hope without faith and love? Just a dream, a bubble that will burst one day. What is love without faith and hope? Just passion, just feeling, just emotion, without any principle or any foundation.

These three virtues are linked together, says Paul, and they abide. What is the meaning of the words "Now abideth"? Surely that "now" in this context is not the same "now" as in verse 12, where it relates to time and not to eternity. Some theological commentators say it is; I am no theologian, but I believe the Holy Spirit has spoken to me about this. These Corinthians thought that their gifts abided, but the whole argument of Paul here is that they do not last. The one thing that lasts is love, and along with love these other virtues: "Now abideth faith, hope and love"—all of them abide. Of course, love is the greatest, but not one of them has the changing, temporary character of the gifts that Paul has been discussing. Here you have to give full force to that word "abideth."

Someone may say, "Surely faith and hope will not abide in heaven, for when I see His lovely face, what do I need with faith then? Will no hope be lost in realization? I will possess everything, then."

> Faith will vanish into sight,
> Hope be emptied in delight,
> Love in heaven will shine more bright...

So says an old hymn—lovely, but you do not find that in the Word of God. The three elements of our relationship with the Lord are faith, hope, and love. When Paul says, "now abideth faith, hope and love," he is trying to tell us that just as our relationship with Jesus is forever, so also are faith, hope, and love. They go on as long as our relationship with Him lasts.

That suggests to me that life here and life in heaven are progressive. In other words, faith goes on possessing God more fully, and hope never ceases to catch new glimpses of His glory in the wonder of eternity. It is a mistake to think that eternity is synonymous with finality. In heaven there is perfection, but there are degrees of attainment just as one star differs from another star in glory. Each of us will have all the blessedness we can contain, but we will have varying capacities and be progressing from stage to stage. "In my Father's house are many mansions," many resting places, the Lord said. These are places for refreshment as we proceed on our journey through the glory-land forever to new and greater discoveries.

Every glimpse of Jesus here prepares us for a greater view in time and eternity ahead. Then we shall see His lovely face—but do you mean to tell me that the first sight I have of Him, five seconds after I have left earth and gone into heaven, is all that I am going to have? Can a mortal being, brought out of the battle and conflict of life into the presence of God, at that moment grasp and comprehend all the glory of God and heaven? No, I believe that in the Bible eternity is presented to us as a continual communication of God whose beauty and glory and majesty are inexhaustible. The resurrected body, united with a redeemed spirit, is brought to live in the very presence of God with a progressive, increasing capacity to receive more and more of His glory. Every new height of glory scaled will reveal more wonderful heights beyond. Faith, hope, love—these three remain. Our possessions and our gifts we leave behind us—only Christian character abides. At the gates of death we will lay down forever the various weapons which God, in His grace, has put into our hand that we might fight His battles—all our gifts and every other capacity of usefulness. But we will carry through the pearly gates of splendor the moral and spiritual character which the Holy Spirit, through the conflicts and testing of life, has developed within us. The three great elements of Christian character are faith, hope, and love.

Paul says that the greatest of these is love. He does not say it is more durable, or that it lasts longer, but that it is *greater*. It is not only greater than those things which pass, but greater than any of these things which also remain. Why? Because love is the home port—faith and hope are means to the end, but love is the goal. You cannot rest in faith and hope, but you can rest in love, as does God. "He shall rest in his love; he shall rejoice over thee with singing" (Zephaniah 3:17).

Love is greatest, also, because it is sacrificial. Faith and hope develop our own Christian character and strengthen us, but love is what we give to others. Love is greatest of all, because God is love. God does not believe, because He knows everything; God does not hope, because He possesses everything. But God loves, because He is love. You will never know the message of God to your own heart until you see, supreme above everything, His love revealed at Calvary.

Love is contrasted with gifts and love is compared with virtues, but most important of all, love is enjoined upon us: "Follow after [love]" (14:1). That means to practice it in daily life, to take every opportunity to encourage one another in the Lord. When we must say something critical and hard, for instance, or think we must, we should ask ourselves such questions as, "Is it true? Is it necessary? Is it kind? Will it help?" If not, then love is silent.

Then this chapter will read: "I suffer long, and am kind. I envy not; I vaunt not myself, am not puffed up. I do not behave myself unseemly. I seek not my own; I am not easily provoked; I think no evil. I rejoice not in iniquity, but rejoice in the truth. I bear all things, believe all things, hope all things, endure all things."

Therefore, follow after love, for God is love.
Love of God, eternal love, shed Thy love through me!
Nothing less than Calvary's love would I ask of Thee.
Fill me, flood me, overflow me,
Love of God, eternal love, shed Thy love through me!

— Amy Carmichael

CHAPTER TWENTY-FIVE

THE GIFT OF
TONGUES

1 CORINTHIANS 14:1–25

Having basked for a time in the refreshing sunshine of the great love chapter of the Bible, we come now to thorny territory, for here is the classic portion in God's Word on the subject of tongues and the use of them. It is so easy for a church to become sidetracked from the main issue; it is so easy for one particular doctrine to be stressed beyond all reason until it is twisted from being truth to being error. Constantly it is the task of the ministry, as far as it is able, to ensure that the main responsibilities of church testimony are always in right focus.

Paul clearly states the two major objectives of any Christian fellowship. First, the edifying of the believers: "Even so ye, forasmuch as ye are zealous of spiritual gifts, seek that ye may excel to the edifying of the church" (14:12). Secondly, the conversion of the unsaved, that because of the united testimony of the Christians, those who come into the church might "report that God is in you of a truth" (14:25). This is the twofold purpose of any Christian fellowship, and nothing must hinder it. At Corinth, the question of tongues had received priority consideration, and Paul takes opportunity in this chapter to put things in right balance.

This is a very useful subject for us to consider, because the tongues' movement in this country is quite popular and widespread. We have a constructive job to do, and I don't believe in hitting at people, but I do want to say this very respectfully to those of you who may disagree with me: In most cases the tongues' movement today, at least as I have seen it expressed, is quite sincere, although misguided and mis-instructed. With the practical teaching of this chapter available, I just cannot see how anyone can go wrong on the subject. It is so clear that everyone ought to be able to understand it.

Paul is really applying here the principle of chapter 13, the triumph of love. He has insisted on church unity in chapter 12, and in the midst of that unity, diversity of gifts and operation. Here he refers back to three of these gifts: prophecy, tongues, and interpretation of tongues (cp. 12:10). Further in that chapter he questions the Corinthian Christians, "Are all apostles? Are all prophets? ... Do all speak with tongues? Do all interpret? ... And yet show I unto you a more excellent way. ... Follow after love" (12:29–30; 14:1). It is in that setting that we are to study Paul's instructions on the subject of tongues.

What is the gift of tongues in the New Testament sense of the word? To answer that question, let me ask another. Where do we find it? We find it first on the day of Pentecost (Acts 2). There appeared cloven tongues like as of fire which sat upon each of the disciples, and they were filled with the Holy Spirit and began to speak with other tongues. We find it in Mark 16:17, where the Lord Jesus was saying farewell to His disciples, and He said to them, "These signs shall follow them that believe ... they shall speak with new tongues." We find it again in Acts 10:45–46, when, following Peter's address in the house of Cornelius, the Holy Spirit fell upon those assembled there and they spoke with tongues. When Paul came to Ephesus he found a few believers who were unrecognizable as Christians. He asked them if they had received the Holy Spirit and they said they had never heard of it. So they did receive the Holy Spirit, and we are told that they spoke with tongues (Acts 19:6). These are the only references in the whole New Testament; I have quoted them all.

Here is a gift bestowed first of all on the *whole* church at Pentecost, then given to *some* of the church on different occasions. The word used for tongues always means "ecstasy," when a man is carried into a realm in which he himself is living completely in mystery. He does not know what he is doing; in worship, he makes ecstatic utterances and speaks in tongues.

Notice this important instruction: "He that speaketh in an unknown tongue speaketh not unto men, but unto God. ... But if there be no interpreter, let him keep silence in the church; and let him speak to himself, and to God" (14:2, 28). In other words, the gift of tongues (and please mark this carefully) is given for the purpose of speech to God and not to man, for ecstatic utterance in praise of God. If this gift of tongues is to be used publicly, it must be used in the presence of an interpreter, and if there is no interpreter, then let him keep silence in the church. Even the man who exercises the gift and who claims to speak in tongues does not know what he is saying at the time: "For if I pray in an unknown tongue, my spirit prayeth, but my understanding is unfruitful" (14:14). Paul knows what he is talking about, for he also has the gift, "I thank my God, I speak with tongues more than ye all" (14:18). So he is not being jealous. But he says, "Follow after love … covet earnestly the best gifts."

As the gift of tongues was given in the first instance on the day of Pentecost to all believers, and then later to other groups of believers it is possible that some may even receive the gift today. I do not deny that. But if they do, they should remember that it is to be used in addressing God; it is not given for the purpose of witness to other people. It is quite beyond the understanding, not only of the people who listen, but of the person who claims to be using it. If it is used in public, there must be an interpreter present. Otherwise, the clear command of the Word of God is to keep silent.

Surely the instruction and definition in this chapter are beyond any misunderstanding. Yet this is quite different from the practice of the gift as exercised in many places today, where there is hysteria and wild enthusiasm, but no interpretation. Sometimes tongues are even demanded of the young convert as an evidence of the fact that he has been born again, before he is allowed to participate in Christian work. This is totally unscriptural; to demand the gift of tongues as an evidence of the fullness of the Spirit has no basis whatever in the Word of God.

Then what is the use of the gift of tongues at all? In the first instance, when it was given on the day of Pentecost, unquestionably it was used to arouse interest. "Tongues are for a sign, not to them that believe, but to them that believe not" (14:22). And on the day of Pentecost, people heard the disciples speak in their own languages the mighty works of God. They were not preaching; they were expressing worship in ecstasy, in languages by which they had never previously spoken. This led to inquiry which, of course, it was meant to do; in fact, the people thought they were drunk. Then Peter stood up and gave the interpretation, "this is that which was spoken by the prophet Joel…" and from that moment, when he had won their interest, he went on to preach the unsearchable riches of Christ.

Will you notice that in the second place there is a distinction to be realized: "For he that speaketh in an known tongue speaketh not unto men, but unto God… he that prophesieth speaketh unto men to edification, and exhortation, and comfort" (14:2–3). At once you have the contrast between tongues and prophecy. Please don't put a narrow definition upon that last word. It literally means preaching, testimony, witnessing in our daily life.

In the teaching of this chapter there is a threefold contrast, very simple but very striking. "He that speaketh in an unknown tongue edifieth himself; but he that prophesieth edifieth the church" (14:4).

In relation to the man himself, and his witness, speaking in tongues is not doing anyone else any good, though it may be doing himself good. But the gift of prophecy, or preaching, or testimony, is for the sake of other people. If a man is going to ask from God that which will only please and edify himself, and make him think that spiritually he has gone further than others, is not his motive selfish? Paul says, "Follow after love." The motive of the Christian should not be to put himself on a pedestal; he is to be a channel through whom the Holy Spirit reaches out in blessing to the world. That is why Paul says that to preach or to witness is far better than to speak in tongues. "I would that ye all spake with tongues, but rather that ye prophesied; for greater is he that prophesieth than he that speaketh with tongues" (14:5).

The first point of distinction is in relation to a man's personal witness, the second is in relation to the church as a whole. Verses 5 to 20 deal with this part of the subject, and we cannot study it in detail, only highlight one or two things. If a man speaks with tongues, he does it to strengthen himself. There may be utterance, but, as Paul says in verse 8, if there is not clear piping of the tune, "if the trumpet give an uncertain sound, who shall prepare himself to the battle?" Who is going to prepare himself for the spiritual warfare as a result of confused ecstasy without interpretation? "In the church," Paul says, "I had rather speak five words with my understanding … than ten thousand words in an unknown tongue" (14:19). That ought to be enough! Five words: "It is Christ that died"—five words to preach the cross and proclaim a crucified, risen Lord!

Then comes a most important distinction, the thing that tongues cannot do in relation to the unbeliever. In verse 23 is a very interesting statement: "If … all speak with tongues … will they not say that ye are mad?" Paul had already warned them not to be childish; they are not to boast of their tongues. Their spirit of worship should be such that the unbeliever "will worship God, and report that God is in you of a truth" (14:25). This is what testimony can do that tongues cannot.

I find here also that there is a demonstration that must be recognized through the testimony of a believer. There is a threefold test of the reality of God the Holy Spirit in a Christian's life.

First, the Holy Spirit is primarily concerned with character and not with gifts (cp. Galatians 5:22–23). When the Holy Spirit comes upon a man at the moment of his conversion, He takes hold of him, as clay in the hand of the potter, to make him Christlike — clean, pure, and righteous. That is the work of the Spirit of God. This is why insistence upon the gift of tongues as evidence of spiritual reality is absolutely without authentic backing from the Word of God. The demonstration of reality is Christlikeness in character and in actions.

In the second place, the Holy Spirit comes to a man's life not to glorify Himself, but to glorify the Lord Jesus: "He shall not speak of himself … he shall receive of mine and shall shew it unto you" (John 16:13–14). If you have been seeking for an experience of God the Holy Spirit that has taken you away from the reality of God in Jesus Christ, you are getting off New Testament ground. The work of the Spirit of God is always to make Jesus known. The evidence that a man is really filled with the Spirit is not that he has some extraordinary emotional experience, but that moment by moment he is conscious of the presence of the Lord Jesus Christ.

The third test of reality is that the Holy Spirit has come to equip us for Christian ministry and testimony: "But ye shall receive power, after that the Holy Ghost is come upon you: and ye shall be witnesses unto me" (Acts 1:8). The evidence of Christ within the life is that upon that man there is the anointing, the power, the authority of the Spirit for his witness.

Therefore seek the Holy Spirit in His fullness today! Seek Him with all your heart. Put things out of your life that get in His way, be earnest, be determined. Never let God go until you enter very definitely into a crisis with Jesus Christ, and know all the fullness of His life with you. Then you will blaze out for Him, and from your life will spread the fragrance of the indwelling Christ.

CHAPTER TWENTY-SIX

SHARING THE
LOAD ON THE ROAD

1 CORINTHIANS 14:26–40

I have a conviction that many of us Christians need to have a new experience of the Lord. I am not going to quarrel with anyone about the terminology, but I am concerned about the reality of the experience. One Christian with reality is worth a thousand who are a sort of library of argument. You never win a soul to Jesus at the end of an argument.

Peter came to Christ because his brother Andrew came after him, just filled up with love. Andrew had spent only about twelve hours in the presence of Jesus. Before that he had been with John the Baptist, who had spoken about the Messiah. Andrew followed Jesus Christ to see where He lived, spent the night, and came out from His presence absolutely bubbling over. He went straight to his brother and said, "I have found the Messiah!" It was all so refreshingly simple.

Today we get so tied up in our doctrine and terminology that we lose the simplicity and glory of Christ and His gospel. We are not intended to be Christ's lawyers; we are His witnesses. Far too often today, I think, instead of being apostolic, we are apologetic: we are on the defense instead of on the attack.

How are we going to remedy this? I think it would be by stopping the things that displease the Lord, and starting what pleases Him. This is exactly what we find in this portion of the Word, something which again may prove to be controversial ground. But the simplest way into a new experience with God is through recognizing and rejoicing in our Christian fellowship.

Let us begin with one or two simple, obvious things. First, here is a principle that Paul reveals: "When you come together … let all things be done to [edify]" (14:26). Now I do not think Paul is describing here what I would call a normal evangelistic service in the church, a preaching service, but he is dealing with a fellowship meeting. This is what earlier Christians would call a "sharing" meeting, in which they shared some of the things the Lord had been saying to them; a practice which has, I am afraid, very largely died out these days.

At such a meeting, everyone comes with something to say, and they are all bursting to say it. The problem is to keep them quiet! One has a song he wants to sing. Another has a doctrine, that is to say, an exposition of truth. Another has a tongue, that is, he wants to burst out in ecstasy and praise. Another has a revelation, a simple testimony about some of the things Jesus has been doing for him. Another has an interpretation, that is, he has come to interpret the man who will speak in tongues.

Now that may seem very strange to us. Can you picture it in an average church today? There is no preaching of a sermon in this particular type of meeting. They did not come to church to receive all the time, but they came also to give out. The song comes from a heart that is overflowing, and the testimony comes from a spirit that just cannot contain itself. But nothing could be more powerful or more infectious than that, and it is the kind of thing that cannot be organized.

Notice also that everything is done for the edifying of one another. That is to say, as each believer expresses something either by song, or by tongue, or by testimony, or by word of doctrine, he is contributing to their upbuilding and to the ministry of the whole church.

The principle of this is not difficult to understand. In Ephesians, Paul elaborates on the unity and purpose of the church: "Endeavoring to keep the unity of the Spirit in the bond of peace. There is one body … one hope of your calling; One Lord, one faith, one baptism, One God and Father of all, who is above all, and through all, and in you all. But unto every one of us is given grace according to the measure of the gift of Christ" (Ephesians 4:3–7). Then later in the same chapter: "For the perfecting of the saints, for the work of the ministry, for the edifying of the body of Christ: Till we all come in the unity of the faith, and of the knowledge of the Son of God, unto a perfect man, unto the measure of the stature of the fullness of Christ" (Ephesians 4:12–13). Here the principle is two-fold. First, there is the unity of the Spirit, then one day we will come to the unity of the faith.

It is a dangerous thing when Christian people try to reverse those two things. There is *first* the unity of the Spirit, oneness of life in Christ. Don't try to demand a unity of faith before you recognize our fellowship in the Holy Spirit. The basic joy of Christian fellowship is oneness in the Holy Spirit, but that will admit many differences in points of view on some matters of doctrine.

The second principle is that no one individual believer ever comes to the fullness of the stature of Christ by himself. It takes the whole Christian church to achieve it in that great day to come. But in that tremendous goal each of us has a part. As you exercise the gifts that God has given you, for which He also gives abundant grace, you are then contributing to the whole of the church, its testimony and its glory.

What positive contribution are you making to this goal? In the fellowship meeting, do you express in song, or testimony, or revelation, that which God has spoken in your heart? You say you cannot do very much as a Christian: you have only a song, or a testimony, just a prayer, or a thought from a text, but it is all part of the display of the glory of the Lord. You can only exercise your spiritual gifts in the fellowship of the church; you cannot live as a Christian in isolation.

Such a "sharing" meeting, however, could obviously lead to confusion, and so Paul begins to correct certain practices. First, in verses 27–32, concerning those who in their enthusiasm would break out into ecstasy all at the same time, Paul says not more than three of them may speak in tongues at a meeting, and please, one at a time! If he has no one to interpret, then let him keep silence.

"But I can't," some may protest, "I can't hold myself in." Paul says you can and must: "the spirits of the prophets are subject to the prophets" (14:32). In other words, don't let this get out of hand — anything else is just lack of self-control. Wouldn't it be wonderful to have to quell the enthusiasm of Christian people who are just longing to express themselves!

He says, moreover, they may all prophesy one by one, that all may learn and be comforted, but "Let the prophets speak two or three, and let the other judge" (14:29). In other words, let not more than three speak in the meeting, and let the others "discern" — that is the word, to discriminate. These limitations should really make us cringe when we think of the silences in our prayer meetings, of the long, painful waiting when nobody says anything! So often the same people pray time after time, and the others never take part.

But here is a little group of Christians just bursting to say something or to sing. Do you know why? Because this chapter is the outcome of the thirteenth chapter. All are cradled in the love of God that has been shed abroad in their hearts. You cannot take this passage out of context; you cannot force it or work it up. This enthusiasm comes because the Holy Spirit has stirred them. What a wonderful thing it would be if such times of sharing together became part of the life of our churches!

Paul now deals with another awkward problem. What are we to say about the ladies? This is another practice he is correcting. "Let your women keep silence in the churches: for it is not permitted unto them to speak; but they are commanded to be under obedience, as also saith the law. And if they will learn any thing, let them ask their husbands at home: for it is a shame for women to speak in the church" (14:34–35). It would seem from these verses to be too bad if she has no husband to ask! In this instance, however, the word means "man": go home and ask a man (for the woman is in subjection to the man). Here Paul is dealing with a situation which could easily get out of hand, and he continues to try to control their enthusiasm: "Don't let everybody speak at once!"

We need to compare this statement with what he has already written: "every woman that prayeth or prophesieth..." (11:5). In other words, he assumes that the woman will both pray and prophesy. In verse 34, he appears to contradict that by saying, "Let your women keep silence."

He has stated quite clearly in the first reference the circumstances under which a woman may pray or preach. She must not do it with her head uncovered for the simple reason that in Corinth for a woman to go around like that was an evidence of immorality. She must do nothing which would bring shame upon her head, and the head of the woman is the man. Therefore, let her pray with her head covered, and let her preach like that too, of course. Now this is local, but the principle of it is with us today. Let there be nothing done that might be misunderstood, in dropping a custom, or let there be nothing introduced into church life that might be irreverent.

In the second reference, where Paul says it is not permitted for the woman to speak, it is the common Greek verb *laleō*, translated about three hundred times in the New Testament with a variety of meanings. It means, "talk, question, argue, profess, chatter." It has nothing to do with prophecy or prayer; it is not public speaking as such. That kind of behavior would disturb any Christian fellowship, of course. Today we admonish our children, "Don't talk in church." Therefore the woman is to keep quiet and ask any questions when they get home, if necessary. We need to understand this, too, that in those times women were in a place of subjection and, in fact, very few were literate. Let her better-educated husband or father explain what she has not understood.

Paul might equally well have said, "Men must keep quiet in the church. Don't chatter, don't talk or gossip, don't argue or question." Elsewhere he says, "I permit not a woman to teach, nor to have dominion over a man." But he might equally well have said, "I suffer not a man to teach by usurping authority," for that is the meaning of the word. Neither the man nor the woman is to teach by usurping authority.

Such statements have been distorted and twisted out of all context until they have brought bondage upon Christian women. I wonder what the mission fields would do without women; I wonder what the Christian church would have done without the ministry of women from the very beginning. What about the woman of Samaria, who preached to a whole city? What about Philip the evangelist's four daughters who prophesied? What about Mary Magdalene, who spread the news of the risen Lord? What about Priscilla, who took the great professor Apollos and put him right on one or two points of doctrine? In the Word of God there in unquestionably a place of ministry for both sexes. What Paul is seeking to say here is that everything must be done decently and in order, without confusion.

In the closing verses of this chapter a plan is outlined for this kind of meeting. Judging by verse 36, people in the Corinthian church were very proud of themselves: "What? came the word of God out from you? or came it unto you only?" In fact, they were so conceited they apparently thought that they had almost originated the Bible! Paul challenges them in verse 37 by saying, in effect, "If you don't agree with me, and think yourself a prophet, or a very spiritual person, then just acknowledge that what I am saying to you is the commandment of the Lord, not my own idea." But the great thing is, "Let all things be done decently and in order" (14:40).

Here is a plan for our lives and all our fellowship. The word "decently" means "with beauty," with comeliness and with honesty. Paul said that our behavior to those that are without God should be sincere; let there be honesty in our testimony. Let there be integrity about all our witness to the outsider, that he may see something of the loveliness of the Christian faith. In the worship of the Christian church, let there be something of comeliness, for this is the same Greek word Paul uses in 12:24 when he speaks about the comeliness of the body. So there should be a beauty, a rightness, a harmony in Christian fellowship and service.

The other word, "order," means "arrangement": let everything be done in beauty and by arrangement. In another connection in the New Testament the writer to the Hebrews speaks of the Lord Jesus being a High Priest after the order of "arrangement" of Melchisedec, with neither beginning nor end. "Perfection" is the full meaning. Let all things be done within the church with sweetness, symmetry and beauty, and with honesty and integrity toward the man outside. Let it be done in perfection, because we have a great High Priest who has an unchanging priesthood, and by whose loveliness and perfection alone we are introduced to our God.

How is this brought about in our lives? The Christian life in the New Testament is portrayed as one of loveliness and integrity. This is only possible when it has been brought into adjustment, into submission to the risen Lord. I wonder if those two words, "decently" and "in order," reveal some glaring failures in our lives today? Have things got out of hand? Is there utter disorder, confusion and chaos? The desire of God is that our lives may have symmetry and beauty, that they may be "in order" after the likeness of our perfect Lord Jesus. There is something very lovely about the prayer life that has orderliness about it. There is something lovely about the private spiritual life of a child of God that has arrangement and discipline. Its perfection is after the order of the Lord Himself.

This is the secret of the fellowship meetings and sharing: you cannot come to such a meeting to pray and sing unless in private you have a heart that is overflowing with love. That only happens when in your life there is the ordered, systematic, personal walk with God. What is your prayer-life like? Is it haphazard? Is your Bible study arranged and disciplined, or is it just hit or miss? It is out of that personal life of sweet communion with God that you can come to a fellowship meeting with a song in your heart and on your lips to give a joyous testimony for the Lord.

CHAPTER TWENTY-SEVEN

YOUR PASSPORT, PLEASE!

1 CORINTHIANS 15:1—11

Paul is now approaching the climax of his message to the Corinthian church. From many different angles, he has challenged them concerning conditions that existed in their fellowship. He has revealed the emptiness of their supposed brilliance and philosophy. He has preached to them the message of the cross. He has rebuked them for their errors of practice and doctrine. He has proclaimed to them the ultimate triumph of love. In all this, he has presented to them what he calls in the opening verse of this chapter, the gospel: "I declare unto you the gospel" (15:1).

The one thing that matters, as he looks back upon his ministry to this church, is whether they have really received the gospel. How many of them are really following on what I have called the royal route to heaven? In this chapter, he brings heaven very near, and the golden gates seem to come into full view across the horizon.

Now the time has come for him to face these people with a verdict. To bring that about, he demonstrates that this gospel of ours is based upon facts, concerning which there is indisputable evidence, so there is no excuse for failing to believe and accept it. Not merely is the gospel based upon facts, but it has immense personal implications for all of us.

You have listened to the facts of the gospel, he says; if you have received it, therefore, you are standing in the power of the gospel: "By which also ye are saved, if ye keep in memory what I preached unto you, unless ye have believed in vain" (15:2). The awful possibility grips his mind as he thinks that the congregation may after all only have believed in vain. This, of course, all depends upon whether their faith has been resting upon facts based upon evidence, and has led to action. I want to give you some of the evidence of the gospel and point out some of its complications in our lives.

What are some of the facts? "I delivered unto you first of all"—that is, first in order of importance—"that which I also received," says Paul, "how that Christ died for our sins according to the scriptures; And that he was buried, and that he rose again the third day according to the scriptures" (15:3–4). That is the whole gospel in a nutshell. The story is simply that there was a man who lived in the Middle East about two thousand years ago and who was crucified outside Jerusalem. He was buried (He did not just disappear) in a fast-secured tomb, and on the third day He rose again. This is the narrative. But when I recognize that He was none other than Christ, the anointed Son of God, and that He died, as Paul says, for our sin, that He was buried, and that His body was raised from the dead on the third day, then this narrative becomes the gospel.

These facts are inevitably linked together: if you take anything away, you have no gospel. A cross without a resurrection is no gospel. These things: He died, He was buried, He rose again, constitute the basic elements of our Christian faith. Twelve simple men, most of them fishermen, could never have turned the world upside down unless all these facts were true.

What about the evidence for the facts? We have no right to expect that any should believe the gospel unless they have evidence.

One line of evidence is that the death of Jesus Christ must have been related to our sin, "For all have sinned, and come short of the glory of God" (Romans 3:23). The Scriptures say that death is not physical cessation from existence, but separation from God for eternity. If these things be true, then Jesus should never have died. Quite clearly His death was not related to His own sin, because even His worst enemies had to admit that He was without fault. Nevertheless, He died, and for that there is no explanation unless you connect it with the fact of sin.

We go back to the very beginning of the Book, when God spoke with such authority to the one who caused our first fathers to fall, and said to the serpent, "I will put enmity between thee and the woman, and between thy seed and her seed; it shall bruise thy head, and thou shalt bruise his heel" (Genesis 3:15). In other words, Christ was to suffer injury, but the wound inflicted upon the devil at the cross was authoritative and final.

From that very beginning of the redemption story, we can trace all through the Old Testament the fact that "he was wounded for our transgressions, he was bruised for our iniquities: ... all we like sheep have gone astray; we have turned every one to his own way; and the Lord hath laid on him the iniquity of us all" (Isaiah 53:5–6). Here is evidence that, as Paul says here, "He died for our sins according to the scriptures."

In that tremendous moment when Jesus cried with a shout of victory, "It is finished!" the hand of God stretched forth from heaven and took hold of the veil of the Temple and ripped it from the top to the bottom. No human hand could have done that: the veil, which kept humanity back from the glory of the presence of God, was torn aside. The veil, through which only one man once a year on the Day of Atonement could pass, in order that he might make sacrifice for his own sin and the sin of the people, was rent so that all might enter the presence of God. Now, because of what happened at the cross, there is a way through to God without any human intermediary: there is "one mediator between God and men, the man Christ Jesus" (1 Timothy 2:5). The evidence that He died for our sins is indisputable.

What about the evidence for His resurrection? Without it, you just cannot explain the existence of the church at all; it would not have lasted one week if the truth of the resurrection had not revitalized that little group of disciples. Immediately after Calvary they were about to separate, their fellowship was collapsing. The birth and growth of the church is one tremendous evidence that Jesus Christ rose again.

Once again, Paul says that Christ was buried and that He rose again "according to the scriptures." The unfolding of God's plan of redemption in the Old Testament is the story of travail and of triumph. It is the story of suffering and yet of glory. In the same chapter from which I have already quoted, Isaiah 53, we read, "When thou shalt make his soul an offering for sin ... he pleasure of the Lord shall prosper in his hand. He shall see the travail of his soul, and shall be satisfied. ... Therefore will I divide him a portion with the great..." (10–12).

There is also the evidence of the disciples themselves. Their incredulity at His resurrection and their unreadiness to believe the message they were going to spread abroad throughout the world reveals the fact that, as the Lord has said, they were "slow of heart to believe." Although they were to be responsible for proclaiming the Christian message, they began by admitting that they did not believe it.

Some have suggested that these early disciples were just being fools, that they knew the story was false. But would they ever have allowed themselves to be martyred for the sake of something they knew was not the truth? If only the Jews or the Romans could have produced the body of Jesus, all the rumors would have been quickly stopped, but they could not produce it.

In the third place, Paul seizes upon personal evidence as the greatest factor of all: "He was seen of Cephas" (15:5a). In an interview about which we know absolutely nothing, Peter met the Master face to face. "Then of the twelve" (15:5b); twice in the Gospels is the record that His disciples meet their risen Lord.

"After that," says Paul, "he was seen of above five hundred brethren at once." Jesus had told them to go into Galilee, where He would go before them. Hundreds of believers, scattered abroad because of their fear after His death, fled to Galilee, and there they met Him as He revealed Himself to them.

"Last of all," Paul says, "he was seen of me also, as one born out of due time" (15:8). One never-to-be-forgotten day, when he was on his way to Damascus to continue his persecution of the young church, God met him in Jesus Christ and brought him upon his face to the ground.

Paul has marshaled his evidences for the gospel; the facts are completely unshakable. But Paul's concern is to know how far these facts have been effective, and how the Corinthian church has responded to this message of the gospel. That is the vital factor today: how far have you and I responded to the implications of this dynamic message of the gospel of Jesus Christ? We may not dispute these basic facts of the gospel, but what is the result in our lives?

What are the threefold implications of the gospel? First of all, to Paul there was a recognition of his own sinfulness: "Last of all he was seen of me also, as of one born out of due time. For I am the least of the apostles, that am not meet to be called an apostle, because I persecuted the church" (15:8–9). That is different language from what this man once used! In giving his testimony before King Agrippa, he said, "I verily thought with myself, that I ought to do many things contrary to the name of Jesus of Nazareth. Which thing I also did in Jerusalem:

and many of the saints did I shut up in prison, having received authority from the chief priests; ... and being exceedingly mad against them, I persecuted them even unto strange cities" (Acts 26:9–11).

In giving a bit of his own autobiography to the Philippians, Paul said, "If any other man thinketh that he hath whereof he might trust in the flesh, I more: ... concerning zeal, persecuting the church; touching the righteousness which is in the law, blameless. But what things were gain to me, those I counted loss for Christ" (Philippians 3:4, 6, 7). Now he is admitting that he did not deserve even to meet the Lord at all. The thing that shook him to the core, as he was confronted with the truth of the resurrection, was a recognition of his own sin — not his immortality, nor his impurity, but the downright arrogance of his proud heart. This was sin at its very root. When he saw that Jesus Christ was alive, he saw what a stubborn, proud, egotistical creature he was, and he fell on his face before the risen Savior.

Unless this implication has really reached you, you are not a Christian, no matter what you say you believe. It is the crossing out of the capital "I," when you begin to recognize that sin is primarily not immorality or impurity. Of course, that is the fruit of it, but the basis of it all is the wretched, arrogant independence of your own selfishness.

The second implication of the gospel is a revolution of character: "But by the grace of God I am what I am: and his grace which was bestowed upon me was not in vain" (15:10). As Paul continued his own statement in Philippians 3:8, 10, he said, "I count all things but loss for the excellency of the knowledge of Christ Jesus my Lord: ... that I may know him, and the power of His resurrection, and the fellowship of his sufferings, being made conformable unto his death." It pleased God to reveal His Son in Paul; in receiving the forgiving grace of God he received the faithfulness and graciousness of the Master.

This man's life was revolutionized in character and personality through the gospel. Is your one concern that you might be conformed to the image of Jesus Christ? A recognition of sin involves revolution of character and habit.

A third implication of the gospel in Paul's life was a redirection of energy. "I laboured more abundantly than they all: yet not I, but the grace of God which was with me" (15:10b). This again is closely connected with Philippians 3:13–14, "I count not myself to have apprehended: but this one thing I do, forgetting those things which are behind, and reaching forth unto those things which are before, I press toward the mark for the prize of the high calling of God in Christ Jesus." Paul does not say he is perfect or that he has attained, but this is his goal, his ambition as he traveled along the royal route to heaven. As if he saw the pearly gates beginning to open, and soon would see the Savior face to face, this truth of a risen Christ has so gripped him that he labored more abundantly than anyone else. He has given himself supremely to the task, above everything else, of making known his wonderful Lord. But once again he says, "It is ... the grace of God." Three times in this verse, you notice, he speaks of grace.

Has the gospel got hold of you, or is this thing just theory to you? I tell you, unless in your life there has been a recognition of sin, which has brought you on your face before Jesus Christ, you are not saved! Until there has come a moment in your experience when God has shown you that sin is not only being immoral or impure, but basically it is *self* in all its ugliness, you know nothing of salvation.

If you can say, "Yes, I have come to recognize sin to be what God says it is," then has there been a revolution of character? Has Jesus Christ, your indwelling Lord, begun to form Himself in you? If there has been a revolution of character and manner of life, then has there been a redirection of your energy? If there have not been these three things, then have you believed in vain?

Paul was a Pharisee, fundamental with the best, but until these things happened, there was not new birth, no Christian experience, nothing to take him through the gates of heaven. I trust the Lord will speak to you through the Word and take you from the sidelines of Christian work into that more abundant labor with Paul, that the passion and enthusiasm that was once used in worldliness or rejecting Christ might be poured out for the salvation of others.

✝

CHAPTER TWENTY-EIGHT

It's Good to
Be Alive!

1 Corinthians 15:12–34

As we approach the climax of the royal route to heaven and look back over the territory through which God has brought us, and as we are reminded of His faithfulness, His mercy, His patience, His love, surely every one of us can say, "It's good to be alive!" That phrase usually expresses delight in some experience which is here today and gone tomorrow. But here it has a deeper significance, and is far more permanent in this connection. I chose it to imply that our subject is that kind of life which lasts for all eternity.

What does it really mean to be alive in the spiritual sense of the word? Adhering to this context, I want to bring to your attention three suggestions concerning the real significance of life in Christ: what it means to be a Christian and what is involved in living a Christian life.

In the first place, a Christian is one who is implanted in the power of God. "For since by man came death, by man came also the resurrection of the dead. For as in Adam all die, even so in Christ shall all be made alive" (15:21–22). Here are two distinct circles, two spheres of existence: in Adam, in Christ. There is no possibility of a third. Everyone who has ever been born has chosen to live in one or the other of these two circles, and there is no neutral ground.

Implanted by our natural birth into the nature of Adam, we can be implanted by the miracle of the second birth into the nature of Christ. We can be born in Adam's circle, living and dying there. Or we can be born in that first circle, then by the regeneration of the Holy Spirit be made alive for evermore in Christ's circle.

"As in Adam all die"; that takes us back to the very beginning of history when one man, our first father, the head of the human race, refused to accept the only limitation put on his liberty, namely, the sovereignty of God. He had been warned that rejection of God's authority would mean loss of his freedom, and he would become a slave to death. He had been told that if he wanted to enjoy freedom, it could only be along the path of submission.

But he took the reins in his own hands, defied God's authority, and promptly died. "Oh no," you say, "he didn't die." Yes, he did! The devil said he wouldn't, but he did, for at the moment of his act of rebellion he died spiritually. His relationship with God, the only source of spiritual life and power, was cut off immediately. The marks of death grew upon him, mentally and physically; there came into his life the fear of God, the sense of sin, the futile attempt to justify himself, the flight to escape from his Creator, and then later jealousy and murder.

So began the story, and so has continued the tragic breakdown of human life at every level, out of proper relationship with God. Each of us, by the simple law of heredity, has become involved in the tragedy; as Paul says, "by one man's disobedience many were made sinners" (Romans 5:19).

It is true that we were not actually there when it happened, but we have all supported it personally by taking sides collectively and individually with that rebellion against God. We have all enthroned the capital "I" where God should be. We have all put self in the center instead of Jesus Christ. Consequently resistance to the will of God becomes natural, and sin in attitude and in action inevitable. The logical conclusion is, of course, that "in Adam all die."

The marks of death are upon each of us today: the stains of sin, of hatred, of all the decaying fruit of the self-life. Unless we move out of the circle in which we were born into the circle in which we are born again by grace, we will go on in rebellion, not only through life but through all eternity in hell.

That is one stream of life, but there is the other: "so in Christ shall all be made alive." Notice in verse 21: "For since by man came death, by man came also the resurrection of the dead." Here is heaven's counterattack, a full-scale offensive, the great invasion into the realm of sin and death.

Man, made like God, has chosen the mastery of the devil and become like him. Now God is made like man in order to rescue man from the domain of Satan, and restore again the beauty of loveliness of the character of God which rebellion has obliterated. Because it was a man who rebelled, it is only by a man that the situation can be recovered, the lost ground retrieved. Only thus can the justice of God's throne be maintained.

Of course, it was not necessary for God to do this. Justice would have been completely satisfied if the whole human race had been allowed to perish forever. But God is not only just, He is loving, and love is only satisfied when it reaches out to seek and to save that which is lost. "But God commendeth his love toward us, in that, while we were yet sinners, Christ died for us" (Romans 5:8).

So Jesus came, the seed of the woman, to bruise the head of the serpent, to launch an attack upon the kingdom of darkness because those He loved were helpless slaves to the enemy. There was nothing attractive in the men for whom Christ died, but He took up the fight alone in hostile territory with not a single individual or circumstance to assist Him. He accepted the path of submission to the will of God. It was to be the only path of freedom for Him, as it is always the only path of freedom for any individual. He chose it deliberately, knowing it meant that He would have to be made sin for us that we might be made the righteousness of God in Him.

For the first time, the kingdom of death was invaded by a Man in whose life there was not sin at all. The Lord Jesus stepped down from the throne to the cross, tempted in all points like as we are, yet without guilt, and attacked death itself. He tore the bars away, as Peter said on the Day of Pentecost, "because it was not possible that he should be holden of it" (Acts 2:24). So as by one man's disobedience many were made sinners, "by the obedience of one shall many be made righteous" (Romans 5:19).

The ground has been recovered and the territory restored, and it now becomes possible for the human race to be put back on center, righteously forgiven by a holy God, with sin atoned for in the blood of the Son of God shed on Calvary. As Head of a new race, Jesus Christ won back for us the privilege of freedom and life by accepting the principle of obedience and submission.

In which circle are you living right now? Have you stepped from death in Adam to life in Christ? This is not something that happens by growth as the years pass by, but it is the crisis of a certain moment in your life. Submission to sin means slavery; submission to Christ means deliverance. Upon the man who is not a Christian are the marks of death. Upon the Christian are the marks of life, "For the law of the Spirit of life in Christ Jesus hath made me free from the law of sin and death" (Romans 8:2).

When you see a gigantic jet plane sitting on the runway, you may well stare and think, "How does a thing like that ever get off the ground at all?" Loaded with more than a hundred people and their baggage, sitting like a great dead weight on the ground, how can it ever fly? But presently, as you watch, the engines begin to whistle and whine, and that aircraft roars down the runway, screaming its way off earth into the sky. Has the law of gravity ceased to operate? No, the law of gravity is unable to control that plane because of the mighty power of a new law of aerodynamics, a new authority that lifts it up even against the gravity which would pull it down. The law of sin and death has not ceased to operate, but there is new law in Christ's death and resurrection which overcomes the power of the old law.

The second implication of being a Christian is that we are involved in the program of God (15:23–28). Brought to life in Christ, the Christian discovers that now he is part of God's plan of redemption. What a great sweep Paul takes here in his theme! He goes back to the beginning of all history: "As in Adam all die, even so in Christ shall all be made alive" (15:22). Then he says, "But every man in his own order: Christ and the firstfruits"—and that goes back two thousand years.

All the program of God's salvation for us depends upon that fact. If Jesus did not rise from the dead, then everything else is a fraud. That is the argument in verses 14–19 which Paul is not afraid to face, and I paraphrase it thus: "If Christ is not risen, then our faith is empty, our preaching useless, and he has failed to deal with sin at all. If he has not been raised from the tomb, we are still in our sins and all his promises are absolutely untrue. He is a fraud, and imposter, and his ashes are buried somewhere in Palestine today. There is no hope beyond the grave for anybody, and those who have died professing faith in him are just left there forever. If in this life only we have hope in Christ, we are of all men most miserable" (15:19). If it is not true that Jesus is alive, you had better be anything rather than a Christian. If you are a professing Christian, and Jesus is not actually living today, you have the worst of everything in life.

"But he is risen!" says Paul. The evidence is indisputable, and Christ is the firstfruits. Then notice that he sweeps over the centuries, instead of looking back to that day when Christ rose from the dead, he looks ahead and says, "afterward they that are Christ's at his coming." There is going to be another resurrection day when all who through the centuries have submitted their lives to the will of God and lived on the principle of submission to the sovereignty of Christ, will be raised from the dead also.

As if Paul couldn't stop there because his theme is running away with him, he continues, "Then cometh the end, when he shall have delivered up the kingdom to God, even the Father; when he shall have put down all rule and all authority and power. For he must reign, till he hath put all enemies under his feet" (15:24–25). That is the greatest glimpse into the ultimate future that the Bible gives to us. Paul goes further there than any other portion of Scripture. It is thrilling to know that Jesus does reign now! Amid all the storms and upheavals, Christ is on the throne. But on that day, He will deliver up the kingdom to the Father.

There is only one Mediator between God and man, the Man Christ Jesus, our great High Priest who ever lives to make intercession for us, and He will continue until His church is complete, until this new humanity of which He is Head, composed of every individual who has submitted himself to the authority of God in Jesus Christ, is redeemed; then He will deliver up that kingdom to the Father and present us faultless before the throne.

We are involved by grace in that program, stretching through all time and eternity. You and I, if we are saved, are members of a new race, and we live under a new sovereignty, for Jesus must reign until He has put all enemies under His feet. But the price of the enjoyment of freedom from self and sin is still the same: submission to the authority and will of God. Lift your sights high, fellow Christian, and understand the dignity and wonder of your position in Jesus!

But there is one more thing here, perhaps the most important of all, the most significant for us today. What does it mean to be alive in Christ? It also means that a Christian is implicated in the purity of God.

Notice the argument of these closing five verses: Paul says if it is not true that Jesus lives, what if the use of being baptized for the dead? The meaning of that phrase is uncertain, but I feel it can only imply one of two things. First, if Jesus Christ is not alive, why be baptized in the name of a dead Savior? Secondly, in Corinthian times there was apparently a practice of being baptized on behalf of those who had already died, and who had themselves never submitted to baptism. If Christ is dead, there is no point in it anyway.

Again, "Why stand we in jeopardy every hour?" (15:30). In other words, if Christ is not alive, why suffer for Him? There is no point in that, either: "Let us eat and drink; for tomorrow we die" (15:32b). What is the point of character, morality, or decency? That is the logical outcome if there is no hope after death.

That, however, is answered by a smashing alternative; He is alive! Therefore these things are true, and because they are, "awake to righteousness and sin not" (15:34). "Evil communications corrupt good manners" says Paul in verse 33. Good behavior is essentially based upon sound doctrine; rejecting the truth and believing in absurdity is bound to lead to bad behavior. If that is true, then the reverse is also true: acceptance of Christ means good behavior. There is no margin between those at all, and therefore a Christian is one who is implicated in the purity of God.

The believer has been implanted in the power of God by his second birth, he has received the indwelling Holy Sprit and a new nature able to overcome the old. He is involved, therefore, in the program of God because the life that he has received in Christ has come to inhabit him in order to take him through death into glory. That is eternal life, which death and the grave cannot touch. But he is also implicated in the purity of God.

Do you see that you are involved in this? All who die perish for the sin of Adam. You are involved in that simply by our natural birth. All who live do so by the merit of Jesus Christ, and you have no part in that either; it is all of grace. You are not condemned for what you are by birth; you are condemned if you do not lay hold of Christ that you may not die. You are not judged because you are born with a nature that is sinful, but because you remain the tool of that nature for the rest of your life, when Christ has offered you life and salvation.

You had nothing to do with your first birth, but you are involved in its sin. You have nothing to do with the second birth, but you are involved in its deliverance. By the one you have been made a sinner, and let's acknowledge that you submitted to it time and time again and never fought against it. Now by the life of Christ and new birth in Him, you are made righteous, therefore you must submit to that. "Know ye not, that to whom ye yield yourselves servants to obey, his servants ye are to whom ye obey; whether of sin unto death, or of obedience unto righteousness?" (Romans 6:16).

It was by submission to His Father's will that the Lord Jesus won the right for us to step out of slavery into freedom. It cost Him absolute obedience; His total submission from the throne to the cross won us the right to His life, His power, His faith, His purity. Who would ever presume to think that it could be otherwise? Yet there are those who say, "Believe, decide for Christ, and that is all." My Bible also uses the words "submit," "yield," "surrender." You cannot go into the glory except you are under the sovereignty of One who has won the right of you to enter. It cost Him absolute submission to win you. Dare you give Him anything less in return?

Which circle are you in? Are you in Christ, or are you in Adam? Are you alive, or are you dead? Are you the servant of sin, or are you a servant of Jesus Christ?

Here is the ABC of the Christian faith: Acceptance of His sovereignty, the Blessing of His salvation, the Character of His suffering. Have you accepted the sovereignty of Christ? If you have, then you are enjoying the blessing of His salvation, and there is being formed in you the character of God's Son. If not, step out of the sphere of death into the sphere of life, humble yourself to the submission and obedience He knew, and meet Jesus Christ face to face.

CHAPTER TWENTY-NINE

WHAT WILL IT BE LIKE
WHEN WE GET THERE?

I CORINTHIANS 15:35–50

We are taking this chapter very slowly to make sure we understand that the royal route by which we have been traveling, in spite of its dangers and trials, but also with its joys and blessings, does indeed lead to heaven.

The chief reason for this fifteenth chapter of 1 Corinthians having been written is the question in the twelfth verse: "How say some among you that there is no resurrection from the dead?" Paul has answered by stating the evidence and showing the implications of the resurrection of Jesus Christ. Then he went on to show the significance of that in the life of each one of us who follows Him.

There still remains two questions unanswered, and they are in verse 35: "But some man will say, How are the dead raised up? And with what body do they come?"

In spite of all that Paul has said, there are some people who are still not satisfied. This is the question of a skeptic, and he is naturally so. Let us not blame him for being like that; at some time most of us have wondered about it, because we have all witnessed death and decay. There is often a lavish expenditure on funerals to seek to delay the certain inroads of disintegration. What about the body that has been smashed to pieces as the result of an accident in the air or on the highway? What about those who have been drowned in the depths of the ocean? What about those that have been blown into a million bits by bombs? I come from a country in which at least seventy-five per cent of the burials are cremations, simply because of lack of cemetery space. What about them?

How are the dead raised up? I am reminded of the question that Paul himself asked King Agrippa, "Why should it be thought a thing incredible with you, that God should raise the dead?" (Acts 26:8). Here we face a great question that is on the minds of many people, because they are convinced that it is completely impossible, not being able to understand the process. How could ashes scattered to the elements, bones in the depths of the sea, flesh that has gone back to mere dust, be brought together again?

How does the Holy Spirit answer these very natural questions? How are the dead raised up? With what body do they come? What will we all be like when we get to heaven?

The revised versions are a little more polite in giving Paul's reply to the questioner: "O foolish man!" (15:36a). Paul, with all his brilliance and understanding of the Scriptures, and of the things of eternity, has not problem in his mind about this. In order to answer the questions of those who are skeptical, he approaches the problem of physical death along three lines.

In answer to the first question, "How are the dead raised up?" Paul gives a simple illustration of a death that is an example, in verses 36–38. To answer the second question, "With what body do they come?" he points out a difference that is eternal in verses 39–43. Then he goes on to show us also a distinction that is essential, in verses 44–50.

If it is true beyond all possible doubt that the dead are raised up, it should make a big difference as to how we live our lives down here. If dust and ashes are in fact the end; if the cemetery, the crematorium, the ocean, are indeed the finish, well, as Paul says, "Let us eat and drink; for to morrow we die." But if the dead are raised up, if a man must, in his flesh, see God, if there is an appointment with Him awaiting every one of us, then our preparation for that day is important.

The illustration Paul gives is that of a simple grain of wheat. He invites us to look at it. First take it in your hand, and then plant it in the ground. What happens to it? It dies. But soon you will see a green shoot, and it unmistakably comes alive again, not the same grain you put in, but another plant. Yet by some amazing miracle, that new plant has come out of the grain that you put in the ground. The two are distinctly different, but they are absolutely connected. The grain which is put into the ground dies, but is quickened into life, for there would be no coming again into life except first that grain has died. As Jesus said, "Except a corn of wheat fall into the ground and die, it abideth alone: but if it die, it bringeth forth much fruit" (John 12:24).

The mystery of the resurrection of the body is not greater than that. If you say that because there are mysteries you cannot understand you refuse to believe the resurrection of the body, then logically you have to say, "I don't believe in harvest, because I don't understand the process."

Look at that bare grain you are putting into the ground, and then in a few months look at the harvest. A new life, a new plant, but out of the old grain that has been planted into death. You can only explain the miracle of its growth if you put God behind it, and say in the words of verse 38: "But God giveth it a body as it hath pleased him, and to every seed his own body." All the harvest fields of the world are eternal witness to the work of God who takes hold of death, brings it to life, gives it a new body, and produces the harvest.

We have seen it in the Lord Jesus Himself, "the firstfruits," as He is called in this chapter. Think of Him after His resurrection in a new body, and yet the old body. It was planted into the ground, dead. It was raised a new body, not subject to the laws of the old body, the limitations of conditions of time and space, not touched by exhaustion and pain. Here is the whole principle. As Paul says, it is no more difficult to believe in the resurrection than it is to believe in harvest. It is not more difficult for God to raise the dead than it was to raise Jesus Christ from the tomb.

You cannot explain how God does all that, but you believe in the "resurrection" of the grain because you see it. Because you cannot see it, don't dismiss the fact of the resurrection of the body from the grave, from the ocean, from the crematorium, from anywhere, for God is omnipotent, and with Him all things are possible.

Paul's answer to the second question is given in verses 39 to 43. We know it is true that all flesh on earth is not the same flesh; there is one kind of flesh of men, another of beasts, another of fish, another of birds. But this distinction is not only true on earth, it is true also in heaven. "There are also celestial bodies, and bodies terrestrial: but the glory of the celestial is one, and the glory of the terrestrial is another" (15:40). Then Paul cites again an example from the wonderful panorama of the skies above us: "There is one glory of the sun, and another glory of the moon, and another glory of the stars: for one star differeth from another star in glory. So also is the resurrection of the dead" (15:41–42a). There is a difference that is eternal.

Isn't it breath-taking when you think about it, that there are not two people alike? There are no two stars alike; there are no two fish, or flowers, or even blades of grass alike. There is an amazing distinction in the glory of earthly forms all around us. "So also is the resurrection of the dead," says Paul.

He is teaching that the difference that exists here will exist forever in the glory. A human personality is not wiped out by disaster; it is preserved forever, with all its distinctions and differences. Just as we have differed in appearance here, so we will differ there. That is why we will know one another when we get to heaven.

But as we have stood by the graveside of a loved one with our hearts utterly broken, what have we seen there? Notice three words that Paul uses to describe what every one of us has realized on such an occasion: "it is sown in corruption … in dishonour … in weakness" (15:42b, 43).

By the grave we have seen the corruption of the human body. No matter how ornate the funeral, and no matter how great an attempt may be made to take away some of the sting by something of fragrance, nevertheless at the graveside we know that there is dishonor. We have witnessed weakness, for as the body is put into the ground the processes of decay are already setting in and the body has to be hurried away.

Paul tells us however, that there is one thing in which we will all be alike. When the trumpet shall sound, we shall all be lifted out from the grave on that great resurrection day. Something will happen to all of us that will completely counteract everything that took place in that grave. There the body was sown in corruption, but it shall be raised in incorruption, with no disease, no decay, no pain, no suffering, no blemish—perfect.

It has been sown in dishonor, it will be raised in honor, a body to glory in. The bodies of men and women redeemed by the blood of Christ have been indwelt by the Spirit here, but the resurrection body will be the greatest glory in heaven. For there the Lord Jesus is to be admired in all of us who have believed; we are to be the jewels in His crown.

In this body we have sinned; in that body we shall be made perfect. In this body we have failed; in that body we shall love and obey God without fault. In this body we have been weak and helpless, full of troubles; in that body we shall be free from all such limitations and defects. So shall it be in the resurrection of the dead.

In the closing verses of our study Paul gives another answer. A literal transliteration of the adjectives in verse 44 would be, "There is a psychic body, and there is a pneumatic body." Right now, you and I are living in a "psychic" body. In heaven we are going to live in what Paul calls a "pneumatic" body.

The natural or psychic body is governed by the soul; of that body Paul says, "I keep under my body." It is a body that has to be mastered, kept in subjection, for in it are all the latent possibilities of sin. "Who shall deliver me from the body of this death?" he cried, speaking of the downward drag of the physical frame in which he lived. If you do not keep this body, with all its natural inclinations, in subjection, it will lead you into endless sin and trouble, defeat and failure.

There is also a "pneumatic" body that comes from the Greek word meaning "spirit." It is therefore a spiritual body, governed by the Spirit, no longer under the mastery of the animal life, but under the complete control of the Holy Spirit of God.

Now here is the miracle: I sow in death the "psychic" body; God raises in the resurrection the "pneumatic" or spiritual body. I sow in death the natural: God raises that which is supernatural. I sow in death that which is of sin; God raises that which is of victory. The two are essentially different, but the one comes out of the other.

Think of Jesus after His resurrection, as He walked along the Emmaus road, when He came to the Upper Room. There had never been a resurrection from the dead, he was revived from the dead, and because he still had a body that was weak and decaying, he went back to the tomb.

When Christ arose, He was beyond all the limitations and weaknesses of the human body. Doors need not be opened, He came through them. He could make Himself known or unknown as He wished.

How was Jesus Christ brought out of the grave a resurrection body, free from every taint of mortality and weakness? "The first man Adam was made a living soul; the last Adam was made a quickening spirit" (15:45). The first Adam was made a living soul: natural, earthly, flesh and blood, and became mastered by sin. The last Adam, Christ, was made a quickening spirit, life-giving, spiritual, heavenly. As we have borne the image of the earthly, so we are to bear the image of the heavenly.

The Lord Jesus bore the image of the first Adam in His flesh; then He brought out from the grave a resurrection body with no limitations. First Christ, in His mighty redemptive power, lived in a natural body; He had to do that in order to redeem us. In that natural body He never sinned or failed; His was the only perfect "psychic" body, and He put it in a tomb. But on the third day He rose again, and now out from the natural has come the supernatural, the spiritual.

You and I have borne the image of the earthly indeed, with all its sin, failure, frustration, pain, suffering, sorrow, heartbreak. As we have borne that image, we can bear the image of the other: "we shall also bear the image of the heavenly" (15:49). By second birth we have received the foretaste of that which is spiritual and eternal. Although we have been made in the image of Adam by our first birth, the Lord from heaven has, in sovereign grace and mercy, stepped into the personality of each of us who has come to Him in acknowledgment of sin, and given us resurrection life, that which is spiritual.

Paul shows us an inescapable conclusion; "Flesh and blood cannot inherit the kingdom of God; neither doth corruption inherit incorruption" (15:50). Of course not! It is of the earth, earthy, living in sin, decay, defeat, and bondage. If, however the Lord Jesus has come into our lives and we have received the quickening Spirit, we have a foretaste of that which is to be forever.

As we face the future, unless Jesus comes first for us, we know we shall all experience death. What happens then? They will put in a coffin, with much respect, that which is of flesh and blood, that in which we have sinned and failed. On the great resurrection day, out from this, and yet different from it, God will raise up that which is spiritual.

If, therefore, you would bear one day the image of the heavenly, you must possess heavenly life now. Beyond the grave only that which is spiritual can enter heaven, that which has already been through death in Christ. Only that life will remain eternally which has begun with the second birth, when in commitment of my life to Jesus Christ, I received His life into my heart.

There is a logical conclusion to this message, which is not found in these verses except by implication. Paul does not mean that the unbeliever can say, "That is all very well for you Christians, but I am not going to bother. It doesn't matter about me, I'll be left there." Oh, no, you won't! The dead who die out of Christ are not left in disintegration and corruption.

"I saw the dead, small and great, stand before God says John in Revelation 20:12. Every one of them will be there from every race and nation: murderers, adulterers, whoremongers, unbelievers—all are included. It does not matter whether they have been moral or immoral, religious or irreligious, sinful, or comparatively righteous, they are unbelievers. They have never received the Lord from heaven, and therefore they die in corruption, and shall not put on incorruption because they have never established a relationship with God in this period of time. "And whosoever was not found written in the book of life was cast into the lake of fire" (Revelation 20:15).

There is a resurrection of the believer, and that is what we are going to be like when we get there. But there is a resurrection of the unbeliever, too. Therefore I must ask you, in the name of the Lord Jesus, are you still in Adam, or has there been a day in your life when the image of the Lord Jesus was implanted into your heart, and you received Him, the second Adam, and a new birth of that which is spiritual? If so, you are able to say, "Though I walk through the valley of the shadow of death, I will fear no evil: for thou art with me" (Psalm 23:4).

CHAPTER THIRTY

The Final Victory

1 Corinthians 15:51–58

I suppose that to the casual observer the royal route to heaven ends as does every other way of life, in death. The language of such a person would be, "If the end is just the same for all of us, why should I bother about being a Christian, especially the kind of Christian depicted in these messages?"

Of course, it is perfectly true that unless there is real assurance of victory at the end of the road, it is pointless to endure everything that is involved in the journey. As Paul has already said, "If in this life only we have hope in Christ, we are of all men most miserable" (15:19). To many people the idea of our earthly bodies, which moulder into dust, or are scattered over the face of the earth, or drowned in the oceans, or exploded into the elements by bombs, being raised and united again to an undying soul seems quite impossible, even fantastic.

But Paul has proved the resurrection of the dead in this chapter beyond all shadow of doubt. He has demonstrated the fact of the resurrection of Christ; he has produced evidence to support it. He has shown its implications for a Christian, and he has declared that Christ is only the firstfruits, and afterwards they that are Christ's at His coming will be raised. In other words, the resurrection of Jesus from the tomb is just the beginning of a great harvest. Within that word "afterwards," are all the hopes, the sighs, the longings, the tears, the disappointments, the tests, the faith and confidence of God's people ever since.

As we have seen in our last two studies, God has equipped us by the indwelling life of His risen Son to bear Christ's image in place of that of the first Adam. Now we will consider the final victory that is to be ours, and may God grant it may be very soon!

I want to point out to you from this portion, in the first place, the victory that confronts us. I have a word to say to the believer, a word to the unbeliever and the skeptic, and also to the one whose heart is heavy with a sense of loss, who longs for that day when he will see his loved ones and the Savior face to face.

First a word to the Christian: look at this victory that confronts us all. "Behold I [show] you a mystery" (15:51). This arouses our attention; it alerts all our faculties to discover what he has to say. A mystery is not something that cannot be explained, but something that you will never prove by intellect, something that you will never reason your way into by sheer process of argument. You do not find God that way; you can argue yourself out of blessing and eternity, but never into it.

Here is the mystery which has been revealed to Paul; "We shall not all sleep." What a lovely word that is to describe the condition of those who have departed from this life trusting in the Savior. They are asleep in Jesus. To be absent from the body is to be present with the Lord, and to be with Christ is far better. They are waiting to be clothed upon with a new body, waiting for your arrival and mine as eagerly as we wait to see them once again. They are waiting for all the purposes of God to be fulfilled; waiting until all those for whom Christ has purchased eternal salvation have received Him and are redeemed through His blood, when the number of the elect is complete and the bride has made herself ready. The dead are "asleep in Jesus," a redeemed spirit without a body waiting for that tremendous moment, that day of resurrection.

Then what will happen? Suddenly, in the twinkling of an eye, the trumpet shall sound and the dead shall be raised incorruptible, and we shall be changed. Notice that we shall not all sleep, but we shall all be changed. There will be a generation which will not die, for in the middle of life, among the ordinary events of human experience, this change will come. They will not go into the valley of the shadow; they will not taste the darkness of death, but all shall be changed. There are no dates given, but it will be at the exact moment which is in the purpose of God. It could happen before this day is out.

In the case of those who have died, corruptible flesh shall put on incorruption, the body that is laid aside in the tomb will be raised a new body. So also, for those who are alive on that great day, mortal shall put on immortality. Corruption cannot inherit incorruption; mortality cannot inherit immortality.

I am reminded of the man who came to Jesus and said, "Good Master, what must I do that I may inherit eternal life?" (Mark 10:17–22). You cannot inherit eternal life. The Lord's answer to that rich young ruler was what Paul is constantly emphasizing: put off the old, put on the new. Put on the new man in Christ and make no provision for the flesh.

You do not inherit incorruption, you put it on. You do not inherit eternal life, you put on the Lord Jesus, and in Him is eternal life. One day the corruptible body shall put on incorruption, because the spiritual body put on Jesus Christ here, forsaking the flesh and its method of life. The Christian has recognized that self-satisfaction, greed for possessions, money, and pleasure, even self-improvement and the desire to be important, have all blocked his view of glory and made him completely earthbound. At conversion these things have been put off. He has repented of them and put on the Lord Jesus Christ, and at that moment there is born in his heart that new nature of incorruption, of immortality.

There comes a day when that incorruptible spirit shall be reunited again with a body that will then put on incorruption, also. The fate of your soul will also be the fate of your body; the two are partners. They separate for a little while, as the body waits for its resurrection. But what happens to your spirit one day happens to your body, also. It is put aside in the grave, but it is raised again incorruptible if it has already, in the course of this life, been the home of a spirit that is incorruptible—the very life of Jesus Christ. Death cannot touch the soul or the spirit of a Christian. It touches the body a bit, for the tent in which we live soon shows signs of collapsing.

Paul uses the same kind of language in 1 Thessalonians: "For the Lord himself shall descend from heaven with a shout, with the voice of the archangel, and with the trump of God: and the dead in Christ shall rise first: then we which are alive and remain shall be caught up together with them in the clouds, to meet the Lord in the air: and so shall we ever be with the Lord" (4:16–17).

We talk about sending a space ship to the moon—what an event that will be! But by that time you and I may have bypassed the moon and be in glory. I don't want to be shot up into heaven by a rocket, but I'm looking forward to being called up by a trumpet from the Lord. Not to be propelled up into space by colossal earthly effort, but to be pulled up by the magnetism of my Lord Jesus coming in power and glory—that is my anticipation.

This is the assurance that comforts us. "O death, where is they sting? O grave, where is they victory? The sting of death is sin; and the strength of sin is the law. But thanks be to God which giveth us the victory through our Lord Jesus Christ" (15:55–57).

Here is the apostle Paul daring to laugh at death and the grave! He stands confronting an enemy which has held in its clutches every human being through all history except two; Enoch who went for a walk with God and never came back, and Elijah who was taken up to the heaven in a chariot of fire. Death would never have existed apart from sin, however, for if there had been no sin, there would have been no death. Death, I presume, would simply have been translation from earth to heaven, as in the case of Enoch.

The law of God passed sentence of death upon Adam, and it still says to every human being, "The soul that sinneth, it shall die." The law of God cannot be set aside. The dominion of death is universal, and the law is as unchangeable as the God who made it. "As by one man sin entered into the world, and death by sin; and so death passed upon all men, for that all have sinned" (Romans 5:12). Because death has power over the whole human race, if justice is to be maintained in order instead of chaos before the supreme court of heaven—the one place where we know absolute truth and justice prevail—the law of God is unalterable, and some provision has to be made for His love and mercy to act.

Therefore the Lord Jesus Christ has put Himself in our place, and has satisfied every demand that God can ever make upon anybody. Does God's law require the death of the man who breaks it? Very well, He has died for the sinner. Does the law demand that the offender of the law shall die? Very well, He was made sin for us, He who knew no sin, and He bore the penalty of a broken law. Must a man have a perfect righteousness to stand before a holy God? Very well, then by Christ's obedience unto death He has established an everlasting righteousness which is credited to every man who comes to Him as a sinner and receives Him by faith.

Then the sting is taken out of death because sin is cancelled, and the strength of the law to condemn us is removed, because it has been fulfilled in Jesus Christ. Therefore death is no longer an enemy to the Christian, but an instrument of freedom from the reign of sin in his body. There will always be that human fear of entering the valley, unless Jesus comes first. Yet, as I think about death and what it means, I think of it as a friend who comes to me and draws aside the veil which has been hiding the full glory of the Savior from my eyes. That is death to the Christian. As Paul says, "Thanks be to God which giveth us the victory through the Lord Jesus Christ!"

If you are a believer, then just put your foot on the neck of the enemy and laugh at him; "O death, where is they victory?" Instead of swallowing you up, praise God, death itself will be swallowed up! Instead of casting you into an eternal hell, death itself will go there: "And death and hell were cast into the lake of fire" (Revelations 20:14). Because of Calvary the tables have been turned. God is just, and yet He is the Justifier of them that believe in Jesus. That is the glory of the gospel; that is the comfort that assures us.

Does that make your heart rejoice? But we have also a call that challenges us: "Therefore, my beloved brethren, be ye steadfast, unmoveable, always abounding in the work of the Lord, forasmuch as ye know that your labour is not in vain in the Lord" (15:58).

I believe that to preach or teach the Bible without applying it to life is sin. The Bible is not a textbook, nor a book of theory and doctrine. It is to be the compass, the chart, the guide for my whole life. If I teach it in Sunday school or preach it from the pulpit, and fail to apply it to my listeners, I am guilty before God of sin.

What is the application of this message? It tells us that we are to prepare for victory on that great day. First, we must give steadfast adherence to the faith and not let anyone rob us of our confidence in God. Hold fast the profession of your faith; don't be moved away from the hope of the gospel.

Then be diligent in the performance of your duty; "always abounding in the work of the Lord." Never be satisfied with just a little bit of service for Him; give yourself wholly to it. Of course, be sure that it is the work of the Lord: ask yourself how much of your service in the past days has been the work of the Lord. He came to seek and to save that which was lost. How much has there been of testimony, of witness, of real earnest endeavor to reach souls that are perishing? How much of it has simply been administration, program work, machinery?

We have the assured promise of reward: "your labour is not in vain in the Lord." Labor means sweat and blood and tears. The Lord is not unrighteous that He should forget your work and labor of love; with His own hand one day He will repay. It is only the man who is really abounding in the work of the Lord who can be assured that his faith is saving faith.

This is the victory ahead for Christians. But may I say to you very solemnly that if you are an unbeliever, death is no friend to you. It is an enemy. If you have never sought refuge in the Lord Jesus Christ, if you have not come to Him out from the curse of a broken law, you are still in sin and therefore must perish. Then death is dreadful. It is just like opening the prison door for a criminal to take him out for execution. For a season your body will sleep in the dust, certainly, but your soul will re-occupy it one day. The body is put in the tomb and the soul goes to the place of the departed dead; but those who have been partners in sin and in rejection of Christ will be partners together in that awful judgment before the throne of God.

But it need not be so. If you would just look to Jesus Christ now, to Him who has fulfilled the law of you, taken away all your guilt by His precious blood; if you would but humble your heart before Him, because he lives, you shall live also. Quit this life of rebellion; put an end to the reign of sin and death. Let Jesus Christ step in and take charge and He will lead you to final victory!

CHAPTER THIRTY-ONE

RESPONSIBILITY TO OTHERS

1 CORINTHIANS 16:1–6

These opening verses might appear an anticlimax to what has gone before. We have been given a glimpse of the glory that awaits us, and an assurance of the victory even over death that is ours through Jesus Christ our Lord. The sound of the trumpet with its call to resurrection has seemed wonderfully real. Surely, anything beyond that must be somewhat reactionary.

"Now concerning the collection." What a coming down to earth! Well, of course — because a Christian is a man whose heart is in heaven, but whose feet are on the ground. Every glimpse of future glory is given to the child of God in order to encourage him to present-day growth in consecration and responsibility. Certainly we do come down to earth here, but I trust we have been refreshed and greatly challenged by all that God has been saying to us in the course of our journey along the royal route to heaven.

As a matter of fact, this chapter is the crown of all the teaching of this Corinthian letter. The epistle begins with the reminder that "God is faithful, by whom ye were called unto the fellowship of his Son Jesus Christ our Lord" (1:9). Because of that, they have also been called into partnership with one another, for through the whole church there pulsates one common life, the life of the indwelling Holy Spirit, flowing through the whole body of the church, whether at Corinth, Jerusalem, Galatia, Macedonia — anywhere.

In both of these relationships, toward God and toward their brethren, the Corinthian church had tragically failed. The whole direction of Paul's teaching in this letter has been to restore their broken fellowship with God, and their broken communion with one another. Once the Christian is right with God, then his relationship with his fellow believer is settled.

These things cannot be interpreted in a local sense, and therefore we find here a fitting climax to this epistle. The whole church comes into view, because the result of our right relationship with God is the glory of that moment when death is swallowed up in victory, and the fruit of our right relationship with fellow Christians is our acceptance of a sense of responsibility to the whole church. Our responsibility is as wide as our fellowship, and our fellowship is as wide as the whole body of Christ in earth. There is no limit to it.

Here, then, Paul refers to the churches in Galatia, Jerusalem, Macedonia, Ephesus, Achaia. Here we find brought to our attention Timothy, Apollos, Stephanas, Fortunatus, Achaicus, Aquila and Priscilla—a world-wide fellowship and a world-wide responsibility.

To get the meat out of this portion, let us look at what I would call "the church and its poverty": "When I come, whomsoever ye shall approve by your letters, them will I send to bring your liberality unto Jerusalem" (16:3). Paul's teaching has been centered upon the church's relationship to the Lord and to one another. Having settled that, he now lifts their eyes to a wider horizon, and asks them to consider their responsibility to the poor church at Jerusalem, the original home base of all New Testament missionary enterprise.

Paul always has a great concern for this church: for instance, "It hath pleased them of Macedonia and Achaia to make certain contribution for the poor saints which are at Jerusalem" (Romans 15:26). The adjective indicates absolute poverty. They were a penniless crowd at Jerusalem, so far as this world's goods are concerned; there was not a rich man among them. If there had been, Paul would have been saying something to him!

The reasons for their poverty are not far to seek. If you link early church history with the Word of God, you find that they were poor for two basic reasons, one they could not very well help, but the other they could. There had been a famine about that time, which made life very difficult for them on the material level, and they were not responsible for that. The other reason is that they had tragically failed in their obedience to the New Testament commission. The Lord Jesus had charged them to go forth to be His witnesses, beginning at Jerusalem, to Judaea, to Samaria, to the uttermost parts of the earth (Acts 1:8). But they did not go out until they were scattered by opposition. They hugged their privileges, they rejoiced in their position, and when they began selfishly to cherish that which God had given them, they lost their spiritual power. God sent persecution to drive them out to preach the gospel. By that time they were reduced to a state of utter poverty.

Here is a great principle: "There is that scattereth, and yet increaseth; and there is that withholdeth more than is meet, but it tendeth to poverty" (Proverbs 11:24). That statement is true in regard to both life and possessions. The Lord Jesus said, "For whosoever will save his life shall lose it: and whosoever will lose his life for my sake shall find it" (Matthew 16:25).

Maybe you have had opportunity to watch this rule in operation. Just let a man hold back from total commitment to the sovereignty of Jesus Christ, and watch him shrivel up spiritually. See how he becomes a critic of everything that is spiritual in the church, because of the front he has to put up in attempting to justify his position.

On the other hand, let a man scatter his life abroad, fling it away for Jesus' sake, then watch him increase in spiritual stature. You can always equate your spiritual growth or lack of it, your wealth or poverty in the things of the Lord, with your obedience to the Master. Just prove it! Obedient living and overflowing blessing are inseparable. And just as inevitably, disobedient living results in the withholding of the blessings of God.

This is also true in relation to material things. To withhold that which ought to belong to the Lord never leads to a man's material enrichment; but to practice Matthew 6:33, "But seek ye first the kingdom of God, and his righteousness," is to experience the faithfulness of God, who never has broken His promise: "But my God shall supply all your need according to his riches in glory" (Philippians 4:19). Here is a principle from which there is no exception. This will always be a reason for the poverty of the child of God, if we have failed to obey the Master and live up to the hilt of His Word. Failure on the part of the church at Jerusalem caused poverty which created a responsibility.

In the second place, I want you to notice what I would call "the claims of the pioneer missionary." Because the lines of communication were very different then from what they are now, the Christians at Corinth could not possibly get to the church at Jerusalem themselves. They could not fulfill their responsibility in person, but they could through their missionary, Paul.

Here you see Paul as a worker, called into fellowship with the Lord and His people, opening his heart to the church at Corinth. There is a glorious uncertainty about his own future in these verses. To those of us who are bound to a program, this is a refreshing breeze from heaven! It would be a wonderful thing if sometimes the Holy Spirit just broke through our little plans and opened our eyes to the far greater purposes of our wonderful Lord. When will we give Him opportunity to do something new in our churches?

Paul did not know when he would get to Corinth or how long he would stay. He did not know when he would leave, nor where he would go next. What a wonderful thing for a missionary to be in a position like that! The one great steadying factor, the source of authority and assurance, was that he was under the command of the Lord: "If the Lord permit."

On the part of the missionary, we see here a sacred responsibility that is twofold. First, freedom of action within the will of God: freedom to move here and there, wherever the Holy Spirit may direct, a complete freedom, not from authority, but from machinery. In the second place, he has a sacred relationship with the home base. I believe absolutely in missionary societies, but the most vital relationship is between the missionary and his home church. The society is the agency through whom the missionary is sent and by whose oversight work is maintained on the field. But the home church is the place of fellowship in prayer and support, without which no missionary enterprise would be possible.

Here, therefore, is the double responsibility. On the part of the missionary there is the opening of his heart completely to the home church, his willingness to serve and work and to have fellowship with them. There may be uncertainty concerning the future; yet the missionary is under the sovereign control of the Lord all the time, and he is sharing this uncertainty as well as the blessedness of this sovereignty with the believers at the home base.

On the other hand, here is the sacred responsibility of the church: to receive their missionary and to "bring me on my journey whithersoever I go" (16:6). As I understand it, this means not merely that support in giving which insures his basic needs, but also support in prayer which assures his safety from all the fiery darks of the devil.

Corinth did not face this challenge alone; Paul applied this principle to all the churches. Wherever he went he expected this fellowship from them, and he laid the responsibility on the local believers so that together they had the privilege of seeing that he took a generous offering to Jerusalem.

A truly Christian man became increasingly interested in missions, and at first he prayed, "Lord, save the heathen." Then, "Lord, send out missionaries to save the heathen." Although he prayed earnestly, this did not satisfy him, so he began to pray, "Lord, if You haven't anyone else to send, send me. But if You can't send me, send somebody else." He still was not satisfied until he settled down to this form of missionary praying: "Lord, send whom You will. If it could be me, how I would love it. But if not, then teach me to pay my share of the expenses." I wonder how far you and I have come along that ladder of prayer and consecration.

There is one thing more, the main thrust of this portion of Paul's letter, what I would call "the collection and its procedure." "Now concerning the collection for the saints, as I have given order to the churches in Galatia, even so do ye. Upon the first day of the week let every one of you lay by him in store, as God hath prospered him, that there be no gatherings when I come" (16:1–2).

Because of the principles of fellowship, the situation at Jerusalem created a demand upon all the churches, not only Corinth. They must feel the suffering of their brethren in Jerusalem, and recognize the immense privilege that God had given them to help. How is this responsibility to be met?

They were to *give*. Money had to be sent to Jerusalem, and Paul had to be seen safely on his journey. This giving has several features I would like to catalogue for you.

First, they were to be systematic: "On the first day of the week." It was to be a real part of their worship and thanksgiving on that resurrection day, which the early church was observing in place of the Jewish sabbath.

Then it was to be very personal: "let every one of you." This suggests that each one was to go away alone, and in an act of worship to settle his account with God Himself.

Thirdly, their giving was to be sacrificial: "as God hath prospered you," says Paul. The exact amount is not stated; that was left between the individual and his Lord: according to God's faithful provision there was to be a real dedication of a portion of their goods.

And it was to be spiritual: "No gatherings when I come." That simply means no whipping up of an offering under pressure at the last moment; no giving under compulsion of any human agency, but all as the result of honest, individual facing of responsibility before God.

It is also my sacred task to face you in the name of our Master with your responsibility in this matter. Do you give regularly to the Lord's work, or is your giving only occasional and haphazard? If so, then there is serious failure somewhere to recognize your responsibility as a Christian to the whole church. I am not, of course, speaking only of the local church but of the fellowship of God's people everywhere. Do you give to missions? In one way or another, is your giving systematic?

Then let me ask you, is your giving personal? Do you ever take five minutes alone with the Lord to thank Him for the provision of your material needs, and to ask His guidance as to what to put into the offering plate on the Lord's day? Is there any worship about it? Do you settle the matter with God first?

Is your giving spiritual — not simply responding when an appeal is made, or your emotions are aroused, but out of the love and devotion of your heart to the Lord Jesus Christ? I honestly believe that if every believer gave like that, there would be no problem in maintaining the Lord's work both at home and abroad.

A certain Christian once said to a friend, "Our church costs too much. They are always asking for money."

"Some time ago a little boy was born in our home," replied her friend. "He cost me a lot of money from the very beginning: he had a big appetite, he needed clothes, medicine, toys, and even a puppy. Then he went to school, and that cost a lot more; later he went to college, then he began dating, and that cost a small fortune! But in his senior year at college he died, and since the funeral he hasn't cost me a penny. Now which situation do you think I would rather have?"

After a significant pause she continued, "As long as this church lives it will cost. When it dies for want of support, it won't cost us anything. A living church has the most vital message for all the world today, therefore I am going to give and pray with everything I have to keep our church alive."

"Now concerning the collection"—you see, this isn't putting giving on a low level, pressuring people to give in a hectic moment of decision. It is asking you to settle this matter as consecrated, surrendered Christians, recognizing your responsibilities. The whole missionary enterprise is impossible without a living church to which all of us contribute with our money and with our prayers. Thank heaven for the privilege, but let us be faithful to it. Otherwise, our individual responsibility may be withdrawn, and our shame will be great when we meet the Lord face to face.

CHAPTER THIRTY-TWO

REASONS FOR
HOLDING ON

I CORINTHIANS 16:7-9

I trust that, as we have traveled together on the royal route to heaven, we have realized that there is more than one road. Paul made it perfectly clear that there is the road of carnality, and there is the road of spirituality. There is salvation, and there is full salvation. There is the forgiveness of sins, and there is deliverance from s-i-n. These roads are different, and God's purpose is that all of us should travel on the "royal route."

The truth of Scripture often lies beneath the surface, waiting only for prayer and study to reveal it to the hungry heart and open mind. This is clearly true of verses like these under consideration.

News of the sad state of affairs in Corinth has been brought to Paul at Ephesus by members of the household of Chloe (1:11). The letter we have been studying is Paul's reply. In closing, he speaks to them of his future plans, especially his hope of returning to Corinth. As to the time of that visit, he is uncertain, for he is sure that at the present moment he is in the will of God where he is. "I will tarry at Ephesus until Pentecost. For a great door and effectual is opened unto me, and there are many adversaries" (16:8-9).

Paul rejoices in this assurance, because God has opened for him a door of opportunity, *and* there are many adversaries. He is not saying, "But there are many adversaries, and therefore I had better quit," but rather, "and there are many adversaries, therefore I must stay." In other words, the adversaries were simply part of the opportunity, and were just as much a reason for him staying at Ephesus as was the open door.

Now I want to consider Paul's open door and his adversaries with you. On the one hand, many of us talk far too lightly about God's open doors for service without ever realizing what is involved in them. On the other hand, we are apt to become much too easily discouraged by the adversaries and give up instead of holding on. We say, "It is wonderful to be serving the Lord here, but it is so difficult and there is so much opposition that the only thing to do is resign."

I trust that our meditation on this may put courage into some faltering life, strength into some soldier of the cross, and insight into all our hearts as to what an open door is, and what it demands of us.

To get the background of this situation, it is well to remember that the door to Ephesus had not always been open (Acts 16:6). A few years previously Paul was forbidden by the Holy Spirit to preach the word in Asia, and was sent to Macedonia. Later, on his way from Corinth to Jerusalem, he spent one day at Ephesus (Acts 18:19), and told them he would return again if the Lord willed.

Many things happened before that door was opened to Paul. For one thing, the eloquent preacher from Alexandria, Apollos by name, arrived at Ephesus. He met that delightful couple, Aquila and Priscilla, who had come with Paul from Corinth on his way to Jerusalem, and had stayed at Ephesus until he should rejoin them. They took Apollos aside" and expounded unto him the way of God more perfectly" (Acts 18:26). As a result of this, his preaching became more powerful and fruitful; Acts 18 closes by telling us that he "mightily convinced the Jews ... showing by the scriptures that Jesus was Christ."

If only you and I could see behind the outward tool to God at work! The door to Ephesus shut to Paul; before he went there God sent another preacher to break up the heavy ground in preparation for Paul's arrival. Ephesus was shut to Paul because Ephesus was not ready for him.

Furthermore, I would suggest to you that Paul himself needed some toughening up for the baptism of fire that awaited him at Ephesus. In between, there was the prison at Philippi: the stripes and beating before the magistrates, the songs in the night, and God's deliverance. There was the uproar in Thessalonica and the scorn of the intellectual populace at Athens. All these experiences were needed to put heavenly resistance and spiritual courage into him.

Now Ephesus is ready, and Paul is ready. It is God's time to strike, and a blow that is struck in the name of the Lord Jesus and in the power of God the Holy Spirit, in His time, is worth a million struck in the power of the flesh. This city was to be the strategic center of missionary enterprise for the apostle Paul. One outcome of his three years there was the founding of the seven churches of Asia to whom the risen Lord sent His messages which are recorded in the early chapters of the Book of Revelation. Here, therefore, behind the closed door, I discover God's reasons for it.

If only we could see behind some of life's closed doors and witness the omnipotent hand of God in our day, patiently working to prepare the door and the worker for His will, how rebuked we would be for our stubbornness and unfaithfulness. The chaos in Christian work is bad enough as it is: mission fields at home and abroad are suffering because of people who blunder their way into some sphere of service for which God has not given them spiritual equipment. Such people are very sure they have what is needed for a particular work, and they are not prepared to wait God's time. They will just put the thing right immediately, they think, and perhaps somebody who has labored patiently for years has his heart broken and his work spoiled. Therefore, if you try to rush into what you want to do, sometimes God slams the door in your face because you are not prepared to go in and the place is not prepared for you.

In the second place, let us look at this door that Paul calls "great and effectual." Apollos has not gone to Corinth (Acts 19:1). It is interesting to notice these little human factors: here in 1 Corinthians 16:12, Paul tells us Apollos did not go there when Paul asked him: "As touching our brother Apollos, I greatly desired him to come unto you with the brethren: but his will was not at all to come at this time; but he will come when he shall have convenient time." I get the impression that Apollos was a strong-minded man; he was not going to be pushed around, even by Paul. Yet he was ready to go to Corinth at God's command, for he was submitted to the will of God.

Now Paul, a prepared man, entered Ephesus, a prepared place. It is a thrilling moment when a man steps into the place of service that is God's will for him. The door is open, and now what will it be like? Will there be overwhelming blessing, mighty revival? No, as a matter of fact, at Ephesus it was a battle from beginning to end. After it was all over, Paul's comment was, "I have fought with beasts at Ephesus" (15:32).

Let us survey this battlefield a moment, and look at the adversaries. To Paul this was a strange city with a huge population, whose methods of thought and culture and background were entirely different from his own. What can he possibly do to stem the tide of sin in that city? What can be done to change the habits of the people spiritually, morally, and socially, and get them to thinking about God? The thing is absolutely impossible; Paul saw that when he faced this great city of Asia.

In Ephesus there was a vast system of organized idolatry in the temple of Diana. The image of Diana had apparently been an early space traveler, supposedly dropped out of the heavens from the god Jupiter, and now was enshrined in a temple (Acts 19:35). "Great is Diana of the Ephesians!" was their slogan, and lavish were the gifts and ceremonies of her worship. In that same chapter of Acts we read of the great trade going on in replicas and charms which every visitor could buy to take home as a memento of his visit to the shrine of Diana. It was a superstitious thing, supposed to preserve them from evil. How could the gospel break into that?

Still further, there was a crowd of wandering Jews who practiced magic, invoking names supposedly potent over people possessed with evil spirits. So deeply rooted were prejudice and superstition in Ephesus that before people made any important decision they consulted these magicians. It is no easy task to turn a savage tribe from confidence in witchcraft and medicine-men to God. But I tell you it is even harder to neutralize the poison of superstition and vice and profit in a city like Ephesus—or Chicago.

But the worst adversary of all was the Jewish synagogue, representing the ancient tradition of the people of God in their unbelief. What trials were to befall Paul by "the lying in wait of the Jews" (Acts 20:19)!

This was God's open door. Was it eager for the gospel? Not a bit of it! Filled with heathenism, idolatry, superstition, demon possession, religious prejudice—such was the open door!

As Paul settled to his trade alongside Aquila and Priscilla, because he worked his passage all the time as a tent maker, he looked far beyond the workshop to victories for the Lord in that great city. How he prayed and how he agonized! Just as William Carey, the great pioneer of modern missions, while he cobbled people's boots and shoes in a little place in England, wept and prayed over a map of the world he kept before him as he worked. If you would step into any work for God, just remember that you will never accomplish anything until God has broken your heart over it.

Are our open doors any different today? I don't think so. Society may be more civilized, with more veneer on the surface, but the adversary is basically the same, even though his manifestations may vary.

If in your experience God has slammed tight the door and you are wondering why, perhaps a little light has fallen on your path. Maybe the place is not ready for you, and you are not ready for that service. The day may come when you are ready, and the place is ready for you; when those two things are timed in the will of God, you step right in. You will then find that you are meeting a similarly tough situation; have you got what is required to meet it?

In the goodness of God, He gives us here some principles for victory. Was Paul what he said he was, more than conqueror in all these things? Turning again to Acts 19:8, you will notice that after three month's conflict with the Jews Paul did what he often did: when he first went into a city he would tackle the Jews, and if they would not hear him, then he would move off and preach to the Gentiles. So now he moved his headquarters to the schoolhouse of Tyrannus and taught there every day. The result was that he continued for two years, "so that all they which dwelt in Asia heard the word of the Lord Jesus, both Jews and Greeks."

Furthermore, the silversmiths who produced the little images of Diana acknowledged that their trade was in danger; they were being put out of business! People were turning from the worship of Diana to the true God. The magicians also were baffled by Paul's miracles of healing. Many brought all their books of magic, confessed their sin, and burned the rubbish in the market place.

The exorcising Jews began trying to use the name of Jesus, only to find themselves answered by the demons — and I can imagine the shock they got! "Jesus we know, and Paul we know, but who do you think you are?" And the man with the demons in him attacked them, making them turn tail and run for their lives, even leaving their clothes behind.

"In all these thing we are more than conquerors," says Paul. What a rebuke this is to our utter ineffectiveness; I do not know of anywhere on earth where such things are happening today. There have been periods in history when a city's life has been completely transformed by the preaching of the gospel. There have been days in the Puritan era when whole towns were moved for God, but not now. In spite of all the big evangelistic campaigns, the city is just the same twelve months after. Its life is not deeply touched, and in spite of the testimony of the Christian church today, social, political, and moral evils just go from bad to worse.

Yet Paul says that in all these things we are more than conquerors. What is the reason? Let us get behind the scenes and look into Paul's private life. What has he to say for himself? You will find records of his battles in several places. For instance, "We should like you, our brothers, to know something of what we went through in Asia. At that time we were completely overwhelmed, the burden was more than we could bear, in fact we told ourselves that this was the end. Yet we believe now that we had this experience of coming to the end of our tether that we might learn to trust, not in ourselves, but in God Who can raise the dead" (2 Corinthians 1:8-9, PHILLIPS). And again, "Every day we experience something of the death of the Lord Jesus, so that we may also know the power of the life of Jesus in these bodies of ours" (2 Corinthians 4:9, PHILLIPS). The source of victory in that open door was not in Paul, but in God; "In all these things we are more than conquerors through him that loved us" (Romans 8:37).

Do you think as Paul faced all that in Ephesus, he overcame his enemies with ease? No, but here is his secret: he was living in daily union with the Lord who loved him and who, because of the life Paul lived, because of the crucifixion of the flesh, because of the renouncement of self, poured into his soul heavenly wisdom, faith, and power. Paul's only concern was lest anything should cut him off from his loving, living Lord. "Shall anything separate me from the love of Christ?" he cried. That was all that mattered to him in his ministry. If nothing could separate him from the love of God in Christ, then nothing could interrupt his supplies of the Lord's strength and power.

That is Paul's secret of victory in the open door: the eternal love of God coming into a crucified life through Jesus Christ. That is the secret and the only hope of the Christian today in any place. But what is the church doing about it? Often demanding more years at the university, raising the standard of education, making men more intellectual. I would not decry such a thing; I am quite sure that the greater education a man can get, humanly speaking, the more he is going to be equipped for the open door in one sense. But I am saying the peril is that in raising these standards of mental ability and understanding, we are forgetting the whole principle of death and self-crucifixion. For it is upon the man bearing his cross for Jesus' sake that God pours out His love, His strength, His grace.

Can anything separate us from the love of God in Christ? Yes, sin can and does. It does not hold back the love of God, for He loves the sinner. But if there is one thing that holds back heavenly supplies of wisdom, strength, ability, power and grace from the Christian, it is man's dependence upon his own ability and education to meet the need of his day. Oh, for grace to repent before God, to receive anew His inexhaustible supplies!

CHAPTER THIRTY-THREE

FINAL
COUNSEL

1 CORINTHIANS 16:10-20

Of all the churches to which Paul wrote in the New Testament, there was none in such trouble as Corinth, none so sinful, none that had failed so badly. None of them received such rebuke as he gave to this church, and yet none of them received such loving counsel. They must have wilted under the scorching fire of his rebuke, but must also have been wonderfully refreshed and restored as this great preacher opened his heart to them and showed them that the way of victory in all things is the way of love.

Now he comes to these closing words of counsel: "Watch ye, stand fast in the faith, quit you like men, be strong. Let all your things be done with [love]" (16:13-14). In other words, "You have many temptations to face, therefore watch. You are going to hear false teachers who would turn you from the truth, therefore stand fast. You will have many trials, therefore behave like men, be strong. There is a lot of contention among you, therefore let everything be done with love."

Paul relates his counsel and advice to the needs of this little fellowship that he knew so well. As we have traveled along what we have called the royal route to heaven in this epistle, I think many of us have found this letter has a great deal to do with our own needs, and therefore we are going to investigate also these closing words of loving pastoral advice which Paul gives to his converts.

I would group Paul's admonitions into three very simple statements as I take these texts in their context, which is the only fair way to deal with Scripture. In the first place, he says there should be a recognition of real Christian fellowship: "Watch ye." They were going to face many temptations, particularly the one of becoming very indifferent and thoughtless of the needs of other people.

Paul introduces some names here that I find most interesting. First of all he speaks about young Timothy, and says, in effect: "Timothy is going to come and see you shortly. He might very well be afraid of all you very clever, intellectual people, but just put him at his ease. Look after him, and send him on his way to me." Paul had written to Timothy, "Let no man despise thy youth." What he really said was, "Don't let your youth be despicable" (1 Timothy 4:12). Now he writes to the church at Corinth, "Don't despise this young believer. He is as much a worker of the Lord as I am." I think one of the wonderful things in the New Testament is this relationship between the aged Paul and young Timothy. It reminds us, and I think we need to be reminded, that old age and youth can get along and can work together in the Lord's service.

Then Paul mentions Apollos: "I wanted Apollos to come and see you, but he didn't want to come." I can imagine Paul saying, "Now Apollos, I do wish you would go to Corinth. If you went, perhaps you could put a stop to all that party spirit and hero worship. I think your presence there might cure them of saying, 'I am of Paul, and I am of Apollos.'"

I think of Apollos turning to Paul and saying, "I don't think it would stop anything at all; I think it would only make matters worse." So they agreed to differ, but they still loved each other: Paul says here, "Brother Apollos." Though Paul didn't get his own way, he knew how to disagree with another Christian and yet to love him just the same.

Then Paul introduces to us three very delightful people, although we know very little about them. One of them was called Stephanas, and he had a little family; at the very beginning of his ministry at Corinth Paul had baptized them (1:16). And then two others, Fortunatus and Achaicus, evidently Christian gentlemen. These three brethren had visited Paul, and he says of them, "They have refreshed me greatly." Indeed, it seems that these people were renowned for their wonderful hospitality, because Sephanas and his household are mentioned in this chapter, that they "have addicted themselves to the ministry of the saints" (16:15). It simply means that they kept open house; everybody was welcome in their home all the time. What lovely people!

And now Paul says, "Acknowledge these people, recognize them for the gems they really are. Watch that you do not slip into the temptation of not recognizing the gifts and fellowship of other Christians." What wonderful ministries are an open home and the refreshment of the saints. As a Christian duty, as a matter of Christian ethics, we must all watch our fellowship, our responsibility to others, and watch our reaction when we disagree with another Christian, avoiding the peril of party spirit.

It sounds very delightful, doesn't it, to have a little group of people like this who are always being friendly? If your house is open for the ministry to the saints, and if you have such a love as Paul had for the young people, what a difference it would make! Christian fellowship is such a lovely thing.

But how do I practice it? What is the power behind it? Look at Paul's second piece of pastoral advice: "Stand fast in the faith." It is impossible to do any of these things as a Christian should unless our behavior stems from Christian principles and Christian doctrine.

Elsewhere Paul says, "Stand fast therefore in the liberty wherewith Christ hath made us free" (Galatians 5:1). He says, "Stand fast in one spirit" (Philippians 1:27), and "Stand fast in the Lord" (Philippians 4:1). Here, when he writes to the church at Corinth, "Stand fast in the faith," though he is saying this important thing, "See that your life is sound," he is also saying, "See that your belief is applied in your life."

For to stand fast in the faith means to stand fast in the liberty with which Christ made us free: "Ye shall know the truth, and the truth shall make you free" (John 8:32). If His truth has dawned upon my mind and gripped my heart, it will set me free from the law of sin and death.

"Stand fast in one spirit," recognizing that a man does not understand his Bible by intellect; he only understands it as the Holy Spirit, the One who has come that he might lead us into all truth, illuminates his mind and guides his heart and life on the track of holy Scripture.

"Stand fast in the Lord, that in all things he may have the pre-eminence" (Colossians 1:18). Sound belief is the only key to sanctified behavior. If I let the one slip, inevitably I become slack in the other. As the apostle John says, "Who is he that overcometh the world, but he that believeth that Jesus is the Son of God?" (1 John 5:5).

The New Testament standard of Christian ethics is only possible in the life of a man whose sound doctrine has been applied to every detail of his experience. It is doctrine that leads a man to submit to the will of

God, and it is submission to the will of God that enables that man to be anointed with the power of the Holy Sprit for daily conduct.

If you turn aside from the principles of the Word of God in just one thing, what happens? You cease to delight in communion with the Lord. You become soured in your fellowship with others. When the Book speaks to your heart and truth comes alive, and the Spirit of God has said something to you from the Word, if you say "no" to Him at any point, if you refuse to apply the doctrine to your experience, immediately your fellowship with the Lord becomes dull and formal, your fellowship with other Christians spoiled. Once you turn away from the Lord Jesus Christ, that in all things He may have the preeminence, immediately you hinder all progress in sanctification.

Your growth in knowledge of the Lord Jesus and in likeness to Him is the goal of all Christian experience. Therefore your graciousness in Christian fellowship, which is the outcome of that growth, is dependent upon your constant submission to the truth of holy Scripture. To grow more like the living Word means constant submission to the authority of the written Word.

This is one piece of advice which Peter, out of the bitter experience of his own failure, also gives us, "Be sober, be vigilant; because your adversary the devil, as a roaring lion, walketh about, seeking whom he may devour: Whom resist stedfast in the faith" (1 Peter 5:8-9).

So may I just put these two things together in your mind: to stand fast in the Lord is to keep your eyes upon the Lord Jesus—that is the greatest source of strength for standing fast in the faith. To stand fast in the faith is to stand fast in submission to the Spirit who is in you to guide you into all truth. To stand fast in one Spirit is to stand fast in the liberty with which Christ has made us free.

Are you failing today in your recognition of fellowship with one another, in your love to others? Are you failing in your responsibility to the faith? I wonder if you have loosened your hold on your Bible—not that you don't read it, but that you've been saying "no," and therefore you have renounced its authority. Remember that this Book does not simply contain the Word of God; it *is* the Word of God, the only thing by which we can live. Looseness in Christian behavior, coldness in attitude to others, lack of desire for fellowship with God's people—all these things go directly back to a depreciation of the authority of God's Word. Stand fast in the faith!

But the third piece of pastoral advice that Paul gives to this church at Corinth is, "Quit you like men, be strong"—be ready to take up the fight.

His complaint against this church at Corinth was, "I could not speak unto you as unto spiritual, but as unto carnal, even as unto babes" (3:1). But now they should have grown up. "If you are grown up, don't behave like babies." Why? Simply because all who *will* live godly in Christ Jesus *shall* suffer persecution (2 Timothy 3:12).

Here is a principle of spiritual life which comes down right into your heart and mine. Satan says we may guard our relationships and friend-ships, and watch our outward course of action and conduct, if we slack off as far as the preeminence of the Lord Jesus and the authority of the Bible are concerned. We can go to any length to be thought a wonderful fellow, as long as we refuse submission to the Word of God. To relax there means that we can go anywhere and do what we like. On the other hand, we may hold on to the preeminence of the Lord Jesus and the authority of the Bible as long as we don't let it affect our conduct and our contact with others. But the moment we put watching and holding fast, belief and behavior together, at that moment we draw the fire of the enemy.

We draw the fire of worldly Christian people and of the unbeliever who cares nothing for the things of God. We cease to be regarded by any of them as a delightful person—no good socially, you know, because we refuse to do the things that are contrary to our Bible.

"Therefore," says Paul, "you'd better be ready for the fight. Be strong, be mature, behave like men." What does that mean? As a man, you will not, as a child would, allow yourself to deviate from what you know to be God's will. As a man in Christ, you will examine every suggestion that is put to you, no matter how fascinating it may be, and compare it with what the Word of God says. In every situation you will resolutely refuse to follow a line of conduct that is contrary to the Word of God.

That is the fight. You have to face it, and so do I, every day. The moment you *will* to live godly in Christ, you find ridicule and scorn, and perhaps most subtle of all, the whispering of Satan, "Don't take your Christianity too far—don't be narrow." From my own experience, I have found that the only answer to these constant suggestions of Satan is the continual soaking of my life in the Scriptures.

There is no short cut to holy living. Whatever suggestion or decision is put to me by friend or foe, before I take action it must be referred to the absolute authority of the Word of God. If I am prepared to do that, I shall be strengthened in the fight: "Quit you like men, be strengthened," is the word.

I want to be very careful that you don't misunderstand what I am talking about. But it is not until a man in his will determines to live godly in Christ that he can claim to be a Christian. If you are not drawing the fire, perhaps it is simply because you are not in the battle at all. And if you are not in this battle, is it because you have never willed to live a godly life? If you have never willed to live a godly life, you are not saved, because that involves turning to God from sin.

I am concerned that we have known so much and experienced so little. Tell me, have you had fascinating suggestions made to you recently? And something has whispered into your mind, "What is the harm in it?" What have you done? Have you gone along with what everybody else does, or have you referred it to the Word of God? And when you did, and the Word of God said "no," did you also say "no," even though you faced the sneers of your friends? God bless you!

Or did you refer it to the Word of God which said "no," but you said, "I think I'll go ahead." What has happened to you since? Your quiet time has died out and your fellowship with God has ceased, because the Word of God is no longer your authority. You have turned aside from the battle.

The people who are really fighting this battle, constantly regarding the Word as their final authority for life, will agree with me that this battle is not a brief one; it is lifelong. Often we are tempted to give way to fear and discouragement, but we have to learn to say with Paul, "None of these things move me, neither count I my life dear unto myself, so that I may finish my course with joy" (Acts 20:24).

Whatever may be your views on eternal security (and I think you know mine), remember it is "he that endureth to the end shall be saved" (Matthew 10:22). It is a mark of reality when you see the sign of endurance in a Christian's life. I believe in the perseverance of the saints because I believe in the perseverance of the Lord Jesus Christ.

The greatest force to inspire us in relating our behavior and our belief together is the thought of verse 14: "Let all your things be done with [love]." It is good to have plenty of zeal, and it is good to have plenty of courage, but they aren't everything. It is very easy for a spirit of bitterness to get hold of us. The Word says we are not to render evil for evil, but on the other hand, blessing.

Perhaps you have discovered that the foes in life are the foes of your own household. Your submission to the authority of God's Book has brought unhappiness in the most precious relationships in life. And you may have gone along with your husband or wife in some issue and compromised for the sake of peace. But there is no peace in your heart—there never is, when you take that policy. Or you may have resisted, but in an unkind spirit. Often the battle will demand that you obey God rather than man, but if you show a bitter spirit you lose the battle, even though you do what you think is God's will. Somehow we have to learn to take up the cross meekly, to bear it patiently, to bless God that we are counted worthy to suffer for Christ, remembering that the Lord Jesus prayed for His enemies. May all things, even our battle, be surrounded by the sweet warmth of love.

The Lord enable you to determine to live a godly life, and to relate what you believe to your conduct, as the evidence of a genuine Christian experience. The Lord give you victory in the battle that must follow when these two things are put together, and enable you to do all things with love.

CHAPTER THIRTY-FOUR

THE VITAL
ISSUE OF LIFE

1 CORINTHIANS 16:21-24

As was Paul's custom in concluding all his letters, he takes the pen in his own hand and writes a farewell greeting. This will receive, from those who get the letter, more attention than anything else. Don't you find yourself, sometimes, looking at the end of a letter before you start it? Perhaps you want to know whom it is from or what he or she really thinks of you. Frequently, what the writer wants to emphasize is contained in the last sentence, possibly even in a postscript.

Now what has Paul to say? How will he sum up his teaching to these Christian people at Corinth? What will he desire that they should remember above everything else? "If any man love not the Lord Jesus Christ, let him be Anathema Maran-atha. The grace of our Lord Jesus Christ be with you. My love be with you all in Christ Jesus. Amen" (16:22-24).

Thank you, Paul, for sending us your love. Thank you for praying that the grace of the Lord Jesus may be with us. We shall certainly need every bit of that as we walk along the royal route to heaven. But this other verse seems rather an ugly tone with which to finish a letter.

Let's look at those two unfamiliar words just a moment. *Anathema* is a Greek word, not even translated into English here. You sometimes find it translated, as in Romans 9:3, when out of the passion of his heart for his Jewish people, Paul exclaims, "I could wish myself were accursed from Christ for my brethren's sake." This is the word: "If any man love not the Lord Jesus Christ, let him be accursed."

The second word is really two words in the Aramaic language, which possibly was the language of Paul's youth. *Maran*—"the Lord"; *atha*—part of the verb "to come." Dr. Ironside says that a free paraphrase of this verse might be: "If any man love not the Lord Jesus Christ, he shall be condemned at the coming of the Lord." Paul is just stating an inevitable fact.

Isn't it harsh to consign to judgment and destruction a man who perhaps is not guilty of any gross sin, and maybe has quite a bit of the form of religion, and yet is destitute of the power of the Christian faith? But how else can you interpret this verse; indeed, how else can you interpret the whole revelation of the Christian gospel?

The unique feature of the Christian faith is that it requires a resolute adherence and a constant devotion to the Lord Jesus Christ. Of course, it doesn't stop there, but it is out of personal devotion to the Lord Jesus, and out of that alone, that there spring all the implications of the Christian life. It is out of a personal devotion to Christ that there arises the social gospel as well as the holy life. That is why Paul emphasized in 1 Corinthians 13 that if I "have not love, I am nothing."

Merely to use a title, to call Him "the Lord," and yet have no personal love or affection, to show no regard for Him in your life, is the worst form of hypocrisy. To love Christ is to put Him before everybody and everything else, and to delight in His presence above all. It means, to use the language of the apostle, that we count all things but loss for the excellencey of the knowledge of Christ Jesus our Lord (Philippians 3:8). It means that we say with David, "As the hart panteth after the water brooks, so panteth my soul after thee, O God" (Psalm 42:1). And again, "Whom have I in heaven but thee? And there is none upon earth that I desire beside thee" (Psalm 73: 25).

When a man truly loves the Lord Jesus, his delight in His presence is always matched by readiness to obey Christ. It was, if you remember, by this criterion that the Lord Himself taught us to judge the reality of Christian experience; "He that hath my commandments, and keepeth them, he it is that loveth me" (John 14:21).

So this is what Paul would underline: the secret of a happy life, a holy life, a victorious life, a Christian life, is a passionate devotion to the Lord Jesus. If you do not have that, you have nothing, and you will stand condemned on the Judgment Day.

As we have been traveling along this royal route to heaven, constantly the burden on my heart has been, "Has the Word had any effect? Has it reached hearts and produced a deeper devotion to the Lord Jesus Christ?" We have been brought back, time and time again, to ask that question. But what matters more than anything else, the thing which is going to be decisive on that Judgment Day, is, "If any man love not the Lord Jesus Christ, let him be Anathema Maran-atha."

I would not discourage the weak, on the one hand, but neither would I confirm the nominal Christian or the hypocrite in his delusion that as long as he has orthodox "religion," he is going to heaven. Let me give you three reasons from the Word of God why not loving the Lord Jesus Christ is so exceedingly sinful, and that if such an attitude is maintained, it brings separation from the presence of the Lord and everlasting destruction.

First, not to love the Lord Jesus Christ means that in my heart I am in rebellion against the highest throne in all the universe. God has spoken in these last days in His Son, and God has nothing more to say. Everything He has for me of blessing is in Jesus Christ. He has commanded us to hear Him in an audible voice that spoke form heaven, "This is my beloved Son, in whom I am well pleased; hear ye him" (Matthew 17:5). God intends us to regard the Lord Jesus with reverence, with affection, and with obedience. And the Lord Himself said it was intended "That all men should honour the Son, even as they honour the Father" (John 5:23).

Are we at liberty to set aside this word of authority from heaven? Indeed not! The essence of all sin is arrogance, setting up the little puppet-god of self on the throne of my heart instead of its rightful ruler, the Lord Jesus. The essence of salvation is the collapse of the regime of self altogether, and the enthronement of another King. There is no New Testament salvation without submission; "If a man love me, he will keep my words: and my Father will love him, and we will come unto him, and make our abode with him" (John 14:23). The Holy Spirit will not enter a heart that is arrogant and self-righteous; He will only come in when there is willingness for the new regime in which Christ is Sovereign. "Not every one that saith unto me, Lord, Lord, shall enter into the kingdom of heaven; but he that doeth the will of my Father which is in heaven" (Mathew 7:21).

This note which I seek to strike has almost entirely disappeared from gospel preaching today. The word "believe" is so abused that it means little more than an acceptance of truth, which still leaves us uncommit-ted when it comes to applying that truth to our lives. To declare that the gospel of Jesus Christ demands submission to Him is to be dubbed a bit peculiar, one of the "deeper life" sect. But this is the gateway to life, at the cross where self is crucified and Jesus is enthroned. There is no salvation apart from that.

The road that takes a man to hell is not only "skid row," not just the indifference of millions of people in this country to the truth — those who never darken a church door. It is much more subtle than that: the road that takes a man to hell can be the path that brings him into church membership without the puppet of self having been dethroned. That is Satan's most clever device.

This principle seems to be utterly strange to this generation. Do you know why? Because it is strange in every relationship of life today.

The Scripture says, "Wives, submit yourselves to your husbands in the Lord" (Ephesians 5:22). In the New Testament, this is the loveliest picture imaginable, drawn for us by the Holy Spirit to illustrate the submission of the Christian to his Savior. To enter into that precious experience with Christ — I would not say it is impossible, but it is a thousand times more difficult when that principle of submission in married life is ignored. Submission one to another is the key to a happy home life. When that principle is refused, what happens? It is not long before the bride says, "I don't see why I should do what he wants; I don't agree with him." And the bridegroom says, "Listen, you've got to do what I tell you." They get into conflict and run away to the divorce court to escape the tangle. If I would refuse to submit to an earthly bridegroom, how can I ever bring myself to submit myself to One whom I have not seen?

Again, "Children, obey your parents" (Ephesians 6:1). That is not taught or practiced in many homes today. Lack of discipline will pro-duce children who have never learned to obey their earthly father, so how can they be expected to obey their heavenly Father? The careless, slipshod bringing up of children has led not only to unhappy homes and juvenile delinquency, but to shallow Christian living. When a child goes out from the shelter of the home in which he has been pampered and spoiled, and he is called upon to submit to the King of kings, do you think he will? All of us are selfish, despicable, wretched creatures unless the grace of God gets into our hearts through submission to Christ's sovereignty. He is the *Lord Jesus Christ,* and to fail to love Him is to rebel against the highest throne of all the universe.

In the second place, not to love the Lord Jesus is to reject the loveliest character of all creation. In Christ is every possible beauty; He is the altogether lovely One. There is nothing lacking in Him that could be for the glory of God and for the blessing of my life. "For in him dwelleth all the fullness of the Godhead bodily" (Colossians 2:9). The great outcome of love for the Savior is that the Holy Spirit comes to dwell within our hearts, that we might know the love of Christ that passeth knowledge, that we too might be filled with all the fullness of God. In other words, to love Jesus is to be like Him.

There is a question in Psalm 115:2: "Wherefore should then heathen say, 'Where is now their God?'" And that is exactly the question people around us are asking. The heathen's god is made of silver and gold; he has eyes that see not, a mouth that speaks not, ears that hear not, a nose that smells not, hands that handle not, feet that walk not. And "They that make them are like unto them; so is every one that trusteth in them" (Psalm 115:8). The heathen becomes like the god he worships.

"Where is your God, Christian? Where is this Lord you say is so wonderful?" they ask. And the Christian has to hang his head in shame, because he has failed to be like Him. Oh, what a rebuke! When an unbeliever sees a Christian, he should be thinking, "There is God, walking in that man, talking through him, living in him, loving through him." That is to be our witness to our God, who is incarnate within our redeemed personality.

To fail to love Christ is to reject this possibility. If I love Him, I worship Him, and if I worship Him, I grow to be like Him. To reject His loveliness is to prefer to be mean and selfish and ugly. It means to become like the material things I worship: cold, ruthless and powerless.

Of what use do you think it is to have a religion that is theologically correct, doctrine that is fundamentally sound, a big Bible that you believe from cover to cover and carry around with you, and yet you are mean and selfish and unlovely? When you are not recognized you resign and walk out—but the trouble is that you come back again. What is the value of a religion like that? Do you love the Lord Jesus? Do you worship Him? Are you growing like Him? Or have you been saved, so you say, for twenty years or more, and you are still as irritable and resentful as ever?

"If any man loves not the Lord Jesus Christ, let him be Anathema." Why? Because thirdly, it is a refusal of the greatest Lover of my soul. Just reflect a moment on what Jesus has suffered for us: "Who, being in the form of God, thought it not robbery to be equal with God: but made himself of no reputation, and took upon him the form of a servant, and was made in the likeness of men: and being found in fashion as a man, he humbled himself, and became obedient unto death, even the death of the cross" (Philippians 2:6-8). And again, "But God commendeth his love toward us, in that, while we were yet sinners, Christ died for us" (Romans 5:8).

Can there be a creature on earth who does not love Him for that? Can you think of His lowly birth in utter poverty, all the toil and labor in His life, the pain and suffering of His death as He was made sin for us, the constancy of His intercession for us at the throne ever since—can you think of it all and not love Him?

Yes, we can, and it stamps upon our character such utter baseness, and it makes the language of our text speak to us with heavenly authority; "If any man love not the Lord Jesus, let him be accursed." When I think about that, I have it in my heart to say, "Amen, Lord. You couldn't do anything else. Hell is no more than we deserve."

In the early days of the church, when the Roman Empire was trying to stamp it out, the Christians had a sign, a fish, because the Greek word was similar to the name "Jesus." And they had a watchword; wherever they went they spread it: "Maran-atha!" Those little groups, harried and chased as fugitives from place to place, scattered by persecution, would follow the sign of the fish, and as the Roman soldiers sought them out, they would encourage each other "Maran-atha!" Hold on, be brave, the Lord is coming!" It was the word of fellowship—"We cannot carry on without Him; we cannot give in." That early church triumphed in spreading the gospel across North Africa and around the Mediterranean world.

Have you been saying to yourself, "But I cannot love Him as I ought"? No, none of us can. But you can ask Him to light the flame of His love within your heart today. Submit to the will of God and the sovereignty of Christ; seek for His character, His righteousness; surrender to this great Lover of your soul. If you do, the love of God will be shed abroad in your heart by the Holy Spirit, and even years of bitterness and heartache, coldness and cynicism—all these things that have gone with so much of nominal Christian profession—will be taken out of your life by the inbreathing of the love of God.

Do you love the Lord Jesus? I'm not asking what your mind says you will believe. I'm asking you what your heart says. If you don't, that is rebellion, refusal, rejection of the Lover of your soul. Make this submission that His love may come in, that your life may be transformed, and that the sweetness of His presence may become a precious reality to you. All along our royal route to heaven, God has said to us, "If any man love not the Lord Jesus Christ, he will be condemned at the coming of the Lord."

If this were my last word to preach this side of meeting my Lord face to face, I would say to you that there is no heaven for any of us without that love for the Lord Jesus. There is no new birth without surrender, no salvation without submission. But there is such joy when His love and life and power are breathed into my heart by the Holy Spirit, so that I may reveal His love to others.

Blessings
Out of
Buffetings

PREFACE

The contents of this book originally formed the basis of a series of messages delivered from the pulpit of Moody Memorial Church, Chicago, over a period of six months. After further prayer and preparation I was in the course of giving them again at Charlotte Chapel, Edinburgh, when I was taken seriously ill. At first this came as a somewhat shattering blow, but soon it was seen to be another evidence of the mercy of God. The contents of this book began to live in a new way, and truths which I had thought to be well learned became part of my experience.

Blessing out of buffeting suddenly became a truth which lived all over again "… every branch that beareth fruit, he purgeth it, that it may bring forth more fruit" (John 15:2) — and out of the painful and trying buffeting of the past months I trust that blessing will flow in a new way out of my life, and out of the pages of this book.

I can say out of a full heart, "My grace is sufficient for thee: for my strength is made perfect in weakness" (2 Corinthians 12:9). I trust that the message of this book will bring strength and the blessing of God to some buffeted and bewildered servant of His who, like me, may be knocked down but not knocked out (2 Corinthians 4:9, PHILLIPS).

My special thanks are due to all who have worked so hard on the manuscripts, and to my wife who once again helped in the revision and correction during the preparation of the book.

Alan Redpath
Charlotte Chapel, Edinburgh

BLESSINGS OUT OF BUFFETINGS

Oh tried and tested Christian,
Beset on every hand
By storms of strife, remember
Thy Father holds command!
E'en though the tempest rages,
Thy chastened heart may sing,
For He doth purpose blessing
Through all thy buffeting.

Be strong and of good courage,
Though foes thy soul assail.
No weapon formed against thee
Hath power to prevail;
For thou shalt share the triumph
Of Christ, thy conquering King,
Who purposes a blessing
Through all thy buffeting.

Rejoice to be found worthy
Of suff'ring for His name,
Who on the cross of Calvary
Bore all thy weight of shame.
When He shall come in glory
His ransomed Home to bring,
Thou'lt know in full the blessing
Attained through buffeting!

—*Avis B. Christiansen*

CHAPTER ONE

BLESSINGS OUT OF BUFFETINGS

2 CORINTHIANS 1:1-11

In commencing what I trust will be a practical and down-to-earth study of Paul's second letter to the church at Corinth, I might point out that the great difference between the themes of First and Second Corinthians is that in First Corinthians we have the account of a church which is being instructed and corrected, whereas in Second Corinthians we have the account of a man who is being disciplined and matured. Nowhere does Paul open his heart to his readers so completely as he does in the second letter as he relates some of God's dealings with him in his inner life. By revealing something of the price he has paid, his ministry is vindicated and his authority recognized.

News has reached Paul from Titus (2 Corinthians 7:7) of the mixed reception of his first letter. There were those, a majority, who had genuinely repented of sin in the church and dealt with it thoroughly; there were others, a minority, who challenged his authority, suspected his motives, and questioned the validity of his ministry. His answer, as recorded here, is an amazing mixture of tender love and stern rebuke.

Notice the language of verses 3–5 of the opening chapter: "Blessed be God, even the Father of our Lord Jesus Christ, the Father of mercies, and the God of all comfort; Who comforteth us in all our tribulation, that we may be able to comfort them which are in any trouble, by the comfort wherewith we ourselves are comforted of God. For as the sufferings of Christ abound in us, so our consolation also aboundeth by Christ."

These verses open to each of us a ministry which is unique. Not everyone is called upon to preach the Word of God in public; not everyone is called upon to bear testimony to Christ before a crowd. But if any of us know the Lord Jesus Christ in reality then God opens for each of His children a ministry which is unique—a ministry of comfort, which simply means the ability to communicate Holy Spirit life to others. Such a ministry is, as we shall see, intensely costly. It is those who experience the suffering of Christ who in turn experience the comfort of the Holy Spirit; these are they who live richly and therefore are used mightily.

Personally, I would rather have the spiritual gift of bringing life to one broken heart than the ability to preach a thousand sermons. Indeed, any public ministry which has not at its heart something of the tenderness which has come because of the personal experience of what Paul calls "the sufferings of Christ" is lacking in the one thing that really matters. I wonder if there was ever a greater need for a ministry of comfort (using that word in the sense that Paul uses it here).

You do not have to look far to find broken hearts, broken lives, and broken homes. Perhaps in a degree far greater than ever before in my life, I have looked recently into the faces of such. Somehow I felt deep down in my soul the awful plight of men and women without God and without hope in the world. I have seen not one but thousands of people with no homes, people who sleep night by night on the pavements of Indian cities without any covering, adults and children all together. As I felt something of the pang of it in my heart, it was then that God began to show me the true meaning of this text, "...the God of all comfort; Who comforteth us in all our tribulation, that we may be able to comfort them which are in any trouble, by the comfort wherewith we ourselves are comforted of God." In other parts of the world the need may be less exposed to the public eye, covered with a veneer of civilization and reserve; yet it is there in all its urgent claim upon every Christian.

You have often heard it said—have you not?—that you cannot bring help and comfort to someone else unless you have been through his trouble. I believe that it is true only in a very limited sense. If it were entirely true, it would put tremendous limitations upon the ministry which Paul had in mind in this letter.

For instance, if you sit by someone who has suffered a deep bereavement and you never have—does that mean you cannot bring any message to his heart? Or you are in touch with someone who has been in desperate physical pain, and you know little of that—does that mean you are excluded from a ministry with such a person? Surely not. But you see, when Paul speaks about his ministry of comfort, he speaks about it having come out of an experience in his own life which has qualified him for such a ministry. Consider therefore the training for this ministry.

Look at this verse again and you will see something of the training through which Paul has passed for this unique ministry when he says, "Who comforteth us in all our tribulation, that we may be able to comfort them which are in any trouble. ..." Paul is speaking about something that has happened to him, an experience of affliction. He might have in mind the thorn in the flesh of which he spoke. He does not betray exactly the nature of the affliction, but I am quite sure that it was something far deeper than a mere physical experience. Indeed, in the fifth verse he says, "...as *the sufferings of Christ* abound in us, so our consolation also aboundeth by Christ." And then you notice how he opens his heart to us in the following verses concerning the training through which he has passed for a ministry of this kind: "...whether we be afflicted, it is for your consolation and salvation..." (v. 6); "...we would not, brethren, have you ignorant of our trouble which came to us in Asia, that we were pressed out of measure, above strength, insomuch that we despaired even of life" (v. 8); "...we had the sentence of death in ourselves, that we should not trust in ourselves, but in God which raiseth the dead" (v. 9).

Clearly Paul is speaking here about some deep experience through which he has passed, for he speaks about the sufferings of Christ abounding in us. And therefore he is making it perfectly clear that if we would ever qualify to bring blessing to one poor needy life, one broken heart, it is going to require a spiritual experience of suffering on a deep level.

I want to try to show you what that means, and I shall introduce it by asking some questions: Have you ever felt the throb in the heart of God over a soul without a Savior? Have you ever felt in your own soul the pain, the agony of the cross, the concern in the heart of God for a soul without Christ? Have you ever been really caused to take hold of God in prayer for someone who seems so helpless, so hopeless, so lost?—perhaps your next-door neighbor? Does it give you five minutes' concern? If it does, you have just begun to enter, in a little measure, into the fellowship of the suffering of Christ.

You can never bring any blessing to someone in need unless first it has touched your own heart. The moment it begins to grip you, you will be led into a school of suffering about which an unbeliever knows nothing. There is nothing in physical pain which in itself produces holiness, but the sufferings of Christ, which are the outcome of our union with Him, become the source of Holy Spirit consolation, and so maturity of character, and this in turn becomes the secret of sharing blessing with others.

Here Paul is speaking about a training which he has passed through for this ministry that he might bring comfort to others. He has himself been comforted in his own tribulation; and he has found that comfort and that experience of God in his time of affliction, not simply for blessing in his own heart, but that he might be made a channel of blessing to another in need.

So, therefore, we introduce our subject by reminding ourselves that the precious and sacred ministry of bringing heavenly comfort and help to one poor, broken, lonely life is not something that we can do lightly with a mere pat on the shoulder. It is something that is going to cost us deeply. The true character of it we will see in a moment.

Let me ask you to look not only at the training Paul faced, but at the enabling God gave him, that is, his resources. If I were to translate the fourth verse of this chapter accurately, you would notice a distinction between two words: "Who comforteth us in all our afflictions, that we may be able to comfort them which are in any affliction, by the comfort wherewith we ourselves are comforted of God." Notice two words in sharp contrast: *affliction, comfort.*

"Affliction" is the word that was used by our Lord when He said, "...in me ye might have peace. In the world ye shall have *tribulation...*" (John 16:33). This is far deeper than mere physical suffering; it is something that was to be the portion of His disciples and the experience of all who would follow Him.

The word "comfort" is the word *paraclete*, which is the Bible word for the Holy Spirit. And so you have the two side by side: on the one hand the depths of tribulation which is the portion of God's people, and which is part of the training for the ministry of comfort to another; on the other hand the ensured enablement and reinforcement of the *paraclete*, the Comforter. Look at that precious verse again: "Who comforteth us..."—that is to say, "Who sends the Holy Spirit, the *paraclete*, to us in all our affliction"—"that we may be able to comfort them which are in any affliction, by the comfort wherewith we ourselves are comforted of God."

See then this simple principle: if you and I are to be a blessing to someone in need, perhaps just to one person whose heart is broken, who is without God and without hope, and if we would have that sacred, precious ministry, we are assured that this is something absolutely impossible to us by ourselves, by any human talent or ability. This is not a ministry that we will acquire at the university, or at a college, or at any school, but it is something that the Holy Spirit will give to us. It is He who will be our strength and enduement. But He will come to us only in the measure that we have entered into the affliction which the Lord said would be the portion of His people.

You do not go far before you find that the people of God throughout the world are going through times of unprecedented pressures and tensions and problems. It would seem as though God is allowing times of testing to come to His people, not that they might despair, but that as they share in the fellowship of the suffering of Christ they may know in a new measure the enduement of the Holy Spirit. Out from this pressure of affliction, the church will begin to fulfill again this tremendous ministry of comfort and blessing which is her unique and glorious task. I am quite sure that these days of pressure upon the church have a very special significance in the mind of our Lord; and I am quite sure that if any of you know something about this in your own life, it has a very special significance for the ministry the Lord has for you.

Paul is speaking about the enablement which will accompany only a man who has really submitted to and accepted the affliction. In other words, in the spiritual sense of the word it is true that the ability to bring comfort and blessing to one life depends not upon having shared their experience, but upon having submitted to the suffering which God imposes upon His people.

Now, what is that suffering? We are not left in any doubt, for again I say that it is something that is not a physical principle, but a spiritual principle in life. We see therefore the sacredness of this personal ministry, and understand that it is going to mean training in a school through which the Lord puts His people. We see that we are absolutely assured of heavenly enduement for it, provided we are prepared to accept the discipline — and what is that discipline?

Let us look at the price of this ministry as Paul gives it in verses eight and nine. Notice the language Paul uses in these verses: what tremendous words they are! "...pressed out of measure, above strength ... we

despaired even of life: ... we had the sentence of death in ourselves. ..."
As Phillips puts it in *Letters to Young Churches*: "...we were completely
overwhelmed, the burden was more than we could bear, in fact we told
ourselves that this was the end." When we ask why this should be, we
have the answer in verse 9: "...that we should not trust in ourselves, but
in God which raiseth the dead"; or to quote from Phillips again: "...we
had this experience of coming to the end of our tether that we might
learn to trust, not in ourselves, but in God Who can raise the dead."

In other words, God has one great purpose for His people above
everything else: it is to destroy in us forever any possible confidence in
the flesh; it is to bring us to the place where self-confidence has passed
into history and has been exchanged for a confidence in God, who raises
the dead. Paul speaks about an experience when he was pressed out of
measure, above strength — as a ship that has been too heavily laden with
cargo gradually sinks under the pressure of the load until it seems that it
is in a fatal condition; or a weary animal that sinks in despair beneath a
burden far beyond its strength.

"Now," says Paul in effect, "I have been through this in the spiritual sense. I have had the sentence of death passed upon myself. I have
despaired even of life. There has been a moment in my experience when
I have been brought to such a place as this. When I came to the place
where I knew in myself I was helpless, hopeless, and could do nothing, somehow everything went to pieces. I had the sentence of death in
myself, and why? So that I should no longer trust in myself. That basis of
confidence was gone, and was replaced by a trust in the Lord who raises
the dead."

In other words, here is the price of this ministry to others. Is it not
amazing? If you would bring blessing to one heart in trouble, one thing
is going to stand in the way and make it absolutely impossible. No matter how you may or may not have entered physically into the sufferings
of another, no matter how much you may be able to share something
through your own experience of that very thing through which another
person has passed — even though you have done all this, yet if in your
life there is still that confidence in the flesh, then your ministry is lost.
For this ministry is a ministry of the Holy Spirit alone, and He cannot
work where there is self-confidence.

Does it not seem to you rather remarkable that Paul speaks about this?
Could there be any man who was more delivered from self-confidence

than the great apostle? He had it all shattered when he met the risen Savior and Master on the road to Damascus, had he not? Yes, but then the Lord knew the perpetual peril of its recurrence! God's ways and methods with His people are always directed along the line of shattering forever any confidence in the flesh. He could not afford to take any risks with a man for whom He purposed such a ministry.

Do you not find in your life that the flesh is very subtle along these lines? For instance, you will say, "I have become so zealous in the service of the Lord!"—and a little voice will whisper, "Yes, you will be able to get through anything because of your zeal." You begin to say to yourself, "My prayer life has progressed so tremendously. I am really growing!"—and self begins to boast of its spirituality: "I have years of Christian experience behind me. I have learned so much!" And so God moves in, for He cannot afford to allow that to go on. By varied ways He will deal with us, as in all sorts of subtle ways there is the whisper within which always makes us want to trust in ourselves.

I wonder if you, like I, have ever walked around the corridor of your own soul. Have you ever examined what goes on there? You can remember the great hopes that you had in yourself—but those hopes have been shattered. Have you ever gone through your life and reminded yourself of imaginations and dreams?—but now it is all a valley of dry bones! Have you ever found yourself with your prayer life gone to pieces, and your Bible become so stale, whereas only recently you had been boasting about how real it was? And all these things seem to be a complete mystery. Why has it turned out like that? I wonder if the Lord is going to bring through these verses new light upon your experience because He wants to turn the mystery of that experience into a ministry.

All along, God has been directing your life until it has come to a place where with the apostle Paul you may say, "…in my flesh … dwelleth no good thing…" (Romans 7:18), and you have lost any trace of confidence in anything self can do. You have the sentence of death in yourself; that is the price of bringing blessing to one needy heart.

To use a simple illustration: if ever you are called upon to rescue somebody who is drowning, I think that you would probably wait until that person is going down for the third time. If you were to intervene at any point at which the man or woman were kicking and resisting and fighting for himself, you would be in great danger of being drowned with him. But if you were to go to the rescue when the drowning person were at the end of his strength and had no confidence left in his own deliverance, at that moment he would be weakened and still, and you could be used to bring deliverance.

God's great purpose with His people all over the world today— through all the pressures and tensions which are being brought upon us—is that we might be brought to the end of self-confidence, where we no longer trust in ourselves but in God, who raiseth the dead.

Look again at verses 3 and 4: "…the God of all comfort; Who comforteth us [that is, who ministers to us by His Holy Spirit] in all our tribulation [affliction], that we may be able to bring comfort [Holy Spirit life and blessing] to them which are in any trouble [affliction], by the comfort [the strength, the enabling] wherewith we ourselves are comforted of God."

Everyone is brought within its scope, and we should be sent out into this world, in all its darkness and need, conscious that each of us has a ministry, a sphere of testimony—perhaps right next door, perhaps in our own home. But it is a ministry so tender and so delicate that you could easily blunder, and perhaps the second condition of the one to be comforted would be worse than the first unless the Holy Spirit were to show you the principle behind such ministry. He will explain to you some of the things which have happened in your life and which are complete mysteries to you, but which are in fact intended to be a ministry—the ministry of Holy Spirit life to another in need.

CHAPTER TWO

NOT FICKLE,
BUT FAITHFUL

2 CORINTHIANS 1:12–24

There are many different ways and means which the Lord uses and applies to His people, that through buffeting may come blessing. One of them is the misunderstanding of our motives, even by our friends. That is a painful kind of buffeting indeed! But what blessing lies at the root of it when we learn to do what Paul did: to apply great spiritual principles to the smallest issues of our everyday life. And after all, unless you and I learn to do that, we will never know how to apply spiritual principles to the crises. The peril which confronts all of us is that of taking even more of life's situations under our own control so that when the crisis arrives, we find ourselves incapable of making contact with heaven.

In this chapter it seems that a very trivial thing had happened to Paul, such as can happen to any of us. He planned to return to Corinth for a second visit, as he wrote in the fifteenth and sixteenth verses. He expected to receive a love gift from the Corinthians that would help him go on in his journey toward Jerusalem. In fact, he had already written to them to tell them to expect him, for the roots of this chapter go back to the last chapter of his previous letter: "Now I will come unto you, when I shall pass through Macedonia: for I do pass through Macedonia. And it may be that I will abide, yea, and winter with you, that ye may bring me on my journey whithersoever I go. For I will not see you now by the way; but I trust to tarry a while with you, if the Lord permit" (1 Corinthians 16:5–7).

But the Lord did not permit. And Paul's concern to get to Jerusalem under the guidance of the Spirit was so irresistible that he by-passed Corinth and left them out. There is always a crowd of folks looking for the slightest inconsistency in a servant of God, and for the opportunity to publish it far and wide; and so those at Corinth began immediately to accuse Paul of being inconsistent and fickle, of saying one thing and then actually doing another.

Yes, our message centers around this very simple thing—failing to keep a promise—for out of that the Corinthians built up a case for Paul's unreliability, and condemned it, saying in effect, "After all, if he cannot be trusted to keep his appointments, how can we ever trust the authority of his ministry?"

Notice how strenuously Paul denies it: "When I therefore was thus minded, did I show lightness [fickleness]? or the things that I purpose, do I purpose according to the flesh, that with me there should be yea yea, and nay nay? But as God is true [faithful], our word toward you was not yea and nay" (2 Corinthians 1:17–18). And he goes on to explain in the closing two verses of the chapter why he did not come: "I call God for a record [witness] upon my soul, that to spare you I came not [forbear to come] as yet unto Corinth. Not for that we have dominion [lordship] over your faith, but are helpers of your joy: for by faith ye stand [fast]."

"Now," says Paul in effect, "that was the reason I did not come to you: you must learn to stand on your own feet; you must not depend upon anybody else for your Christian strength and character. The prop must be removed."

I do not wish to digress, but I must interject here a very deep conviction that some of the props that are being taken away now in the withdrawal of missionaries from many parts of the world may be overruled in the sovereignty of God to teach us that national Christians are to stand on their own feet; for that reason Paul by-passed Corinth. But behind it all there is a spiritual principle, a principle upon which he lives his life every day, without any moment of change, and he gives it in verses 20 to 22, in effect: "I live my life in the absolute conviction of the certainty of God's promises. How many soever be the promises of God in Christ, is the yea. And because I am so sure of God's promises in every issue of my life, therefore I have responded to them in the total commitment of my life to God who has promised me everything. Wherefore through Christ is the amen to the glory of God by us."

Because in his life he is sure of God's promises, Paul is saying, and in answer to that conviction he has said "Amen" in his soul to all of them, there has been communicated into his life the very character of God. For he says, in effect, "He that established us with you in Christ and has anointed us is God; who also has sealed us and given us the earnest of the Spirit in our heart."

All of this simply means that a man who has believed God's promises, and has said "Amen" to them in the depths of his soul without any hesitation, is a man to whose life has been communicated the divine character of the Holy Spirit. Therefore the charge of fickleness in such a man is a sheer absurdity. For a man of God to be a double-dealer in his relationships with other people is an utter contradiction of terms.

Let us look at these precious truths a moment, recognizing that here is a man whose life has been so gripped by eternal reality that the faithfulness of God has become part of his character. Because God has proved Himself faithful to him, Paul must be absolutely faithful in his dealings with others. Here is a simple lesson that lies at the very root of the exposition of this portion of Scripture. When God says "Yea" and my heart says "Amen," His character by the Holy Ghost is implanted in my life to make fickleness with other people, even in the smallest detail, a sheer impossibility. Is it not amazing how out of a simple little issue like this comes to us some of the greatest truths of the Word of God?

In the *King James Version* of 2 Corinthians, you would almost feel that both the "yea" and "amen" are on God's side: "...all the promises of God in him are yea, and in him amen..."; that is to say, His promises are both given and confirmed by the Lord Jesus. But surely the *Revised Version* throws a different light upon this passage, and another slant upon this verse. True, every promise of God is "yea" in Christ: it is centered in the Lord Jesus; it is made known and made real because of Him. The "yea" is the voice of absolute authority, of absolute assurance. But the "amen" is my voice, your voice—the voice of absolute faith and complete obedience. The one has to do with divine revelation, which is unshakable; the other has to do with personal faith and commitment to it, which should also be unshakable.

Consider some of the things that are "yea" in Jesus Christ, some of God's certainties which are made known to us in the Lord Jesus. How many they are!—but I can only mention one or two. I think about the certainty of God's heart. How would I ever know that God loved me?

How would you ever know that God is love, except for a place called Calvary concerning which the apostle John says, "Herein is love, not that we loved God, but that he loved us, and sent his Son to be the propitiation for our sins" (1 John 4:10). The fact that God is love carries with it the "yea" of Calvary, the absolute certainty that He is love demonstrated at the cross.

What about the certainty of forgiveness? Perhaps some people who read this book have not troubled themselves too much about these things, but I believe that even the most superficial of lives, the most thoughtless and heedless of people, come to recognize their urgent need of a clear message concerning sin and forgiveness. There comes to every life the haunting reality of eternity, of judgment, the memory of a past which has been full of bitterness and shame. And the only message upon which any soul can hang its whole weight with absolute confidence is that "we have redemption through his blood, the forgiveness of sins…" (Ephesians 1:7); "…Christ has suffered… the just for the unjust, that he might bring us to God…" (I Peter 3:18). When God does forgive the soul, is there any limit to His forgiveness? Is God not only a God of love, but a God of forgiving mercy? The cross of Calvary where He died, the Just for the unjust, sends down to us through all the centuries the great "yea" of Jesus Christ to the fact of God's forgiveness.

But then I think also about the certainty for my life, for in the Lord Jesus there is One who is the way, the truth, and the life. Not only is He the Way into life, but the Standard for my life. There is a standard set for me and for all who would claim His pardon; for if I would claim His forgiveness and take my place happily and gladly under the blessedness of the "yea" of God's forgiving mercy, then I must also take my place happily under His leadership and under His dominion, and accept His standard for my life, the pattern for every one of His followers, to which all who would rest in the Lord Jesus must conform.

Perhaps one day in Christian living there will be uncertainties about some things; but the great lines of moral character, the great standard of Christian living, the great ethic of what a Christian ought to be is traced for us by a firm hand of the Lord Jesus in, for example, the Sermon on the Mount. That is why we sing:

Be like Jesus, this my song,
In the home and in the throng

Be like Jesus all day long,
I would be like Jesus.

Has your heart said "amen" to that?

The certainty of life, the absolute, clear, unshakable certainty is that if I am to rest in His pardon, then I must accept His standard unswervingly. Furthermore, in the Lord Jesus there is a certainty for the future. Apart from Christ everything about the future would be so dark. We would not know a thing beyond this brief spell we call life. But there is One who has gone over the gulf and come back again, and who brings us the tremendous assurance from His Word: "I am the resurrection, and the life: he that believeth in me, though he were dead, yet shall he live" (John 11:25).

You see, "How many soever are the promises of God: in Christ is the yea." They are all in Christ, and in Him is the "yea"; and Paul presents to us, as the reason for his consistency and absence of fickleness in daily living, that in his heart there has been the "amen" to all the promises of God.

Today deep calls unto deep and claims the response of your "amen" and my "amen" to the promises of God which are "yea" in Christ. Let us look therefore at this second thing, the commitment of my life. "…wherefore also through him is the Amen unto the glory of God through us." Do you see how this is so important for our daily life? There ought to be some kind of correspondence, some kind of mutual likeness between the "yea" of God in Christ and the "amen" of our hearts. The stability of His promises that are all settled in Jesus ought to be answered by the stability of our "amen" without any hesitancy or reservation. Surely it is a poor compliment to meet the promises that have been sealed in heaven by the blood of Jesus with a faltering "amen" that almost sticks in our throat. Surely it is an insult to the Lord in His great faithfulness and goodness to respond with hesitancy in our hearts to the "yea" that is so sure.

Paul is saying that the charge of inconsistency leveled against him is a sheer impossibility because God's unswerving "yea" in Christ has been met by an unswerving "amen" from his soul. He has looked up into the face of his Lord concerning pardon, concerning God's love, and concerning God's standards for his life, and he has said, "amen, Lord," unreservedly. Therefore, because he is so gripped by that relationship, he cannot be faithless in his relationships to other people. In other words, truth has so gripped this man that the one thing that matters to him is that he should be obedient to it, for that transaction must spread its influence to every part of his life.

Now I would underline something here for your heart. Somehow I think it is just along this line that the church today—that is you and I—is guilty of some measure of failure. What a fantastic contrast there is between the great "yea" of God and the half-hearted "amen" of our hearts! The reason, I believe, is party moral and partly intellectual. Many of us are so afraid of giving unhesitating conviction in response to spiritual things, in case we are thought dogmatic or narrow. We think it looks like an attempt to boast of advanced education to say, "Well, I think— perhaps—it may be." But the language of the Christian church when it has been living in real victory in relation to the promises of God has never been, "We infer—we calculate—we think." It has always been, "We know." Whatever uncertainties may lie beyond us concerning some of the great issues of life, yet the love of God, the pardon of God, the standards for life that come to us in Jesus Christ—about these things there is no doubt. We know. And therefore our "amen" is to be as sure and as final as is God's "yea" forever.

From that moment when a man says "amen" to the Lord in these matters, his life is to be gripped constantly by the reality of the promises of the Word of God. That is one thing that I believe the Christian church lacks today—a grip of eternal truth upon our souls—so that when God says, "Thou shalt not," something rises in us that says, "Why?" When God forbids a certain course of action, strangely enough Satan can come along and persuade us that a course of action contrary to the teaching of Scripture may be completely right. I grieve in the instance of a Christian who can placate himself (or herself) that it is right to marry a non-Christian, and convince himself that it is right in order that he might satisfy the loneliness of his heart, and convince himself that that kind of thing is permissible to a child of God. Satan does that today to the people of God.

Oh, but when God says "yea" concerning standards of life, my heart has to bow down before the throne of all the universe and say "amen." And until it does, eternal truth has never gripped my soul. Until that happens, I shall be constantly fickle, unreliable, and unstable in my relationships with other people.

The church today is lamentably weak in its grip upon eternal reality, and therefore Christian homes are lamentably weak in their testimony because they are permitting things that are contrary to the testimony of the Word of God.

Have you said "amen" to the Lord in your soul? I believe that God waits for every one of His children to have a day when they crash! Have you had your crash? That crash is not something emotional, nor it is a moral breakdown; it is the moment when from the depths of your soul there is an "amen" to all the will of God. And heaven resounds with rejoicing because it has heard the "amen" to His pardon, the "amen" to His standards, no matter how narrow the world may think they are. By the grace of God, His standard is to be our standard, and therefore to Him we say "amen." Has that happened in your heart? If so, observe the inevitable spiritual outcome of that great moment in life: the communication of his character.

Paul's argument is simply this: How can I, with such a message burning in my soul, ever be guilty of fickleness? Surely the message must make the messenger like it. Surely communion with a faithful God whose promises are "yea" must make a man faithful in all other relationships. As I have said, for a man to be a Christian and a double-dealer is an utter impossibility. Why? Because God, whose promises are "yea" in Christ and who hears the "amen" of our hearts, thereupon without delay—at that moment, instantaneously—communicates His character to make us stable.

Notice Paul's precious words in the two closing verses: underline them, and test your Christian life by them; *establish, anoint, seal, earnest*. He establishes us in Christ; that is to say, the fixity with which the Lord Jesus set His face towards Jerusalem, the constant and tenacious purpose of obedience to His Father's will—that becomes a part of my life, too. Days of broken promises and hesitancy of obedience become less frequent, for He establishes us.

How does He do it? He does it by the anointing of the Spirit. John says, "…ye have an unction from the Holy One …" (1 John 2:20), and the man and the woman who have said "amen" in happy, glad abandonment to the will and Word of God have received this. The anointing of the Holy Ghost which enabled Jesus to obey His Father in heaven unswervingly is the same anointing of the Holy Spirit that has come upon the child of God who has said "amen" to all God's will. It is Christ in us, and only Christ in us by the anointing of His Spirit, who can deal with the fickleness of our nature and the wandering of our hearts, and bind those wandering hearts to Him.

278 / Blessings Out of Buffetings

Having anointed us, see what He does: He seals what He anoints. The seal impresses its likeness upon everything it touches. So a man sealed with the Spirit is made strong with the strength of Christ, wise with the wisdom of Christ, gracious with the gentleness of Christ, holy with the purity of Christ. Sealed! And all these are marks of His divine ownership, the mark of the moment when God raises the flag of heaven over the territory of the soul and seals with the Spirit.

If every inward profession of faith is matched with an outward righteousness of life, then we make it plain that truly we are genuinely His. So we have the earnest of the Spirit, the down payment which guarantees—with evidences that are unmistakable in a man who is living a life that is faithful—that he will one day see His lovely face. And there is no such guarantee in my Bible for any other kind of life.

Thus Paul brings all these great principles to bear in answering a simple charge—"Paul, you broke your promise! Paul, we cannot trust you! Paul, you are completely fickle!" To all of which he tells them that he uses the greatest principles of life to direct his conduct in the smallest detail, and therefore fickleness is impossible.

There may be two kinds of people reading this book. The one kind, like the chaff with no roots, is swept by every wind, unstable. Christian principles are at the mercy of passion and whim, and are forsaken when it seems more convenient. Oh, they would not call themselves unbelievers, because they believe everything most Christians believe. They would not call themselves anything but fundamental, conservative Christians—but in reality they are chaff! Principle is thrown overboard at a moment when it is inconvenient, because their hearts have never said "amen" to the Lord.

Then there are others, and they are like the tree rooted deep and rising high; their roots go as deep underground as their branches spread up into God's sky. They have echoed in their hearts "amen" to Jesus. It could be said of them: "I have set the Lord always before me: because he is at my right hand, I shall not be moved" (Psalm 16:8). There has come into that life such a stability by the unction of the Spirit that it bears the seal of His ownership—all because there was a day. And there is many a day when, sometimes with tears, sometimes with the flesh in rebellion, sometimes when everyone around you says you are narrow, extreme, bigoted, yet nevertheless in your soul alone with God you say, "Lord Jesus, amen. Amen to Your love, amen to Your pardon, amen to Your standards, amen to all of Your will, Lord!" Therefore, because you have said "amen," fickleness and unreliability have gone forever.

> So let our lips and lives express
>> The holy gospel we profess;
> So let our works and virtues shine,
>> To prove the doctrine all divine.

> Thus shall we best proclaim abroad
>> The honors of our Savior God,
> When His salvation reigns within,
>> And grace subdues the pow'r of sin.

> Our flesh and sense must be denied,
>> Passion and envy, lust and pride;
> While justice, temp'rance, truth and love,
>> Our inward piety approve.

CHAPTER THREE

VICTORY THROUGH CAPTIVITY

2 CORINTHIANS 2:14–16

Most expositors of this particular portion of the Word of God seem to be in agreement that, from the twelfth verse of this chapter right through the sixth chapter, Paul digresses in order to open his heart, as he very seldom does (so completely at least) in any other of his letters, concerning what it really means to him to be a minister of the gospel. He reveals something of what it has cost and some of the things that have brought him much joy. As we shall see later, he does not digress completely from what he has just been saying in the previous verses of this chapter; there is a very real relationship between the triumph of which Paul speaks here and the application of it to the situation in the church of which he has been speaking a few verses previously. What then has Paul to say about his ministry?

Whatever the experiences through which he has passed, somehow he would not let us think anything else than that from beginning to end it has been a glorious victory. "…thanks be unto God, which always causeth us to triumph in Christ. …" One version of the New Testament translates it this way: "Thanks be unto God, who through our union with Christ, leads us in one continual triumph." Paul is going to speak to us in succeeding chapters of the heartaches, the pressures, and the burdens he has borne, but he would underline from the very commencement that all through the story of his life there has been, because of his union with Christ, one continual victory. It is a victory along a particular road—as suggested by our title to this chapter—a victory through captivity, and what Paul says about his life as a Christian should, I am sure, be true about the lives of each one of us today. Amidst the heartaches and disappointments, the burdens and trials, as well as the joys of Christian living and all that is involved, nevertheless because of our union with Christ the story should be one of continual triumph.

"...thanks be unto God, which always leadeth us in triumph in Christ" (RSV). I think it is important to notice that that is the word—"who always *leadeth* us in triumph"—because it is quite clear that Paul had a very graphic picture in his mind as he used this language. It would be a picture—very familiar to Corinthian Christians—of a victorious Roman general returning from battle in his chariot, indeed with a whole procession of chariots and soldiers. A large crowd would gather to acclaim the victory in the battle, and the most significant thing everyone would notice would be the prisoners chained to the chariot wheels and dragged along the ground to their complete degradation. As the general rode by in his chariot, followed by soldiers in other chariots dragging more prisoners, bound and chained, the crowd would break out in a tumultuous roar as they rejoiced in the victory, and the air was filled with the odor of incense which was being burned and offered in thanksgiving to heathen gods. Such is Paul's picture in these verses. "Thanks be unto God," he says, in effect, "who drags me, not reluctantly but so happily, at the chariot wheel of His victory, and causes the air around me to be filled with the fragrance of His knowledge and His presence because of the victory that He has won by grace in my life."

Bear in mind the background of the man who is triumphing in this situation! Paul was not an immoral man or a degraded man, but a very self-righteous, proud, and arrogant Pharisee. Such a man is sometimes more difficult to face with the claims of the gospel. One day in his life he had a personal interview with the Lord Jesus, and from that day he began to count all his righteousness as but filthy rags in the sight of God. He had exchanged all that for the righteousness which God had offered him through faith in the Lord Jesus; and everything else he counted gladly as refuse, that he might win Christ. Because of this there had been a day when he held out his hands to the Lord and said, "Lord Jesus, today put Your chains upon my heart. You know how my heart is so prone to wander, and how wilful and stubborn and proud it can be. Lord, please, I want You at this moment and for the rest of my life to chain me up to Your chariot wheel. I want to be enchained and enslaved by Your love, because I know that is the road to liberty and freedom. Put Your chains on me, Lord, and never let me away!" What an amazing thing that such a man, so proud, should have such a complete capitulation as that! That a man who was considered a paragon of virtue and goodness of life and morality of living should one day hold out empty hands to the Lord and ask Him to put His chains upon him! He had found no freedom in his religion, no joy in his self-righteousness; it was all utter bondage. But one day the love of Calvary had begun to melt his heart, and just as the warmth of sunshine begins to melt the ice until it is reduced to water, so as he gazed and gazed upon the Savior and came to understand something in his own soul of the meaning of those nail prints and of what it cost God to die in his place, Paul said, "Lord Jesus, chain me to Thyself!"

> Make me a captive, Lord,
>   And then I shall be free;
> Force me to render up my sword,
>   And I shall conqueror be.
>
> I sink in life's alarms
>   When by myself I stand;
> Imprison me within Thine arms,
>   And strong shall be my hand.

Triumph by captivity! Liberty in bondage! Freedom through slavery! Triumphant living by union with a crucified, living Lord! A triumphant life meant all that to Paul. It is the only way of triumph for any of us.

He goes on to say something else, however. Because it has been a life of triumph, it has been a life of testimony.

"...[God] maketh manifest the savour of his knowledge by us in every place" (v. 14). Just for a moment, go back in your mind to the picture which Paul put before the Corinthian Christians, and see the prisoners of war being dragged along the ground. That which was their degradation was to Paul, in terms of spiritual experience, his greatest honor: that he could be a slave of the Master. As you see these prisoners being drawn by their chains and listen to the roar of applause, you might ask yourself, "Why the cheering?" The cheering was not for them but for the honor of the general who had captured them. Every chain that was put around them and tied to his chariot wheels was the symbol of his power. No doubt, as they were dragged along the road, they carried with them broken spears and shattered arrows. Every weapon they had once used in their defense was shattered and drawn along with them, symbolizing the general's total area of authority.

So Paul says, "Thanks be unto God! In Jesus Christ He has chained me to His chariot wheel, and for the rest of my life, I am His slave and, because of this, inevitably—not by sermons I preach or by words I use, but by my life—in my daily routine there is made manifest and clear the savor, the scent, the fragrance of His knowledge by me in every place." Or as the *Revised Version* puts it: "…thanks be unto God, which always leadeth us in triumph in Christ, and maketh manifest through us the savour of his knowledge in every place." "I am so happy," says Paul, in effect, "since the chains were put on me and since the Lord manacled my hands and took hold of my life and made me His slave. I am so thankful that, as I am taken along the journey of life, inevitably other people will see the weapons I once used to trust in are now destroyed and shattered. Whereas I once trusted in my self-righteousness and my ability, in my sheer determination and will power, now I gaze upon my lovely Lord, and these others are all lying shattered around me. Because I have been put in chains by the Master, therefore wherever I go I carry the savor of His knowledge in every place." This is a witnessing life! When the Christian has really stretched out his empty hands, recognizing the futility of his own life, and he has been chained with his whole life to the Lord Jesus, other things in which he once trusted for life, for salvation, for death, and for eternity, lie shattered and ruined around him. He has seen the emptiness of everything that he is—except for grace and the cleansing of the precious blood—and the self-life lies in ruins. He has come to the point of no return and has crashed before God. He has seen the things in which he once trusted lying as utterly useless, but because he is chained with chains that no man can see and is bound by cords of love to the altar, wherever he goes there is something about him that brings the savor of the knowledge of the Lord, and the people do not become conscious of the human channel but of Him. So Paul witnesses to the fact that this life, no matter what it has meant in terms of testing and affliction, is a triumphant life, a testifying life. But he also says that it is a fragrant life.

"For we are unto God a sweet savour of Christ, in them that are saved, and in them that perish" (v. 15). In the paraphrase of Phillips'

Letters to Young Churches the meaning is conveyed dramatically: "Thanks be to God Who leads us, wherever we are, on His own triumphant way and makes our knowledge of Him to spread throughout the world like a lovely perfume! We Christians have the unmistakable 'scent' of Christ, discernible alike to those who are being saved and to those who are heading for death. To the latter it seems like the very smell of doom, to the former it has the fresh fragrance of life itself." Paul is saying that since he has been made a captive of his wonderful Lord, he leaves a scent wherever he goes. The real Christian, the genuine believer who has passed through this very same thing, also has a scent about him. Paul is careful to say that the scent is breathed in heaven; but not only there, for it is breathed down here on earth. He says, "For we are unto God a sweet savour of Christ." One day the Father looked down upon the Son and said, "This is my beloved Son, in whom I am well pleased; hear ye him" (Matthew 17:5). He said it at the moment of His obedience and submission to all the will of God, and He said, "This is my beloved Son." The scent, the savor, the obedience of His life and the surrender of His will went up to heaven. Your life carries with it a scent, and the aroma of it is going up to glory. I wonder if it is pungent; I wonder if it is pleasant, I wonder if it is something which reminds the angels and the Father in heaven of the day when Jesus was down here; and as He could look down upon this little planet which was in rebellion against Him, and say, "This is my beloved Son," I wonder if in some measure heaven can look down upon your life and mine and say that very same thing. Since you and I have been captive for the Lord and bound in chains to His chariot, God the Father looks down and sees you in Christ, and Christ in you, and says, "There is my beloved Son!" This is the scent of a life that is triumphant by captivity; but it is not only mounting to heaven, it is going out into the world. "...we are unto God," says Paul, "a sweet savour of Christ, in them that are saved, and in them that perish: To the one we are the savour of death unto death; and to the other the savour of life unto life." What a responsibility this is for the child of God! No wonder Paul exclaims, "...who is sufficient for these things?" Wherever he goes (as Phillips puts it) to some people he carries the very smell of doom. To those who have no use for the things of God, to the unconverted and the ungodly (not necessarily the immoral, though any man who is ungodly is immoral just for that reason), a Christian who has been made a captive of the Lord Jesus, his self-weapons lying in shattered ruins around him, carries with him the smell of doom. At least that man who is not born again, and who has not cared for the things of God, will be brought abruptly to a halt in his life as he meets a man who is a captive to the Lord. A captive is triumphant, fragrant, attractive, and the ungodly man will either have to get right with God or get rid of the Christian altogether. The smell of doom reveals to him the fact that unless he gets converted, the judgment of God is upon him.

Moreover, not only is the captive a savor of death unto death as a Christian, but he is a savor of life unto life. What fragrance, comfort, and joy come to us when, from time to time, God gives us the privilege of fellowship with captive Christians! Theirs is the scent of life! I put the question in its spiritual sense: "What sort of aroma goes up to heaven and around on earth from your life? Is it the savor of Christ, or will He have to say, as He did to Simon Peter, "…thou savourest not the things that be of God, but those that be of men" (Matthew 16:23)?

Let us return to what is perhaps the most significant thrust of this portion, and its most challenging application. It is, as I have said, a digression from the main theme of Paul's letter, and is the beginning of his great statement about what it means to be a Christian. That is evident from this whole passage, yet somehow I cannot think that we get to the real heart of our text if we consider it apart from the earlier verses of this chapter.

Why has Paul written the second time to the church at Corinth? Not simply to explain the reason why he had not come to see them again. He has written to them once more in order that they might fulfill their spiritual duty concerning a brother who had been excommunicated from the church. I do not need to go into this passage in great detail, but you will recall that while the church at Corinth was arguing and protesting about denominationalism and a thousand and one other things that caused them to be full of strife and division, they were blind to one dreadful sin that was going on in the life of at least one of their membership, the sin of immorality.

Paul had already spoken about this sinning brother: "…deliver such an one unto Satan for the destruction of the flesh, that the spirit may be saved in the day of the Lord Jesus" (1 Corinthians 5:5). In other words, Paul had already written to them concerning the absolute necessity of discipline concerning the brother who had sinned. Sin cannot be tolerated within the fellowship of the church, and the offender must be dealt with and delivered to Satan for the destruction of the flesh (but ultimately, remember, for the saving of the soul).

Now Paul writes to them again as he has something else to say to them about this. He writes from the experience of a Christian life that has been made captive to Christ and therefore is witnessing and, above all, is fragrant. (There is an area today which, I admit, is very dangerous, very delicate ground, but it is an area which desperately needs the fragrance of a Christian.) Paul says to them, concerning a brother, "Sufficient to such a man is this punishment, which was inflicted of many" (v. 6). In other words, "I am grateful to you Corinthian Christians, for doing what I asked. I am glad that you faced the necessity of discipline of the man who is excommunicated, but this punishment has gone far enough.""...contrariwise," he goes on to say, "you ought rather to forgive him, and comfort him, lest perhaps such a one should be swallowed up with overmuch sorrow. Wherefore I beseech you that you would confirm your love toward him ... Lest Satan should get an advantage of us: for we are not ignorant of his devices" (2 Corinthians 2:7–11).

Do you realize what Paul is saying? "I want something of the fragrance of your Christian life to penetrate into this area. Here is a man who has been excommunicated because of his sin. This was dealt with immediately; but now remember that God's last sentence upon a man who is repentant is never judgment but always grace. Therefore we need to be careful lest our brother be overcome with much sorrow. We are not ignorant of the devices of the devil; we must be careful that having disciplined the man we do not slay his soul. We did it for the salvation of his soul; now let us be careful, having completed one side of the treatment, that we adopt the other, lest Satan get an advantage of us. There is nothing that the devil would like to do more than, having exposed the man's sin, to keep on reminding him of it and telling him that he is of no use and never will be of any use, that he is finished for the rest of his life and quite possibly will end in hell. Now, I want you to go to that man and confirm your love to him by forgiving him and by comforting him." Do you see what we are getting at here? May the Lord help us to see that whereas—and let us confess it before God—we certainly are very neglectful these days of church discipline—afraid perhaps because of embarrassment—we are far more neglectful concerning the exercise of forgiveness of the brother who is in the wrong. Of course there must be discipline. Of course there can be no excusing sin in the name of a false kind of sentiment. Love which simply goes out in sentiment to the man who has been tripped up by the enemy is not the love of God. Love will never be shown at the expense of holiness. *But*, holiness must never be shown at the expense of slaying love.

I wonder if this is not an area into which many of us need to move. Paul says, "Forgive him and comfort him." There is a kind of forgiveness which is worth literally nothing, in which perhaps the church might welcome the man back into fellowship and then put him on probation for five years or so. His reinstatement is a sort of legalistic welcome which will always remind him that he is a failure, and which will always point a finger of accusation at him, reminding him of what he used to be. There is a kind of forgiveness which is almost like that which David offered Absalom, and because of which Absalom never saw the king's face for two years. But Paul says to this church, in effect, "I want you to forgive him and comfort him," and when forgiveness gets into the realm of comfort, I tell you that forgiveness forgets.

I am so thankful that I am a man whom God has forgiven and, praise God, whose sin has been forgotten. That is the only kind of forgiveness that would give my heart a moment's peace. When God forgave, for Jesus' sake, He buried my sins in the depth of the sea to remember them no more against me, as if they had never happened. What kind of forgiveness am I offering to others who offend? What kind of mercy do I show to the man whom Satan has tripped? Do you not see that when Paul says, in effect, "Thanks be unto God, who always leadeth us in one continual triumph in Christ, and maketh manifest the savor of His knowledge in every place, we are a savor of life unto life or death unto death," the fragrance of the Christian life is needed most in the area I have just discussed? That is the area it seldom reaches, because at that point all that the man who has stumbled may feel, at least from many of us, is the sentence of condemnation.

I pray God that as you conclude this chapter, it may be indeed as men and women who have held out their hands and their wills to be chained up by the living Christ, to live in that perfect liberty which is the outcome of bondage; and that, as the fruit of this, in your life there might be poured out the inevitable fragrance, the scent that will remind people of the Lord; and that it may be evident most of all in our forgiving mercy to those with whom, for one reason or another, we are out of fellowship. That will only be possible as we recognize that our sufficiency is of God and it is He who always leads us in triumph in every place (especially in this place of forgiveness) in Christ and so makes our knowledge of Him spread like a lovely perfume.

> Fill me with gladness from above,
>   Hold me by strength divine;
> Lord let the glow of Thy great love
>   Through my whole being shine.
>
> Make this poor self grow less and less,
>   Be Thou my life and aim.
> Oh, make me daily through Thy grace
>   More meet to bear Thy name.

CHAPTER FOUR

THE TRANSFORMED LIFE

2 CORINTHIANS 3:1–18

"**B**ut we all, with open face beholding as in a glass the glory of the Lord, are changed into the same image from glory to glory, even as by the Spirit of the Lord" (2 Corinthians 3:18). In the succeeding chapter Paul begins to open his heart concerning some of the buffetings that he has taken because he is a Christian. But before he does so, he has something to say about the resources he has found in Jesus Christ in order that he can stand the test when the buffeting comes. That is why he is able to say (4:8–9) that although he is troubled, he has not been distressed, although he is perplexed, he has never been in despair, although he has been persecuted, he has never been forsaken, and although, as Phillips put it, he has been knocked down, he has never been knocked out! Paul has been able to take the buffetings because he has made a great discovery and received a great ministry, described in the words of our text, where we too can find spiritual resources adequate for any buffeting.

This is a very practical subject, because any of us who would be followers of the Lord Jesus Christ must expect the buffetings: from within and from without; from our foes and from our friends; from Satan, who would seek to attack on every possible quarter the man who is set upon being the best for God. I am sure that none of us escapes something of the buffeting. Life is full of it, and the question that arises when the buffeting comes is, "Have I really got what it takes to stand it, or am I to become a spiritual casualty?"

As Paul opens up this subject, he contrasts what the Jew had and what the Christian had—a contrast of the revelation of the Old Testament with the revelation of the New. This is the theme of the third chapter. Notice some of contrasts between the Old and the New, contrasts which led Paul to say that in this new covenant he had discovered resources adequate for every pressure of life.

Verse 3: "...the epistle of Christ ministered by us, written not with ink, but with the Spirit of the living God; not in tables of stone, but in fleshy tables of the heart"; in other words, the revelation of God is not something which is legal or external or outside of Paul, but something that has come into the every depths of his soul, that has touched the hardness of his heart and melted it. Verse 5: "Not that we are sufficient of ourselves to think anything as of ourselves; but our sufficiency is of God"; not something that causes Paul to boast in himself, but rather something that has caused him to renounce all self-confidence and put his confidence in the Lord. Verse 6: "...not of the letter, but of the spirit: for the letter killeth, but the spirit giveth life"; not a ministry which has brought him under a sense of condemnation and guilt, but a ministry of grace which has set him free from all of that and given him life and righteousness, purity and victory.

Finally, verses 13 and 18: "And not as Moses, which put a veil over his face, that the children of Israel could not stedfastly look to the end of that which is abolished ... But we all, with open face beholding as in a glass the glory of the Lord..." Notice the contrast: not the one but the other; not the condemnation but the deliverance; not the letter but the spirit; not an external God but an internal reality; not death but life; not a veil of uncertainty concerning the things of glory and heaven, but an open face beholding the glory of the Lord.

"Now," Paul is saying, "I can take any buffeting in the reality of that experience!"

To make this simple and practical I would take three words to sum it all up as we ask, What are the resources which are adequate for any buffeting and which enable us to say, as Paul says in chapter 4:1: "...seeing we have this ministry, as we have received mercy, we faint not"? Seeing that I have this ministry—this about which he speaks in the third chapter—that is such a glorious reality to him, and has made religion not just an external obligation but an indwelling life, that has brought him out from death into liberty and joy, that has taken away the veil from his face and enabled him to see God—seeing I have received this ministry, I faint not. I have something which enables me to take it in the face of all the buffeting that comes my way, for I can always find resources that are adequate to take the knocks.

The first word is "contemplation": "…we all, with open face beholding as in a glass the glory of the Lord…" I do not think that the *King James Version* quite conveys what Paul had in mind. "…beholding as in a glass…"—if that is all I can see of the glory of the Lord (as it were, in the dimness or possibly even the distortion of a glass), this is not superior to the Old Testament, because Moses saw God face to face. Therefore I go to another translation of the New Testament to help me to get at the root of this. Actually there is one word in the Greek New Testament which is translated in all these words, "beholding as in a glass," and it is suggested that a better rendering would be "reflecting, as a glass does," the glory of God." Or again, "All of us, as with unveiled faces, we mirror the glory of the Lord" (Weymouth). Ah, that helps me! If I look into the mirror, it will only reflect that which it sees. It receives something upon its surface and then reflects that out into the world around it. We all, with unveiled faces, beholding as in a mirror, catch the light and reflect the glory of the Lord. We reflect, as a glass does, and we do it with unveiled faces.

"This," says Paul, in effect, "is my first and dynamic secret which enables me to take all the buffeting that comes my way. I have a clear view of my Savior, with open face." But, you say to me, this is impossible! What about the veils of sense and sin? What about the things that would hide our Savior from our eyes? Surely no man could look with an open face upon God!

Wait a moment—who is the One we see? Is it not the great luster of that mighty throne of all heaven? One day we will see that; one day Jesus our Lord, who has washed us in His blood and indwelt us by His Spirit, will present us faultless before the throne of glory with exceeding joy; one day we will be so transformed that we will be able to see God face to face and not shrink from the vision; but not now in this human body. Well, then, how is it Paul says he sees the glory of God? Is it not what the apostle John says to us in the opening verses of his first epistle and in his gospel: "That which was from the beginning, which we have heard, which we have seen with our eyes, which we have looked upon, and our hands have handled, of the Word of life…; That which we have seen and heard declare we unto you…" (1 John 1:1, 3); "And the Word was made flesh, and dwelt among us, (and we beheld his glory, the glory as of the only begotten of the Father,) full of grace and truth" (John 1:14).

This, claims Paul, is the One he has seen, the One who said, "...he that hath seen me hath seen the Father..." (John 14:9). He is saying, "I have had a clear view of God as He has revealed Himself to my heart in Jesus Christ, and what have I seen? I saw in Him the glory of a life lived in total abandonment to the sovereign will of His Father in heaven. I saw a life lived in utter poverty yet in absolute contentment. I saw a life triumph over every temptation that ever tempted me, and I saw Him victorious at every point where I have failed. I have seen Him come so near to the poor, to those who are sick, and to those who are in need. I have seen Him holy, separate, harmless, and undefiled; so close to the sinner yet never contaminated. Ah, but most of all I have seen His tears, I have heard His crying, and I have listened to the cry where He said, 'O my Father, if it be possible, let this cup pass from me: nevertheless not as I will, but as thou wilt' (Matthew 26:39). I have seen the nail prints, the marks in His hands and His side; I have seen the thorns on His brow. And yet, I have heard the cry, 'My God, my God, why hast thou forsaken me?' (Matthew 27:46). I have seen Him made sin on my behalf, God in Christ, reconciling the world to Himself. I have seen the glory of God in the face of Jesus Christ and, bless His holy name, I have seen an empty tomb, an ascended Savior, and I have met Him face to face when He said to me, 'Saul, why persecutest thou me?... it is hard for thee to kick against the pricks' (Acts 9:4–5).

"I have had a clear view of Jesus. I have seen Him, felt Him, and I have known Him in a far deeper way than simply by the outward physical appearance; I have felt the reality of His life begin to burn in my heart. I have seen in Christ the glory of a life that is totally submitted to the sovereignty of God. That glory has begun to take hold of me, and I have begun to see that this is the one life that God expects of any man He made in His own image. I have seen the marks of the cross upon Him, and by His grace the marks of the cross have been put upon me and I am no longer my own; I am bought with a price, redeemed by His precious blood. Yes, I have seen Him—not in the outward physical sense only, but in the inward sense of a deep spiritual reality. I have had a clear view of Jesus and my life will never be the same again."

But who has seen Him? Is it only the giants, like Paul? "...we all, with open face beholding as in a glass the glory of the Lord...." *We all*—not merely the Moseses, the Elijahs, the spiritual aristocracy of the Old Testament times and the whole multitude afraid at a distance in the valley; not only Paul on his face on the Damascus road, blinded by the vision—*we all*, the weakest, the poorest, the most sinful, the most defiled. The spiritual aristocracy of the church of Jesus Christ is not the preacher or the prophet, but the sinner saved by grace. It is the soul who has come like the publican of old and said, "God be merciful to me a sinner" (Luke 18:13), and it is the soul bowed before Calvary and seeing (as Paul saw) the glory of God in the face of Jesus Christ. As the epistle to the Hebrews reads, "Having therefore, brethren, boldness to enter into the holiest by the blood of Jesus, By a new and living way, which he hath consecrated for us, through the veil, that is to say, his flesh...; Let us draw near with a true heart in full assurance of faith..." (10:19–22). Paul's resources are dug deep in the fact that he had a clear view of his wonderful Lord.

Let me pause to ask you solemnly in the presence of God—you are taking the buffetings, aren't you? The buffetings of the devil in your soul? The buffetings in the home life which is perhaps so utterly and hopelessly confused and divided? The buffetings of lack of understanding from your friends who couldn't care less, and perhaps from your parents too? You are taking the buffetings? Beloved, have you got what it takes? Have you now a clear view of Jesus? You see, we all, with open face—the veil removed, rent in two by His cross—draw near in full assurance of faith, and we see Him. Have you looked into His lovely face in contemplation? Oh, not just a moment's glance while upon your knees with your Scripture portion and then a dash out into the world. Not just a long time spent in preparing the fashion of the body to come to the house of God, or to meet the onslaught of the day—but a long time in preparing the heart as you have gazed upon your lovely Lord. Have you met Him like that today? A clear view of Jesus Christ is that which is needed to take all that comes across our path.

My second word is "reflection" and, as I have said to you before, what a mirror sees it reflects, and it can reflect only what it sees and what it receives. We, all of us, with unveiled faces, mirror the glory of the Lord. You see, in the life of a man who has seen Christ—the glory of God in the life, death, and resurrection of our Lord, the glory of God in a life submitted to the sovereignty of His Father—inevitably truth begins to dominate character, and the life of Jesus Christ begins to be reproduced in and through him. Don't you think it is a very lovely thing? Have you watched it through life? When a husband and wife live together for many years and they are devoted to each other, finding the center of their affection in the living Lord Jesus, don't you think it is a wonderful thing that, as they live and pray together, walk and talk together, they become not only like Him, but like each other? Put an iron within range of a magnet and the iron becomes magnetized.

> Turn your eyes upon Jesus,
> Look full in His wonderful face;
> And the things of earth will grow strangely dim
> In the light of His glory and grace.

Turn your eyes upon Jesus not with the quick look but the gaze, and believe me, that which you see becomes a very part of your life and character—"...reflecting as does a mirror."

You see, the whole argument and force of this is simply, as Paul says, "In whom the god of this world hath blinded the minds of them which believe not, lest the light of the glorious gospel of Christ, who is the image of God, should shine unto them" (2 Corinthians 4:4). That is the fate of a man who is unsaved.

My friend, you don't blame people for living as they do. You cannot hold up, as it were, holy hands in horror as you see the world live. What do you expect? That is the way the natural man does live—you don't expect him to live on any higher level! It may be expressed in different ways, but the root of it is that the god of this present world has blinded the eyes, the minds, of them that believe not; and I ask you, who in the name of heaven has the power to take the veil from ungodly faces, to take the blindness out of an ungodly man's mind? Do you think that a university education will do it? It will not. Do you think that brilliance of intellect will do it? Never. Do you think that an outstanding grasp of theology will do it? No. I will tell you what will: "For God, who commanded the light to shine out of darkness, hath shined in our hearts, to give the light of the knowledge of the glory of God in the face of Jesus Christ" (2 Corinthians 4:6). That is what will do it.

The man who gazes upon and contemplates day by day the face of the Lord Jesus Christ, and who has caught the glow of the reality that the Lord is not a theory but an indwelling power and force in his life, is as a mirror reflecting the glory of the Lord. Wherever he goes, people begin to ask questions as to why he triumphs when others fail; why it is when at business everything is at sixes and sevens and all is upset and confused, he maintains a sense of poise; how it is, when facing buffeting of one kind or another, he reacts with such patience; how it is, when the general level of conversation is so impure he is never dragged down, and how he stands above it, not in a sense of rebuke to others but in a sense of testimony to the fact that, because he belongs to God, he cannot descend to another level. He has caught the glow and is reflecting it. *We all* reflect as in a mirror. Has anything been getting through to your life?—any light, any reflection, any glow?

It was over thirty years ago that the Lord Jesus met me when I was far away from Him, and I came to Christ through the testimony of an office colleague, who did not preach at me but lived Christ before me, and by whose life I was condemned. I met him recently at Keswick, and again it was my privilege to be alongside my spiritual father and listen to some of the things he had to say. He rose to the top of the tree in business, becoming very successful, but as we talked together, I was reminded of some words he had spoken years previously: "I have found in my life that as far as business success is concerned, with all its pressures, the price in terms of eternity is too great to pay."

Is there any light getting through? Is any of the glory of God getting through to others through your life? If not, perhaps it is because the pressures upon you are so great. In your home, in the care of that precious little family, in your responsibilities in business life, in the pressure of study—be careful that the price in terms of eternity is not too great. Be careful to recognize that if the light is not getting through, it is because you are not looking at Him long enough.

Our third word is "transformation": "But all of us as with unveiled faces we mirror the glory of the Lord are transformed into the same likeness, from glory to glory, even as derived from the Lord, the Spirit" (Weymouth). Here Paul is saying that the secret of his ability to stand in the power of the Lord against all of the buffetings of life is not simply that he has beheld Him in Jesus Christ and therefore reflects Him to others, but that as he beholds Him he is being transformed into His own likeness. "...ye shall know the truth, and the truth shall make you free" (John 8:32), said our precious Lord, and that word "set you free" is the same one as is used here for the word "liberty"—"...where the Spirit of the Lord is, there is liberty" (2 Corinthians 3:17) — freedom, deliverance. Paul tells us that our ability to take things and to stand against all that Satan flings at us means we are learning the secret as we behold Jesus. He lifts us up above it all, and by His power we stand where once we used to fall; and so we are transformed.

Maybe the great concern in your heart today is that this life might be your life, that this ability to take things might be yours. I wonder if that statement which I have just made comes to you as good news? Are you battling with yourself, defeated in life, going down under the buffeting? You face so many battles! None of us stands above you in this, because we know it all in our own hearts, but we would gladly tell you the good news that you overcome not by battle but by faith. You overcome not by inward struggle but by upward look. Any battle for victory, power, and deliverance — from ourselves and from sin — which is not based constantly upon the gazing and the beholding of the Lord Jesus, with the heart and life lifted up to Him, is doomed to failure.

If I could just get across to you the word that the Holy Spirit would quietly speak to you, it would be: "Give up the struggle and the fight; relax in the omnipotence of the Lord Jesus; look up into His lovely face and as you behold Him, He will transform you into His likeness. You do the beholding — He does the transforming. There is no short-cut to holiness."

"...Changed into the same image from glory to glory..." (v. 18) — this is a lifelong, glorious experience, and it will be perfected one day in heaven. Paul tells us (Philippians 3:21) that He "shall change our vile body [this body of sin in which dwells no good thing], that it may be fashioned like unto his glorious body. ..." Yes, He will do that!

It will all be perfected one day. In the language of Ephesians 4:13: "Till we all come in the unity of the faith, and of the knowledge of the Son of God, unto a perfect man..." — not unto multitudes of perfect people but unto a perfect man. It takes all of the church through every generation every color, every race, all living in contemplation of the Lord Jesus, reflecting His glory and being transformed into His likeness; it takes every one of us, redeemed by blood, the whole temple of the Spirit, the whole body of Christ, one day to be made a perfect man like Him. It is going to be perfected one day.

Meanwhile, day by day, through this life in which you live amid all the pressures of circumstances, are you able to say with the apostle

Paul, in effect, "Therefore having received this ministry, I faint not" (2 Corinthians 4:1)? Buffeted, knocked down but never knocked out, cast down but never in despair, persecuted but never forsaken, because — praise the Lord! — you have found the answer to what it takes to stand in the ministry you have received: a clear view of Jesus, in contemplation; in reflection of His glory in the midst of the battle; and then being made like unto Him as day by day your heart is lifted up to the Lord Jesus and He imparts to your life the sweetness and loveliness of His character. Oh, may that be your portion this day as you are able to say, "Thank God, by grace, I have got what it takes!" I have received a ministry: contemplation, reflection, transformation.

———————————— ✝ ————————————

CHAPTER FIVE

The Price of Fruitfulness

2 Corinthians 4:1–12

"For God, who commanded the light to shine out of darkness, hath shined in our hearts, to give the light of the knowledge of the glory of God in the face of Jesus Christ" (2 Corinthians 4:6). Phillips puts it like this: "God, Who first ordered Light to shine in darkness has flooded our hearts with His Light. We can now enlighten men only because we can give them knowledge of the glory of God, as we see it in the face of Jesus Christ."

In this chapter Paul has some tremendous things to say concerning the ministry. It is here that he opens his heart and speaks to us regarding what it means to him to be a minister of the gospel. This chapter is a tremendous challenge, a great comfort, and a great revelation of God's purposes for each one of us as His servants.

Paul speaks first about the character of the ministry in the words of our text. What is this ministry? "The ministry which I have received," he calls it, and this, in effect, is what he received: "God hath shined in our hearts to give the light of the glory of God in the face of Jesus Christ."

But this ministry which has been received must be communicated, and I notice that in the fifth verse he says: "…we preach not ourselves, but Christ Jesus our Lord; and ourselves your servants for Jesus' sake." And then Paul explains that we can only communicate this truth and this ministry at great personal cost: "So then death worketh in us, but life in you" (v. 12).

Our subject, therefore, is this whole matter of Christian ministry, and I would remind you that this is something which involves every one of us. You often hear it said of a particular individual that he has had a call to the ministry, and of course we know what is meant by that: such a person has given his life for training and preparation for preaching the gospel. But the truth is that from the moment the Holy Spirit reveals to us Jesus Christ and comes to live in our hearts and we are born again, life becomes a ministry. It is no longer a self-seeking, aimless, purposeless existence, but it is a ministry. Just as a rug is laid on a floor, so a man who has met God in the face of Jesus Christ begins to lay down his life in the service of Christ and of others. "For even the Son of man came not to be ministered unto, but to minister, and to give his life a ransom for many" (Mark 10:45). This is the principle which must grip not only those who may be called into the ministry in the first and primary sense, but all who have been redeemed by the blood of Christ and who share the life of His indwelling Spirit. To all such, life becomes a ministry. As we think about this ministry, we must ask ourselves if we really are in the ministry. Is God using it and blessing it for His honor and for His glory?

First of all, let us consider the character of this ministry: What is it that we have received? "…God, who commanded the light to shine out of darkness, hath shined in our hearts, to give the light of the knowledge of the glory of God in the face of Jesus Christ." As in the creation, God's first words were, "Let there be light," so in that tremendous moment when we were born of the Spirit of God, the light dawned and shone into our hearts. It shone not merely as an influence, not only as a doctrine or creed, but it shone in the revelation to our hearts by His Spirit in the person and in the face of Jesus Christ. As Paul says, (Galatians 1:15–16), "…it pleased God. To reveal his Son in me…"

Think now about the face of Jesus Christ. Have you ever looked into His face? This is a theme that would baffle any preacher, and even an angel in heaven would seem to be inadequate to proclaim it, but I would try to talk to you about the face of Jesus Christ. For it is only those who have gazed into His face and understood something of that revelation who know anything of life as a ministry.

As you look into the face of Jesus Christ you can see it from so many different angles and viewpoints. For instance, I look into the face of Jesus Christ when God became a Baby, and I think of Him in a manger, and

I see Him there as One who has turned aside completely from all self-seeking and all things that fill our minds and dominate our lives. It could have happened in a palace, it could have taken place in a mansion, but surely there is a tremendous glimpse of the glory of God in the face of Jesus Christ as in poverty He came to Bethlehem.

Again, I think of Him as a child of twelve as He sat and taught in the Temple, and with a Spirit-instructed mind He baffled all the learned professors of His day. They "were astonished at his understanding and answers" (Luke 2:47). I see the glory of God in the face of Jesus Christ as He taught there.

I see Him in a carpenter's shop in Nazareth, standing among the shavings. I see something of the glory of God in the face of Jesus Christ, in the divine leisureliness in the heart of our Lord as He was content to await God's time there, knowing that His hour had not yet come. In quietness and confidence in all those surroundings He worked in that carpenter's shop. He became the Carpenter (no *a*, as one of many, but *the* carpenter of Nazareth). Nothing imperfect ever came from His shop.

I think of Him too in His ministry as He fed five thousand people with a few loaves and fishes, and met every need. I hear the word of authority as it comes from His lips, and I see the devils begin to tremble and acknowledge His absolute sovereignty. I see the glory of God in the face of Jesus Christ as He rebukes the powers of sin. As He ministers, every tone of His voice and every look on His face, and every word He speaks—whether it be a word of tenderness and gentleness or a stern rebuke—reveals the glory of God in the face of Jesus Christ.

But I see Him most wonderfully on the cross, for surely there is no place that the glory of God in the face of Jesus Christ is revealed more clearly as at Calvary, where He laid down His life for us. I see the glory of the love of God that stooped so far in order to save us from our sin; and I see the glory of the justice of God in the face of Jesus Christ who allowed Himself to be made sin for us rather than that sin should go unpunished or that the Lord God should be dishonored. To those who have eyes to see, the glory of God in the face of Jesus Christ is revealed, as nowhere else, at the cross of Calvary.

But I think of Him too on the third day when He arose again triumphant over the grave and over all the powers of evil. As He ascended into heaven, all heaven's host fell down to worship the Lamb of God who had been slain, and who had risen again. Here is the glory of God in the face of our ascended Lord! And in my mind I see it even more glorious on that day when He shall come as King of kings and Lord of lords, and before Him every knee shall bow and every tongue confess that He is Lord; and I can see that same Lord Jesus and the glory of God shining through.

"Now," says Paul, in effect, "This is what I have seen, this is the revelation that has come to my heart, this is the ministry that I have received. As the sum and substance of it, there is a person, there is a life, there is God manifest in Jesus Christ. The light of the knowledge of the glory of God in the face of Jesus Christ has shined into my heart and I have looked into His face. I have seen His lowliness, His leisureliness, His authority over the powers of sin, His release of life from the empty tomb, His ascension into heaven—and one day I will see Him come back. Yes, I have seen the glory of God in the face of Jesus Christ, and I have received this ministry, for because of Calvary there has been a Pentecost, and the ascended Lord has brought me in repentance to His feet, and now it is Christ *in* me."

Such is the character of our ministry: the glory of God in the face of Jesus Christ. Have you seen God in Jesus? All that you could ever know of God you will find in the Lord Jesus Christ. Have you gazed into His face and recognized His grace and love, His tenderness and authority, His atonement, His resurrection, His ascension, and His reign in glory? One day He is coming back. All the sum and substance of what God has to say to this world is said when He has spoken in these last days in His Son. Have you looked into the face of Jesus Christ like that, and has that look brought you in submission to His feet to receive His Spirit into your heart, or the life of an indwelling Lord? We have nothing to say or to give to a poor world today except as we have received that ministry in the person of our Lord. I think that if we gazed into His face, we would be a lot more reverent in our living; we would be more careful in our speech and more dignified in our bearing as Christian people. There would be about us the marks of men who have met God in the glory and in the face of Jesus Christ in all His greatness, and this would take the lightness and the superficiality out of our living. The church which broke the Savior's heart was full of hard work, sacrificial service, patience, and sound doctrine, *but* it had lost its first love, its paramount love. Has something happened to cool *your* ardor? All affection dies if it is not nourished. The beginning of breakdown occurs when we take each other for granted. Love withers if it is not fed, for then it cannot stand up to the strains imposed upon it. That is true spirituality. Your ministry can go to seed or to externals. You may have all the mechanisms, but if the white flame of love has gone, you have fallen. You can be a fallen Christian without a stain on your moral character if the fire has gone out.

If you have seen the glory of God in the face of Jesus Christ, you will never be the same again. But this is not something to enjoy selfishly, for Paul speaks about the communication of this ministry: "For we preach not ourselves, but Christ Jesus the Lord; and ourselves your servants for Jesus' sake" (v. 5). This is Paul's concern constantly, for he adds, "...that the life also of Jesus might be made manifest in our body ... that the life also of Jesus might be made manifest in our mortal flesh" (v. 10–11).

Paul has received this ministry—and so have you—not for selfish enjoyment but for its communication through you to others. And it is the unique responsibility (I say "unique" because nobody else is capable of doing it) of the man redeemed and indwelt by Christ to communicate Him to others. That which lies at the root of all suffering and unhappiness, that which is at the bottom of so much tension in personal living and church life, is not so much some things outside ourselves, but it is ourselves, individually. It is the self which is always seeing to be exalted, praised, vindicated, with the result that Christ Himself is put into the background. This is the principle of life upon which the world lives, in which it exalts self and dethrones God. Now, when you become a Christian, you are redeemed in order that this new principle of life—in which you no longer proclaim yourself but proclaim Christ Jesus the Lord—becomes that which is communicated to others.

Let me ask you lovingly and earnestly, Whom are you proclaiming, not only by speech but by living? Let us remind ourselves of the glory of God in the face of Jesus Christ; this glory must shine through the Christian, this ministry must be communicated so that we may make manifest in these mortal bodies of ours the life of the Lord Jesus. In other words, there is a life to be revealed—not just a system of theology, but a life, a character, a principle of action—through the Christian church which is the only hope amid the darkness, immorality, and spiritual bankruptcy of the world today.

We have seen a little glimpse of the glory of God in the face of Jesus Christ as He lay in a manger, as He despised things that we hold so important in life, as He went right through in His great stoop down to poverty. I wonder if we have anything of that in us today—of that character which despises things that the world holds very close, which enables us to hold lightly all that people hold so tightly to themselves? I wonder if the spirit of the manger, the lowliness and self-humiliation that took our precious Lord right down to such depths, has gripped our hearts and lives as Christian people?

Consider the glory of God in the face of Jesus Christ as He taught and confounded the so-called intellectualism of His day. The Spirit-taught mind is the portion of the person who, through waiting upon God, has been taught by the Spirit of God, and in whose life it is equally true that the foolishness of God is wiser than men, and who has within him the light and enlightenment of soul that can never be obtained from any university anywhere. It has come because it has been imparted by the Holy Spirit into the heart from heaven, "For he shall take of the things of Christ and reveal them unto you ... He shall guide you into all truth," in effect, said our Master. He it is who will take of the things of Christ and reveal them to you. He imparts truth to you as no other ever could. Is yours a Spirit-taught mind, a life with the ability in the Holy Spirit to teach what only He can impart?

Again, is there about our lives, as there was about the Lord Jesus (and how this hits home in these days of haste and feverish rush!), a leisureliness of spirit, a quietness of heart, a readiness day by day to wait upon Him for His guidance and direction? Or are we just blustering our way through at our own pace and in our own time, far outmatching the pace of God and leaving behind altogether the guiding of His Spirit? Is yours a leisurely heart today? Spiritual leisureliness and human pressures are not necessarily antagonistic to each other. If there was anybody who knew pressure upon Him, it was the Master, but in the midst of it all there was a divine leisureliness of soul. And this is what a feverish world needs to see and to have revealed to it: that quietness of spirit, that absence of strain and tension, that sense of release in the Spirit of Christ.

> Drop Thy still dews of quietness,
> Till all our strivings cease ...
>
> ... And let our ordered lives confess
> The beauty of Thy peace.

Is there in your heart, as there was in the life of the Lord Jesus, that same sense of authority and power to say "no" to the devil and "yes" to the Lord? Is there the same absolute authority that can keep the flesh in subjection when Satan tempts with all his fiery darts, and that ability to say "yes" to the will of God? As Jesus rebuked the powers of evil, is He by His Spirit rebuking them in your life? Because He has come to dwell in your heart, is there that word of deliverance, that word of power so that when you are faced with all the pressures imaginable, you can stand in the power of God and say "no" to the thing you know is wrong, and "yes" to the Lord?

Is Christ by His life being made manifest through you? Is there any communication of His character through you today? This is why we have had the revelation, and this is why God has shined into our hearts in the light of His knowledge in the glory of the face of Christ. Are you communicating? Whom are we preaching? "We preach not ourselves," says Paul, "but Christ Jesus our Lord." This life is manifest in our mortal flesh so that every child of God, wherever he goes, is a living replica, in some measure at least, of the life of Jesus. This is the great means of communication for which the church exists, and for which you and I are to live day by day.

If there is to be any communication, however, it will prove to be a costly business, and Paul takes the rest of this passage of Scripture to speak to us about the cost of such a life.

J. B. Phillips put it so graphically: "This priceless treasure we hold, so to speak, in a common earthenware jar—to show that the splendid power of it belongs to God and not to us. We are handicapped on all sides but we are never frustrated: we are puzzled, but never in despair; We are persecuted, but we never have to stand it alone: we may be knocked down but we are never knocked out! Every day we experience something of the death of the Lord Jesus, so that we may also know the power of the life of Jesus in these bodies of ours. We are always facing death, but this means that you know more and more of life."

Here we have brought to us the cost of communication. If we would communicate the character of Jesus (and this is the purpose of our salvation), there is a price we must pay: "So then death worketh in us, but life in you" (v. 12). See it again in the opening part of verses 10 and 11: "Always bearing about in the body the dying of the Lord Jesus, ... we which live are always delivered unto death for Jesus' sake...."

So Paul tells us a little bit about what it meant to him in order that the character of Christ may get through him, and be communicated to others. Why should this be so costly? Because the whole principle of Christian living is totally contrary to the principle on which everyone else lives. The principle of the world is "self-glorification," and the principle of the Christian is "self-crucifixion." The principle of the world is "exalt yourself," and the principle of the Christian is "crucify yourself." The principle of men is greatness, bigness, pomp, and show; the principle of the cross is death. Therefore, whenever a man has seen the glory of God in the face of Jesus Christ and recognizes that this is for communication, at once he comes right into a head-on collision within his own personal living, with all of his principles and motives upon which he has lived until this moment. For, you see — and I hope that every one of us will get this in our souls and that it will burn there like a fire from the Word of God — if there is to be a continual manifestation of Holy Spirit life, there must be a constant submission to the crucifixion of the flesh, not simply sometimes, but *always*.

There is the cost. And the cost in the Christian life does not mean that of necessity the Christian has to give up things which he once enjoyed. You may never go near a motion picture theater; you may be very selective in your use of the television; you may have put a taboo on tobacco and alcohol — but none of these things touches this issue of the price to be paid to communicate the life of Christ to others. It is far deeper than that, for deep down in the Christian's life, always and all the time, there is to be a "no" to every demand that the flesh may make for recognition, and every demand that the flesh may make for vindication. Always the Christian must bear about in his body the marks of the Lord Jesus. There is never a breaking through of communication of His life in your heart and through you to others in heavenly conviction and authority which will challenge or bless them unless at that point there has been a personal Calvary.

Remember the tremendous statement our Lord Jesus made on the last day of the feast: "If any man thirst, let him come unto me, and drink. He that believeth on me, ... out of his belly shall flow rivers of living water" (John 7:37–38). And then later, by explanation, John said, "...this spake he of the Spirit which they that believe on him should receive: for the Holy Ghost was not yet given; because that Jesus was not yet glorified" (John 7:39).

Do not let ourselves be involved in a dispensational argument at this point; this is not what is at stake. The issue is whether the life of Jesus

Christ is being communicated. Is the Holy Spirit getting through? Is the life of Christ manifest in you day by day in your contact with others? If it is not, it is because Jesus is not yet glorified.

He received of the Father the promise of the Holy Spirit *after* Calvary, and there is no Pentecost without a Calvary. It is of no use crying to God for the unction and power of God the Holy Ghost, because He will constantly point you back again to the cross, and say to you, "If you are prepared to face this principle of always bearing about in your body the death of Jesus Christ, then inevitably the Spirit will get through." That is a heavenly principle.

But somebody may ask, "What do you mean by 'bearing about in the body the dying of the Lord Jesus'?" I could not possibly quote this in terms of personal example to any of you in the situation of your life, but I can give you a simple principle, and I believe you can relate it to your own personal context. Whereas in a given situation of circumstances up to this point, there would naturally and normally be an immediate reaction which reveals self, there is now a reaction which reveals the character of Jesus Christ. Where once you showed resentment, now you are long-suffering. Where once you were angry, now you are gentle. Where once you demanded vindication of your position, now you are happy to leave it all in His hands.

I heard a Christian saying to another Christian, "You know, when so-and-so spoke about me like that, it was only natural for me to react as I did." Exactly—only natural! And that is the level upon which so many professing Christians live. The result is that the Holy Spirit never gets through, and there is no communication or manifestation of the life of Jesus.

Now I complete the circle of the message by going back to the point at which I began. I spoke of the ministry of the Christian life being like the laying down of a rug upon which other people walk and receive comfort and are helped. The whole principle of Christian living as a ministry is a life which reacts like that. In all situations and in every circumstance, there is death to my likes and wishes, to my ideas and ambitions and my rights, for a Christian's only right is to do the will of God. And immediately there is the communication of the life of Jesus Christ!

When Satan comes in like a flood, as he did in attacking our Lord, what is your reaction? Do you reveal self and lose the battle? Or do you reveal Christ and so gain a victory? There is always victory through the simple principle of accepting death and saying, "Lord, in this thing I am helpless, and I die to every effort to overcome. I look up into Thy face and I expect the communication of Holy Spirit life upon the altar of self-crucifixion."

It all comes to this: I see the glory of God in the face of Jesus Christ, in the measure in which I am prepared to die. Upon a crucified life there comes the authority of the Holy Ghost and the communication of the life of Jesus Christ in blessing to others. Why is it that so many Christians behave like kindergarten children? Because they have not seen His face! That is the only hope for the church today. That is basically the only answer—the life of Jesus manifest in this mortal body.

May the Lord give you a ministry that sees the glory of God in the face of Jesus Christ. Then the Lord will enable you to communicate that life as you yourself face the price of it in death.

> And all through life I see a cross—
> Where sons of God yield up their breath;
> There is no gain except by loss;
> There is no life except by death;
> There is no vision but by faith,
> No glory but in bearing shame,
> No justice but in taking blame.
> And that Eternal Savior saith,
> Be emptied now of right and name.

In an art gallery there is a portrait of the great General Booth, with radiant, glowing face, bent in prayer over an open Bible. One evening, as the janitor was closing that room for the day, and all the crowd had gone, he found an old man gazing at the picture with tears streaming down his face and saying over and over again, "Lord, do it again, do it again." Would you say that to Him now?

CHAPTER SIX

Strength for
the Battle

2 Corinthians 4:17–18

In our previous chapter we underlined the fact that the Christian ministry is not a question for the man in the pulpit only, but because from the moment we receive Christ into our lives as Savior and Lord, life becomes a ministry. No longer is it an aimless existence to satisfy ourselves; it becomes a ministry for the blessing of other people. The church is the only organization in the world which exists entirely for the sake of those who are not members of it.

Naturally, then, in the sequence of his thought, Paul, having exposed to us the real nature of the ministry and what is involved in it, now tells us how he receives strength for the battle; and that is what we all need to know. If the ministry means that Jesus Christ is to be communicated by the power of His Spirit, and if it is to involve us day by day in the principle of the cross and death to ourselves, how do we receive strength for the battle? What is the secret of motivation? May the Lord make the answer very real and personal to us.

It is fascinating to notice how Paul describes this battle. Let us look at his *description* in verse 17: "For our light affliction, which is but for a moment, worketh for us a far more exceeding and eternal weight of glory." This is what he says the ministry is to him. It involves affliction, and the trouble with so many people is that the affliction has seemed so great and the battle so strong that they have fallen by the wayside. There have been casualties—on the mission field, in home ministry, and in Christian testimony. The battle has been too hot; the enemy fire has been too heavy.

But Paul speaks of the struggle as only a trivial affliction. We are tempted to say that if it was only a light affliction to him, he could not possibly have known our suffering. He could not have known how you have suffered from pain for years, could he? He could not know anything about what you've been through! Light affliction? He's no man to tell us about this if he has known only light affliction. Look at what we've faced!

Oh, but wait! Was this the kind of thing about which Paul was speaking? Not at all. If you want to spell out affliction, you can spell it out over Paul's life in these words: "Are they ministers of Christ? (I speak as a fool) I am more; in labours more abundant, in stripes above measure, in prisons more frequent, in deaths oft. Of the Jews five times received I forty stripes save one. Thrice was I beaten with rods, once was I stoned, thrice I suffered shipwreck, a night and a day I have been in the deep; In journeyings often, in perils of waters, in perils of robbers, in perils by mine own countrymen, in perils by the heathen, in perils in the city, in perils in the wilderness, in perils in the sea, in perils among false brethren; In weariness and painfulness, in watchings often, in hunger and thirst, in fastings often, in cold and nakedness. Beside those things that are without, that which cometh upon me daily, the care of all the churches" (2 Corinthians 11:23–28).

Light affliction? Do you notice that nothing on that list is the kind of thing about which we talk and complain that we have to endure? Remember, though, that Paul was not free from such things. He could speak about "a thorn in the flesh," but this light affliction, as he calls it, is a realm of suffering that came to him simply because he was a Christian. It is the kind of thing that is inevitable the moment a man takes his stand in his life for the thing that is right; the moment his life and character begin to be governed in the light of eternity—from that moment there is affliction, multiplied affliction. This is the kind of thing Paul is talking about. And yet, all that he went through was not really necessary! He could have avoided and escaped every bit of it. So can you; so can I; but if he was to be true to his Master, if he was to be real in his Christian profession, inevitably and constantly this must come to him. And he calls it "light affliction"!

It comes to you when in a godless home you bow your head at a meal and ask a blessing; when for the first moment in a home where people do not understand, you give a word of testimony; when those who love you most begin to laugh at you. It happens in a business when you stand clear of the thing that is disreputable. It happens on the mission field when you refuse to allow yourself to descend to the level of the average Christian life. It happens in daily life, constantly, when a man recognizes that because he belongs to the Lord he must live according to a new principle. From the moment he begins by grace to live Christ, there comes upon him what Paul calls "light affliction."

Because we know that some of this is inevitable, some of us have flinched from it at one time or another. What Paul calls "light affliction" perhaps has been too heavy for us. There have been moments when the affliction and the pressure of it all has been so great that we have given in. We feared the loss of prestige, or the loss of popularity, and because of that some are no longer in the fight as Paul was. They have no heart for battle any more. But this light affliction is purely trivial, that is all. Not only is it trivial; Paul says it is temporary: "…light affliction, which is but for a moment…" (v. 17).

"Well, Paul, when do you expect to be free from it?"

"At the moment when I see Jesus face to face; not until then. I have in the name of the Lord declared myself on His side. That has meant for me the renouncing of sin, the renouncing of a self-seeking existence, and the beginning of life as a ministry. And because of this I am expecting all through my life to know this light affliction. There will be no escape, but it is only for a moment. In the light of the truth, as I see it, in the light of eternity, it is not going to last long—perhaps a decade, perhaps two decades, I do not know. But how short a time in comparison with eternity! It is only temporary."

Not only that, but it is a transforming affliction, for Paul says it "worketh *for* us a far more exceeding and eternal weight of glory" (v. 17). Notice the contrast: affliction, glory; light affliction, weight of glory; light affliction that is but for a moment, weight of glory that is eternal. This affliction, this thing that happens inevitably because I am a Christian, this constant sense of attack from without and within because I am true to the Lord, is working for me—as it were, hammering out for me—an eternal weight of glory. That is Paul's description of the affliction. That is how he describes the battle: trivial, temporary, transforming. Oh, that heaven could be so real to us that we could live in that sense of liberty and power!

But if this is how he describes the battle, I want to look more closely at the context to learn how Paul finds the secret of deliverance in it. From where does he get his strength? What is it that makes him feel it is so worthwhile to be on the Lord's side even though it brings affliction upon him every day? The kind of suffering about which the unbeliever knows not a thing is happening to the Christian constantly. And Paul says it is working *for* him. It is worth every minute of it, and he is thankful for it. How do you get strength like that for a battle?

Paul would tell us he found it because he looked somewhere. He has looked at the things that are unseen, eternal, not at the things that are seen because they are merely temporal. The word used for "look" in this verse does not mean a casual glance; it is the word you would use if you were to pick up a telescope and try to bring something far away into view and into focus. It is a word that suggests an intense examination, a constant scrutiny, a steady gaze.

Now, Paul says, because I have looked and understood, because I have taken the time not to glance casually at spiritual things, but sat down and thought them through and examined them with my mind and my heart until they came into clear focus, something tremendous has happened in my life. Because I looked so intensely, that look brought conviction. What sort of conviction? "We having the same spirit of faith, according as it is written, I believed, and therefore have I spoken; we also believe, and therefore speak; Knowing that he which raised up the Lord Jesus shall raise up us also by Jesus, and shall present us with you" (vv. 13–14).

"I have looked long into the face of my Lord," says Paul, in effect, "I have looked beyond this earthly life. As I have gazed, I have thought about heaven, and because of this I have a faith like they had in Old Testament times. As they believed, so I believe, and therefore I speak. I have been gripped by this same spirit of faith because this has become a conviction that the God who raised Jesus from the dead is going to raise me also together with you. And one day we are going to meet again in heaven, and stand beside each other as we have ministered to each other here upon earth. We are going to stand together before the judgment seat of Christ to give an account of the things done in our bodies. Because I believe this, I can never be the same man again. No longer can I hold the truth as a mere theory; no longer can I simply discuss the correctness of doctrine. I have been gripped by the realty that one day I am going to meet God face to face. I am going to stand before the judgment seat of Christ, and you will stand there too."

But somebody says, "That is not a place to be afraid of—that is the believers' prize day! I shall never be afraid at the great white throne of judgment!" No, bless God, if you are saved by grace and redeemed by blood and your name is written in the Book of Life, you will not be. But surely, then, this place is a place to look forward to, this judgment seat of Christ, where I receive my reward and I am given a position of privilege in heaven.

It is not only that. I ask you to observe what Paul said of it in the following chapter: "Knowing therefore the terror of the Lord..." (5:11). This is the thing that grips the heart of the apostle. One day he and the Corinthian Christians are going to stand together before the judgment seat of Christ. He has said some things to them and said them very plainly. He talked to them about a brother who had to be excommunicated from the church, and pleaded with them about carnal Christian living, that they might recognize that it is spirituality and not carnality that is going to count. He has done this, and they have misunderstood his apostleship and his message. One day he is going to give an account for his ministry before the judgment seat of Christ, and they are going to give an account concerning their response to it. Because he believes, this eternity has gripped his soul, and the things of time do not matter except that one day when he stands before Christ he shall by His grace be without blame.

"...we look not at the things which are seen, but at the things which are not seen. ..." (4:18). My friend, it may only be one decade, it may be two—I do not know. But this much I do know—one day pastor and people will stand together before the judgment seat of Christ. That is a very solemn thought to me as I look back over twenty-five years of pastoral ministry. How have I acted? Have I been kind, have I been loving, have I been gracious, have I been Christ-like? Have I lived in a way that is worthy of a servant of God? Have I prayed behind my ministry as I ought to have done? Would there have been far more blessing in London, Chicago, and in Edinburgh than there has been if I had been the man I ought to have been? These things I have been asking myself as my soul has been gripped with this verse.

Lovingly, let me ask—How have you reacted and what has been your response to the message through the many years that you may have sat under the ministry of some servant of God? What has been your conversation outside the church concerning the preacher and the leadership? How have you received the ministry? Has it been kind, has it been Christ-like, has it been gracious? God who raised up Jesus shall also raise me up together with you, and we shall stand and look into His face. Will I have cause then to hide my head in shame for my failure to pray, my failure to speak as God would have me speak, my failure to love as God would have had me love, my failure to respond in terms of a crucified life? Will you have cause to be ashamed because you have failed to respond, failed to love, and failed to pray? You never attend a prayer meeting; you never stand with others at an open-air meeting. You have not really been behind your pastor. Have you thought about it in relation to eternity and the judgment seat of Christ? I think I can truly say I have taken a look in some measure as Paul did, and I have gazed long into the face of Jesus, so that the greatest reality is not the things of time, but the judgment seat of Jesus Christ. Somehow your life and mine must be regulated by that conviction.

A conviction, yes, but not only as he looked did Paul become possessed of a conviction; he came to know a compassion in his heart: "For all things are for your sakes, that the abundant grace might through the thanksgiving of many redound to the glory of God" (4:15).

Paul's light affliction! But he does not want any self-pity, or the pity of people who come and say, "Paul, I feel sorry for you because you are going through all this, and you are doing so only because you are so out-and-out as a man of God. If only you would lower the standards a little, you would take the heat off. 'No,' says Paul, 'it is only a light affliction, and I must go right through—and you see, it is all for your sake.'"

"Why?"

"So that as you watch me going through it you will see that as I face it every day of my life an abundance of grace is sent down to me from heaven. And because that is so, it will result in thanksgiving on your part, thanksgiving for the one who has faced it and gone through with it, and so it will all redound to the glory of God. Ah, yes, I have taken a long look as I have thought about the judgment seat of Christ, and eternity has come very near. Because of that I have started loving in a new way, and all things are for your sakes."

Not only is he possessed of this deep conviction that has fashioned all his life, not only has it resulted in a wonderful compassion as he recognizes that it is all part of the ministry for their sakes, but he is possessed of a new courage: "For which cause we faint not; but though our outward man perish, yet the inward man is renewed day by day" (v. 16).

Yes, the outward man is perishing, and we can all say the same! It is so hard sometimes to keep going and maintain the pace while the outward shell in which we live is decaying.

But something else is also happening: the inner man is being renewed every day. I am receiving strength for the battle, strength to bear the affliction. For this cause I never faint because day by day I am finding an abundance of grace to meet my every need. And therefore, though the outward man is perishing, it is so wonderful to have day by day that fresh touch from the Lord, that fresh supply of manna from heaven, that fresh strength for the daily duties so that I know I shall never faint: "…as thy days, so shall thy strength be" (Deuteronomy 33:25); "…they that wait upon the Lord shall renew their strength…" (Isaiah 40:31). So Paul would speak to us as he describes the secret of how he finds his strength.

Let me recapitulate. This light affliction which is going to last all our lives has come to us because we have accepted the cross, we have received Christ and crowned Him as our Lord. From henceforth we are living for Him and Him alone, and for His glory. And we know that the gospel of the grace of God makes even greater demands upon us than the law of the Old Testament ever could. The grace that we have received ensures further grace so that we might obey, and this calls for the incessant affliction which comes to a man who, in a world that is all out of gear, is standing for the right, and who in his soul is fighting a battle.

Are you in the battle? Or are you so foolish that you have only looked at the things that are seen? Are you completely given over to things that are temporal, to the making of money, and to the prosperity of business? Once things were different; you did stand true, but you thought the price was too much to pay, and look at you now—no testimony, never at a prayer meeting, no zeal for God! Yet one day you will lay all aside and leave everything behind, and you do not know when. Have you given yourself to the temporal? Are you in the fight or have you given up? I wonder if there was a point where the heat was turned on in your soul and it proved too great; and you did not listen to the Word which says, "Ye have not yet resisted unto blood, striving against sin" (Hebrews 12:4). When Satan put the pressure upon your life—perhaps in a moral issue or perhaps in a personal one—and the temptation came at you, you gave in and took your eyes off the Lord Jesus. You settled with the enemy, and gave in to the flesh. So, I repeat, are you in the fight today, or have you given up?

It did not begin at the moment when the heat was really on, or at the moment of some great temptation. Do you know when it began? It began when you preferred the temporal to the eternal. It began when you robbed God of His tithe (Malachi 3:10). So many give to Him a few spare coins, but how many give what He demands? But I would not speculate. You know and God knows the moment when you turned away from the principle of the cross. You ceased to look at the things that are unseen. Oh, how you have suffered, and how others have suffered! How many have never heard the truth from your lips and will spend eternity in hell because you have failed to speak? You could not speak because your heart was cold. How many men of God (including the preacher) have suffered because you have opposed them at every turn simply because of the stand they take for truth?

It began with a look, as it did with Eve, but it did not end there. And alas! O tragedy of tragedies!—you may be a child of God, redeemed by the Spirit, one who looked to Jesus! But now you have taken your eyes away and you are no longer in the fight. Do you want to get into the fight again? "Turn your eyes upon Jesus, look full in His wonderful face!" And from that moment life takes on a new meaning. Suffering?—yes, but only trivial, merely temporary, and wonderfully transforming. For with that look comes conviction—and life is lived in the light of a judgment day; compassion—and life is lived for Jesus' sake; courage—you faint not, for the inner man is renewed day after day.

CHAPTER SEVEN

CONFIDENCE AT THE END OF THE ROAD

2 CORINTHIANS 5:1–10

We have seen some of the things which are involved in the commitment of our lives to Christ as revealed by Paul. Nobody—or certainly very few—has ever been buffeted so severely as the apostle, and similarly very few have had such blessing and have been so triumphant in the midst of their buffeting. The reason was that Paul had learned to look away from things that are temporary to things that are eternal. And this deep gaze brought conviction, enabling him to see that the light affliction is but trivial and temporary, and that it has a transforming power about it because it is working together for the glory of God.

One day, however, buffetings will come to an end, and so will blessings, at least as they are experienced on this earth. Life has a terminus to it, sooner or later. This is the great certainty of the future amidst so much that is uncertain. Therefore I am so glad that Paul, in logical sequence to what he has been saying, now opens his heart to us concerning his attitude toward what lies at the end of the journey. Because of this we find him living in absolute confidence. For instance, we read: "Therefore we are always confident, knowing that, whilst we are at home in the body, we are absent from the Lord" (v. 6); "We are confident, I say, and willing rather to be absent from the body, and to be present with the Lord" (v. 8). For him life down here meant being present in the body, but absent from his Lord and exiled from heaven. He anticipated a day when that situation would be reversed, when he would be absent from the body and present with the Lord, and concerning this event he had absolute confidence.

As we look at the testimony of this man, we are constrained to ask whether we share the same confidence concerning the end of the journey. And if we do, how has this affected our daily life? Does it make any difference as to how we live and our sense of responsibility toward others and toward the Lord?

Observe first, therefore, that Paul introduces into the picture the possibility of catastrophe. He says, "For we know that if our earthly house of this tabernacle were dissolved..." (v. 1). Notice the language he uses to describe his body: this earthly house, this tabernacle—this tent in which he lives.

There are two important things about that statement. In the first place, "... if"—he is not quite sure about something. In other words, it is just possible that he may never die at all because he is a believer in the Lord Jesus Christ; and He may come before that day. Therefore, says Paul, he really does not know whether he will go through the valley of the shadow at all.

In the second place, he does not say, "...if *I* be dissolved"; he says, "...if the earthly house of this tabernacle be dissolved..." In other words, he is out of harm's way altogether. "...if our earthly house of this tabernacle were dissolved, we have a building of God, an house not made with hands..."—the essential man is going right through the experience without harm, unscathed. This is how Paul regards the possibility of catastrophe, the future, the thing that we call death. "...if our earthly house of this tabernacle be *dissolved*..."—I pause a minute at this word. It is the strongest word he could use. It is the same word that was used, for example, by our Lord Jesus when He referred to the destruction of the Temple. In Matthew 24:2 He said, in effect, "Not one stone left but that would be *thrown down*." This is the word Paul is using as he envisages the worst possible thing that could ever happen to him, the possibility that he would suffer a violent death. Remember, it was very possible that such a thing might happen to him. Paul never pampered his body, he did not care for it unduly, he did not bother with it except to buffet it and keep it in subjection lest he should fail in self-discipline. In fact, he used his body simply to blaze out his life as a missionary, that was all. It was a vehicle through which the life of Jesus was being made manifest to others.

As we have already acknowledged, the outer man was perishing. Every day brought a sense of weakness and fatigue, tiredness and exhaustion. Paul knew what it was to be lonely, to experience shipwreck, to be hungry, to be desolate and downtrodden, to be beaten, and to suffer constantly. And his body was being buffeted as very few others ever have been, and always for the cause of Christ.

Therefore he envisages this tremendous thing that might happen: one day his body might be completely destroyed, one day it might be hurled to the ground, one day he might be stoned to death. It is a very good thing, is it not, to bring to your mind the worst possible thing that could ever happen to you and look it in the face? That is the way to deal with your fears. And that is what Paul is doing at this point.

Notice that Paul immediately switches from catastrophe to what I have called the preciousness of a very wonderful contrast.

What does he say? "...we have a building of God, an house not made with hands, eternal in the heavens" (v. 1). He does not fear that he is going to roast in purgatory for two thousand years. He does not alarm himself about the possibility of any intermediate stage between this life and heaven. He just contemplates the moving out of one department of life into another—out of a tent into a home; out of a temporary building into a permanent one; out of one that was quite suited for earthly use into one that will be admirably suited for use through all the ages in glory. You ask what it will be like? I dare not embark on that theme except to say that in it you will never be weary, never have pain, never be thirsty or hungry; you will never sin, *and* you will see God face to face and yet be unafraid (Revelation 7:14–17).

During one of London's air raids in 1944, a lovely house was reduced to a heap of rubble. Buried beneath it was a fine Christian family. The next day a poster was found on a tree in the garden; it said: "He that dwelleth in the secret place of the most High shall abide under the shadow of the Almighty" (Psalm 91:1).

In the face of the possibility of what could happen to us, here is the contrast. We have a building, one of those mansions about which Jesus spoke: "In my Father's house are many mansions: if it were not so, I would have told you" (John 14:2). "And I know," says Paul, in effect, "that this is what awaits me. This is that which has been promised to me, and therefore if the worst possible thing happens, I will just go straight out of this tent, leaving it on one side, into a building in which I will live for all eternity—not a building of bricks and mortar, but a body that is gloriously indestructible because it is fashioned like unto His glorious body."

That is a tremendous confidence to have for the last moment of life, is it not? I wonder if you and I have that same confidence concerning death? If we can look it full in the face, if we can consider the worst possible thing that could happen, and yet face it without fear, without any sense of trembling, then we must have absolute confidence that if Jesus does not come first, death—no matter how violent or painful—will simply be the moment when we lay aside this tent in which we live and enter a building which God has prepared for us.

If a man can speak like this, the question that comes to mind immediately is twofold: What is the basis of his confidence? Is he on solid ground? If he *is* so sure of himself, what difference is it going to make for the rest of his life down here? Let me answer the first question first, as Paul tells us about the pledge of his confidence.

Look for instance at verse 5: "Now he that hath wrought us for the selfsame thing is God, who also hath given unto us the earnest of the Spirit." As Paul thinks about the tremendous possibility that confronts him, the experience of leaving a tabernacle and entering into an eternal building, he has absolute confidence about that experience because he knows that God has made us for that purpose. We are not made for this world. This is just a temporary experience, a training ground; this is the place where eternity is decided for all of us; this is the place where decisions are made and characters are formed which affect eternal destinies. But it is only a temporary situation, and God has not made us for this earth. He has made us for heaven. He has made us for Himself. He has wrought us for this selfsame thing. He has formed us for this very purpose. And in order to prove it, He has done a very wonderful thing. He has deigned, in His condescending love, to come to be with us in the tabernacle in which we now live. Therefore, Paul says, he has the earnest of the Spirit. He has the assurance in his heart because within him he had the indwelling of the Spirit of God, the foretaste of glory—"...Christ in you, the hope of glory" (Colossians 1:27). Therefore he never ceased to be confident because in his heart there dwells the living Christ. One day the Comforter whom He has sent to be with him and in him—well, He and Paul will leave this earthly tabernacle together! The Comforter will never leave Paul, for Christ said so: "...lo, I am with you alway, even unto the end of the world" (Matthew 28:20). There is coming a day, Paul says, when the two of them will leave this tabernacle behind, and will go straight into the presence of the Father.

Because of this, says Paul, we groan while we are in the body: "For in this we groan, earnestly desiring to be clothed upon with our house which is from heaven: If so be that being clothed we shall not be found naked" (vv. 2–3). To explain that, he says, "For we that are in this tabernacle do groan, being burdened: not for that we would be unclothed, but clothed upon, that mortality might be swallowed up of life" (v. 4).

Do you see the argument? Paul says that he has the earnest of the Holy Spirit, and because of this he groans—not that one day he will be stripped of everything and left spiritually naked, but that everything that is mortal within shall be swallowed up in life. He has that life now, and the Spirit of Christ within him is battling in his heart for truth and righteousness. There is a constant warfare going on in the soul between good and evil, between right and wrong. But there is coming a day when the Spirit and Paul will leave this body of sin and enter the presence of the Father. Then mortality will be swallowed up in life. There will be no more battle and struggle against temptation, no more crying out to God for deliverance, no more confession of failure and breakdown and sin. That will all be past history, for everything that is mortal within him, says Paul, will be swallowed up in life.

So he has the earnest of the Spirit and His presence is expressed with a sigh that goes up to the throne in heaven from Paul's heart day by day—"Oh, Lord, for that day when this mortal shall be laid aside, when this corruptible shall have put on incorruption, and everything that is mortal in me will be swallowed up! Then there will be no more enemy, no more battle and warfare, no more struggle and temptation!"

Does that sigh ever go up from your heart to heaven? If a man is content with life as it is—content with his earthly surroundings and with temporal things—what evidence is there in such a life that there is the Spirit of God? Is there within your heart that longing to be delivered forever from the conflict and from that which Paul describes as he writes, "...the flesh, lusteth against the Spirit, and the Spirit against the flesh ... so that ye cannot do the things that you would" (Galatians 5:17)? It will be all over on that day.

Paul says that one basis of assurance is the Spirit within him, the cry that makes him know that this earth is not his home, and he longs for the day when he will meet his Savior face to face. But that was not the only basis of his assurance. He had met Jesus Christ face to face, and the assurance that one day the tabernacle would be changed for a home was contained in the promise of the Lord when He said, in effect, "I go to prepare a place for you, that where I am there you may be also. And I will come again and receive you unto myself" (John 14:2–3). This was the promise vindicated by the fact that on the first Easter morning Christ rose from the tomb. Some little while after He spoke personally to Paul: "Saul, Saul, why persecutest thou me? ... I am Jesus whom thou persecutest" (Acts 9:4–5). And from that day on, Paul belonged completely to Christ. He had met the risen Savior. He had been assured that one day the tabernacle would become a home because he had the earnest of the Spirit within him, he had the promise of Christ, and because he had met the Lord Jesus personally.

As you face the end of an earthly journey, do you have that same pledge of confidence? Have you met the risen Lord? Has there been a moment in your life when you have seen that He indeed has vindicated all His claims to be the Savior of the world, and that He is alive from the dead? That resurrection demands God's future judgment, and unless you clothe yourself with God's offer of salvation through faith in a crucified, risen Savior, you become part of that judgment and will be condemned. Have you met the risen Savior and turned to Him, receiving and trusting Him? Have you that same basis of confidence?

Furthermore, Paul was absolutely confident because of a family relationship: he had received the Spirit of adoption whereby he cried, "Abba, Father!" He knew God so intimately, not as a stranger but as a Father, because he believed in Christ. He was a member of God's great family, and he knew that the Father would one day welcome him home. You see, this man was sure, and he had grounds for his confidence because Father, Son, and Holy Spirit witnessed to him of the absolute assurance that one day he would be with Jesus.

I imagine that most of us—indeed all who read this book, I trust—have that same assurance. You can say, "Yes, I have met Jesus Christ personally in life's journey. He has cleansed me from sin and I have received Him into my life and heart. He is my Savior. I have the earnest of the Spirit within my heart, and in some measure I know the groaning and discontent with this earthy life—the loneliness, the frustrations, and the longing to be with Christ and with those whom I have loved and who have gone before me. I know all these things, and life becomes more and more restless in my desire to be with Him. I am one of His family and call Him 'Abba, Father.' I have these evidences."

Very well. Let me come to the thing that presses upon my mind and heart most of all. If we have such absolute confidence, then we are able to say, "...for I know whom I have believed, and am persuaded that he is able to keep that which I have committed unto him against that day" (2 Timothy 1:12). If we can face death not as an enemy but as an angel, that will take us out from a life of frustration into a life that is full and complete in the presence of the Lord. If that is so, what difference does it make to us right now?

I want you to notice the priority claims that came to Paul's life. In the face of the tremendous possibility that confronted him, and with the absolute confidence that it would simply usher him into the presence of God, what has he got to say? "Wherefore we labour, that, whether present or absent, we may be accepted of him" (v. 9). Let me clarify one thing lest you misunderstand from the translation of that verse in the *King James Version*. Paul is not suggesting that he is working as a Christian now in order that one day he might be accepted before God. That is what you might think he says, but certainly that is not what he says. The matter of his acceptance before God was settled when he met Jesus Christ and he was "accepted in the beloved." The basis of your acceptance before God is not on the basis of your work or service, but on the basis of His precious blood, of His work for you on which by faith you rely. This is settled.

But what is Paul actually saying? Weymouth's translation is very helpful: "Wherefore we labour, that whether we be present or absent we may be pleasing to Him."

In other words, Paul is saying, "I am sure of heaven, because of what Christ has done for me. I have within me the earnest of the Spirit; I know that God is my Father. But this has not sent me to sleep; it does not carry me to heaven on flowery beds of ease. It has put into my life one master ambition, and I care for nothing else; wherefore I labor that whether I be present in the body or absent, I may be well pleasing to Him."

This is the Christian's concern now. Every other relationship and every other interest of life is motivated by this one: "Will it please my Lord? Is this something that I may do because it pleases Him, or is it

326 / BLESSINGS OUT OF BUFFETINGS

something that I just cannot do because it would displease Him?" That is the test.

I wonder how many of us apply this principle in our daily lives — especially, may I venture to say, young people? For instance, what about entertainment, recreation, the motion pictures? People will recommend that you see a film because it has a religious emphasis, and therefore you cannot afford to miss it. Are you quite sure about that? I am not going to spend one penny of the money that God entrusts to me in supporting an industry which is basically rotten, even though occasionally it may produce a film with a religious flavor to satisfy its own conscience. I know perfectly well the kind of thing that the film industry uses as bait to get people inside the theater, and that is no place for a child of God. Can I afford to miss it? Rather, can I afford to go? Does it please Jesus? These are the basic questions.

A man, especially, a Christian man in leadership, has to pay the price of leadership and there are some things he cannot afford to do at all. If he is not prepared to pay the price of leadership and walk with God and seek in every decision to please Him, and if he is in any doubt whatsoever to avoid it, the sooner he resigns from the Christian leadership the better. The example is going to count more than anything else.

These are days when a Christian has to watch his every step. With all solemnity I ask you, Does the same tremendous motivating passion grip your life? Do you say that, whether you are present or absent, you labor constantly, and from this you have no vacation? Are you laboring so that one day you may be acceptable to Him, and that every day you may please Him and have His smile upon you? Is the ambition of your life narrowed down to that one thing? And therefore, in every decision you make, every place you go, and everything you think about — your dress, your books, your money, your circumstances — first of all do you ask yourself whether it is pleasing to the Lord? This is not restrictive; rather it is the only way in which Holy Spirit power is released in your life. Fail there and you may have many "things" while lacking the supreme thing — the mark of a man of God.

As I prepared this chapter I asked, "Lord, what have I done this week that has been pleasing to You?" And that question went like a stab into my heart. Has there been a friend who has been in need, and have I spoken to him or her about Christ? Has there been somebody sick or lonely, and have I visited him? Has there been a single thing done this week that would please the Lord? Has there been a word spoken for Jesus in situations which demanded a testimony? Or have I been silent?

Does this motivating passion really grip our hearts because we are sure of the end of the road? If this motive does not grip your life, if there are not accumulating evidences of grace and the life that lives to please the Lord Jesus, if these things are not to be observed at all, then you may talk about faith and you may boast of your spiritual experiences, but you have very serious reasons to question whether you have any life at all. If faith is your assurance concerning death and glory, if your experience of the Spirit of God dwelling within you has not created a flame that burns in your heart until you live for one thing alone — to please Jesus your Lord — then what business do you have to claim to be His child?

Paul was sure about heaven, but he had a great fear, even a terror in his heart. Look at one verse beyond that which we read: "Knowing, therefore, the terror of the Lord..." (v. 11).

Why? Because we must all appear before the judgment seat of Christ, and do you know what that word "appear" means? It means that our motives will be exposed; the things that have lain behind our actions will be revealed; the things that have really governed our lives will be demonstrated. We must all have our lives laid bare before the tribunal of Christ (NEB). And on that day the verdict of Jesus Christ concerning His people will meet with a unanimous "Amen" from the whole universe.

When God promotes or demotes on that day, when He exalts or humbles, when He clothes or strips us of everything we have by profession, the whole creation will acknowledge His justice. "Knowing, therefore," says Paul, "the terror of the Lord, we persuade men..." Is it not strange? A man with confidence, a man with absolute assurance, a man to whom death was simply an entering into a home from a tabernacle, was gripped in his soul by one great ambition — to please God — and yet gripped in his soul by the fear of that day when every motive would be revealed.

God grant that your assurance may be precious to you, that your confidence may be absolutely basic and soundly grounded upon the Word of God, and above all, that there may be evidences in your life which justify your confidence that your one ambition is not to please other people, not to do the thing that is popular, but to please Him who is your Savior and Lord.

CHAPTER EIGHT

THE JUDGMENT
SEAT OF CHRIST

2 CORINTHIANS 5:10–11

Before studying the verses in 2 Corinthians 5, I wish to direct your thoughts to other passages which throw some light upon our subject.

First, Romans 14:10–13: "But why dost thou judge thy brother? or why dost thou set at nought thy brother? for we shall all stand before the judgment seat of Christ. For it is written, As I live, saith the Lord, every knee shall bow to me, and every tongue shall confess to God. So then every one of us shall give account of himself to God. Let us not therefore judge one another any more…"

First Corinthians 3:12–15: " Now if any man build upon this foundation [Jesus Christ] gold, silver, precious stones, wood, hay, stubble; Every man's work shall be made manifest: for the day shall declare it, because it shall be revealed by fire; and the fire shall try every man's work of what sort it is. If any man's work abide which he hath built thereupon, he shall receive a reward. If any man's work shall be burned, he shall suffer loss: but he himself shall be saved; yet so as by fire."

Now, our text in 2 Corinthians 5:10–11: "For we must all appear before the judgment seat of Christ; that every one may receive the things done in his body, according to that he hath done, whether it be good or bad. Knowing therefore the terror of the Lord, we persuade men…" I wonder if there is any other verse in the New Testament which at once comforts and challenges the believer as this one does. Certainly when the Holy Spirit begins to apply the truth of this verse to a man's life, it begins to burn and scorch in his conscience until he begins to see that there is not a day, sevens days a week, fifty-two weeks a year, when he lives but that it must be related to that day of which this verse speaks—"For we must all appear before the judgment seat of Christ. ..."

Of course it is well that we should understand (and I am sure that most of you do) that the judgment seat of Christ referred to in 2 Corinthians 5 and in the other portions has to do with Christian people. The judgment which awaits the unbeliever (which, for example, is dealt with in Revelation 20) is something very different. Here the issue at stake is our response to the love of God revealed to us in Jesus Christ; in the judgment of the unbelievers, the issue is the ultimate rejection of that love. In the judgment of the believers, God is dealing with people who have established a relationship with Christ; unbelievers have never established that relationship.

That this is so is confirmed, I believe, by the word used in connection with this reference to the judgment seat. The word is different from that which is used in connection with the judgment of the unbeliever. In the case of the unbeliever (Revelation 20) it has to do with punishment and penalty; in the case of the believer the primary meaning has to do with awards, or loss of them, in heaven. But at the same time, having said that, let it also be said that any conception of the judgment seat of Christ which gives us the idea that it is going to be—what shall I say?—a happy prize-day for the Christian when everything else about his life is completely overlooked and forgotten, is far from the truth.

Put the main thoughts together from the opening verses: "...every one of us shall give an account of *himself* to God" (Romans 14); "...the fire shall try a man's *work* of what sort it is" (1 Corinthians 3); "...we must all appear before the judgment seat of Christ; that every one may receive the things done in his *body*..." (2 Corinthians 5). Our body, our work, ourselves—this is an inclusive situation in which the whole redeemed personality of a man indwelt by the Spirit of God is brought personally before the judgment seat of Christ.

The Scriptural emphasis on this subject presents it to us as solemn, indeed, and yet one (if it is rightly understood) which puts passion into our prayers, sacrifice into our service, and a real dedication into our daily living. Are not these qualities—passion, sacrifice, dedication—conspicuous by their absence today? Is that not why our witness is so ineffective? Why are they lacking? Surely because we do not really live in the light of the great day of which we are now thinking. As we seriously consider this appointment with God which awaits every one of us, you will notice some *facts* about it in our text and in the following verse. Just because these facts have gripped Paul's heart, there has come into his soul a holy *fear*: Knowing therefore the terror of the Lord…" And because of the fear his whole life has been gripped with a new *fervency*: "…we persuade men…" To Paul the greatest reality of life is that he is going to account for himself before God. He speaks therefore, about the certainty of this day. He says we *must* appear before the judgment seat of Christ. This is not a possibility, but a certainty; not even a probability, but a definite appointment on the calendar with God.

If we ask why this should be so, we do not have to go very far for the answer. The absolute injustices of life on earth demand that there shall be a day when right is vindicated and wrong is condemned. How many Christian people—and maybe you are among them—have suffered because of motives that were misjudged and actions that were completely misconstrued! How many Christians have lived a whole life of suffering simply because of the damage that has been done to them by somebody else! Many have gone through life with a wound in the soul from which there seems to be no deliverance, no recovery, no forgetfulness! How many have served faithfully and yet have had no recognition, but rather a great deal of abuse! Yes, there is a wonderful comfort in knowing that we *must* appear before the judgment seat of Christ. And many who have spent a lifetime with a sore heart and a sense of utter frustration may find wonderful solace in the assurance that, among the great things that will happen on that day, right will be vindicated and wrong condemned.

But wait a moment—how readily do we pass final judgment upon somebody else when we have very little knowledge of the facts? It is this with which Paul challenges us when he says, "…why dost thou judge thy brother? or why dost thou set at nought thy brother? for we shall all stand [together] before the judgment seat of Christ. … Every one of us shall give an account of himself to God. Let us not therefore judge one another any more…" (Romans 14:10–13).

In other words, Paul would say to us, "Silence that critical tongue, for we must appear before the judgment seat of Christ. Stop that hobby of judging another, which has become the practice of so many lives, because Christ Himself is at the door. And remember, the one we are judging is our brother. Let the world condemn him if it will, but simply because we are intimately related in Christ let us get alongside him and love him, or at least overlook his failures without seeking to condemn him for his faults. Let no man judge another because one day, in the light of the judgment we have passed on others, every one of us must stand before the judgment seat of Christ. Silence then the censorious tongue. Cast the burdens of the misjudged motive and the misunderstood action at the feet of the Lord and leave them until that day when He shall vindicate, for vengeance is His and He will repay. Such is the certainty of the fact that we must appear before the judgment seat of Christ.

Notice in this verse the universality of it. We must *all* appear. Romans 14:11 says: "As I live, saith the Lord, every knee shall bow to me, and every tongue shall confess to God." The strong Christian and the weak Christian will stand, for no imagined progress in piety or holiness will exempt us from this personal interview at the judgment seat of Christ, and no weakness will excuse us from it.

The man who has been entrusted with only one talent will appear before the judgment seat of Christ along with the man who has been entrusted with ten. And the leaders, the teachers, the ministers, the elders, the deacons, as well as the more obscure church members (and perhaps the Christian who never had the courage to join any church) must all appear before the judgment seat of Christ to give an account of their stewardship. Not one shall escape, nor will there ever be the possibility of the omission of one from this date on the calendar. We must *all* appear—without exemption or excuse.

You will also note the authority of this day. It is the judgment seat of *Christ*. He will make no mistake, because He discerns the heart. He will impute no wrong where it is not due, and He will give no credit for something that appears to be right while the motive has been sinful. He will search to the very core of every matter, and there will be a standard of perfect justice as the Lord examines the motives for every action of every one of us on that day. "For God shall bring every work into judgment, with every secret thing, whether it be good, or whether it be evil" (Ecclesiastes 12:14).

Think of the absolute authority of that judgment from which there is no court of appeal—a judgment that is final, and just, and absolutely true; a judgment based not upon appearances, but upon the infinite knowledge of our God and Savior. Oh, the dreadful, awful, solemn authority of the judgment seat of our Lord!

Further see the individuality of it. "...That *everyone* may receive the things done in his body, ... whether it be good or bad." There is nothing indiscriminate about that. It is not a question of God calling people before Him in terms of a church fellowship or even a Christian family. It is a man and a woman being separated even from the context of their family and standing alone to give an account of himself and herself before God. This is husband and wife, parent and child, separated from each other.

The account is to be given not of a group, but of an individual, and the account is to be given not only of the individual's deeds and thoughts and intentions, but of *himself:* "...every one ... shall give account of himself to God" (Romans 14:12); "...as he thinketh in his heart, so is he" (Proverbs 23:7); "Thou hast set our iniquities before thee, our secret sins in the light of thy countenance" (Psalm 90:8). The issue on that day is not the amount of work I have done or the quantity of service I have rendered, but what kind of person I have been as a believer and a Christian.

It is then that we will also have to given an account of our judgment of other people because, the Lord Jesus told us, when we judge another, we lay down His standard of judgment upon us. You remember that He said (Matthew 7:1–2): "Judge not, that ye be not judged. For with what judgment ye judge, ye shall be judged: and with what measure ye mete, it shall be measured to you again." Very often those who are most censorious in their judgment of other Christians are the very people who need the greatest mercy from God, but their very censoriousness invites God to deal with them in the very same measure that they have dealt with others.

The final fact here is the impartiality of God's judgment—the deeds done in the body, whether they be good or bad.

Do you really feel, as you read the language of these verses and put the teaching together that you can exempt a Christian from the judgment of his sin in that day? Can you possibly escape the conclusion that at the judgment seat of Christ it is the sins of a Christian that will come before His throne for judgment? Of course, I know that our eternal destiny and the eternal punishment of sin was settled when we met God in Jesus Christ at the cross. If that was a real and genuine experience of a new birth, then the sin question in terms of eternal banishment from the presence of God was settled for ever. But as to eternal loss in heaven—that is not settled. The issue is before us. How can you possibly separate sin from works? For the Holy Spirit says that everyone shall give an account of himself, that man's works shall be tried by fire to prove what sort it is, and that every man shall give an account of the deeds done in his body.

You cannot separate sin from works and deeds done in the body, for here is the total judgment of a redeemed soul at the judgment seat of Christ. It is this that confronts every child of God: the things done in the body, whether they be good—gold, silver, and precious stones—or whether they be bad—wood, hay, and stubble.

I like a little comment by Dr. Harry Ironside on this subject. In his study of Paul's First Letter to the Corinthians he said, "Just look at that little word s-o-r-t, sort. It is not how much we have done that is going to count, but it is the quality of what we have done that is going to matter." Every man's work, of what *sort* it is: that which has been for the glory of God—gold, silver, and precious stones, that which has been in the power of self and for the glory of man—wood, hay, and stubble.

We sum up, therefore, what the Bible teaches concerning the judgment seat of Christ which every Christian must face. On that day, the Lord will go over the Christian's life from the moment when His grace met him and saved him from the bondage of sin into salvation in Christ. And the whole of his Christian life will be brought before him as one great panoramic picture. Furthermore, the character of Christ's judgment will be based on a man's judgment of others. When he has been merciful, Christ will be merciful with him. When he has been severe, Christ will be severe with him. When he has forgiven others, Christ will forgive him. When he has not forgiven others, neither will Christ forgive him (Matthew 6:14–15).

Everything which has been done in dependence upon the Holy Spirit and for the glory of God will merit the "Well done" and receive the reward. Everything which has been done in the energy of the flesh and for the glory of self will be burnt up and destroyed to one's eternal loss. Only that which is of the new life and of the new nature, and which is the outcome of redemption, will get through the fire of that day to the very presence of the King of kings where it will stand forever. But that which has been done in the body, that which has been sinful, that which has been of an unworthy motive, that which has been for the glorification of the flesh shall be on that day destroyed like wood, hay, and stubble.

Do you say, "I am conscious in my life that there has been so much selfishness and carnality and sin, so much of sheer un-Christ-like behavior. What can I do about it if I am going to face this tremendous day of which you speak?" There is one thing you can do, and you can do it today, right now. You can go into the presence of God in the name of the Lord Jesus and you can judge yourself on every one of those things known to be contrary to His will. Do you remember what Paul says in 1 Corinthians 11:31? "…If we would judge ourselves, we should not be judged."

In the face of that great day which will come to all, there is one thing that will take the fear out of it, and leave only hope and confidence. If you are prepared today to judge unquestionably in the presence of God that which you know in your life to be out of His will, and that which is sinful and contrary to His purpose for you, then you can trust Him for the cleansing by the precious blood of Christ.

I would say lovingly but firmly that if you are not prepared to do that, you need to question yourself very seriously concerning the genuineness of your conversion. The apostle John says that he who is born of God does not continue in the practice of sin (1 John 3:9). It would be a sheer contradiction, an impossibility, in the light of the teaching of the Word of God.

If in the course of your Christian life Satan trips you up and causes you to fall and to be ashamed, what must you do? At that moment, in the presence of God, you must judge it as sin; do not ally yourself with it, but judge it and condemn it. Look up into God's face and trust Him for forgiveness and cleansing, pardon and restoration, and power to overcome. But if you refuse to do that, and continue to allow yourself to be the victim of habit and sinfulness, then you will face a dreadful day when you come to meet with God. The time lag between the moment of sinning and the moment of forsaking and confessing is a sure indication of the true nature of a man's walk with God. No one who has enjoyed the intimacy of His presence and the power of His Spirit can endure His absence for long!

Yes, it is a tremendous moment about which Paul speaks and which brings fear into his heart! So, in the light of these facts, let us see the fear that came upon him. It is a fear which is the outcome of recognizing the facts of the great judgment day.

What was the fear that gripped Paul's heart? Well, he has just been speaking of absolute confidence concerning victory over death, so it could not be that. No, Paul's fear is not of hell; it is a fear of heaven. It is a fear of being ashamed at the coming of the Lord. It is a fear of those eyes which are like fire piercing him through and through, of finding himself in the presence of God with sin in his life which has never been judged and put away, and which has never been destroyed in the name of the Lord. It is the fear of meeting the scorching gaze of a pure and holy God who died and who lives to keep him. It is the fear of meeting such a God, and (as he says in 1 Corinthians 9:27) finding that, having preached to others, he himself might become a castaway. It is not a fear of eternal judgment or of eternal punishment, but the fear of an eternity in heaven reflecting upon a life that has failed to deal adequately, in the power that God gives, with the sin which has constantly beset.

"I fear, therefore I buffet my body and keep it in subjection," says the apostle, in effect, "lest having preached to others, I myself might be disqualified at that great day. I fear; therefore I hasten to forgive others lest He will not forgive me. I fear; therefore I hasten to judge all He shows me to be sin in my life and to cease to judge others." This is a fear of getting into the very presence of God when the opportunities of confession and repentance are gone, of knowing that in your heart there has been sin unjudged, and that you have not been willing to face up to it. I repeat, any man who can face that happily, and go through life knowing that he is bound by habits which he has never brought out to be judged, has every right to question his conversion. Sin, if it is to be forgiven, must be forsaken. Any other doctrine of forgiveness is a fallacy.

With Paul's fears there came a new fervency: "Therefore, knowing the fear of the Lord, we persuade men…" (2 Corinthians 5:11, RSV); "…every knee shall bow to me, and every tongue shall confess to God" (Romans 14:11)—and there is the whole purpose of the judgment which confronts us all: it is always with the view toward the total submission of our hearts to His sovereignty and the confession of His authority. Before Him every knee shall bow, and every life in the process of time must either bend or break. It must either bend before the throne or be broken before the justice of an almighty God.

I am reminded of the language of the apostle Peter when he says that the time has come that judgment must begin at the house of God. If it first begins with us, what shall be the end of those who obey not the gospel of God? And if the righteous scarcely be saved, where shall the ungodly and the sinner appear (1 Peter 4:17–18)?

"Therefore, knowing the fear of the Lord, we persuade men,..." says Paul. And the greatest power in his ability to persuade others is that "we are made manifest unto God; and I trust ... in your consciences." In other words, it is plain to the Lord—and we trust it is also plain to you—that this fact of the judgment seat of Christ has so gripped our hearts that we could not go on living as we have been. The fear of God has brought us to a judgment of sin in our own lives, to a confession and a forsaking of it. We are therefore manifest to God, and we trust that we are manifest also to your own conscience.

This is a solemn subject, and yet it is one that brings great comfort to our hearts if we are prepared to do what Paul did. Are you ready for that accounting day? It could be today, and this may be your last opportunity to confess, to break, to judge yourself, to get right with God, to purify yourself as He is pure, to show mercy and forgiveness to others, that you may qualify to receive all these things from Him. When the opportunity is gone and suddenly (for these things happen unexpectedly) you are ushered into the presence of God, will you go into His presence with sin that is unconfessed and unjudged? With resentment unbroken, with wrong unforgiven, with broken fellowship unrestored? Dare you face that judgment seat with a life that is not right with God? This may be—God only knows—your last opportunity to judge yourself so that you will not be judged.

I am persuaded that if you are prepared to do this, knowing the fear of the Lord, then your power of persuasiveness with others will be tremendous. Remember that the power of your persuasion in other people depends upon your self-judgment in the light of the judgment seat of Christ. Have you ever tried to give testimony to others and to speak to them about Jesus, and found your tongue tied? You have been helpless to speak a word and you have know why, because as you have tried to talk you knew that there was a sin your life that was unconfessed and unjudged. At that moment you lost all your authority and ability to persuade others.

It is out of the heart that the mouth speaketh. I trust that if this is the last moment any of us might have here on earth, before we stand before the judgment seat of Christ, that in our hearts we have judged ourselves, condemned our sins, refused to live with them, and trust in the blood of Christ to cleanse us, that we might walk with God. So we shall look forward to that judgment seat not as a place of fear, but a place of comfort, where we will look into His face and hear, "Well done!"

CHAPTER NINE

WHAT KIND OF PEOPLE ARE WE?

2 CORINTHIANS 5:12–17

Paul's definition of a Christian is one of the most dynamic and revealing to be found anywhere in the New Testament: "If any man [not a few people, some of whom would live on one standard and some on another; but—*if any man*] be in Christ [in whose life the great miracle of the new birth has taken place and who has been born from above; like the branch is in the vine and the tree is in the soil, he is in Christ], he is a new creature…" "New," is not used to convey the sense of something recent, as you would buy a new coat to replace an old one; it is used in the sense of becoming a totally different kind of person. At the moment of his new birth there has come to live within him a new life; and because of this he is now governed by a new principle, arrested by a new motive, moving in new company, surrendered to new objectives. This is not a question of a man having reformed his life, nor of some new things that have been added to old things. He has not merely changed a few practices or habits; Paul says that if any man be in Christ, he is a totally different kind of person: "…old things are passed away; behold, all things are become new." Notice the contrast: *if any man—all things have become new.*

Here then is the New Testament definition of a Christian. It prompts the question, "What kind of people are we?" In the light of some things that confront us, I believe it is the most significant question of the hour. We, who claim to be in direct succession of the church—in this line of inheritance in which we are also in Christ—and therefore have this same experience, what kind of people are we?

You will notice the sixth verse begins with the word *therefore*, and which obviously implies the outcome of reasoning and argument. Paul has come to this inevitable conclusion and summation of his argument: if any man is in Christ, then he is a totally different kind of person; and because of it he has certain evidences and characteristics about him. Going back to the context, Paul says in verse 11: "...we are made manifest unto God; and I trust also are made manifest in your consciences." In other words, there are some things about us which are so self-evident that we do not have to argue for them; they are manifest to God, and we trust they are manifest to others. But remember, as Paul goes on in his argument, that we are not commending ourselves to others; we are not boasting, but we are giving others some reason to glory on our behalf, and we are answering those who simply judge by outward experiences and profession instead of inward reality.

What are these evidences? First, in Paul's life there is a fervor which was revealed constantly: "...the love of Christ constraineth us..." (v. 14). In the previous verse he said that some people thought him mad, beside himself (I doubt if that upset him one little bit!). Festus said he was mad when he gave his testimony before the court on one occasion; but Paul no doubt reminded himself that the Lord Jesus was said to be beside Himself. But he gives the reason for this fervor that is revealed in his life; the love *of* Christ, not Paul's love *for* Christ, the love of Christ is the love eternal, having no beginning or ending. The love of Christ was long before the foundation of this world. The love of Christ was so utterly selfless, for He had nothing to gain by stooping from the throne to the manger. The love of Christ—why, the highest place that heaven affords was His by sovereign right, but He forsook it all and humbled Himself, and made Himself of no reputation. The love of Christ was so patient; it went on loving even though He came to His own and His own received Him not; yet He loved them to the end. The love of Christ took Him right to the cross, and bared His heart to a spear and the sword of the justice of God that was buried in the body of our Lord Jesus. The love of Christ took Him through all the shame, the reviling, the despisings; and, as Paul sums it up in the last verse of this chapter, this is the love of Christ who was made sin for us.

The Holy Spirit has shown this to Paul; it was no theory to him. He had seen something of the glory of God's love and he knew it was this love that constrains us. The word *constrains* is difficult to translate from the original into the English language as it has many meanings. It could be used to mean, "the love of Christ restrains"—as the reins upon a horse hold him back, hold him in check, keep him on the right path, guide him round the bend. Paul says, in effect, "His power has so got hold of me that the love of Christ keeps me back from doing the thing that otherwise I would do, a thing that would be so shameful as to bring disgrace upon His name."

Another meaning of *constrains* in this verse could be translated, "the love of Christ coerces me." Jamieson, Fawcett, and Brown's commentary upon this verse says that "there is an irresistible object which has so controlled the life of a Christian that he lives with one objective in view to the elimination of any other possible consideration." Just as a river in flood is dammed up and restrained in order to be constrained, taking all its power in increasing flow until it bursts into the ocean, so the love of Christ constrains the man of God.

Something has gripped the Christian and possessed him till the world says he is a fanatic. But someone may be saying, "That is not so; it is faith that saves." Faith does it by love, faith worketh by love, and if your faith has not so got hold of you that in some measure you are gripped like this by the love of Christ, then I say your faith is not saving faith, no matter how orthodox it is. Love always blooms on the plant where faith has taken root in the soil of redemption; and where faith takes root, love springs up and bursts out. This is the fervor that is revealed in Paul's life.

Any man who counts for anything in the world, whether good or bad, is a man controlled by one principle. People who are something for a little while, then something else for a little while longer, and nothing for very long, are just like the jet stream which follows a jet plane and disappears in a moment; it does not count for anything. But there are men who are gripped by one principle—your Caesars, your Alexanders, your Napoleons, your Stalins, your Mussolinis, your Hitlers, your Khrushchevs, and others like them. True, they have been bad men, but they are men of one passion, one principle, one concern. And you also have your Wesleys, your Whitefields, your Judsons, your Finneys, your Moodys, your Studds, your Taylors, your Bonars—men of one passion, but good men.

Paul had looked with Spirit-enlightened eyes into the heart of God, and Christ's love for him gripped him, propelled him, impelled him along one line of life to the exclusion of any other attraction. If any would say that this is awful bondage for the Christian, Paul would answer that he found that which he loved to do was the will of God. That which consumed his whole life and governed all his principles of living, seven days a week, was so tremendous that he had no room for any secondary consideration. There were no rivals in his life; therefore he was the happiest man in the world! Some would say that this kind of religion is too emotional; but wait; for another evidence of this man in whose life there is a total and complete transformation is not only a fervor that reveals, but facts that are recognized. This fervor springs from facts. "…Because we thus judge [with the Spirit-enlightened minds and eyes], that if one died for all, then were all dead" (v. 14). Paul rejoiced in his constraint; that which gripped his life was not emotion, because it was based upon two dynamic facts, substitution and identification.

> Bearing shame and scoffing rude,
>   In my place condemned He stood.
> Sealed my pardon with His blood,
>   Hallelujah! What a Savior.

He died for all! "…he was wounded for our transgressions, he was bruised for our iniquities: the chastisement of our peace was upon him…" (Isaiah 53:5). The great fact of the substitutionary death of our Lord Jesus is basic; it puts fire in the heart.

The Christian's fervor also springs from the fact of his identification: "…if one [Christ] died for all, then were all dead." Paul explains, in effect: I see in the cross that just as by my first nature I was involved in condemnation, guilt, sin, and judgment, so by my second birth in the Lord Jesus I am involved in a new nature, a new life which has died and risen, I died in Him, I was buried with Him, I rose with Him and ascended with Him; though my feet are on the ground, my heart is in heaven, and the spirit of the risen Christ governs my personality. I am identified with Him. Therefore His victory is my victory; His triumph over temptation is my triumph; His resources are my resources; His grace is my grace; His patience is my patience; His meekness is my meekness; His strength in adversity is mine; His power to overcome is mine. I was one with Adam by my first birth, but I am one with Christ by my second birth.

To illustrate, as Paul was saying, here is a slave who escaped from prison. A search is organized to find him, but when the news is received that the slave is dead, immediately the search is called off. Because of the fact of the slave's death, the law has no more hold on him. It has no more power to enforce its condemnation or its judgment. The man died and therefore he is free. When I was a slave of sin, I had no power, no ability to overcome. Once the things that I would I did not, and the things that I hated I did. Once I was poor, wretched, and vile; and by myself, in the flesh, I am no different now from what I was then. But hallelujah! in Jesus one day I died, and from that moment the law had no more encroachment, no more power—it could not touch me. I was free from it, and in Jesus Christ I was set free not only from its penalty but, praise the Lord! indwelt by a new and mightier power that could overcome all the power of sin in my heart. Do you think I can keep quiet about that?

The thrill of our redemption in Christ is like the constraining force in Paul's life. It burns in us because we have been set free by the blood of Jesus. These are facts, not emotions, that are recognized; and because of them the love of Christ has pressurized our lives along one channel.

In the third place, there is a fellowship that is recognized by the Christian in daily life: "...he died for all, that they which live should not henceforth live unto themselves, but unto him which died for them, and rose again. Wherefore henceforth know we no man after the flesh: yea, though we have known Christ after the flesh, yet now henceforth know we him no more" (vv. 15–16). Perhaps you have never noticed the significance of these two verses. Here is a fellowship that is recognized in the life of a man who is a new creation: a fellowship God-ward and a fellowship earthward; it is vertical and horizontal.

The love *of* Christ for me has been answered in the heart in which He has come to dwell by the love *for* Christ burning like a fire through me. Love begets love. The love of Christ shed abroad by the Holy Spirit brings a response from the regenerate heart. "Love knows no limit to its endurance, no end to its trust, no fading of its hope. It can outlast anything. It is, in fact, the one thing that still stands when all else has fallen" (1 Corinthians 13, PHILLIPS). That is the love the Spirit of God has begotten in us because we have been born again with a new nature capable of reloving and sending back to heaven the flame of consecration, devotion and love to Him. It is expressed so beautifully by F. W. Faber:

> O Jesus, Jesus, dearest Lord! Forgive me if I say,
> For very love, Thy sacred Name a thousand times a day.
> I love Thee so I know not how my transports to control;
> Thy love is like a burning fire within my very soul.
>
> Burn, burn, O love, within my heart, burn fiercely night and day,
> Till all the dross of earthly loves is burned, and burned away.
> O Jesus, Jesus, sweetest Lord, Who art Thou not to me?
> Each hour brings joy before unknown, each day new liberty.

Is there in your heart such a fellowship? Love has answered love, deep has called unto deep, and in a life which was so barren, cold, and dead the Holy Spirit has come and kindled a flame of sacred love upon the heart. Not that our old nature loves God—it is incapable of doing so; but the new nature by the Holy Ghost has put the old in subjection, and love is going up to the throne. We say to Him:

> My Jesus, I love Thee,
>   I know Thou art mine,
> For Thee all the follies
>   Of sin I resign.

That fellowship is revealed earthward, too; "…henceforth know we no man after the flesh: yea, though we have known Christ after the flesh, yet now henceforth know we him no more" (v. 16). If only the church could get hold of this today! What does it mean? The old things that marked our friendships and dislikes in our unconverted days put barriers upon our love, and made forbidden territories of certain areas: distinction of color, distinction of race and nationality. And Paul says that we used to know Jesus that way—but not any more. There was a day when our wonderful Lord, referring to His crucifixion, looked into the faces of His disciples and said, in effect, "Now it is better for you that I should go away" (John 16:7). I can imagine them saying, "Lord Jesus, that takes some believing. We talked and walked with You, we have been to Your college for three years; and is it better for You to go away?" And Jesus answered, in effect, "If I do not depart, the Comforter will not come. But if I depart, I will send Him to you, and in that day you shall know that I am in My Father, and you are in Me, and I in you." Henceforth we know not Christ after the flesh. Now we know Him in terms of a spiritual union and oneness which is far greater, far richer. Therefore, because there is a fellowship recognized in heaven, there is a fellowship recognized here. I am not going to know men and love them simply because one is white and another is black. I am going to love them regardless of the color of their skin; I will care for them regardless of their background and race, because this flame has burned through background, tradition, prejudice, and everything until I love my fellow men in Jesus' name as He loves me.

As we ask this question, "What kind of people are we?" I say most earnestly that the future of mankind is in grave peril unless there is to be a revival of Protestant religion. I want to be kind, but I want to express what I believe is the Word of God for this hour when I say that in the last several years Satan has had a wonderful millennium in so-called Christian lands. People have forgotten their spiritual obligations in their enjoyment of material luxury, and they think that they can do anything they please as long as they set aside their quiet time. They can plan any program for young people, or play the fool in any way, as long as they gather around the Word at the end of it. Oh, if ever the devil has done something to the church, he has done it today! The mark of distinction of the child of God (apart, of course, from his attendance at church and membership in Christian organizations) is completely eliminated in our daily living. I say, therefore, that there is a desperate need at this moment for a revival of the kind of Christian faith that brought Luther and others like him to be the men they were.

In the book *Come Wind, Come Weather*, written by Leslie T. Lyall of the China Inland Mission, there is the story of a decade under Communism in China. It tells of the day when Communists came in as angels of light and proposed self-government, self-propagation, self-support for the church. They also promised religious freedom. Communism worked for a while, and then the pressure began and it was discovered that Communism meant total allegiance to the régime and its outlook on life. It meant, too, that Christians who were true to the Word of God lived in fear of imprisonment or banishment to some climate that would probably kill them. In that little group of men and women who have been brainwashed until they have nearly gone mad, there have been those who even today stand for their faith and are true to the Lord. When they meet each other on the street, they say, "Goodbye, we will see you inside next time"—"inside" meaning prison. One girl (whose story is told in the book) was arrested because of her fearless testimony, and when the police came to put the handcuffs on her she held out her arms, her wrists close together, and said, "I am not worthy."

What kind of people are we? I never believe in frightening people, but no one needs to be reminded that Communist power is an ever-present threat. If they do not attack because they fear retaliation by force, they try to do it by corruption from within. There are deadly forces at work in this world, forces that would squeeze the vitals out of our Christian living. It is time some of us stopped playing at Christianity.

What kind of people are we? Is there a power, something that has you in its grip, something that will push you through without any possible alternative? It is the love of Christ! That is the quality the church of Jesus Christ needs now, for survival, in this hour of human history. The one thing that is going to cripple a nation beyond hope of recovery is the failure of Protestant Christians to be constrained by the love of Christ.

Would you hold out your hands to Jesus today, and let Him put the handcuffs on your wrists, and say, "Lord, I am not worthy, but for Thy sake today I am Thine altogether, driven by one master passion with no rival claim outside the will of God"? I beg of you to consider your daily life in the light of this. I beg of you to consider the rival claims that put you out of God's will and enable you to live a lighthearted, happy-go-lucky Christian life with no burden for living in the center of the will of God. I beg of you, for Jesus' sake and for the sake of your testimony, that you will review these things before it is too late, and that you will bear the mark of a man who is constrained by one mighty principle, the love of Christ. Are you that kind of person?

CHAPTER TEN

GET RIGHT
WITH GOD

2 CORINTHIANS 5:17–21

What wonderful words these are! I believe it is upon the reception of such words spoken with authority from the throne of God in heaven that our future in this generation and for all time depends. Indeed, without them, any promise of man—whoever he may be—is merely a straw in the wind. They are wonderful, not only because of what they reveal to us of the servants who are described as His ambassadors, but because of what they reveal of God Himself: "…as though God did beseech you by us…" Here is God pleading; and with whom is He pleading? You notice in this verse that the word *you* is set in italics in both instances, and the verse would really read this way: "Now then we are ambassadors for Christ, as though God did beseech by us: we pray in Christ's stead, be ye reconciled to God."

Paul was speaking in verse 19 of a world that was already reconciled to God. Notice therefore that the plea here is not to a few people; it is as world-wide as God's tremendous power to reconcile the human race at the cross. The Corinthian church had already been reconciled; that is the whole implication of the message. They had experienced something of the buffeting as well as the blessings of the Christian life, which is what Paul has been talking about and what we have been considering. They have known something of the affliction which is but for a moment—a lifetime on earth—the affliction that comes from being a Christian, from standing for God against sin. They face the judgment seat of Christ to give an account of the deeds done in their bodies. Consequently, it is the whole ransomed, redeemed church—reconciled, pardoned, Spirit-filled—that is now committed to the ministry of reconciliation. In other words, the "all things" that are new (because we now belong to the Lord Jesus) combine together with this one supreme purpose to extend to the whole world and are committed to this ministry of reconciliation. This word is to be proclaimed by the church of Jesus Christ, by every redeemed man and woman in whose life all things have become new, and therefore all things are committed to this ministry. From the lips of every child of God there is going out to the millions in the world, "Be ye reconciled to God!" for the pleading of the heart of God is only made known through the lips of ransomed men and women.

Here then is the voice that I pray all may hear at this moment. It is the voice of God, greater and mightier than any man's voice could ever be. Here is the voice that comes from the throne, and it is the pleading voice of the Lord Jesus, because when God pleads, Christ pleads, and when Christ pleads, God pleads. The two are one, as revealed in the language of verse 20: "...ambassadors for Christ, ... we pray you in Christ's stead, be ye reconciled to God." Notice how Paul interchanges *Christ* and *God*; the two are absolutely one. Here is the deity of our Lord revealed; and the great voice that comes from the trinity in heaven declares, "Be ye reconciled to God."

I would stand in a sense of awe and worship, and in reverent amazement. Here is God the omnipotent, pleading Almighty God, our fortress, our deliverer, our strength, to Whom the nations are but drops in the bucket, Who has all power in heaven and in earth committed to Him—pleading! Surely this plea for the love of another, this begging that an enemy would put away his enmity, is the part of the one who is inferior, the one who has offended, the offender rather than the offended. It is the place of the rebel, not the King, to plead. But here is deity in the person of God in Jesus Christ breaking through all the patterns of human relationships and human precedents; here is God omnipotent in heaven bending down to this little planet in which there has been a total rebellion against His rule, and saying to the rebel race who lie helpless at His feet, "I beg you to be reconciled to God."

Why should God do that? Because the rebel, though he be helpless, chained, and absolutely powerless, is unconquered by heaven until his heart lies broken before God. Can you imagine it? Would to God I had the lips of a Martin Luther, or a John Wesley, or a Dwight Moody, to bring into focus this picture of deity bending down at the feet of rebellious humanity.

Can you imagine the President of the United States taking a trip across to Cuba and paying a visit to Dr. Castro, and saying, "It was very wrong of you to steal all our property; but now, let us be friends, I beg of you"? Can you imagine the Prime Minister of England going to Egypt and saying to Mr. Nasser, "It was extremely bad of you to take all our property at the Suez Canal; but come, let us be reconciled"? Of course, these are impossibilities. They could not happen because both sides distrust each other, and would have motives that were not perfectly selfless.

Here, however, is God lowering Himself to plead with rebels that they might accept His pardon. Did I say "lowering Himself"? I ought to have said "exalting Himself," because the greatest thing about the love of God is that He stoops down from the throne to where I am today, and He pleads that I be reconciled to God. This represents, if it represents anything, that in the heart of God there is a great longing that the creature He has made might be reconciled to Him.

"...We are ambassadors on Christ's behalf..." (v. 20, RSV), or "we pray on Christ's account," suggests that it means so much to God if the rebel is reconciled. God, who is absolutely self-sufficient and complete in Himself, yet could see only the travail of His soul and could be satisfied only when one man allowed the love of God in Jesus Christ to subdue his heart and silence the rebellion of his will. God is ready to stoop to any humiliation to achieve the reconciliation of the human heart, not for His sake, but for our sake. So intent is His desire for our love—because when we give it to Him and yield it to Him, it means our salvation—that He stoops to any depth in order to sue for our hearts rather than to lose us eternally.

This may raise an objection in the minds of some, and they may say, "I do not know what you are talking about. God is completely silent to me. The thing that baffles me is that He says nothing, He seems indifferent to all our problems and troubles." But wait a moment; if you think that, you are wrong. The message God speaks at this time is, "Be ye reconciled to God," for only in such a reconciliation can there be your deliverance.

But how does God do this? Observe the method He uses. I would remind you of the tears the Lord shed as He looked upon Jerusalem and said, "O Jerusalem, ... how often would I have gathered thy children together, even as a hen gathereth her chickens under her wings, but ye would not!" (Matthew 23:37); and it was He who said, "Come unto me, all ye that labour and are heavy laden, and I will give you rest" (Matthew 11:28). Oh, the intensity of the desire in the heart of our Lord, and the pain of disappointment as He wept over the city that refused Him!

Consider also the travail that God has experienced. One thing, more than anything else, shows us what God is, what sin is, and what I am—the cross. Paul concludes the great argument of this portion of his letter by saying, "...he hath made him to be sin for us, who knew no sin; that we might be made the righteousness of God in him" (v. 21). Is not that the most earnest entreaty of all, the voice that would seek to pierce the darkness of these days? Christ was made sin for us to make reconciliation possible, to banish our rebellion, to put sin out of the sight of God forever. I do not understand it—and I do not expect that any of us will until we get to heaven—but I do know that whereas the offence of one man could involve the whole human race in rebellion, sin, total corruption, and failure, so the obedience of one Man, even obedience unto the death of the cross, can involve the whole human race in a glorious deliverance from the effects of our sin. His obedience can bring us back as reconciled to God, for the whole ugly load of it has been heaped upon His head as He cried, "My God, my God, why hast thou forsaken me?" (Matthew 27:46). Oh, the travail God experienced to welcome us back!

You may say, "That is all history; it does not work today. I do not think God is speaking now, in spite of what you say." Is He not? Do you mean to tell me that God has not spoken to this nation in the past two decades? How often a very fond and loving mother would seek to draw her little child's heart away from its faults and its sin by redoubling her kindness and love! How eager she is to overlook the faults, if not to excuse them, and to shower love and affection from her mother-heart, so that the little one may respond to her love and despise the things that are spoiling that little life. Is not that what God has done?

We have all deserved His anger, but He has showered upon us in the past quarter of a century providential blessings that are unprecedented in the life of men anywhere in the world. In so many parts of the world you will see poverty, a lack of many of the things that we possess, and you cannot help but come to the conclusion that our merciful Creator has given us good measure, pressed down and running over. He has been doing for us that which He tells us to do: "…if thine enemy hunger, feed him; if he thirsts, give him drink; for in so doing thou shalt heap coals of fire upon his head" (Romans 12:20). In the providential mercy of a loving Creator-God, coals of fire have been heaped upon the heads of many millions of people in this part of the world during recent years. Do you mean to tell me that God has been saying nothing?

You say, God is silent; He has not spoken. Think of the tears God has shed; think of His travail. Then think of the providence God has given; think of the pricks of conscience He has sent to every one of us. How many an inward prick of conscience has accompanied these outward tokens of God's blessings? Do you mean to tell me that you could stand up and deny this? Has there never been a moment in your life when perhaps in time of loneliness, failure, disillusionment, disappointment, sadness, or bereavement there has not been a voice saying, "My son, give Me thine heart"? I am sure that every individual who is loved (and all of us are loved by a loving God) has known moments when God has supported the overwhelming outward evidence of His care by the inward stab of conscience.

How many a strange longing has swept across your soul in the course of your brief life—a longing for companionship, for love, for friendship, for assurance, for someone to whom you could take every care? Have you known a longing to find the strength to get you through, to pick you up and send you on the road again when you are conscious of so much failure and disappointment? Do you mean to tell me that you have never known such a thing? Of course, you have—we all have! How our hearts have echoed the words, "Jesus, Lover of my soul"! We have known it, and have heard His voice and His pleadings, but we have recoiled from it, misunderstood it, because we have not recognized it. We have silenced it and turned away from Him, resisting the spirit of conviction. Yet, while there is yet time, the word is "Be ye reconciled to God!"

What a mystery that a poor little speck of humanity like you or me has the power to lift its puny little self before the throne of God and say "no" to all His beseeching love! God beseeches because He has no settled relationships between Himself and creatures like us, and He wants to win our love. He cannot force us, He cannot pry open the human heart and force an entrance; the door opens from the inside. "Behold, I stand at the door, and knock: if…" (Revelation 3:20). Ask a theologian to explain that *if* and he cannot; none of us could. The living God, who pleads and beseeches, stands at the door and the rest is left with the man on the inside. A mysterious prerogative, an awful responsibility is placed upon every one of us, and the act of refusal is so simple—just do nothing about it and you have done everything.

There are millions of people today, in and out of churches, who, all of their lives, have unconsciously been refusing the pleading of God. They are indifferent and passive; they hear it all often, but it does not produce any effect. This is the sort of thing they expect a preacher to say—he has been taught to say it, and they wonder why he gets so excited and concerned about it. Then, after church, they discuss the weather or some other subject. Once more, not recognizing it as the pleading of God, they recoil against it and refuse it simply by doing nothing. That is the climax of all folly, for refusing His highest and best is choosing certain ruin.

Why is God so persistent? Why is He so patient, so passionate in His entreaties? Why must Jesus Christ die? Why was it worth His while to bear the punishment of our sins? Why does He let us go through this and that? Why does He speak to our hearts, time and time again, in spite of our refusals? I will tell you why. Because He says, "…they that hate me love death" (Proverbs 8:36).

There is no alternative. "Be ye reconciled to God," for enmity is ruin and destruction. There can be no stronger proof of the sinfulness of the human heart than that God should plead and I should steel my heart and deafen my ear to His voice. The crown of all sin, the disclosure of what we really are by nature, the secret of all true character is that light has come into the world, but men have preferred darkness to light because their deeds are evil. "…Choose you this day whom ye will serve…" (Joshua 24:15). I beg you, in Christ's stead, be ye reconciled to God!

CHAPTER ELEVEN

A CALL TO CONSISTENCY

2 CORINTHIANS 6:1–10

Paul's first letter to the church at Corinth had as its great concern the discipline of the church. His second letter has as its chief burden the discipline of a Christian, and the first five chapters, which we have already studied, have had to do with this great theme of discipleship.

In 2 Corinthians, chapter 1, is the price of discipleship: "...we had the sentence of death in ourselves, that we should not trust in ourselves, but in God which raiseth the dead." The theme of the second chapter is that of the privilege of discipleship: "...we are unto God a sweet savour of Christ, in them that are saved, and in them that perish." What a privilege!

Then in the third chapter there is what I call the practice of discipleship: "...we all, with open face beholding as in a glass the glory of the Lord, are changed into the same image from glory to glory. ..."

In the fourth chapter we have the power of discipleship, "For our light affliction, which is but for a moment, worketh for us a far more exceeding and eternal weight of glory," and we recalled in that chapter that what Paul called *light* we would call almost overwhelming. But such was Christ's power in Paul's life as a Christian that it was to him a light affliction which lasted but for a moment and worked for him a far more exceeding and eternal weight of glory.

The fifth chapter has as its theme the purpose of discipleship. In order that every Christian who has been trained in this school, who has been facing the implication of the Christian life in the day in which he lives, that from each one there may go out to a world that is rejecting the Lord Jesus and upon which the judgment of God is surely coming imminently, the great appeal, "...we pray you in Christ' stead, be ye reconciled to God."

Now Paul turns in chapter six to the church with another great appeal: "We then, as workers together with him, beseech you also that ye receive not the grace of God in vain"—receive not in vain the grace of this privilege of discipleship, and all that has been made known to us in Jesus Christ. In this chapter his appeal is centered in the first ten verses upon the call to consistency in the Christian life, and then, in the closing part of the chapter, to an appeal for consecration in the Christian life.

As we consider these opening verses, the first thrust to our hearts is introduced to us by the very suggestiveness of our text. It is a peril that lies in the path of every believer, that of dissipating the grace of God: "I beseech you ... that you receive not the grace of God in vain." All His fullness of blessing, all that is ours in Christ that Paul has been describing, this wonderful life with its ministry of reconciliation, with its price of discipleship and its privilege, its practice, its power—take heed that you receive not these things in vain. I repeat, there is a tremendous peril to the Christian that he may dissipate the grace of God.

I suggest that Paul brings to us here two ways in which this dissipation occurs, and by which we fling away God's grace until it becomes utterly irrelevant and meaningless to us. The first way is suggested to us in the second verse of this chapter, enclosed in brackets, when he is quoting from Isaiah 49:8, "...I have heard thee in a time accepted, and in the day of salvation have I succoured thee: behold, now is the accepted time; behold, now is the day of salvation." While that verse may say many things to many people, it has been saying one thing to me that I know it will say to anyone who is not a believer in Christ, that God's time for reconciliation is now. God's time for receiving life in Jesus Christ is today. If you shall hear His voice, harden not your hearts. The devil's time is always tomorrow; God's time is always today.

Yes, the verse says that. But the Spirit of God has been saying more to me: it is saying that God's grace is always coming to my heart and life in a very wonderful and blessed experience of now. Yesterday's grace is totally inadequate for the burden of today, and if I do not learn to lay hold of heavenly resources every day of my life for the little things as well as the big things, as a Christian I soon become stale, barren, and fruitless in the service of the Lord. Now is the day of salvation. This is the moment in which God's grace is available to me, in any emergency and in any situation. Thank heaven that whatever the surprises, disappointments, and problems that may come to me at any moment of any day, I do not have to look back and say, "What did the preacher say last Sunday that I should do at this moment? What was it that I did when I faced that situation last week?" No, for any situation, at any moment, as I live day by day in His will, now is the day of salvation.

Charles Inwood has described this in a lovely way: "It is a constant appropriation of a constant supply from Jesus Christ Himself. As I believe, I receive; and as I go on believing, I go on receiving." Speedily I will dissipate the grace of God, its supply will become stale and ineffective in my life, and I will become totally barren if I am always looking back upon the past, drawing upon past experiences and old deliverances, ... if I am not proving that the God of Jacob and the God of Elijah and the God of Moody and Taylor is my God today, with grace sufficient at every moment to meet every need. Beware that you do not dissipate the grace of God by failing moment by moment to lay hold of a heavenly supply.

There is another way that the grace of God can be dissipated suggested to us by the third verse. It occurs when we make the grace of God the ground for continuation in sin, "Giving no offence in any thing, that the ministry be not blamed." When he uses the word *ministry*, Paul is not speaking specially of a few people who are called ministers. I reminded you previously that when a man is born again he enters into a life of ministry and service. "...As the Son of man came not to be ministered unto, but to minister, and to give his life a ransom for many," so every Christian is called upon to live sacramentally, as broken bread and poured-out wine, in the service of the King of kings and for the blessing of his fellowmen. Now, says Paul, let this ministry of yours never be blamed and held in low repute: "give offence in nothing." You will speedily dissipate the grace of God if you imagine that all His fullness of supply is being given to you to excuse you and to allow you to continue living in sin and failure.

I know full well that God's grace comes to us as a free gift and His salvation is His precious gift through the blood of Jesus in response to our repentance — I am fully aware of this — but I am also aware that my Bible tells me that though the law of God may make heavy demands upon an individual, the grace of God makes bigger demands. If a man would live day by day by grace for the glory of God, the demands made upon him are of a deeper and a more complete and fuller level than the law could ever make. We will see in a moment the wonderful fact that when the grace of God makes the demand, grace meets the demand with heavenly supply. Therefore I must be careful that I do not dissipate the grace of God by making His grace an excuse to continue living in sin.

So Paul, in his appeal for consistency, begins by disclosing the peril of dissipating the grace of God. Let us learn, moment by moment, to lay hold upon heavenly supply; let us learn to regard the grace of God as a great lever that gets underneath and lifts us up constantly to a deeper, higher, fuller life in Jesus Christ that enables us to say, "…in all these things [by His grace] we are more than conquerors…"

If Paul makes this appeal for consistency, warning us of the peril of dissipating the grace of God, I find myself asking a question: "Where would I expect that in normal situations the grace of God would be revealed in my life?" The answer to that question is found in verses 4–10, which provide a platform for the display of God's grace in your life. To be quite honest with you, I have to admit that Paul leaves me right behind! As I listen to him opening his heart about what it means to be a Christian, somehow he is far ahead and I have to stand back and admire it all, and recognize that this is an experience through which I have never yet passed and to which I have never yet come. Nevertheless it is an ideal my heart would long to attain. I am sure that I am in the same school and that I understand this principle, therefore I am careful to say, not as though I had already attained, or were already perfect, but this one thing I do, I press toward the mark.

What is the platform upon which the grace of God is displayed in a man's life? What are the areas in which one might expect to see grace working itself out in that life? Is it in some time of great crisis? Is it in the ministry of a pulpit? Is it in some great public work, through some business career or public situation? No, for I find that Paul opens his heart and draws aside the veil to show us some things that are the platform upon which grace is being displayed, things that lie right behind the scenes, that tell us about the reactions of the man, not when he is in the public arena, but when he is alone with God.

In the first place, there are conditions in our lives which have to be borne patiently, conditions which are the theme of verses 4 and 5. As by grace we learn to bear such conditions patiently, so too there are characteristics in our lives that are going to be revealed (vv. 6–7). As these characteristics are expressed in our lives, there will be contrasts which will be accepted gladly (vv. 8–10). I want you to notice this very carefully: the first of these conditions has to do with what happens to a man in his body. The second of these conditions is what happens to a man in his mind. The third of these conditions is what happens to a man in his spirit.

Here is the whole platform upon which grace is going to be displayed, upon which all the fullness of God—of which I may lay hold every day so that I will not dissipate His grace—is revealed in power to lift me up and enable me to triumph in every area. Here is the platform, and here is a man, as it were, exposed to the gaze of people, and, most of all, exposed to the scrutiny of heaven. Such is the picture of what grace can do for us today, if we receive it not in vain.

What about the conditions that we must bear patiently? There is a group of nine such conditions; note them carefully: affliction, which means physical suffering; necessities, which means that physically you are put on a spot where there is a desperate need and you do not know how to meet it; distresses, which implies that physically you are in such a place that you do not know where to turn; stripes, which means taking punishments. Do you remember that the apostle says on one occasion that he took forty stripes five times save one for the gospel's sake, one hundred and ninety-five lashes altogether? One hundred and ninety-five strokes of the whip because he was a Christian. You say that is unknown today. No, it is not. The church in China is going through it all the time, and probably the church in Russia too. This is not history but present-day experience in some places. We may just regard them from a distance in this land, but God only knows what the future holds for the people who are true to Him. Here, however, Paul continues with the conditions to be borne patiently: imprisonments, tumults raised by both Jew and Gentile against him; labors, which means the traveling and work in the spreading and preaching of the gospel; watchings, which means his prayer-life as he watched and waited; fastings, which means his personal life of self-denial, as he denied himself the legitimate for the sake of the Lord Jesus.

358 / Blessings Out of Buffetings

Do you see why I say that Paul leaves me behind? I suppose he has left you behind too! Yet there are principles here, which must be learned in daily living, which we must be ready to take, conditions that we must face patiently. If I learn to face them, there are characteristics that are to be exhibited daily. They are given in another cluster of nine conditions. Pureness: let us remember there is no piety without purity; no pious phraseology, no evangelical language, however good it may sound, is adequate or has any meaning at all unless it is supported by purity. "Blessed are the pure in heart: for they shall see God." A man who is pure is one who is unspotted from the world. Knowledge: zeal without knowledge is a dangerous thing, and therefore Paul says these characteristics are to be exhibited if the grace of God is not received in vain. Long-suffering means tenderheartedness, bearing hard treatment kindly. Kindness: the word is love, charity. By the Holy Ghost, this is the power and fruit of grace, its very character. Love unfeigned, in which I love not for any wrong motive but simply for the blessing of the other. The word of truth and the power of God, that is the best attack against sin. The armor of righteousness on the right hand and on the left, here is the best defense against temptation that I know. Here then are characteristics that are going to be exhibited on this platform on which a man is living his life.

Paul finally moves on to speak of contrasts that are going to be suffered gladly, and there is another cluster of nine such contrasts. Honor and dishonor: evil report and good report; deceiving and yet true; unknown yet well known; dying and behold we live; chastened but not killed; sorrowful but always rejoicing; poor but making many rich; having nothing but possessing all things—the contrast.

Put yourself in the place of the man on the platform in the arena of his life as he is observed both from heaven and from earth. From the standpoint of this world the man is dishonorable, deceiving, nobody knows a thing about him (he never gets his name in the headlines!), living a perpetual death, constantly suffering, sorrowful, and so poor he does not possess a single thing. That is the aspect from the standpoint and judgment of the world upon the man who is a disciple and who is receiving not the grace of God in vain. He is not held in a great deal of repute by the world, but heaven looks down upon him and observes not only that he is bearing conditions patiently and revealing certain characteristics, but that he is suffering some contrasts gladly for the gospel's sake. Heaven holds him in high honor, and says that he is true, and though he is being chastened, it is bringing forth fruitfulness in character; though he is dying, the inner man is being renewed day by day; though he is being persecuted he is not being killed; though he is sorrowful, inwardly there is a joy that perhaps the world does not detect. Also he is poor, yes very poor, not merely materially but in so many other ways—but I will tell you something that the Lord sees though the world does not: each night when he goes to bed he is so poor that he has not one little drop of grace left! All the grace of God for that day has gone, he is exhausted and without any reserve for tomorrow. But he just goes to sleep for he knows "…as thy days, so shall thy strength be," and he waits until the next morning to be filled up again with God's daily grace. But in the process of being poor, he is making many rich: and though he possesses apparently nothing, yet he has access to the treasure in heaven, and nothing can ever touch that or ever take it away.

Here then is the platform upon which grace is being displayed, the platform of a man's life as he is being surveyed by an unfriendly world. As he is not receiving the grace of God in vain, he is bearing physical suffering patiently, and in his outlook, his thoughts, and his attitudes, he is exhibiting characteristics daily, and he is bearing contrasts between himself and the world gladly.

There is one further thing to say that seems to round it all up concerning this appeal for consistency. I have admitted—and perhaps you have too—that in terms of experience Paul has left us a long way behind. However, in the principle of the thing, by the grace of God, I think I can say that I am following in his track—are you? I see in this passage what I would call the principle of dispensing the grace of God. There is not only the peril of dissipating it and throwing it away, not on the characters of the platform upon which I can display it in every area of life, but the principle upon which God dispenses grace.

In this tremendous, open-hearted statement concerning God's dealing with him, Paul has shown us what a contrast there is between the Christian and the unbeliever—different contrasts and different phases of life—and if there is one thing that seems to me to stand out, it is the spirit of his absolute detachment from the world around him. He holds the things of time so lightly and is concerned about one supreme thing: a life of consistency in which there is detachment in every area of life. This consistency includes several characteristics. It is exhibiting characteristics that are totally contrary to the spirit of the world. It is bearing these things patiently while the world would be impatient. It is suffering contrasts where otherwise he would feel himself so out of place, and doing this because in his spirit he is a man who is detached.

What do I mean by that? God expends His grace day by day, not in the public arena or in the crowd, but as He sees His child alone with Himself. He observes His reactions and his thoughts to suffering and depression, to pressures, and to the whole spirit of the world in which he lives. He is advancing in his study and reading of the Bible; he is advancing in his prayer life; he is advancing in his witness. In all these contrasts and under all these pressures God watches this man and sees the discipline of his life.

You may be a woman—He watches you in the kitchen and as the mother of children; He watches you in your home and longs to see one in whose life His grace is not be dissipated, but rather a life where grace is being received gladly, as you live day by day on the platform of the world.

I want to ask you this very personal question: I do not know what your life has been like during the past week, or what your circumstances are at all, but have you advanced? Have you advanced in your prayer life and your devotional life? Have you gone deeper, and has there been progress behind the scenes? Has the grace of God dissipated this week, or has it been laid hold of? Amid all the pressures that have come upon you and the contrasts you observed because you are a Christian, and the afflictions which have been yours, have these things caused you to advance in the things of God? Has that housewife advanced in grace in her kitchen, in her home as a mother of children? Has that businessman, in his office with all the problems that beset him, experienced a week of progress? God has been watching and has seen you upon the platform that only He can see. God dispenses fullness of grace every day to the man who is (do not misunderstand me) learning to squander it and to come to Him day by day for more. Such a man is not dissipating God's grace because he is relying on the past. But he is going deeper every day into the Word and into prayer, deeper into the Lord, that there may be further and greater supplies of grace. Thus he is advancing.

If ever there was a time when the church of Jesus Christ needed to advance like this, to take root downward and to bear fruit upward, it is in these days. What has your Bible study been like this week? Just a little casual reading with a casual time of prayer, hurried, unbalanced, unmeaningful, which has not put anything into your life and has not helped? Have you been dissipating His grace by saying to yourself, "Well, I remember at the last Keswick Convention I got a blessing. I will rely upon that and ask the Lord to make it real again"? He will not. It has gone forever, but there is Jesus Christ, who is the same yesterday, today, and forever, waiting to dispense grace to those who are prepared to live on this principle, to those who bear outward circumstances patiently, to those whose lives express certain characteristics daily, and in whose lives there is the glad acceptance of the contrast between the spirit of the world and the will of God.

Are you making progress in a life of true consistency?

CHAPTER TWELVE

A CALL TO CONSECRATION

2 CORINTHIANS 6:11–18

I am sure that a minister never appears in so forbidding a form, especially to young people, as he does when he comes to deal with this subject of separation, and with the relationship of the Christian to the world in which we live. Many people are almost ready to account him an enemy of their happiness, and call him a kind of promoter of gloom and misery. Immediately they will put up all sorts of defenses, and there springs to their minds a torrent of ideas to refute every argument from the pulpit. For instance, "Narrowness! Legalism! Why shouldn't I? What is the harm in it?"

Now before any of you withdraw into a bomb-proof shelter, I would show you the spirit of Paul when he wrote these words to the Corinthian Christians, for at this point in the letter he suddenly breaks into a passionate appeal for them to separate themselves from every worldly entanglement. They simply must maintain the fundamental opposition which exists between the Christian way of life and that of the world. The two are as irreconcilable—and Paul uses some tremendously graphic contrasts—as light and darkness, God and the devil, faith and unbelief. He well knew that the Christians lived daily in heathen surroundings, and were in grave danger of falling prey to the spirit of the world around them.

This appeal immediately follows the most wonderful outpouring of love from the heart of the apostle that you would find anywhere in the New Testament, so much so that he almost seems to apologize for it. "Oh ye Corinthians, our mouth is open unto you, our heart is enlarged." (v. 11). In other words, we have told you about our life and how we live it in the opening part of this chapter. We have spoken to you about conditions that we bear patiently, characteristics that we reveal daily, contrasts we accept gladly, for Jesus' sake and for your sake. We have opened our heart to you completely, not to boast for our spirituality, but to show you that we love you and long for God's best in your lives. "Ye are not straitened in us, but ye are straitened in your own affections [bowels]" (v. 12). In other words, there is no coldness in our hearts towards you; we love you. "I beg of you as my children," Paul says, in effect, "do not be cold in your response! Do not be suspicious of our motives! Let your heart be as wide open to the message of the Word as ours is to you."

It is in that very same spirit that I would minister to you in the things of the Lord, as one member of God's family to others. As one member of the family would warn another member of the family of the things that are likely to throw him off-center in relation to his service for God, so I would speak to you in His name, and ask that you, too, might be enlarged. Do not hide behind some shelter as we come to think of this great subject. Come prepared to receive everything that God has for you in His Son, who purchased you at Calvary. Come as believers, persuaded that there is an experience of the fullness of blessing in Christ if we are prepared to walk God's way.

A text like this, if it is to be understood, has to be seen in a far wider context than in its local meaning to the Corinthian church, or even in the immediate situation surrounding us today. If you use these verses simply as an argument for negative approach to almost anything, resulting in a Christian's shutting himself away in a nice little corner all his own labeled "Separated," you do a gross injustice to the whole teaching of the Word of God. I want you to see the greatness and dignity of this text, and therefore to see the greatness and dignity of the Christian life. I want you to see something of its urgent application to your life today.

Is it not a wonderful thing that God has made us a part of His great program of redemption? Surely that is something that must compel our uttermost response in love to Him. Therefore here is a word that is based upon an Old Testament command. It is as old as the dawn of redemption, rooted in Old Testament history. Indeed, it is the substance of the call of Isaiah the prophet: "Depart ye, depart ye, go ye out from thence, touch no unclean thing; go ye out of the midst of her; be ye clean; that bear the vessels of the Lord" (Isaiah 52:11).

It was the call of the prophet to the exiles in Babylon. It was the Word of God to Solomon as he dedicated the Temple: "If my people, which are called by my name, shall humble themselves, and pray, and seek my face, and turn from their wicked ways; then will I hear from heaven, and will forgive their sin, and will heal their land" (2 Chronicles 7:14).

In essence it is the subject of innumerable prophetic appeals in the Word of God, and underlying them all is God's conception of His people as a peculiar treasure for His own enjoyment. He claims Israel for Himself, and He sets them apart from all others. He began it, of course, in a covenant with Abraham, but it was initiated in that day when they were brought out from Egypt under the covering of the blood, and brought through the Red Sea, guided through the wilderness, and brought into the land of fullness of blessing. This was the people who were bound to God by solemn obligation and by sacred rights. He gave them first of all His commandment which was "I am the Lord thy God, which have brought thee out of the land of Egypt, out of the house of bondage. Thou shalt have no other gods before me" (Exodus 20:2–3).

God and His people have always been intended to be all in all to each other. Nothing must ever come between them, and if anything threatens to break that bond, it must be destroyed. Therefore the Canaanites must be rooted out; the high places of idol worship must be cast down; there must be no intermarriage with the heathen. This principle was enforced by prophetic teaching and by bitter experience, until it became the passion of the heart of every Jew. This applies to the appeal of God in Isaiah 52 that carries the conviction—often, I am afraid, in a fanatical spirit—that they stood above all other nations in their separation to God.

You might ask why should this be so? What is God's motive in it all? Well, it is twofold. First, it was for their preservation. They were to be hedged in like a walled garden in order that it might be kept from weeds and from thorns that would choke it. If they were not so sheltered, it would not be long before they would lose their faith, adopt heathen customs, and walk in heathen ways until they became as corrupt as the heathen people around them, and nobody could distinguish the difference between them.

The whole history of Israel is a powerful testimony to that very danger. Time after time, you recall, they were seduced from their real faith, to their own sorrow and bitter experience. Even Solomon had his heart turned away by the fascination of heathen women. How much more easily then could it happen to the ordinary people? Here was the lifelong struggle of the Jewish people with their tragic failure and downfall; against this the voices of the prophets were raised consistently. It is this that gives a wonderful sense of pathos to the prayer of Ezra. As he came back from captivity and chastisement into the land, and found God's people mingling again in marriage with the heathen, he says with a broken heart as he prays to God, "And after all that is come upon us for our evil deeds, and for our great trespass, seeing that thou our God hast punished us less than our iniquities deserve, and hast given us such deliverance as this; Should we again break thy commandments, and join in affinity with the people of these abominations? wouldest not thou be angry with us till thou hadst consumed us, so that there should be no remnant nor escaping? O Lord God of Israel, thou art righteous: for we remain yet escaped, as it is this day: behold, we are before thee in our trespasses: for we cannot stand before thee because of this" (Ezra 9:13–15).

It was for the sake of their preservation that God marked them out as a separated people.

But not only so. Second, it was because—may I say it reverently, in the presence of the Lord, and with such a sense of awe in my soul?— of the exclusiveness of God's love. You see, love is possessive, and when the whole heart is given, then the whole heart must be returned. It will be satisfied with nothing less. When God empties heaven of all the glory and gives Himself to the point of bankruptcy, as He gave everything in Jesus Christ at the cross, He will not accept less than all in return. That was the demand that God made upon His redeemed people. His love would have no rival: "...the Lord thy God is a jealous God..." In case you think that is an ugly thing to say about God, may I remind you that He was not jealous of other rivals for His sake, but because of what the rivals would do to His people. It was for their sake.

In Old Testament picture language, how wonderfully that love is portrayed to us. It is the love of a father: "...Ephraim is my firstborn" (Jeremiah 31:9). It is the love of a husband: "...I am married unto you, saith the Lord" (Jeremiah 3:14); "...thy Maker is thine husband..." (Isaiah 54:5). And that wonderful love of God could stand the strain of His people's sin apparently without limit. It could forgive and restore, because in the amazing drama of Hosea, He says, "…behold, I will allure her, and bring her into the wilderness, and will speak unto her; … I will even betroth thee unto me…" (Hosea 2:14, 20). Can ever that love of God be satisfied with less than the whole heart, that His people should keep themselves for Him alone?

You see that this great text is rooted in Old Testament revelation, in the purpose of God for our preservation, and for the satisfaction of His loving heart. But there is a New Testament interpretation also, and in this sense the same call is made upon the Christian. The Jew, of course, gave it a meaning that ministered to their racial pride, as an excuse for contempt of other people, but all that is done away in Christ. Yet the same call for separation — not racially or socially, but in spirit and manner of life — runs right through the Book. Jesus said, "If the world hate you, ye know that it hated me before it hated you. If ye were of the world, the world would love his own: but because ye are not of the world, but I have chosen you out of the world, therefore the world hateth you" (John 15:18–19).

That is the whole significance of the cross, the place where Jesus died! It reminds us that the Lord whom we follow was rejected and cast out because the spirit of His life, His way and manner of life, were so totally contrary to the spirit of the world. He said to His disciples, "…if any man will come after me, let him deny himself, and take up his cross daily, and follow me" (Luke 9:23). We are called to take sides with Him against a world that crucified Him.

The New Testament church had no misconception of what He meant. The writer to the Hebrews says, "Wherefore Jesus also, that he might sanctify the people with his own blood, suffered without the gate. Let us go forth therefore unto him without the camp, bearing his reproach" (Hebrews 13:12–13). The apostle James takes up the theme, saying, "Pure religion and undefiled before God and the Father is this, To visit the fatherless and widows in their affliction, and to keep himself unspotted from the world" (James 1:27). Almost in a burst of indignation — which I feel, not knowing him personally but reading between the lines, James was quite capable of — he writes, "Ye adulterers and adulteresses, know ye not that the friendship of the world is enmity with God? whosoever therefore will be a friend of the world is the enemy of God" (James 4:4). I think his pen nearly took fire when he wrote like that! He was indignant at the possibility of a Christian's getting mixed up with worldly things.

Paul's whole view of the Christian life rested upon this principle. "But God forbid that I should glory, save in the cross of our Lord Jesus Christ, by whom the world is crucified unto me, and I unto the world ... let no man trouble me ... for I bear in my body the marks of the Lord Jesus" (Galatians 6:14, 17). And to Paul the gulf between himself and the world was as wide and as final as was death itself.

The Christian is to reckon himself dead unto sin and alive unto God. He is a soldier on active service and therefore he must not entangle himself with the affairs of this life. He is part of a colony of heaven living in an alien, enemy country. He must be subject to the laws of the kingdom of which he is a member, and if you want to know what they are, read the Sermon on the Mount.

The motive in the New Testament is exactly the same as the motive in the Old Testament. First, for our preservation, not racially but spiritually, Jesus prayed — oh that you would catch the anguish in the heart of our precious Lord as He prayed in the last days of His earthly life: "I pray not that thou shouldest take them out of the world, but that thou shouldest keep them from the evil. They are not of the world, even as I am not of the world" (John 17:15–16). I was included in that prayer, so were you; is not that wonderful?

God's motive is not only for our preservation and purity, but it is for the satisfaction of the heart of God, for Jesus declared that the first and greatest commandment is, "...Thou shalt love the Lord thy God with all thine heart, and with all thy soul, and with all thy mind ... Ye cannot serve God and mammon." There can be no rival in the heart to this supreme passion of the love of God, and as Christ loved His own unto the end, He must have our whole love in return. The Holy Spirit uses, in the New Testament, exactly the same symbol of marriage as He uses in the Old Testament: "...I have espoused you to one husband, that I may present you as a chaste virgin to Christ. But I fear, lest by any means, as the serpent beguiled Eve ... so your minds should be corrupted from the simplicity that is in Christ" (2 Corinthians 11:2–3). What daring language!

Our text is as great, as deep, as wide, as long as all the revelation of God. It is a part of God's mind, heart, and purpose for His people, from the day when He flung the stars in space until the day when we shall see His lovely face, and we are part of that great plan. Therefore, come ye out from among them and be ye separate, saith the Lord Almighty.

Now, wait a minute, that is all very well, but what is the modern significance? The great question is, how are we to apply it today? I hope you read John Bunyan's books: *Pilgrim's Progress, Grace Abounding, Holy War*. Do you remember how Bunyan describes his pilgrims in Vanity Fair? He says of them that they were so different from all the others in their dress, in their speech, in their behavior, and in their contempt for the merchandise of the Fair. Is that relevant in our day? Many would reply no! Oh, that was all right in the dark ages of ancient civilization, but when Christian principles are applied to society in which we live, the call is obsolete.

That is the most dangerous attitude a Christian can take today. It is an attitude that pulls the dynamic power of the church of Jesus Christ right down to the level of a godless, sinful, Christ-rejecting world until she is powerless to lift the world up. We have set aside the call to separation.

To what extent do you think Christian principles are really applied in modern society? I suggest to you that the veneer is very thin, not even more than skin deep. It is the same world that rejected Christ, and it does so still. It is a civilization which is under the judgment of God, and it is doomed to destruction. The Babylon of the Old Testament has its counterpart today, and in the great last Book of the Word of God, in the picture of the overthrow of world civilization, God says: "…Come out of her, my people, that ye be not partakers of her sins, and that ye receive not of her plagues. For her sins have reached unto heaven, and God hath remembered her iniquities" (Revelation 18:4–5).

It is fantastically absurd—it is worse than that, it is sheer downright sin—for one generation for the sake of its worldly convenience to imagine that it can lower the bars of separation, which are rooted in divine history, and revealed in divine prophecy, when we live in a world that is under God's judgment and doomed to destruction, and when Jesus Christ is returning to take His people home. Yet most Christians are satisfied to conform to custom, to dress, and to the opinion of the day in which we live, and the great command, "…be not conformed to this world: but be ye transformed by the renewing of your mind…" ceases to grip our hearts, and is regarded as archaic. Indeed, it even creates resentment on the part of those who argue that you must conform if you would live. I wonder who spread that devilish doctrine into the church of Christ today? The great church historian, Honeck, records this: "The church never had so much influence on the world as when she kept herself aloof from it. A church conformed to the world will never lead it; she must separate if she would live."

Now if that principle is true for this day—as it has certainly been true in every other, and it is certainly yet to be true in those to come till Jesus comes again—then how do I apply it in daily life? Do you know where we have gone wrong, and why we have brought down upon us the scorn of an unbelieving world? We have laid down mechanical rules and lifted a whole row of things that are taboo. Life is far too complex for that. You cannot lift certain things and make separation from them a mark of Christian discipleship. Let me be careful to say, nevertheless, that what Christian people found to be harmful in days gone by, they are most likely to find harmful today. On the other hand, separation such as I am talking about is not a negative thing; it is a positive thing. It is not simply living contrary to the world, as I have said before, putting yourself in a little compartment labeled "Separated," and making everybody mad at you. It is living in harmony with the passion in the heart of God for a world that is lost. That is separation.

Separation is investing every moment of your day, wherever you may be, in the ministry or in secular life (and that is a ministry anyway), to the glory of God in a commitment to His authority and power in your life without reservation. This means that day by day you live in such a way that you refrain from doing anything which would disturb your harmony with God. I am not concerned if people do not like me, and I am unpopular down here. But I am very concerned if I lose the harmony of my relationship with the Holy Spirit. He is a very sensitive Lord.

It is not a question simply of trying to empty your heart and life of every worldly desire—what an awful impossibility! It is rather opening your heart wide to all the love of God in Christ, and letting that love just sweep through you and exercise its expulsive power till your heart is filled with love.

One would think that a fundamentalist group of Christians ought never to need to be told this, but they do! Surely the all-sufficient incentive for a holy life is not legalism but grace, not saying to a young Christian, "Thou shalt not do this or that; thou shalt not go here or there." No, it is saying, "Do you not recognize what God has done for you in Jesus Christ, the privileges that are yours, what it cost Him to forgive you? That which you have taken so easily as God's gift was purchased with a broken heart, with the God of all the universe giving His life for you outside Jerusalem. You are the temple of the living God."

You see, this is Paul's basis for it (v. 16). A temple is set apart for holy use. In Old Testament days it was in three parts: the outer court of service, the holy place of sacrifice, the holiest of all of worship. You are the temple of the living God and the outer court of your body (the place of service), the inner place (the holy place of your soul where you make decisions, the place of sacrifice), and the holiest of all (your spirit, the place of worship), every bit of you, is set apart in the sight of heaven for holy use. The conduct of the people in the outer court and in the holy place of the Temple was regulated twenty-four hours, day and night, by the awful sense of the presence of the living God in the holiest of all. "I will dwell in them, and walk in them; and I will be their God, and they shall be my people." The whole temple is set apart for His glory.

Are you going to argue about motion pictures? Do not be so absurd! You are set apart for His glory, every bit of you, every minute of every day. Bunyan—forgive me for quoting a favorite author again—says of his unconverted days, "I well remember that though I could myself sin with the greatest delight and ease, yet even then if I saw wicked things practised by those who professed godliness, it made my spirit tremble."

I am not going to lay down any rules for you for it is not law but grace, but I am going to suggest principles about anything in your life which is a problem: Is it to the glory of God for you to do that (1 Corinthians 10:31)? Has it the appearance of evil (1 Thessalonians 5:22)? Is it a stumbling block to a weaker Christian? Beware how you use your liberty in Christ lest a younger brother be caused to offend. Is it a weight? Does it drag you down? Does it make your prayer-life more difficult? Does it dim the vision of your wonderful Savior? Does it make you less than your best when you are praying and reading the Word? Does it destroy all that, or does it help you see His lovely face? Can you ask His blessing upon it? "The blessing of the Lord, it maketh rich, and he addeth no sorrows..." If you are honest and concerned enough, and deeply devoted enough to the Lord Jesus, when you apply those principles, you will have no doubts whatsoever about anything.

What a promise there is here for obedience (v. 18). What does the Lord offer to His child who is really prepared to face this? Relationship with God is established by faith and commitment to Jesus Christ as Savior and Lord; but sonship and friendship are the rewards of obedience

(John 15:7). Such a reward is the result of an intimate relationship with the Lord that makes us sensitive to sin. Nothing else matters too much except that there may be in your heart an intimate sense of His nearness and love, His protecting care, His presence and joy. How urgent it is that you might hear His Word, for the church of today has lost its savor because it is conformed to the pattern of the age and is no longer marked out as being a separated church. The spirit of the world has poisoned our life and paralyzed our testimony, and on that level the church of today is powerless to do a thing. In the light of the majesty, dignity, and greatness of this text at the very heart of divine revelation, respond to His great love in terms of the cross, and say to Him, "Father, I yield!"

CHAPTER THIRTEEN

REVIVAL THROUGH REPENTANCE

2 CORINTHIANS 7:1–16

At this point in our studies a remarkable transformation has taken place in the church at Corinth. What wonderful blessings, what things have been happening, how this church has been revived! Once it was carnal, though not when it was founded. No Christian is ever carnal when he begins his Christian life, but he can sink into carnality. And this church had sunk into carnality, but now it is living in great blessing and victory, so that Paul can say, "I rejoice therefore that I have confidence in you in all things" (v. 16).

What a contrast! You remember in 1 Corinthians he said, "...there is among you envying, and strife, and divisions, are ye not carnal...?" (1 Corinthians 3:3). And in chapter 4 he said, "...some are puffed up..." (v. 18). Phillips uses the expression "like inflated gas bags"! In chapter 6 Paul says: "...ye do wrong, and defraud, and that your brethren" (v. 8). But now, "...I have confidence in you in all things." What a tremendous transformation! What has happened?

Let Paul tell us in his own language, as I paraphrase the opening verses of this chapter. In the fourth verse he says, in effect, to them, "I speak to you boldly and I glory in you, for you have given me so much comfort. I am joyful in the midst of all my testings and afflictions and tribulations in the ministry. What has happened to you has filled me with joy, and I can tell you when it happened.

"One day I was in the very depths of despair. I was in Macedonia at the time, actually in Philippi, and while there I had no rest for my body, and I was attacked on every side. Without were fightings and within me were all kinds of fears. I was at a low ebb. I was really with my back to the wall. But God knows just when to bring us a word of encouragement when we are like that. And at that moment, Titus arrived on the scene, having come to me from Corinth. Not only was I refreshed because he came to talk and pray with me, but I was so refreshed because of what he told me about you. He told me how you had received my first letter. It had rocked you, and grieved and hurt you. But it had brought you down not in anger, but in utter repentance—not merely sorrow, but real godly repentance. You have dealt with the thing about which I had spoken to you, and you have borne ever since all the marks of repentance and the fruit of it in your lives. Because of this, I am both refreshed and encouraged. Why? It's worth all that I have been through in my ministry," says Paul, "to know that this has happened to you."

In other words, here is a church that had existed for quite a while which had slipped from the vision into carnality, but now was living in victory and revival because it had taken a shattering blow in the power of the Holy Spirit from the preacher who himself loved those people so deeply that he says of them in the third verse: "You are in our hearts to die and live with you"—or as the *Amplified New Testament* says: "You are nestling in our hearts, we love you so much."

Paul, who spoke to them like this and loved them so deeply, nevertheless had to face them with some important issues, but they had accepted his rebukes, had listened to his word, and had responded with broken-hearted repentance. Because of this, God had brought them right through into revival. What a wonderful thing true repentance is! Indeed, I believe that all of the gospel can be included in this simple statement: "...repentance toward God, and faith toward our Lord Jesus Christ" (Acts 20:21). True repentance is not only a momentary act, but a constant attitude of the heart.

Do you know this experience? Do you understand it? You cannot separate faith and repentance. True, repentance inevitably must lead to saving faith. But saving faith can never exist without constant repentance. The gospel which talks much about faith and little about repentance will be free from offence, and will certainly be much easier to preach, but it will be deprived of all heavenly power. For the preacher to say, "peace, peace," when there is no peace is to make himself an ally of unrighteousness, and to make himself guilty of allowing indulgence in sin.

Let us look, therefore, at the significance and the qualities of true repentance. Keeping closely to the context of this chapter, see first the root of repentance. But let me say, by way of explanation, that in thinking about the root of repentance in the Christian life you can never have uniformity of experience. No two people are alike. Perhaps it is just as well! But you are unique, you are different from every other person, and because you are different, your experience with Christ is different.

Isn't it wonderful to think that in the eons of eternity—it will take all eternity to tell—as you meet people in heaven, each one will be able to tell you about the road he came along to meet God in Christ at Calvary, for everyone has come along a different road. There will not be two people with the same testimony in heaven, even among the countless multitudes. There are as many roads that have led people to faith at Calvary as there are Christians. Inevitably there is a big difference between the life of a man who has spent most of his life on skid row before his deliverance, and the boy or girl who has had the privilege of the sheltered home and a Christian upbringing. Yes, there may be big differences, but there is always, in every true experience, an element of what Paul calls in this chapter "sorrow toward God" (vv. 9–11).

Quite evidently it is possible for us to be sorry, to be chagrined, to be full of remorse without ever being repentant. It is possible for sorrow to have nothing at all to do with God. That is the difference between true and false repentance. The one puts our sin in the light of God's judgment; the other ignores God altogether. The one grieves with a broken heart over the sin itself; the other is embittered with the consequences of sin, but has never been made to grieve over the act.

You see, crime is one thing, wrongdoing is another, and sin is still another. Crime is an offence against the law of the nation, wrongdoing is an offence against the law of your conscience, but sin is an offence against the law of God. If there is a God and I have personal relationships with Him and His law, to break God's law is much more than offence, it is much more than crime; it is sin!

Repentance begins when a man faces the law of God—the Ten Commandments as amplified in the teaching of the Lord Jesus on the Sermon on the Mount—examines his life alongside that law, and begins to recognize the awfulness of his sin. Nobody ever enters into grace before he has felt the thunder of the law of God and the condemnation of guilt which he cannot escape by any effort of his own. I want to speak confidently in the name of the Lord Jesus, although it is not easy to say: until I have seen my sin in the light that God sees it and have repented of it, I have never entered into the straight gate and the narrow way that leads me to life. No matter how much I have stressed my faith in Jesus, or how much I have said that I believe in Him and His work on the cross, unless I have seen my sin as He sees it and have repented of it, I have never entered into His Kingdom.

It is failure not to submit to that truth, and that failure has led to some desperately superficial expressions of so-called conversion. It is like the parable of the sower and the seed of which the Lord Jesus spoke in St. Matthew 13:20. The seed fell on stony ground and for a while it sprouted and grew, but then was shriveled by the heat of the sun, and having no root, it withered away. As He explained the parable, the Lord said these are they that have received the Word and for a time have rejoiced in it and are thankful for it, but because they have no root in themselves, they have withered.

Unless a man's faith in Jesus Christ is rooted in a soil which is bathed very often with tears, soil that has been broken up from its hardness, soil that has felt the melting and moving of God's Spirit in conviction of sin and has cried, "Oh, God, be merciful to me a sinner"—unless faith in Christ is grounded on that soil, it has no root and it will die.

Someone might say to me, "That's all very well. I understand that but, you see, I don't ever feel that I am sorry enough for my sin."

How sorry do you think you have to be? What is the purpose of your sorrow for sin? It is to bring you to trust in the atoning work of our Lord Jesus Christ. It is not your sorrow that cleanses you from sin, but His blood. It is the goodness of God that leads a man to repentance. Has your sorrow for sin led you at one time or another to fling all the burden of it at the feet of a crucified, risen Savior? If it hasn't, anything short of that is what Paul here calls sorrow that leads to death. This is the root of repentance.

Let me take you to the next step in what Paul has to say about this. Consider the reality of repentance. Clearly this text separates sorrow and repentance. This sorrow is not merely for sin. There are some passages in Scripture which actually attribute repentance to God. For instance, you will recall in the story of Jonah that after he had recovered himself, and set his face again toward Nineveh, he preached there in the power of God and Nineveh repented. And so what happened? "...God repented of the evil, that he had said that he would do unto them; and he did it not" (Jonah 3:10).

Godly sorrow that leads to repentance, therefore, is a sorrow that leads to a change of purpose, of intention, and of action. It is not the sorrow of idle tears; it is not crying by your bedside because once again you have failed; nor is it vain regret, wishing things had never happened, wishing that you could live the moments again. No, it is not that. It is a change of purpose and intentions, a change of direction and action.

Here is the whole difference between the sorrow of the world and that of godly sorrow. The sorrow of the world, the sense of remorse, the sense of failure, the sense of defeat which has come upon every-one of us many times I am sure in the course of our lives—that kind of sorrow leads to despair and unbelief. It often leads to an attempt at reformation, ... when you set out bravely into a new day saying, "It's never going to happen again!"

But it has happened again. Frustrated by inner corruption and the hopelessness of the battle against inbred sin, many people have been driven to the extreme limit of taking their own lives. When I read in the daily paper the verdict that is passed by the court, "Suicide while the mind was disturbed," my heart aches. I wonder if on that day when the truth is known, it will be the story of some poor fellow or girl who has battled with himself, with his temperament and the downward drag of a sinful nature, who has given it all up as hopeless, and has ended it by committing suicide. That kind of sorrow leads to death.

When sorrow for sin has swept over your heart, and you have been deeply convicted of that which you have done and you have cried like David of old, "Against thee, thee only, have I sinned"; when you have seen your sin not simply as an offence against the law of the land or a rejection of the voice of conscience, but as sin against God; when it is all over and your heart has been broken about it, will you then still be facing the same way? Is it right-about-turn or is it as you were? Has there been a right-about-turn and a complete switch around and now an upward look into the face of the Lord Jesus? This is the reality of repentance—something that has led you to His feet, that has changed the direction of your life, that has caused you to turn right around, and with a broken heart come to Him for cleansing and forgiveness. What is the result of it all? The next step is the main thrust of what Paul has to say: "Godly sorrow worketh repentance to salvation not to be repented of."

What do you think is the connection between repentance and salvation? Let me answer that question by two sentences which may seem to be contradictory, but which nevertheless get into the heart of the matter. First, you cannot have salvation without repentance. Second, you are not saved because you repent. Does that sound like a hopeless contradiction? Is it simply picking at words? No, it is touching at the heart of the whole matter. You cannot be a Christian without repentance, but you do not become a Christian because you repent.

Let me deal with the first: there is no salvation without forsaking of sin. Beware of making a scapegoat of the grace of God in order to permit you to continue living in personal failure. This is not in our Bible. It is no use for a preacher or for anybody else to say, "Believe! Believe! Believe!" unless he also says, "Let the wicked forsake his way, and the unrighteous man his thoughts: and let him return unto the Lord, ... for he will abundantly pardon."

It is an absolute, absurd contradiction, a denial of the great purpose of redemption. Surely, it is impossible for God to save a man and to give him deliverance from his sin while at the same time the man insists on holding on to it. Unless you turn from sin as resolutely as you would turn from a serpent if it crept into your room, you cannot enter into the kingdom of God. May the Spirit of God write that upon your heart!

But you do not get salvation by repentance.

> Could my zeal no respite know,
> Could my tears forever flow,
> All for sin could not atone;
> Thou must save, and Thou alone

We fight and struggle with this, and we will do everything under the sun rather than see this precious truth, that there is repentance in one hand and faith in the other, and repentance hand-in-hand with faith leads a man into the presence of a crucified Christ from whom peace will come immediately into the darkest and lowliest of hearts.

It is not my repentance but His death that is the ground of my salvation, and yet repentance is a condition of being saved. There is not true repentance which does not lead you to a complete trust in a crucified, risen Savior and the committal of your life to Him. But there is no trust in Him such as that trust without the absolute forsaking of all the things that you know to be wrong.

Now see the result of this in experience, expressed by Paul in the language of verse 11: "...behold this selfsame thing..."—here is the evidence that you sorrowed after a godly sort. What carefulness! Since that day how careful you have been of the company you keep, of the places you go, of running ahead needlessly into temptation! You have steered clear. You haven't given up friends; they have given you up. You have refused to get yourself involved or entangled again in a situation which would lead you back into the path. What carefulness!

What clearing of yourselves, not in any sense to vindicate yourself by self-justification, but by putting the whole business away forever, dealing with it, finishing with it without compromise. You have been careful not to leave one possible line of retreat. You may have written the letter stopping a friendship or correspondence, ending the whole affair. You have dealt with it at depth drastically and finally without compromise.

And what indignation! I am glad the Bible allows me to get mad, mad with the devil! To think that he had the audacity to pull me down and make me do that! What indignation, what fury at sin and all the agencies of Satan!

What fear, what reverence, what watchfulness! People will notice a difference in the way you walk and talk, for this experience with God has knocked the flippancy out of your life. It has removed the superficiality and froth from it, and it has made you one who walks in godly fear that Satan might trip you up again.

What a vehement desire, what hunger for a deeper relationship with God! Your concern now is that you might walk with God. And what zeal, what love, what anger for sin, and what zeal for Christian service! Why, the lethargy in service is all gone now. What zeal, what passion is being put into you!

What revenge against sin in all its ways and against your own folly! You are determined that, even though the hour be late, the Lord will restore the year or years that the locust has eaten. These, says Paul, are the things that have happened to you. I rejoice that I have confidence in you in all things. It has been worth all the buffeting that I have taken in my ministry to be able to say this of you again.

If these words have touched your heart, I beg of you do not trifle with the conviction of the Spirit. For if you do, you will only be hardened and will come one step nearer to the sorrow which worketh unto death. Do not trust to your tears, or your resolves, but yield yourself today to the Holy Spirit who convinces of sin and points you to Jesus' blood, and to a trust in Him. Let Him bring you to such repentance that you cast it all at His feet, One whose death for you and life in you by His Spirit gives you deliverance. Then you will have a salvation never to be repented of.

CHAPTER FOURTEEN

HEAVEN'S MISSIONARY PROGRAM

2 CORINTHIANS 8:1–9

In this last half century we have seen two world wars which have rocked civilization to its very foundation; if ever we stood at a critical moment in world history we do today. One crisis seems to follow another until we live in such a moment when either the Lord must soon be coming back, or disaster confronts us. There is just one other alternative and that is, that the Protestant church must recover its vision of God's plan for missionary enterprise that the gospel may reach out to every land in this generation. Another generation would be too late! The return of our Lord, the ruin of our civilization, or the revival of our Protestant faith, resulting in an outpouring of men, money, and equipment to the uttermost parts of the earth while there is yet time—these, I firmly believe, are three alternatives which face us at this moment.

Such revolutionary world changes as have taken place in these last years have left missionary enterprise lagging behind, both in terms of method and in terms of men. Never has there been a time when the church needed more than now a word from the Lord in heaven as to His will, plan, and strategy for this tremendous hour. So much of our Christian living these days lacks any sense of goal or of heavenly directed motive: so much of it is haphazard, without concern, and indifferent to the vital issues of the day.

I was interested to read that the United States spent no less than four billion dollars on what is called "religious and welfare activities," but it spent sixty and a half billion dollars on tobacco and alcohol a year. I wonder if there is any connection between that shattering statement and the fact that they spend seven times as much on church buildings as they do on foreign missions. In a poll of seventy Bible colleges, seminaries, and institutes for the past ten years of about thirty-three thousand graduates, only 9½ per cent have gone to the foreign mission field, 36½ per cent to the home ministry and no less than 53 per cent to secular work. I wonder if there is some connection between indulgence in tobacco and drink in the world, and the lack of vision and of real Holy Ghost concern and a lack of a sense of spiritual values that exists in the church today. The task is overwhelming, but we have a God-given opportunity to seek His face concerning His plan for His people at this moment. God grant we may not miss it, and God grant that as He speaks to us, we may not only hear but that we may respond and take action.

The most vital issue of all is to see to it that our lives are totally adjusted to the principles of heaven's missionary program, and that therefore the over-all missionary enterprise is in line with the pattern and purpose of the mind of God. Only as that is so can we expect to see the unfinished task completed, because He gives His Holy Spirit without measure to them that obey Him, and only Holy Spirit strategy can be adequate for a day like this. In this task we are engaged in a total spiritual campaign against a ruthless and powerful enemy: a spiritual enemy and a powerful foe, whose only superior—let this be noted and underlined—is God the Holy Ghost.

Our text, originally given as the motive for the Corinthian church in a matter of financial responsibility, is in fact the whole principle of the Christian life, and the secret of our strength and strategy for this great moment of missionary opportunity. Paul has spent a good deal of time in appealing for funds for the church in Jerusalem. This is evidence, incidentally, that the church is one and has a world-wide responsibility. Paul quotes the example of the churches in Macedonia, of whom we read in the second verse, in the rather startling paraphrase in Phillips' *Letter to Young Churches*: "Somehow, in most difficult cir-cumstances, their joy and the fact of being down to their last penny themselves, produced a magnificent concern for other people." What a statement! But how did they come to have such a concern, to give so recklessly and in their poverty? It was because they were gripped by the principle of heaven's program as outlined in the ninth verse. It was nothing less than that, and the understanding of what was involved in it, that brought them to the uttermost in surrender and sacrifice. For they "...first gave their own selves to the Lord, and unto us by the will of God" (v. 5). Not only did they give themselves to the Lord in commitment but then, and only then—after having made a total commitment to the Lord in response to the grace of our Lord Jesus Christ—they gave themselves to His church as His ambassadors and His servants in total availability for whatever the will of God might be. Surrender to Christ was followed by abandonment to the church of Christ in carrying out the church's program for world evangelization.

Now that same spirit of all-out dedication on every level must somehow catch all of us, for it lies at the very heart of heaven's strategy, and for lack of such dedication the cause of Christ is in a tragic condition today. But how can these things be accomplished? How can Christian people be stabbed awake and into alertness? Is it by the high pressure of financial appeals? Is it by masses of impressive statistics of world needs? Is it by fearful and horrifying stories, albeit true ones, of the advance of Communism?

No, not by any of these things will you stab the conscience of a Christian to get into the will of God. You will never do it by impressive statements concerning the need of the world, or of the shortness of funds. You will do it only when every child of God catches the glow and the fire which is in the heart of God in His love shed abroad by the Holy Spirit. You will do it only as you see the grace of our Lord Jesus Christ that He launched at Bethlehem, continued at Calvary, and continues today from the throne of heaven, and one day will complete when He returns. We shall only catch the glow and fire, and be stabbed awake, when we see what was involved in God's mighty counterattack against sin and Satan. No, if the church is going to arise to the tremendous opportunity and challenge of these days, it will be only as we see and know the grace of our Lord Jesus Christ, who though He was rich, yet for our sakes became poor, that we through His poverty might be rich.

Think first of the position of Christ, the pre-eminence of Christ, if you like. "...though he was rich..." How often I have tried to peer through the mystery of that statement; I have tried to plumb the depths, but I have to confess to you that my effort has been in vain. At least this much I can say: He was rich, rich in possession, the whole universe was His. He had only to speak one word and a new world would be created. He could put

His finger on every star. He could put His finger on anything and every-thing throughout all of His great creation and He could say, "Mine!" "...by him were all things created, that are in heaven, and that are in earth, visible and invisible, whether they be thrones, or dominions, or principalities, or powers: all things were created by him and for him: And he is before all things, and by him all things consist" (Colossians 1:16–17).

Jesus Christ was rich in honor. I think of the multitude of heavenly hosts that bowed before Him in praise and adoration. From time to time you catch a glimpse of it in the Word of God. Isaiah saw something of them, the Lord sitting upon the throne high and lifted up, and His train filling the Temple and above it the seraphim. Each one had six wings, and with twain he covered his face, with twain he covered his feet, and with twain he did fly—fly to the rescue of this spoiled and corrupt humanity that it might be cleansed from sin. Jesus was rich in honor with a great heavenly host around Him. A host only too eager to fly at His bidding.

He was rich in love, the love of His Father and of the Spirit. What human being could ever speak of the love which existed within the Trin-ity, between Father, Son, and Holy Ghost? The love of the Father—the Lord Jesus prayed in John 17:26 that "...the love wherewith thou hast loved me may be in them..." He was loved by the whole host of heaven. I sometimes wonder (and if this is but a flight of imagination, forgive me, but I am quite sure that when we speak on a text like this, one day when we meet the Lord, we shall be ashamed of our efforts) if heaven has held in history what we might call "a court day," when hosts of angelic beings and those who have not fallen into sin like this human race, visit some planets and stars, and return into the courts of heaven to bring their tribute of honor and glory and worship to the Lamb who was slain and who liveth again. Words fail me, but I know that He was rich, and the best place that heaven affords is His by sovereign right.

Oh, the pre-eminence of Jesus Christ! He was rich, yet He because poor. Oh, let us speak with bated breath! What amazement there must have been in the courts of heaven when the announcement was made that He was about to depart. Can you see Him stripping Himself of His glory? Can you see Him preparing for that journey? Can you see how they followed Him as far as they could into outer space, and even into the heaven around us, crying, "Glory to God in the highest, peace on earth, good will to men"?

Then see Him upon whose shoulders all this universe rested—for all things are upheld by the word of His power—being carried as a Babe in the arms of a peasant woman in Bethlehem. See Him in a dirty stable, and see Him in a carpenter's shop; no ray of glory now, none so poor as He.

We are told that His garments were woven from the top throughout—a mark of extreme poverty. See this wonderful Lord Jesus, who one day long ago in the councils of eternity dug the bed of the ocean, go to a sinful woman and say, "Give me to drink." He saw the foxes and the birds going back to their nests and resting-places, and He had to say, "I have nowhere to lay My head." Once He had been honored by the "Hallelujahs!" of heaven, and all the courts of glory had shouted His praise. Now He is stripped naked; He is put upon a cross to bleed and die; He is spat upon and struck.

Who can measure the gap between the throne and the cross? "He who was rich became poor": and poverty is always worse when you have known better days. If you want to know extremes of poverty, visit India and the cities of Calcutta and Madras and Bombay and other places, and you would see the poor outcasts in their thousands all suffering, perhaps getting two or three meals a week. But they have been like that since their birth; they have lived with it, and are used to it, and everybody else seems to live with it too. But one day Jesus was rich and He became poor. Oh, the grace of our Lord Jesus Christ! Cursed by everybody, for He became a curse of us.

What was the purpose of it all? For your sake, "…that ye through his poverty might be rich." For your sake, not just a certain group, not Christians *en masse*, but you, husband and wife, parent and child, young man and lady, one by one, for your sake, "He who was rich became poor."

Those eyes of yours, which He gave for vision, have seldom looked upon Him. That tongue or yours, which He gave for speech, has rarely spoken a word in His name. That life of yours, which He gave for His use and to be available for His purpose, is being used for anything but that. That heart of yours, which He gave that He might love through you, has loved anything and anybody except the Lord—for your sake, He who was rich became poor that you through His poverty might be rich.

When I have responded to this tremendous truth and to His mighty work, I discover in it possession. He became poor that you might have within our heart a fountain of life that would never dry up: not simply a little cistern or pool, but a fountain that would overflow in blessing to the world — God the Holy Ghost incarnate in your life that you might be rich in possession, that out from you might flow rivers of living water. Rich in promises, for every promise in the Book, sealed by His precious blood and absolutely unbreakable, is yours to claim by faith! "Go ye," He says, "into all the world and preach the gospel to every creature." Rich in promises and rich in power: "...ye shall receive power, after that the Holy Ghost is come upon you: and ye shall be witnesses unto me..."

Through His poverty you might become rich, and this is heaven's counterattack against sin, and this is still the only principle of heaven's missionary program — the grace of our Lord Jesus Christ, communicating Himself, a love that was never turned away by sin, a love that never held back because of unworthiness, a love that is not moved by anger, that is not easily provoked, content to give nothing less than a total, complete surrender and an absolute impartation of itself — that is heaven's counterattack. Oh, that we might know the glow of that love in our hearts!

> Fill me with gladness from above,
>   Hold me by strength divine;
> Lord, let the glow of Thy great love
>   Through my whole being shine.

Heaven's missionary program was that He became poor, assumed all the poverty of our manhood in order that through His poverty we might be made rich. He stooped to earth, veiled His deity in His humanity, in order that He might lift us right up into heaven, and clothe and veil our humanity in His divinity. He became like us that He might make us like Him; and "the Son of man came not to be ministered unto, but to minister, and to give his life a ransom for many."

This is not only an object for our worship, but it is the pattern and principle for our lives if we are to get into the heart of God's program today; for this same necessity that brought the Lord Jesus down to our level to lift us up to His level, to communicate Himself, to give nothing less than all for our sakes, to love and never to be turned away by sin, or by anger, or by provocation, is the principle upon which you and I are to live our lives if we are ever to get into God's plan for the world. For Jesus said, "Except a corn of wheat fall into the ground and die, it abideth alone: but if it die, it bringeth forth much fruit." Unless somehow this principle gets into the heart of Christian testimony before it is too late—when really and truly, not as a theory but as a principle for life, we die to ourselves for the sake of others—we are in solitude and in fact die while we think we are living, utterly fruitless; but if we die, then He lives in us to communicate His life and power and principle through us.

It was this principle of which the Lord speaks that had taken hold of the church in Macedonia. If you glance at the opening verse of this chapter again, notice how these churches were plunged into sorrow and trouble and deep poverty, that they gave far beyond what they could afford, for they could afford nothing. They gave far beyond prudence, and without waiting to be asked or pleaded with, they begged Paul that he would receive this gift. Just think of it! A church, financially bankrupt, unable to do a thing, so poor and unable to afford to keep themselves, yet this church comes with a gift and begs Paul that he might receive it on their behalf! Why? Because they had yielded themselves to the Lord, and they had seen and known the grace of the Lord Jesus Christ. They had given themselves up to Him entirely, and when a man comes to a place where he knows he does not own himself, when he comes to that moment in his life when he knows that the grace of the Lord Jesus is such that it did all that for him and therefore he does not own himself, he will never again say that he owns his money. He will never again say that material things belong to him. He belongs to the Lord Jesus Himself and therefore everything that he has is Christ's also.

And yet we argue about a tithe. God forgive us! We argue about how much we should give. Christian giving is never by commandment, by human pressure or by appeals—what an ugly, paltry level all that is—for the giving of money and of life! If the Holy Spirit is talking to us now, we are moving in an area far above all vulgar appeals for the raising of funds to meet the need of missionaries. We are in a place where we know the grace of our Lord Jesus Christ, and therefore we give ourselves in utter self-surrender to Him and, not only that, we follow through in the commitment of our lives to church of Christ for His use wherever He may lead. In other words, we become poor in every bit of self-confidence that we might make others rich.

I believe with all my heart, though I put this case so inadequately, that this principle of the cross lies at the very heart of heaven's missionary program. Alas, it is a principle to a large extent discarded and

388 / Blessings Out of Buffetings

gone out of use, and in place of it we major in higher education, better techniques, and development of talent, only to find ourselves in the thick of the spiritual battle tragically and helplessly inadequate to take the pressure of the hour. But alas again, instead of recognizing the reason for our failure, we leave the mission field or retire from Christian work and service for a prolonged furlough, and take further studies and more degrees, and we are bent on the same devil-misguided goal to educate the self-life till we fondly imagine we shall have what it takes. Then often after one term on the field and more often still, after two, we are added to the list of casualties.

When the grace of the Lord Jesus Christ captures the heart, and when you yield yourself with total, complete motivation which has stemmed from a revelation of His grace, to the Lord and to the church, what happens then? You begin then to say (if I may take this word as applied to the Savior and apply it in another setting to your own life), though you were rich, yet for the sake of others you became poor that they through your poverty might be rich. Once you were rich, not as Jesus was rich, but in self-esteem, in self-importance, in self-righteousness, in pride, and in arrogance, but now having known the grace of the Lord Jesus Christ, who though He was rich became poor, and having marveled at that mighty dynamic counterattack against sin, you have become poor. For what things were gain to you, those you counted loss for Christ: reputation, education, religion, everything; "...I count all things but loss for the excellency of the knowledge of Christ Jesus my Lord..." Then out of that utter poverty of spirit you desire that others too might become rich. Paul puts it—"For we which live are alway delivered unto death for Jesus' sake, that the life also of Jesus might be made manifest in our mortal flesh. So then death worketh in us, but life in you" (2 Corinthians 4:11–12).

Only when that principle gets back into the heart of our living, nothing on earth or in hell will prevail against another counterattack from heaven in the name of the Lord Jesus, for it is upon such a principle of life that there will rest all the authority of the Holy Ghost. "Blessed are the poor in spirit: for theirs is the kingdom of heaven." Blessed are they who have renounced all their self-life, important as it was, and have come in poverty to the foot of the cross with nothing to offer but their desperate need. Blessed are they who have given themselves like that in total poverty of spirit, and have then followed through and have abandoned themselves to all the sovereign purpose of God until one day they meet Jesus face to face. Oh, that God in these days would bring His church back on to resurrection ground, to give every one of us a new vision, a new venture, a new faith, and a new obedience up to the hilt, until one day Jesus comes and reigns as King of kings! "...the grace of the Lord Jesus Christ, that, though he was rich, ...he became poor, that you through his poverty might be rich," and therefore, "Lord Jesus, all I have and all I am, without argument, without debate, without committee, without question, without any possible contradiction, all of this is Yours now and forever."

I believe that will loosen purse strings. I believe that will warm hearts and cause to go out, while there is yet time, a great recruitment to the mission fields to intensify heaven's counterattack in this day. God grant that you and I might be found part of heaven's program.

—

CHAPTER FIFTEEN

THE TIME TO
ACT IS NOW

2 CORINTHIANS 8:10–24

At this time in his missionary service Paul was especially concerned about the condition of the church in Jerusalem, a church which had grown poor. There might have been spiritual reasons for its material poverty, but that is another issue. He was concerned that other churches which he visited, and through which he passed in the areas in which he traveled, should recognize their sense of responsibility to the church at Jerusalem. A prominent part, therefore, of Paul's teaching in the two following chapters has to do with the great subject of Christian giving, and I trust you will ask the Holy Spirit to speak to you upon this important matter of Christian stewardship from this portion of God's Word.

For those of you who are following the teaching of this letter, will you please notice that this chapter is really divided into three separate sections. This is an automatic division of this chapter, in no way artificial. You find in the first six verses what I have called the principle which we must follow. From verses 7–15 there is a promise we must fulfill and in verses 16–24 there is a practice which we must foster.

First of all, the principle to follow in this matter of giving. There is one word which occurs over and over again here, and when the Holy Spirit repeats Himself frequently, it is always because He desires this to be the emphasis. And the word which finds frequent repetition in this chapter is the word *grace*.

Note the repetition. In chapter 8:1, "…we do you to wit of the grace of God…"—we want you to know of the grace of God bestowed on the churches of Macedonia. Then again in verse 4: "Praying us with much intreaty that we would receive the gift…"—and that word *there* is the same word that is translated *grace*, "receive the grace." Again in verse 6: "That [Titus] would … finish in you the same grace also." Verse 7: "…that ye abound in this grace…" In verse 9: "…ye know the grace of our Lord Jesus Christ, that, though he was rich, yet for your sakes he became poor, that ye through his poverty might be rich." In verse 16 we read: "But thanks be to God,…" and again in verse 19: "…but who was also chosen of the churches to travel with us with this grace, which is administered by us to the glory of the same Lord…" So seven times in this chapter you have the repetition of the word *grace*.

Now what does that word *grace* mean? You have often heard it defined as the unmerited favor of God. Well, that is a definition, but it is only a limited definition of the word. It is the word from which we get our English word *charity*.

Now the word has taken on many different meanings down through the years. When this word was used in the early stages of history, it meant a desire to bring to other people goodness, health and strength, beauty, and loveliness. Later it became a little more pregnant in its meaning and began to mean the actual activity which expresses the desire to bring to others goodness instead of evil, health instead of sickness, beauty instead of ugliness, glory instead of punishment. This of course is outstandingly so as we think about the manger and the cross: "…the grace of our Lord Jesus Christ [as it is mentioned here in verse 9] who, thought he was rich, yet for your sakes he became poor, that ye through his poverty might be rich."

Here then is the activity of heaven, desiring to bring to all that which is good, that which is wonderful, that which is glorious in place of all that is unpleasant and unsavory and unhappy. What a wonderful word is this word *grace*! Once you see the matter of giving is centered in this lovely word *grace*, it lifts the whole act away from mechanics, from pressure and duty, from obligation and mere legalism. It lifts us up into the most lovely atmosphere of an activity which seeks by giving to convey to others all that is lovely, all that is beautiful, all that is good, and all that is glorious. What a lovely word this word is!

Paul, you notice, quotes a human example of *grace* in the opening verses of this chapter as he refers to the churches in Macedonia, where he speaks of their action as "…the grace of God bestowed on…" them. And you notice the measure of their giving, "How that in a great trial of affliction the abundance of their joy and their deep poverty abounded unto the riches of their liberality." What glorious language that is!

The title of this series of messages is *Blessings Out of Buffetings*, and there is no area in the Christian life in which there is a greater blessing coming out of severe buffeting than in the area of Christian giving. For there is no area in the Christian life in which grace shines out so much, so beautifully, so delightfully, and so happily as when giving comes from the background of poverty.

The churches of Macedonia, who had been so poor, had been through so much affliction, and, out of their poverty, had given so generously. This was the measure of their giving, and you notice that they gave far beyond the bonds of discretion, far beyond what they could afford. Paul says, "…I bear record, … and beyond their power they were willing of themselves,…" (v. 3). This was the measure of their giving. They were rash. They went far beyond the limit of discretion. They gave out of what they could not afford; they gave out of deep poverty. The grace of God was upon them.

You will observe what merit their giving had, because we are told that far from any pressure being brought upon them to give, they were the ones who put the pressure on Paul to receive their gift: "Praying us with much intreaty that we would receive the gift, and take upon us the fellowship of the ministering to the saints" (v. 4). What a refreshing atmosphere! There was no pressure put upon them to give. It was those who were giving who were putting the pressure on the others that they might receive their gift and take it from them.

What was the method by which they did this? And they did even more than I expected, says Paul, in effect, because first of all they "…gave their own selves to the Lord, and then unto us by the will of God" (v. 5).

Here then, is the principle to follow. It was giving out of poverty; it was giving without any pressure; it was giving by a specific method, by which, before they gave anything to others, first of all they gave themselves to the Lord and then having done that, everything they had belonged to Him. So they gave to the fellowship of the church. Here then is the background for our message, the principles which we must follow in this whole grace of giving.

Now see, in the second place, the promise that has to be fulfilled. Paul is referring here in verses 10 and 11 to an occasion about a year previously, apparently, when the Corinthian church had made what we would call "a faith promise." They had indicated their willingness to help the church in Jerusalem. They had given their faith promise, but now was the time to act.

Twelve months had passed by and while they had been willing, they had not acted upon their willingness; there had been no performance. So I am very interested to know how Paul goes about the task of seeing to it that people who have promised and yet have not fulfilled that promise, actually put their promise into action! How does he persuade people that being merely willing to give does not get one anywhere. It must be followed by action. Well, this is how he does it.

What do you know about tact? Well, here you have it, for in the first place he gives a word of praise. "Therefore," says Paul, "as ye abound in every thing, in faith, and utterance, and knowledge, and in all diligence, and in your love to us, see that ye abound in this grace also" (v. 7). Here is the acme of tactfulness, is it not? He begins by praising them for all their good qualities rather than exacting their promise by pressure.

He tells them they excel in faith, which is a great quality. They excel in utterance, having the gift of speech and expression. They excel in knowledge, knowing the doctrines of the Bible. They are diligent and sacrificial in their service and supreme in their love for the apostle. He was so grateful for this, and for their warmth in fellowship, and in all these things he praises them. Now see to it that you abound in this grace also!

There is a complete absence of any pressure upon the people, for he says, "I speak not by commandment, but by occasion of the forwardness of others" (that is, the example of the Macedonian churches) "and to prove the sincerity of your love" (v. 8). In other words, I am not going to say you must do this, I am not going to issue a command. No, not at all; but I give you my advice. Paul continues, "…for this is expedient for you, who have begun before, not only to do, but also to be forward a year ago. Now therefore perform the doing of it…" (v. 10). Following the word of praise, there is a reminder here of the necessity of performance: "…perform the doing of it…"

In what measure must they give? Now, I want you to notice this gift. Listen very carefully, for this goes to the very heart of the whole matter. Therefore, "…as there was a readiness to will, so there may be a performance…" I want you to perform. This is my advice to you, he says, out of that which you have. "For if there be first a willing mind, it is accepted according to that a man hath, and not according to that he hath not." So I am expecting, says Paul, in effect, that you would give, not according to what you have not got—that is not expected of you—but according to what you actually have.

This hits very hard at the modern idea of tithing. I have no objection to tithing, but I would suggest to you that in the light of the atmosphere of this teaching and in the grace that centers here in this chapter as the whole principle of New Testament living, tithing in many instances would be totally inadequate.

Let me give you a simple example. Supposing a man in this country, living in this country permanently, earns $3,000 a year. And let us assume that this man gives $300 to Christian work, not necessarily to his own church, but to Christian work. Well, I would suggest that this man was being generous. But let us suppose there is a man somewhere earning $10,000 a year, and this man gives $1,000 to Christian work. I would suggest to you that he is not being very generous. And if you have another man who is earning $20,000 a year and he is giving $2,000 to Christian work, that man is being quite mean!

I am suggesting to you that tithing is totally inadequate. And you cannot preach a gospel of tithing in the light of New Testament principles and views, because tithing simply means to suggest that having given my tenth, I keep the ninety per cent and everything is lovely. I am to give according to what I have, not what I have not. And this I believe necessitates that at least once a month a man will sit down with his bank book, he will examine it and say to himself, "Now this past month I have made so much more or so much less than the previous month. Therefore I will regulate my giving accordingly. I will give according to what I have."

This, then, is to be the performance of our giving. Not giving by the standard of the mechanical, legalistic tithe which may be totally inadequate, but by a standard whose character is grace and love, giving in the consciousness that having first given myself to the Lord, I am altogether His. And because I am altogether His, then nothing I have is my own. I must give according to what I have.

The basis of this gift is simply that of a recognition of partnership. You see, in considering this promise that Paul must fulfill, he has begun by praising the people, then he has reminded them of the necessity of their performance on that basis, and now he shows giving is the result of one's recognition of partnership.

What do I mean by that? Look at Paul's words: "For I mean not that other men be eased, and ye burdened: But by an equality, that now at this time your abundance may be a supply for their want, that their abundance also may be a supply for your want: that there may be equality: As it is written, He that had gathered much [and of course he is going back to the wilderness journey and the gathering of the manna] had nothing over; and he that had gathered little had no lack" (vv. 13–15).

Now here again let me ask you to notice a very important principle on this matter of giving. I do not believe God ever intended all men to possess equally of everything of this world's goods, because this would immediately dispense with the whole principle of charity and of sacrificial giving on the behalf of others. But Paul is teaching here that there needs to be a recognition that the church is one, that there is a need for fellowship, and that there needs to be a recognition that this is a partnership for life.

Paul then says, "...your abundance ... their want..." (v. 14). Then following in the same verse, "...their abundance ... your want..." Your abundance; that is the abundance of the Corinthian church. Their want; that is the church of Jerusalem. Their abundance; that is the abundance of the Jerusalem church; your want; that is the want of the Corinthian church.

We might ask ourselves, what abundance had the church at Jerusalem? It had a great deal of want, it was very poor. What abundance had it? If it had not been for the church at Jerusalem, there would not have been any other church at all. Other missionary churches were formed because from Jerusalem they went everywhere scattering the Word. I think that it could be substantiated that the Jerusalem church failed in its responsibility as it hugged itself too much, and probably lost a great deal of its missionary zeal. But nevertheless, the truth remains that had it not been for the disciples from Jerusalem who scattered the Word everywhere, there would have been none of the other churches, who owed everything they possessed of spiritual life, of vision, and of understanding of the gospel, all their spiritual wealth, to what had happened in Jerusalem.

This is not simply the strict confines of one little church family. It is the partnership of the whole church everywhere. And here, then, because of this recognition of partnership, there must be, says Paul, an immediate performance of what you promised a year ago. So then, there is our promise to fulfill.

Now let us look at the third thing I have called a practice we must foster. I am now interested to know how Paul carries this performance out in terms of its practical outworking. How does he collect the money? How does he make sure that people give? How does he regulate it? For there must be some administration of the whole matter, and indeed you find that this is just exactly so.

In the first place in the closing portion of this chapter, there is an immediate delegation of responsibility, and here we have mention of the name Titus: "But thanks be to God, which put the same earnest care into the heart of Titus for you" (v. 16). "And we have sent with him the brother, whose praise is in the gospel throughout all the churches…" (v. 18). "And we have sent with them our brother, whom we have oftentimes proved diligent in many things…" (v. 22).

So Paul, recognizing that this was not his task, delegates to three people the responsibility of the gathering of the funds on behalf of the Jerusalem church. The first of them is named Titus; the second and the third are not named. Tradition has it that the second one, whose praise is in the gospel throughout all the churches, is none other than Dr. Luke. And the third one, "…our brother, whom we have oftentimes proved diligent in many things,…" is Apollos. But this is merely conjecture. However, we can be quite sure that here is one young man whom Paul has entrusted with this sacred responsibility, Titus.

I want to leave the thought with you, because it is worth following through in your own personal study: in the course of Paul's journeys and preaching he was used of God to bring many young people to Christ. Two outstanding men were Titus and Timothy, two very different types. And at this particular moment in his life he says, "Titus, he is my partner and fellowhelper concerning you…" (v. 23).

Why should Paul entrust this man with such tremendous responsibility? As we think about this young man, Titus, he is not mentioned in the Book of Acts at all, but he is found in the second chapter of Galatians, where he is the test case which Paul used concerning the whole matter of a Gentile convert submitting to the rite of circumcision. Paul refused to allow Titus to go through this: he was a Gentile by background, and so Paul says no, this man must not be submitted to a Jewish ceremony.

This is in distinction, incidentally, to Timothy. When Paul won Timothy to Christ, one of the first things he did was to see to it that he passed through this rite of circumcision. Timothy's father was a Gentile, his mother and her ancestors were Jews. And so in order to validate his testimony, to authorize it and give it approval among Jewish circles, Paul has Timothy circumcised.

Later on, you will recall, it was Titus who was entrusted with one of the most difficult tasks of all missionary enterprise, because he became bishop of the church of Crete. And there as its first bishop was entrusted with looking after a situation in which he needed all heavenly wisdom and grace and understanding. But to train him for that great task which would require all heavenly strategy and wisdom and understanding, this man was the one to whom Paul delegates the responsibility of raising funds from the church at Corinth. Titus, Luke, and Apollos (if we accept what tradition tells us) were the three chosen of God to whom Paul delegates responsibility.

Furthermore, he does it because he has something in view: he has a reputation to safeguard. "Avoiding this, that no man should blame us in this abundance which is administered by us" (v. 20). In other words, says Paul, in effect, I am not going to lay myself open to any charge of dishonesty because I as one individual would handle so much money on my own. This is going to be a big offering, so I am going to see to it that responsibility for handling it is going to be handed over to someone I can trust, and someone you can trust also.

Titus had already been to Corinth. They already knew him, they trusted him, they loved him, and he had meant much to them. And so Paul makes his wise choice of men whom he could entrust with this sacred responsibility in order that he might guard his reputation, for he says this must be done: "Providing for honest things, not only in the sight of the Lord, but also in the sight of men" (v. 21). This is to be a matter of absolute integrity. It must be above reproach or suspicion; the accounts must be beyond any possible cloud of doubt, and so it must be undertaken by men of transparent honesty.

To ensure that the Corinthian Christians will receive them, Paul now gives them their references: concerning Titus, he says, "...he is my partner..."; and Paul says, in effect, "if you want to know who the other brethren are, they are messengers of the churches, and they are men indeed who are the glory of Christ."

Here is the whole question of Christian giving put before us without any human mechanism, without any pressure, without any prolonged appeals. It is lifted up into an atmosphere of heavenly grace. You are brought face to face with an example of another church which gave out of poverty, and most of all the supreme example of our Lord Jesus who for our sakes became so poor that we might be made rich.

Then very tactfully, graciously and lovingly, Paul reminds them that now is the time to act: you promised, you have intended, you willed, you decided, you declared; now is the time that you must perform. And you must give not according to some legalistic percentage, but you must perform out of that which you possess. In order that this may be collected I am going to delegate responsibility. There will be a treasurer, and others who will be chosen for this task, men of integrity, so that everything will be done in the open without any suspicion; and the accounts will be audited and available for your inspection. This is the whole principle of giving.

Let me tell you a story. In the country of Palestine there are two seas, both fed by the same river, the river Jordan. If you went alongside one of those seas, you would find children playing by the banks, trees growing alongside, and life apparent everywhere. But you find people avoid traveling anywhere near the other sea; they take another route and go in another direction. There is no sign of life or vegetation—there is nothing at all but barrenness.

What is the difference between the two? There is no difference in the source of supply, for the same river supplies both. But the difference is this: that for every drop of water that goes into Galilee (that, of course, is the first sea) another drop goes out. What it receives, it gives. It takes in, it gives out. And all around it is life, blossoming fruit, abundance. But the other sea jealously hoards its resources and refuses to let out a single drop. It keeps everything it takes in. And its name is *Dead*.

To give is to live. To restrain, to hold, to guard, to hoard, is to die. The same river of life in the power of the Spirit of God comes into your heart and into mine, and I would leave that parable with you. Freely you have received; the Lord help us to freely give.

CHAPTER SIXTEEN

HEAVEN'S LAW OF SUPPLY
AND DEMAND

2 CORINTHIANS 9:1–15

This gem of a text comes right at the heart of an earnest appeal which Paul is making on behalf of the Christians at Jerusalem for financial help from the church at Corinth. He has boasted everywhere of the generosity of the Corinthian believers, and now he writes very tactfully about the matter in case his boasting proved empty, and to ensure that their promised contribution would be ready when Titus arrived and not be exacted and wrung out of them by pressure. God loves, as Paul says here, a hilarious giver, and each one must give as he purposed in his heart.

But finance is certainly not the burden of this message: that is secondary. Nor was it the burden of Paul's message. He is lifting up this secular matter, if you could call it such — though it is certainly a deeply spiritual one — into a wonderful spiritual area of truth, and he is laying down a principle which lies at the very heart of our Christian life, that I have called "heaven's law of supply and demand."

Notice first, a provision which is inexhaustible: "…God is able to make all grace abound toward you…"; a practice which is inevitable, "…that ye always having all sufficiency in all things, may abound unto every good work"; and third, a principle which is inescapable: "…He which soweth sparingly shall reap also sparingly; and he which soweth bountifully shall reap also bountifully" (v. 6).

Consider first the provision which is inexhaustible. The Christian life, as depicted in the New Testament in all its various experiences, is no more and no less than the outflow from a fountain of life which has its source at the very throne of heaven, an outflow that comes from the great giving of the heart of God in Jesus Christ our Lord (John 4:14). Such is God's plan for you.

Notice how Paul piles on the superlatives here: "...God is able to make *all* grace abound toward you." This word *abound* is exactly the same word that the Lord used when He said, "...except your righteousness shall exceed the righteousness of the scribes and Pharisees, ye shall in no case enter into the kingdom..." (Matthew 5:20). In paraphrase, Paul says, "God is able to make *all* grace exceed toward you; abound toward you that you always might have *all* sufficiency in *all* things." This is the provision for your life from heaven today, right now in your immediate circumstances, a provision that is inexhaustible; it is all grace and it is, moreover, abounding grace.

What does Paul mean by grace? It is just one word which sums up all the blessings which come to our lives undeservedly from God through Jesus Christ our Lord. Primarily, the word *grace* describes a disposition in the very nature of God, in His character, which is revealed in His eternal, unchanging, and pardoning love. This is grace: a kindness, an overflowing disposition in the heart of God. But then God's dispositions are never passive or inactive, and grace therefore means love that is expressed and displayed in action: "Love knows no limit to its endurance, no end to its trust, no fading of its hope: it can outlast anything" (1 Corinthians 13:7–8, PHILLIPS).

It is still more than this. Grace is never fruitless. It is always fruitful, and therefore the greatest meaning of grace is all the blessedness that comes, and all the lovely and beautiful things that take place and happen in the life of a man who has come to know the indwelling Christ and the very nature of God dwelling in him by the Holy Spirit. Grace is love, joy, peace, longsuffering, gentleness, goodness, faith, meekness, self-control. Thus, Paul, in effect, says, "And God is able to make *all* grace abound toward you; in order that you might have all sufficiency in all things."

Very briefly and inadequately, that is the New Testament meaning of grace: love in action in the heart and passion of God expressed supremely at Calvary's cross. Love in action as expressed in the passion of each of God's own redeemed family, expressed in redemptive living, in sacrificial, sacramental living, in a life that is broken bread and poured out wine.

God is able to make *all* grace abound toward you. You see, there are not many graces. There is only one. What is it that God gives to each one of us and calls grace? It is not an "it." It is a Person, and His name is Jesus. When God gives grace, He gives Jesus, and that grace in Jesus Christ has many-sided expressions in our living, but it has only one source. It is from the throne and from the heart of God that there is poured out, in the name and virtue of Jesus Christ, by the power of His indwelling Spirit, grace; and it is abundant grace, for Paul says, He is able to make all grace abound toward you.

When God gives grace, He does not reluctantly open a little finger and maintain a clenched fist full of gifts. I would tell you today that God's hands are nail-pierced hands and they are wide open. This fountain of grace is always pouring itself out with no limitation on heaven's side at all. No wonder Paul concluded this chapter with a doxology: "Thanks be unto God for his unspeakable gift"! God's grace is a provision that is inexhaustible.

Because this provision is inexhaustible, and is to be found and expressed by love in action, to be demonstrated by every member of God's family — that means you and me, if we are redeemed by the precious blood of Christ — then, in the second place, there is a practice that is inevitable. "…God is able to make all grace — all the fullness of His grace in Jesus Christ — abound [exceed] toward you; *that ye* always having all sufficiency in all things, may abound to every good work."

The inevitable result of this constant and exuberant giving (may I use the word in relation to heaven? I don't wish to be irreverent, but when God says He loves a hilarious giver, He has set the example Himself and He has given hilariously; He has given gladly, happily, thankfully, and with exuberance in Jesus Christ) — from the fountain of life in the very throne of God — is that the basin of my life, which receives from the fountain in heaven, must always be full.

Now that is God's intention: "The water that I shall give you shall be in you a fountain springing up, bubbling up, overflowing into everlasting life." "He that believeth on me, … out of his belly shall flow rivers of living water." The man redeemed by blood and indwelt by the Spirit is receiving from a fountain that is inexhaustible, from a provision that is limitless, and therefore God expects him always to be full. God says in this word to our hearts "…that ye having all sufficiency,…" in other words, His grace is sufficient.

Is that rather an anti-climax? Certainly in days when we have to exaggerate everything to make anybody believe anything, it sounds rather like it. Sufficiency—couldn't He have used a stronger word than that? But then, how much more do I need for my life than sufficiency, and where else do I get sufficiency for anything except I get it from the very heart of God? He "...is able to make all grace abound toward you; that ye..." may have *all* "...sufficiency in *all* things," and the grace of God and the supply from the fountain of heaven is always proportioned to the need of each one of His children.

Could you not bear testimony with me when I say that there is nothing in life so wonderful and so satisfying as day by day to receive from the fountain strength for the task? Strength to carry the cross, to bear the sorrow or the persecution, strength to stand in the day of adversity, strength sufficient for every demand that could ever be made upon me, as I live in God's will, and all this out of the fullness in Jesus Christ.

> He giveth more grace when the burdens grow greater,
> He sendeth more strength when the labors increase,
> To added affliction, He addeth His mercy,
> To multiplied trials, His multiplied peace.

Thomas Fuller once prayed, "Lord, please either lighten the load or strengthen my back." The word from heaven is, "...as thy days so shall thy strength be." God has never hurled a battalion of His soldiers into a blundering attack against some impregnable situation to stand and watch them defeated and discomfited. He lays His command upon them to do this or that, then He infuses His strength and His power adequate for the task, and He makes the back to carry the load. There is never one bundle of affliction that can come into the life of any of His children, but that when you unwrap it, you will discover sufficient grace. For every increasing responsibility in life, God gives spiritual maturity and manhood. Therefore, the basin should always be full, full because it isn't there simply for your own enjoyment of grace, but for the blessing of other people.

"...the service rendered ... does more than supply the wants of the saints, it overflows with many a cry of thanks to God. This service shows what you are, it makes men praise God for the way you have come under the gospel of Christ which you confess, and ... they are drawn to you and pray for you, on account of the surpassing race which God has shown to you" (vv. 4–12, MOFFATT). Grace, all sufficient and abounding, in order that I may abound to every good work and supremely that I might become an attractive person! I don't mean necessarily physically, but I mean that, by a character transformed by the surpassing grace of God, other people will see this that is caused to rest upon us, and they will be drawn to us because of it. The church then glows with a spiritual attraction because every basin is filled up. That is why God gives grace, that we may abound unto every good work.

Now please follow me very carefully. There have been terrible evils arising from the way in which some evangelical preachers have talked as if the end of God's dealings with us is a vague sort of experience which we call salvation, which means little more than dodging hell. The New Testament declares that the purpose of God is that we should be filled with all the fullness of God, and that the basin of our life should be full because of the fountain being inexhaustible. We have received of His fullness that we may abound unto every good work. "…we are … created … unto good works, which God hath before ordained that we should walk in them" (Ephesians 2:10).

A correct creed is intended to become a Christ-like character, and if it does not do so, then the creed is worthless. The avalanche of grace that rushes down upon us from the throne of God in Christ is supremely for the reproduction of character and conduct which will make men see our good works and glorify our Father which is in heaven. We are not saved *by* our good character. We are saved *from* our character to demonstrate our salvation. The evidence of it will be in the display of the character of Jesus Himself whose grace abounds in His children. Any profession of salvation which does not issue in this is certainly not authentic.

How could it ever be possible for the grace of God in Jesus Christ to be in Him and not in His people, when He is actually living within them? It is fantastic to think about it. This inexhaustible provision—all grace abounding that you might have all sufficiency, and all things abounding to every good work, reaching the life, touching the heart, filling the soul—must result in this inevitable practice.

I suppose every preacher, if you asked him, has a burden on his heart. He is not worthy to be a preacher if he doesn't, for he has a major concern which brings him constantly to God, upon his face in prayer, a burden that is with him not merely days but nights as well. I can truly

406 / BLESSINGS OUT OF BUFFETINGS

say before the Lord I have that, and if you want to know what it is these days—it changes, I suppose, but this has lain upon me now for some years with increasing heaviness—my soul is burdened for all those whose lives are a complete contradiction of this principle, who profess to glory in the fact that salvation is all of grace and who claim to rejoice in forgiveness by grace, but whose lives are utterly bereft of that quality in which they boast.

To claim to have experienced the grace of God in forgiveness and yet to be ungracious is a fantastic contradiction of New Testament thought. To claim to have experienced the grace of God in forgiveness, yet fail to display the grace of God in action is a total contradiction of New Testament truth, and let me say it, though I die in the saying of it, such a man is as lost as a man down on "skid row," in fact, more so, for in that memorable, immortal parable of the prodigal son, the man who was in the far country knew it. When he was starving and knew (as Paul later came to know) that in his flesh dwelt no good thing, he said, "I will arise and go to my father." But there was an elder brother who geographically was very near his father and under the sound of his father's voice all his life, but spiritually he was in a far country, far worse and far more final than that of the prodigal. He was in the far country of self-righteousness and religious formality and correctness of creed which was unsupported by the passion in his heart for his brother who was without God. Oh, you who are so near geographically to the sound of the gospel, who have been brought up under the sound of fundamental teaching, who claim forgiveness by grace, are you really saved?

So we see, there is a fountain that is inexhaustible, and because of that there is a basin which is my life, and it must always be full. Because it is filled up from the fountain, that which is in the basin must be of the same quality and character as that which is in the fountain, and therefore it will be displayed in love, in joy, in peace, and in the grace of Jesus Christ. Now observe the principle that is inescapable, because there is something in our text that is quite shocking: "God is able to make all grace abound toward you…" Paul does not say, God *will do* this: he says, God *is able* to do it. He puts the whole weight of responsibility upon us to make God's ability to do this mighty work an operating factor in each life, seven days a week.

God is able! I pause to think about the marvel of it, that He is able to make all grace abound toward me that I might have all sufficiency in all things. But there are conditions. I may have access to this fountain from the throne in heaven, but it may gush by my side and pass me by, and the reason is not that I am straightened in God but that I am straightened in my own life.

Does not what I have said to you make you ask the question, as it certainly does me, why the breakdown? Why the lack of display in your life of all this which heaven supplies in Christ? Why the ungraciousness? Why the un-Christlikeness? Why the doctrine without the practice? Why the defeat and emptiness? Ask why until He gives you the answer.

You have learned something, I trust, about heaven's law of supply, but what about the demand? There is a principle here, and it is that of harvest. I cannot take a text like this out of its context. "…He which soweth sparingly shall reap also sparingly; and he which soweth bountifully shall reap also bountifully." Here is a principle of harvest, of sowing, and of reaping. "…He that soweth to his flesh shall of the flesh reap corruption; but he that soweth to the Spirit shall of the Spirit reap life everlasting" (Galatians 6:8). If you want God's supply, this great harvest of grace—or to change the metaphor for a moment, if you want this fountain of life and want to be supplied with an all-sufficiency—then you must show God that you are desperate for it, and you must sow, and sow that you might reap.

Oh, how sparingly we have sown in the Spirit! How little we pray, how little time we give to meditating upon the Word, how rarely do we witness to others. Examine your sowing, and if your sowing is poverty-stricken, no wonder the supply is held up. Even in Christian work, you can sow to the flesh and reap a harvest of corruption. You can make the church the opportunity to demonstrate your authority, and you can use it in the flesh and substitute service in the house of God for nourishment of your own soul in quiet alone.

God is able to make all grace abound toward you that you may have all sufficiency in all things and abound unto every good work, but does heaven hear you knock at the door? "…Ask, and it shall be given you; seek, and ye shall find; knock, and it shall be opened unto you." God's supply is there, but the door is shut because He has never heard the cry of your heart.

Consider God's principle of supply and demand: "…concerning the work of my hands command ye me" (Isaiah 45:11). He is able, but

His doing depends upon your sowing; His supply depends upon your demand. "Let us therefore come boldly unto the throne of grace, that we may obtain mercy, and find grace to help in time of need" (Hebrews 4:16). You see, you don't ask and demand and knock until heaven's door is opened and the fountain gushes out, do you? God is not going to display and dispense heaven's treasury upon a self-satisfied individual.

Perhaps someone says, quite frankly, "If I would be honest with you, I've lost every bit of desire to sow to the Spirit. I have no heart concern for other people. I just couldn't care less. As a matter of fact, from all practical realities, I'm learning to live without God, even though I profess to be a Christian." In other words, my dear friend, you are prepared to settle for the delusion, for the mockery and travesty of a salvation that is not real or genuine, one that will land you in a lost eternity, simply because you profess such and such a thing and have been in a fundamental church, but now you don't really care.

You say to me, "Are you telling me that for this fountain to flow into my life, then there must be desire and demand? I haven't got it, so I am lost and it is hopeless." Is it? Listen to Paul: "...he that ministereth seed to the sower both minister bread for your food, and multiply your seed sown, and increase the fruits of your righteousness" (v. 10). When you have no desire and no heart for God, when your appetite for the Word has turned sour, when your prayer life has gone shattering apart, when you have shown to everybody and to God especially that you don't really care, when you neither witness nor really pray nor show any deep heart concern, what does God do about it? Does He leave you to perish eternally? No, He ministers seed to the sower. If that isn't the overplus of grace, I do not know what is.

When He sees someone who has lost his spiritual appetite and concern, one who has recognized the provision as being inexhaustible, but one who has seen that the basin of his life is so empty—he has no desire and no heart for the things of God any more, and therefore the supply to his soul has broken down because the demand is never going up to heaven—does God deliver him up completely to perish? No, He holds out His hand with the overplus of grace, and He ministers seed to the sower.

There was a corn of wheat that fell into the ground and died that it might not abide alone, and because it died, it shall bring forth much fruit. That seed which fell into the ground and died and rose again is the seed which He offers to us in our desperate spiritual poverty in the overplus of

His grace. He does not leave the sour appetite of the professing believer, who settled for a salvation that is not real, to descend to a lost eternity. He gives the seed of His life, and if you will come to Him today with all the sourness of your appetite, the ungraciousness of your life, the evidences that have abounded, that show you are not a genuine Christian at all in spite of all your profession, if you will come like that, He will put into your heart the seed of His crucified, risen life and create within you the hunger which is the longing of the Holy Spirit Himself to express Himself through life.

CHAPTER SEVENTEEN

VICTORY IN
THE BATTLE

2 CORINTHIANS 10:1–18

I am sure that nobody would dispute the statement that the Christian life is essentially a conflict, and in various areas and in different ways this conflict expresses itself in the experience of every one of us; but when we begin to think about the real nature of the conflict, what it is basically, and the secret of victory in it, then we would have various ideas upon that subject. As we consider from this chapter the conflict of the Christian life, I would seek to show you what is the real basic nature of it, what it stems from, and, therefore, the secret of victory in it.

"…The weapons," says Paul, "of our warfare…": our warfare, and right from the very beginning you will recall that the Lord Jesus Christ always made plain to His disciples that He was calling them to a battle, and if we are to understand this text, we must not only see it in its context, but we must compare Scripture with Scripture.

When Jesus began to speak to a group of people who were seeking to commit themselves to Him and to follow Him, He said, "Blessed are they which are persecuted for righteousness' sake: for theirs is the kingdom of heaven. Blessed are ye, when men shall revile you, and persecute you, and shall say all manner of evil against you falsely, for my sake. Rejoice, and be exceeding glad: for great is your reward in heaven: for so persecuted they the prophets which were before you" (Matthew 5:10–12).

At the very moment when He was beginning to gather together a little group of disciples, He announced that this was what discipleship would involve. He enlightened them on this subject and elaborated on it again when He commissioned them: "...I send you forth as sheep in the midst of wolves. ..." He spoke to them about kings and governors being against them, but they were to take no thought of what they would say, for in that hour He would give them what to speak, and then He said, "And ye shall be hated of all men for my name's sake: but he that endureth to the end shall be saved" (Matthew 10:16, 22).

Then for further enlightenment He told them the parable that we know as the wheat and the tares (Matthew 13:24–30), and spoke to them about the reality of the wheat and counterfeit of the tares that looked so like the wheat in its early growth, but ultimately there was no possible mistake as they were so different. His method of teaching them was to say, "Now, let them alone. Don't try to root up the tares, don't counterattack in that manner, but leave them alone until harvest time."

He did not only enlighten His disciples, however; He explained Himself to them, and you find the Lord Jesus using words like this to that little group of men, "If ye were of the world, the world would love his own: but because ye are not of the world, but I have chosen you out of the world, therefore the world hateth you" (John 15:19). And then He gave them a word of encouragement: "These things I have spoken unto you, that in me ye might have peace. In the world ye shall have tribulation: but be of good cheer; I have overcome the world" (John 16:33).

So from the very beginning the Lord Jesus was calling out to Himself a little group of men, of whom you and I claim to be in direct succession as His representatives here on earth, and He enlightened them concerning the conflict to which He called them. But He also said, "...my yoke is easy [or, my yoke fits] and my burden is light" (Matthew 11:30) — don't be afraid of it; this is the kind of life to which I am calling you! He gives them a word of enlightenment, a word of explanation as to why this is so, and then He gives them a word of encouragement proclaiming that He has overcome the world.

In this way our Lord calls His disciples to a new principle of life altogether. What a strange kind of battle it was, and as He spoke to them about it, there seems to me to be one thing that stands out perfectly clearly: they were to win the battle by apparent defeat. By crucifixion they were going to be crowned. By refusing to counterattack they were to find the way of victory. By apparent failure they were going to conquer; and by allowing themselves to be identified with His cross, they were going to find the way of triumph. The paradoxes of the Christian life! Thus the Christian faith had, in its birth, a new principle at the very heart of it—the principle of sacrifice, the principle of love, the principle of non-retaliation, the principle that was to lead to absolute victory.

So we come to our text, because we find Paul explaining this more fully. If that is the fact of conflict, what is the nature of it? The strange thing that we notice about this verse is that it is written to a Christian church, and it soon became apparent in the early days of the Christian faith that the simple issues were godliness on the one hand and godlessness on the other; but not simply godlessness in a pagan world, but godlessness found inside the sphere of the Christian church.

It is interesting to notice that these verses come in a context in which Paul is defending his apostleship. The Corinthian church had challenged his authority! "For his letters," say they, "are weighty and powerful; but his bodily presence is weak, and his speech contemptible" (v. 10).

Here was Paul, finding himself faced with contention and dispute and a questioning of his authority in the church at Corinth, so he answers them in the words of our text and says, in effect, "I want you to understand that the weapons of our warfare are not carnal, but mighty through God to the pulling down of strongholds; casting down imaginations, and every high thing that exalteth itself against the knowledge of God, and bringing into captivity every thought to the obedience of Christ."

What is the nature of this Christian battle? Paul spoke of it to the church of Ephesus in these words, "For we wrestle not against flesh and blood, but against principalities, against powers, against the rulers of the darkness of this world, against spiritual wickedness in high places" (Ephesians 6:12). The conflict into which the Christian is introduced is first a spiritual one, and in its essence it is one which stems from our minds and from our thought-life. So the child of God, responding to the call of Jesus Christ, and duly warned by Him that he is entering into a battle, finds himself in a warfare, the nature of which is spiritual and the source of which is in his thought-life. Paul describes the problem of carnality in the church as that which stems from corruption in the mind and which results in captivity of the soul.

We will consider these things in their setting. First of all consider carnality in the church. The Christian church is a very wonderful body, composed of a group of people who have received Jesus Christ as Savior, who have been redeemed by His precious blood, and who share together in the fellowship of His Spirit. Therefore, they are a group of people who share, or ought to share, in each other's burdens, who comfort each other along the journey of life, and who stand together in the name of the Lord against a common enemy. The problem is that although they have been born again, although they have entered into the fellowship of the Christian church, they don't come by some magical process to be saints all in a moment! Paul's concern for the church at Corinth (as it would indeed be for us) is simply that the imagination of the mind, the process of thinking, the way of reasoning, the method of logic, the understanding of things which a man adopted in his unconverted days, become projected into the fellowship of the church, and the church begins to fail in its spiritual battle because it adopts carnal procedures. Alas, there is so much carnality in the church, but Paul says, "...the weapons of our warfare are *not* carnal..."

The process of victory which our Lord taught His disciples was this: that if you cease to resist in the realm of carnality, then you are resisting automatically in the realm that is spiritual, and in this way you overcome the enemy. Resist, counterattack, deal with the situation upon the same level that the world deals with it, and you are defeated. But refuse to follow that principle of life; take up rather the principle of the cross, and by non-combat in carnal levels you are combating the enemy is spiritual levels and therefore you will overcome.

To illustrate this, turn to Simon Peter and the incident in which the Lord Jesus began to show to him this principle of the cross (Matthew 16:21–23). Christ spoke to him about the cross, about the blood, about the way of sacrifice and death. He had spoken earlier about the corn of wheat falling into the ground and dying, and if it die, it brings forth much fruit, but if it did not die it would abide alone; and Peter's answer was, "Not so, Lord, not that way, not the way of the cross and death!"

Christ's reply was shattering: "...Get thee behind me, Satan: thou art an offence unto me: for thou savourest not the things that be of God, but those that be of men."

But Peter did not learn his lesson. In the Garden of Gethsemane up goes his sword, out goes his arm, and off goes the man's ear. He is still resisting the principle of the cross, still following the procedure of carnality, and taking the line of resistance instead of the line of meekness and submission. He did not learn his lesson until after Pentecost (and it took him some time then), but this is the lesson which the Lord Jesus sought to teach him, and the very lesson which Paul is bringing to bear upon the church at Corinth.

You find this principle today in the church in terms of the theological outlook upon the Bible, though I have no wish to get involved in a controversial issue. The difference between what we call today the fundamentalist or the conservative evangelical and all others in their approach to the Book is that we as conservative evangelicals submit ourselves to the criticism of the Word of God, whereas all others submit the Book to their own criticism. This is the basic difference of approach to the whole subject of theology, so much so that in some circles it is said that if you are orthodox you are out-of-date; you are an obscurantist, and it is an impossible position to hold in the light of modern theology and modern science.

These are some of the high things that Paul said exalt themselves against the knowledge of God, and because the evangelical conservative holds to a position in which he submits all his criticisms and life to the authority of Scripture, and refuses to move from that position, while he is only too glad to discuss and consider all enlightenment upon the Book, he is therefore called out-of-date.

Now this I believe is the form of carnality in the church which stems from corruption of the mind; not necessarily moral corruption, but the mind which insists in submitting the Word of God to its own criticism and only accepting that which the human intellect can understand and believe. This corruption of mind leads to carnality in the church and to captivity of spirit, for by that means there is that which exalts itself against the knowledge of God. That, in the theological area, is exactly the modern counterpart of our verse.

I wish to come much closer to home than that, as I bring this right down to where we live. What is the nature of this conflict? It is the battle which goes on in the personal life of every one of us in ordinary, everyday, down-to-earth, practical living — the battle to forsake the principle of carnality and to accept the principle of spirituality. It is the battle to take the line of refusing to resist along the human level, and by so doing, resisting in terms of spiritual warfare, and therefore overcoming. This is something which works itself out in terms of our relationship with one another, as well as in terms of our relationship with God.

If, therefore, it is true that the weapons of our warfare are not carnal, if God is calling us to be His followers and to live the Christian life here and now on exactly the same principle as that which was followed by His disciples — in other words, the line of non-resistance, of meekness and crucifixion and death, the line of submission one to another in the fear of God — what then are the weapons a Christian must use, and how does he use them?

I remind you of words which Paul wrote in his letter to the church at Ephesus. We must arm ourselves, because in paraphrase he says, "…the weapons of our warfare, though they are not carnal, are mighty through God to the pulling down of strongholds." In other words, there is a way of life, there is an armor, there are weapons which the Christian church (and by that I mean any group of Christians) can use today in ordinary everyday life which will be so invincible that, to quote the words of our Lord Jesus, "…the gates of hell shall not prevail against them."

If this is true, then it behooves us surely to give very prayerful attention to this fact, because the fact of the matter is that apart from a mighty awakening and revival in the church, we are fighting a losing battle because we are resisting on carnal levels. This is not something you settle at denominational headquarters or in the high courts of the ecclesiastical world. It is something you begin to settle here and now that causes the tide of Holy Spirit power and life to flow once again through the church, which has been blocked because we as individual believers have rejected God's principles.

What then are the weapons which are mighty through God? "…take unto you the whole armour of God, that ye may be able to withstand in the evil day, and having done all, to stand … your loins girt about with truth, and having on the breastplate of righteousness; … your feet shod with the preparation of the gospel of peace; … taking the shield of faith, … and take the helmet of salvation, and the sword of the Spirit, which is the word of God: Praying always with all prayer and supplication in the Spirit, … for all saints" (Ephesians 6:13–18).

Here is the Christian armor. Now will you please notice this: it is not armor to protect the body, for it is not designed to keep the Christian from physical harm, but it is armor designed to protect him against all spiritual attack. It is not something with which he clothes his body, but something with which he clothes his soul. It is hidden from the outward scrutiny of others, but its existence in the realm of a man's soul will be revealed in his daily life. That is why Paul says "…though we walk in the flesh, we do not war after the flesh…" (2 Corinthians 10:3). Yet our whole activity and our actions in the flesh, in the body, in daily conduct, are governed by this inward clothing, the armor of the spirit.

Let a man neglect putting on this armor and he will soon reveal carnality to everybody else in his conduct and behavior. But let him go into the robbing room each day with God in the name of the Lord Jesus, and let him there in prayer put on the whole armor of God—truth, righteousness, faith, peace, the helmet of salvation, the Word of God as the sword of the Spirit, and the armor of all-prayer, clothing that the world cannot see—and it will soon be evident to all by his daily conduct in his daily life that he has clothed himself with the whole armor of God. the absence of a time he takes to clothe himself with the armor of God is revealed in his approach to the Bible, in his criticism of everything, in his refusal of every authority, in his hesitancy to accept the Word of truth, and in his carnality of daily behavior. Here, then, is the answer to the area within the church where the greatest battles are to be fought, in the weapons of our warfare that are not carnal, but mighty through God to the pulling down of strongholds.

You may ask, how do they work? They work in the realm of the mind. How is the victory won? It is won in the realm of the thought-life. Does this mean merely asking God to do something while we do nothing at all ourselves? No, indeed. What then is the secret of it? Jesus said, "As a man thinketh in his heart, so is he," and it is our leisure thoughts, our meditative life, that decides our conduct.

Alas, how much time we give to the life as it appears before men, and how little do we give to the life that appears before God! Yet it is that life that shines through everything, it is that life which is lived with the Lord Himself and which is clothed with heavenly armor that reveals itself in spirituality. It is that life, when it is lacking, that displays itself in carnality. The world, you see, sees the expression on a man's face, hears the tone of his voice, studies his actions whether they are selfish or unselfish, and by these he is judged inevitably and rightly. In spite of all his efforts to hold it all in check, he is conveying transparently to other people that his Christianity is all in the shop-window, and he is painfully lacking in being clothed with the armor of God in the soul.

To be specific, it works something like this. Somebody says an unkind word about you, or you are accused falsely of something you have not done, or somebody is spiteful in his comments and critical in his attitude. You begin to think about it, you repeat it to yourself over and over again with increased indignation, and because it begins to fill your mind, you tell your friends (with additions of course) until at last, by frequent repetition, you have been insulted twenty times instead of one. You have determined to counterattack, to retaliate, to answer back, to vindicate yourself, and to prove that they are wrong and you are right. This is the carnality in the life which has happened because of corruption in the mind, because in the thought-life you have been defeated before you have to counterattack.

What then is the answer? As a Christian engaged in this conflict, knowing that the weapons of our warfare are not carnal but mighty through God to the pulling down of strongholds, there is the law of exclusion. How does it operate? When the thought comes and the person is reported to have said what he has said, and the unkindness has been passed over to us, and the criticism has been made, whereas carnality would say, "Counterattack!" spirituality has the mind which was in Christ Jesus and humbles itself and recognizes that nothing that any person could ever say about any of us is really one hundredth part as bad as the truth if he only knew it. Therefore, we have no reason to counterattack, but one good reason to submit and to forget. That is the law of exclusion.

But there is the law of attention. "…Whatsoever things," says Paul, writing to the church at Philippi, "are true, whatsoever things are pure, whatsoever things are lovely, whatsoever things are of good report; if there be any virtue, and if there be any praise, think on these things." When carnality arises in our hearts, causing us to answer back, to retaliate, and to fail to follow the principle of discipleship laid down by the Master, then at that moment we must think on these things, and answer the enemy by saying, "I'm sorry, my house is full, I have no room for you and I have no time to listen to you." That is the law of attention.

I quote some lovely words from that wonderful book, *The Imitation of Christ* by Thomas à Kempis: "Many thoughts have risen up against me, and great terrors which afflict my soul. How shall I pass through them without hurt? How shall I break them in pieces before me? I will go before Thee, O Lord, and I will bring low the proud boasters of the earth and I will open the gates of the prison and reveal to Thee the hidden secret. Do, Lord, as thou saidest and let all wicked thoughts flee from before Thy face. This is my hope and only consolation — to put my trust in Thee, to call on Thee from my inmost heart, and to wait patiently for Thy help and for Thy strength."

Yes, truly, the weapons of our warfare are not carnal, but they are mighty through God to the pulling down of strongholds; and they cast down imaginations and every high thing that exalts itself against the knowledge of God and bring into captivity every thought into the obedience of Christ. That is the principle upon which the church was founded; that is the principle that was followed by the Master when He stepped from the throne to the manger and from the manger to the cross. That is the obedience He expects from each of His followers. But let us confess with shame, today in the realm of the intellect, the mind, the thought-life, the church — that is, you and I as believers in Christ — has followed the carnal method, and therefore she has divested herself of spiritual power.

God grant that you and I every day may go into our personal robing room alone with Him, and put on all the armor of God which is mighty to the pulling down of strongholds of the enemy.

CHAPTER EIGHTEEN

The Jealousy
of God

2 Corinthians 11:1–4

This statement of Paul's is very unusual, striking, and somewhat challenging. Of all things that has brought misery upon the human life it is jealousy. There is nothing that has done so much harm in homes, in personal and national relationships, in international situations, in church life, as the ugly, devilish poison of jealousy. This has been true all through history, not only in secular history, for at the beginning of the story of redemption, as you will recall in the Word of God, Cain is jealous of Abel and slays him; the children of Israel are jealous of Joseph and sell him; Saul's jealousy of David results in his trying to murder him.

In the New Testament, to carry the picture through, the disciples become jealous of the man who cast out devils in the name of the Lord, and try to destroy him; the scribes and Pharisees are bitterly jealous of the Lord Jesus Christ and stirred up the emotions of the crowd to crucify Him. Everywhere in the story of God's Book and in the story of human life, you have this fearful, ugly business of jealousy, which is the seed of murder, and which usually has led to it, preeminently in the case of our Savior Himself. Against this background, therefore, I find these words of the apostle Paul very striking. "...I am jealous over you with godly jealousy...."

I would never have dared to think it possible that God could be jealous, and yet I am reminded that the moment God begins to lay down the pattern of His relationships with human people, He reminds them, "...I the Lord thy God am a jealous God. ..." And if I might carry the analogy further, in laying down the basis of human relationships by the implication and standard of the Ten Commandments, the Lord not only declared His jealousy but He said, "Thou shalt have no other gods before me."

In other words, it is as if Jehovah in effect says, "I refuse to consider the possibility of a rival, I must be master, I must be supreme. I must be Lord, total Lord of all, or I will not be Lord at all. I am not going to compete with another for a place in your affection; I am not going to attempt to bargain that you should decide upon a syndicate or by the resolution of a committee that you should follow Me. I will be your sovereign, I will be your Master, your God, or I shall be nothing."

But this is surely the very thing that has wrecked human living, that has broken marriages and wrecked homes, and this ugly business has smashed its way into churches. "I will have no other friends nor will I allow other friends to come into your life, but me," says one to another. Is this the thing of which God is responsible? Oh, no, but at least I have said enough to make you realize that this word *jealousy* needs examination and explanation.

What is the jealousy of God? I will answer that question in the first place by reminding you of the character of God revealed to us in His Book, and then I will answer it for you by reminding you of the context from which our verse is taken.

First of all, what does the Bible say about the character of God? It has always been the belief of non-Christian religions that their gods are jealous and must be appeased by sacrifice. But this is not our God. The Bible reveals that our God is essentially moral and just, essentially pure and holy, and His jealousy—which is the greatest flame that burns in the heart of deity—is the flame of love in action. His jealousy is a concern for the purity, the holiness, the greatness, the glory of His people. His concern—and you need only refer to your Bible and you will see there His purpose to call out a peculiar people unto Himself who will be His witnesses, and whose lives will demonstrate His beauty to the world—is a consuming flame, burning eternally in His heart, the flame of love in action.

No sooner does He lay down the law in the Ten Commandments than He declares His jealousy for His people. His eyes are too pure to behold iniquity, yet He declares that the whole basis of His people's holiness and happiness is centered in their loyalty to Himself.

In case I am getting on debatable theological grounds, let me say this to make myself clear, that the ceremonial law of the Jew was finished in Jesus Christ. God made the first sacrifice in the Bible, and God made the last. The first He made in the garden; the last He made on a rugged cross outside Jerusalem; and there the thin trail of blood which has flowed from Genesis all through human history was stopped. Christ's finished final work was the last complete sacrifice for the salvation of the human race. But the moral law of God as defined by the Ten Commandments was not put away by Christ. It was fulfilled in the person of Jesus Christ completely in order that in the twentieth century, in civilized "Christianized" lands as well as in the uttermost parts of the earth, there might be a great company of people redeemed by the blood of Jesus Christ, indwelt by the Holy Ghost, in whose lives the righteousness of the Lord is fulfilled by the Spirit (Romans 8:4).

God's jealousy, therefore, is a concern for the holiness, integrity, purity of ethics, and Christian standards for His people. Because of this, He will refuse to brook a rival in our affections for Him, not because of a selfish greed which wishes us all for His own possession, but simply because He knows that His great purpose for us of purity and holiness of life depends on our personal surrender and submission to His purpose, and because God would make it known (and we are very slow to believe) that happiness without holiness is impossible.

God is fearful lest His people bestow their affections on some alien thing or on some other master, and therefore I say to you that the jealousy of God stems from a tenderness and passion that burns in the heart of God for the welfare of His people.

To put it another way, the jealousy of man is selfish and self-centered. It usurps the rights of others, it is blind to their happiness, and it involves their ruin by leading to tyranny, and it cares nothing for anybody else as long as he gets through.

Observe carefully that God is not jealous *of* you; He is jealous *for* you, and that is the big difference. If you want proof and demonstration of this in reality, I take you to the cross and ask you to remember that there God, instead of destroying the race that deserted and rebelled against Him, has allowed that very race to rebel against Him in order that through that very act He might win back their love. That is the jealousy of God.

Think about that; let it get into your heart and into your soul: God jealous for His people and displaying it. Instead of wiping out of existence those who had deserted Him and treated Him so basely, He allowed them to murder Him on the cross of Calvary that He might win back their hearts. Glorious, life-giving jealousy!

Does this then throw some light upon this passage? I believe it does, for it introduces us in the second place to the jealousy of Paul. What an amazing thing that here is a man who says, in writing to a group of Christian people, "…I am jealous over you with godly jealousy. …" He says, in effect, "I wish that you could bear with me in my folly; please understand, for this flame that burns in my heart for you and eats up my life, possessing my personality and gripping my soul, is something that has got hold of me until nothing else matters." "…I am jealous over you with godly jealousy…"

Elsewhere Paul said, "My little children … I travail together in birth … until Christ be formed in you." I am jealous, not of you, but I am jealous for you. I care nothing for anything else, says Paul, except that those to whom I minister might fulfill God's purposes in their hearts.

I would remind you at this point of the terrific thing that has taken place in this man's life. Consider for a moment what happened as he went down the road that led to Damascus. In Acts 9 is the account of this experience, and as this great Pharisee went on his way, he was just eaten up with anger and fury. What was the matter with him? He had secured letters of authority to slay every Christian, and to put to death everyone who followed Jesus of Nazareth. Paul's whole life was a consuming jealousy against every Christian, so much so that he was determined to wipe them out. That was all that was wrong with him: he was eaten up with jealousy and bent on murder. Ah, but on that road he came face to face with the risen Lord. "Who are thou, Lord?" he asked.

"…I am Jesus of Nazareth, whom thou persecutest; and in your attempted destruction of My people, you are fighting against Me."

"Then, Lord, what wilt thou have me to do?" and from that moment a wonderful revolution took place in Saul's personality. He was still jealous; he was still consumed with the passion of jealousy as a Christian. Ah, but it had been transformed into a jealousy not *of* people, but *for* them. "…I am jealous over you with godly jealousy. …"

Has that transformation ever happened in your life? People are so afraid of what they call "the crucified life," and when they hear it taught that we must die to ourselves that we might live unto God, they say, "What a miserable thing to die like that! This is negative teaching, this is passive — this is agony! Fancy dying!" Does this mean that God wipes out your personality? No, indeed. He does not; but I will tell you what He does, much to the discomfiture of the devil: He takes hold of that twisted, warped life of yours that is eaten up with jealousy, and He fills it with Holy Ghost jealousy. Instead of your being jealous of people, you become jealous for them. You live with one great burning motive that others might be blessed and helped along life's road. God takes hold of the tongue that has been so critical and maliciously talkative, and what does He do — cut it out and silence it? No! He gives you a new tongue that speaks with love and gentleness, grace and meekness. Here is the fruit of the gospel, when a man's weakest point is transformed by the Holy Ghost, taken to the cross, brought into resurrection life, and purified for the glory of God. What a gospel!

Oh, what discomfiture in the regions below! What awful panic in hell when a man who has served the devil successfully (often, alas, in good fundamental churches) by his jealousy, by his tongue, and by his gossip, and for long has been a wonderful vehicle of the enemy right inside the camp of the King of kings — what discomfiture when the devil finds such a man suddenly revolutionized by the power of the Spirit of God, with a new flame burning in his heart — the flame of love — and a new tongue talking through his lips, a tongue that has been touched by the grace of the Holy Spirit!

The jealousy of Paul has been transformed, but now in this Scripture passage is seen the subtlety of Satan: "...I fear, lest by any means, as the serpent beguiled Eve through his subtilty, so your minds should be corrupted from the simplicity that is in Christ" (v. 3) — the simplicity that is in Christ.

That is an arresting phrase because in these days there is scarcely anything that is simple; everything is so complicated. What am I to believe? What is right? What is wrong? In every area of life the old simplicities have vanished from us until even this word *simple* has changed, and I do not think people like being called *simple* because it has an association that is a little unpleasant! It would mean that you are not quite one-hundred per cent! That is not the meaning of the word in the New Testament, for simplicity means single-hearted, crystal clear. As a matter of fact, the actual word would be "like a bit of cloth without a crease in it."

All the great men of God have been so simple, just as little children. I could bring an array of them (I wish I could in person) to your mind — Isaiah and Paul from the Word of God, Bunyan, William Carey, Handley Moule, Hudson Taylor, D. L. Moody, Adoniram Judson, to mention just a few, but these men with brilliant minds were basically as simple as little children in their walk with God. A man may be a saint without having many of the qualities which the world today rates very highly, but he will never be a saint without the simplicity of soul, a simplicity that is in Christ. It was this that burned in the heart of Martin Luther in the days of the Reformation when he said, "Let us get through to God. Give us a basic, dynamic, personal simplicity of faith in Jesus Christ."

Let me put in a warning here. When people go around saying, "All we want is the simple gospel," let us be careful. That could be an excuse for sheer mental laziness. The gospel is simple, but it is profound; and when Paul speaks about the simplicity that is in Christ, we will see that the *Revised Version* alters it slightly.

Look first at the simplicity that is in Christ. How simple was His life! He had nowhere to lay His head. The only legacy He left was a seamless robe that His mother made Him. There was no connection in the life of Jesus between wealth and happiness. And His speech, never shallow, was always simple. He could stand against the best intellects of His day and confound them, but He was never above people's heads. Is it not significant, the common people heard Him gladly. His way of salvation, too, is so simple, only two words, "Follow Me."

His cross was so simple, so clear, yet we try to improve on it today, of course. It is not enough to say, some people would tell us, that "there is life for a look at the Crucified One." This needs a new intellectual approach to the gospel for these days. Rubbish, my friend! What this world needs is an enlightenment of the Holy Ghost, such a breathing upon our hearts of His conviction that we recognize that it is revelation and not education that gets a man into the kingdom. Yes, so simple was Christ's way of salvation; so simple was His whole soul, His inner life.

Have you ever thought about how worrying the life of Jesus could have been? What about the disciples who just would not learn their lessons, who were so slow, so disobedient, so backward? How worrying! But He was never distracted. How loud were other voices that dinned upon His ears: "...come down from the cross!"" ... Art thou then the Son of God...?" But through all the contention and strife that surrounded His person, He was never dismayed. How threatening and dangerous was the whole situation, but He was never disturbed. "...My peace I give unto you,..." that is the simplicity that is in Christ. If you ask me the reason, I would give it to you in the words that He Himself spoke when He said, "My meat is to do the will of him who sent me, and to finish his work." In other words, you see, in the person of Jesus our Lord the jealousy of the heart of God the Father was completely satisfied. No rival claims at all to the will of God can be found in His life, and godly jealousy found perfect satisfaction in the total submission, total commitment, and single-heartedness of our precious Savior.

Now look at the *Revised Version*: "I fear lest Satan should corrupt your minds from the simplicity that is toward Christ." In other words, our attitude which is the governing relationship of everything else toward the Lord Jesus is to be utterly simple. Here is the only thing that will work in the rush of modern life and glorify God in the tremendous controversies and testings that face us today. There is one thing that will end simplicity, and that is divided loyalty.

What is the simplicity that is toward Christ? I give it to you in a nutshell: it is a faith that looks to Christ crucified and risen exclusively as the source of salvation and life; not Christ plus the church, not Christ plus ritual, not Christ plus ceremony, not Christ plus works, but Christ: crucified, risen, glorified, coming again. It is a faith that looks to Him exclusively and says, "Lord, in days like these to whom shall I go? Thou alone hast the words of eternal life." A faith that is exclusively resting in and centered upon Jesus our Lord alone, a love that is clear from every competing affection: "I am jealous over you with godly jealousy: for I have espoused you to one husband that I may present you as a chaste virgin to Christ" (v. 2). God's purpose for His people is union with Himself as between man and woman like this: a chaste, pure, spotless bride, absolutely separated and devoted to the claims of Jesus Christ.

I suppose one of the greatest delights of a bride or a bridegroom is to keep himself or herself chaste for the other, and neither of them would brook the incoming of a third party who would take away that sweet, precious, sacred relationship. No, and neither will heaven. That does not mean that in my love to Jesus I am not to love other people. Of course not. But it does mean that if I cannot take any human love into His presence and have His smile, or if that love deflects me from my devotion to the Lord Jesus Christ, that is the end of simplicity, that is the end of sweetness, that is the end of power, that is the end of graciousness, that is the end of reality in my Christian life. It must be a love that is clear from every rival affection.

Is that true of you? You love other people rightly, but are you being presented, as Paul says, as a chaste, pure virgin to Jesus, washed in His blood, consecrated, dedicated to His service, yielding to His loving heart? Can you say that every other affection that you have has been taken into His presence and He has smiled upon it, or if He has said "no" then you have put it away? Every human love that is real, far from taking away from devotion to your Lord, is being sanctified, made pure, beautiful, lovely, just because Jesus is in the midst of it.

There must also be an obedience, unqualified obedience to His commands, for the Lord Jesus said, "If ye love me, keep my commandments." This is the simplicity in Christ. Have you got it? This is what we need, this is the only answer in Christian living today—a faith, I repeat, that looks to Him exclusively, a love in which He is totally supreme, an obedience which is unreserved. Anything short of that is totally unworthy of the cross.

So many people today have got enough religion to prick and sting their consciences, but not enough to make them forsake their sins or bend their wills in submission to the will of God and say "no" to the thing that is wrong. How much of a dose of Holy Spirit authority do we need that people's consciences may not merely be pricked, but that their wills may be broken to the will of God?

In the days of the First Word War, in London, a regiment of soldiers was about to go out to France. In those days war was slaughter, and before they went, they were entertained at a concert in a theater in London by a group of people who wished them well. When the concert, which was given very well, was ended, the captain in charge of the regiment stood up, thanked the people for their kindness, and then with a broken voice said, "Ladies and gentlemen, is there anybody here who can tell us how to die?"

There was a moment's embarrassed silence until one lady, an artist in the concert, a Christian, came forward, stood up before the whole regiment of men and sang, "Oh, rest in the Lord, wait patiently for Him." There were few dry eyes that night.

In what you say to other people, have you so lost your way in theological argument that you can no longer tell people how to die? For the simplicity that is in Jesus Christ is to rest in the Lord like a little child rests in the arms of a mother. Are you there?

CHAPTER NINETEEN

TRANSFORMATION
OF THE DEVIL

2 CORINTHIANS 11:5–14

In the course of our studies we now come to the words of Paul's which I cannot possibly pass by. They are almost terrifying as well as tremendously challenging. When seen in the context of the whole teaching of the Word of God and in the light of current events, these words expose the true nature of the battle in which you and I are engaged: "…Satan himself is transformed into an angel of light." Therefore, instead of looking at the chapter itself, I want to bring to bear upon this one verse other passages from the Word which will illuminate it for us. At the same time, may God help us to understand, as perhaps we have never understood before, the desperate plight of modern civilization, the awful grip of the devil upon the world at this time, and the one hope that yet remains for us who are God's children.

There is no need for me to argue for the existence of Satan, or his personality, not simply as an influence or as an evil thing, but as a person who is just as real as Jesus Christ Himself. Indeed, if we accept the personality of Christ upon the revelation of the Word of God (and that is how we do accept it), we must also accept the personality of the devil upon the same evidence.

In Isaiah 14 he is revealed as one of God's heavenly host long before the existence of civilization on this planet, who set himself against the will of God and said, "I will ascend into heaven, and I will exalt my throne above the stars of God..." Before there was rebellion on earth, there was revolt in heaven.

Satan stepped into the record of human history as the serpent seeking to ally the human race in his purpose to become self-centered, self-sufficient, independent of God (Genesis 3). He was one hundred per cent successful, and ever since then submission to that principle of life, as he calls it, has become the very nature of the human race as we know it, transmitted down from all posterity to this generation.

Further, Satan is seen as one who has access to the throne of God (Job 1:6). Then we find him in face to face, direct combat with Jesus the Son of God, offering to Him all the kingdoms of this world if He would only worship him, and acknowledge that there is a possibility of life that can yet be achieved for the human race out of relationship with the Lord of all creation (Luke 4).

Now please notice that it is perfectly plain from the teaching of Scripture that it is not the aim of the devil to destroy humanity. That may surprise you, but his plan rather is to realize his ambition for world dominion through men yielded to him. To such he promises that they shall know good and evil. On the other hand, God, the Lord of all glory, power, and authority, upon a throne above all His created universe, far above Satan, declares that life on that principle will bring doom. Satan says it will not. God says it will. God says one thing, Satan says another thing. Satan says, "Believe me, yield to me, accept the principle of self-existence, self-sufficiency, independence of God, and I will show you life." God says, "Believe him and you will die, but believe on the Lord Jesus Christ, and you shall be saved." The whole of your life here and your destiny in eternity depend upon whom you believe.

In this great spiritual warfare there is one factor that weighs heavily in the devil's favor, for because the human race basically has submitted to this principle he has an ally in every human heart; there is that within each of us that will assent to this principle of evil. Because of a nature that is born in sin and therefore demands its self-existence and self-dependence, Satan has a powerful ally in the heart of each of us today.

There is also another factor in this spiritual warfare that weighs heavily against him. It is the course of human history which has abundantly proved, never more so than today, the awful tragedy and disaster which God said would happen if we rebelled against Him, and allied ourselves with the enemy. Furthermore, human history records that heaven has launched a full-scale counterattack against this hellish principle of life in the person of Jesus Christ, and in spite of all the efforts of the devil—in that he fought and battled with Jesus face to face—at the cross our Lord has stripped from Himself principalities and powers and made a show of them openly, and ascended into heaven to the right hand of all power, from whence He shall reign till every enemy becomes His footstool.

This mighty counterattack from heaven against all the powers of darkness is a factor which weighs heavily against the enemy. Yet in spite of it Satan successfully blinds the minds of them who believe not, lest the light of the glory of the gospel of Christ shines into them. He holds the whole of modern civilization, as the *Revised Version* renders 1 John 5:19, "he holds the world unconscious in his arms." What a plight for a soul made in the image of God, unconscious in the arms of the devil!

It follows, therefore, that the enmity of Satan is never with the unbeliever—they are already his—but it is with the man who has revolted from his rule, turned to God in Christ, and found himself by that blessed act of turning inspired by the Holy Spirit, and wonderfully free from the grip of the enemy. He is free to do the will of God, free not for license or lust, not to live as he pleases, but free to live in submission to the whole principle God has laid down, and in living that way to find His liberty. All the fiery darts of the enemy are hurled at the child of God simply because the Christian is indwelt by His divine nature, Satan's deadly enemy. The attack of the enemy against the Christian is not against flesh and blood, but it is against our relationship to Jesus Christ. Satan is not primarily concerned to make a Christian descend into moral filth. Oh no, for, in fact, that would rather defeat his object. But he is concerned to make the child of God fail in prayer, be bankrupt in his testimony, defeated in his spiritual life, deprived forever of being a channel of communication of God's principle of light into this world. Now it is just here that we see the transformation of the devil.

"…Your adversary the devil, as a roaring lion, walketh about, seeking whom he may devour" (1 Peter 5:8). I somehow feel that kind of language rather suited the man who wrote it—Peter is of a lion-hearted temperament! In Bunyan's immortal book he writes of Apollyon in this way: "Now the monster was hideous to behold, clothed with scales like a fish, wings like a dragon, feet like a bear, and out of his belly came fire and smoke; his mouth was as the mouth of a lion." And that is how Satan comes upon us sometimes, as an undisguised, hideous, evil monster, ready to devour us and throw us down. But he is easy to detect, and if he always came like that, the Christian could take his sword and beat him off.

Paul speaks of the devil much more seriously, and in many passages of Scripture he refers to him as a serpent, who comes with subtlety and guile. Listen to his language, "...we are not ignorant of his devices" (2 Corinthians 2:11). "Put on the whole armour of God, that ye may be able to stand against the wiles of the devil" (Ephesians 6:11), "...the snare (or trap) of the devil..." (2 Timothy 2:26). To Peter, a roaring lion; to Paul, a serpent which beguiles and still fascinates men with his glittering eye, and then slowly winds his slimy length, coil after coil, around their lives, because he fashions himself as an angel of light.

That is exactly what he once was, an angel of light, and that is what he pretends to be today. That is what he was before creation when he rebelled; that is what he pretends to be while still living in rebellion. He offers men light on that principle, and by every counterfeit imaginable he offers a way of life without any relationship to God.

As you observe Satan's basic place of attack and his counterfeit, notice that his master-stroke in this twentieth century, as far as an ungodly world is concerned, is the strategy of communism. Never has Satan achieved anything so powerful, so successful, and so overwhelming as this in all history. It was practically unknown fifty years ago, and is now sweeping the world, threatening to engulf western civilization. The fear for lands of freedom and civilization, as we know it, is not from an onslaught of nuclear bombs, but from the collapse of the whole moral fiber from inside. The thing we are fighting today is not over in Moscow or Peking, but right here where we live. Our enemy is not flesh and blood, but a spiritual foe.

If this be so, notice the strategy of the devil. He has the world blinded by this devilish system, but where is the focal point of his attack? It is upon the Christian church, for his only enemy really is the divine nature, Jesus Christ, who only lives in born-again people. Therefore Satan's first and primary target is the church of Jesus Christ.

He attacks in three ways: first, in the realm of the Spirit by false teaching. It is this which Paul has strictly in view in this passage: "...if he that cometh preacheth another Jesus, whom we have not preached, or if ye receive another spirit, which ye have not received, or another gospel, which ye have not accepted, ye might well bear with him" (v. 4). "...Such are false apostles, deceitful works, transforming themselves into the apostles of Christ" (v. 13). In other words, the first basic attack of the enemy upon the church of Jesus Christ is in the realm of our souls by false teaching.

There is no doctrine of the church which is free from abuse. When Satan attacked the Lord Jesus Christ, you will recall, he turned himself into a preacher with a text from the Bible (Psalm 91, Matthew 4) and dared to use the Word of God to attack the Lord of glory. Satan is adept at preaching a form of religion based on Scripture [texts] and incorporating many of the doctrines of the Christian faith; indeed every doctrine of the faith except one. There is one he is afraid of, because he knows it is this one which will defeat him.

We read in Revelation 12:11, as the whole of this universe celebrates the triumph of our risen and returning Lord Jesus, "...they overcame him by the blood of the Lamb, and by the word of their testimony." If there is one doctrine that Satan cringes before, it is redemption by blood. It is justification by faith and not by works. It is atonement by the blood of Jesus. It is the free grace of God that puts a man right by God's unmerited favor, and not by our working to achieve salvation. Because Satan is afraid of this, he does his deadliest work not by ignoring this cardinal doctrine, but by perverting it. Then he makes this wondrous, precious, glorious truth of the gospel an excuse for self-indulgence until you have the antinomians saying today, "It does not matter how I live; all my sins will be washed away by the blood of Christ." So Satan would, if he could, deceive the very elect.

There were very few things that could make Paul cry like a child. He had the Roman scourge upon his bare back, but he ignored it and was glad that he was counted worthy to suffer for Jesus. He could be in the midst of a Mediterranean storm, driven to shipwreck, but he praised God and believed Him for deliverance. He could have the executioner's sword raised above him, about to behead him, and he could say, "I have fought a good fight, I have finished the course, and kept the faith." Ah, but there was one thing that made him sob, that broke his heart—it was when he saw men take the gospel of the grace of God and make it an excuse for sin, saying, "Let us continue in sin that grace may abound!" for of such, Paul says, "...I tell you even weeping, they are the enemies of the cross of Christ: whose end is destruction, whose God is their belly, and whose glory is in their shame..." (Philippians 3:18–19).

Satan's masterpiece in the church today is an attack upon the stronghold of evangelical testimony to make us abuse the gospel of grace, and make us permit it to allow us to continue in disgusting sin, and yet say, "I am a Christian." Friends, in the name of heaven, this has to stop before it is too late, or else the church will be doomed! That is what is happening in fundamental circles in western lands today, when people exploit the grace of God, make use of it to say, "By grace all is well!" and then live like the devil. The thing is a sheer impossibility.

Second, the enemy attacks in the realm of the imagination, by unholy thinking. Here it is that temptation is dressed upon in its most attractive garb. There is no gift so exalting as that of our imagination; it can rise to great heights. But there is no curse so debasing, so degrading, as an imagination which is defiled by the enemy. Therefore, Satan, who knows exactly the moment to attack, will come with full force at the best time. At times of sickness and depression, when low in spirit and health, he fills our mind with doubt, with questionings, with self-pity. When we are well, strong, and prosperous, he fills our mind with self-confidence, self-love, and self-admiration. In times when we relax and seek to rest our mind, he will fill an empty mind with foul thinking and imagination. When we seek the face of God in prayer, he will invade the holy place with thoughts of which we are desperately ashamed. For every mood or condition he has his weapon.

But most subtle of all are the moments when he withdraws altogether from the field of action and you are left numb, no longer with any love for God's work, doing it because you have to do it. No sweetness is found in God's Word; you may be stirred by the sermon occasionally, but never stirred into action—that is dealt with five minutes after the service by the conversation that takes place. You are completely without any susceptibility to the things of heaven, immoveable by the most powerful message except vaguely stirred in your conscience. Life is just a round of duty, and there is a dead calm in the soul, with no hunger or longing for God and heaven, you seem to be just cruising along spiritually without life, without any semblance of concern, and Satan has conveniently withdrawn. He stands back and watches the soul that he has ceased to tempt because he does not need to bother.

You say temptation is hard. I know, but I tell you what is worse; when Satan has stopped bothering, and he leaves the soul without troubling anything, and with no heart-concern for the things of God. If you are just going through life with no reality, no power, no grace, no hunger for God, everything a duty and performance, I plead with you, go to

God and say to Him, "Lord, let the devil loose on my life again!" It is a dangerous thing to pray, for He will do it.

Satan's transformation into an angel of light is, in the third place, in the realm of conscience by self-interest. Oh, how subtly Satan puts on the apparel of an angel of light! As he is well dressed in the garb of heaven, he makes himself to appear in the soul as the very voice of heaven. You sometimes find it hard to know whether it is the devil or the Lord talking to you—of course you do, if you are honest. It is not always so easy to know when you are being "clearly led" about this or that. Satan is always working in the realm of conscience to cloud the issue, and when self-interest would call for me to go in a certain direction, he would tell me that is the path of duty. Have you ever heard him say this: "Friend, there is no harm in it! It does not pay to follow Jesus too far. After all, you have got to have a good time, you know"?

So by false teaching, by imagination, by conscience, the Christian is deceived by the devil transformed into an angel of light. I would say that one of the most amazing things about him is that he is so united. He has a thousand agencies all ready for his use, and while the church of Jesus Christ is always quarreling and indulging in the luxury of civil war, I never learn of any civil war in hell. All Satan's hosts are united on one full-scale attack upon the place where he can find the nature of Christ indwelling a child of God. God help us, for when the church fights within its own ranks, Satan has a field day.

What is the answer to it? Have I uncovered Satan in your own life? Is this your experience? Then how do you think he can be detected and overcome? I would remind you that the ultimate doom of the devil is certain (Revelation 12:7–11), but we do not have to look into a vague future. Go back to the cross and see there One who cast from Himself principalities and powers, and made a show of them openly (Colossians 2:14–15). The defeat that was predicted from the very moment the rebellion began, when the Lord promised that the seed of the woman would bruise the head of the serpent (Genesis 3:15) has actually happened in human history as Jesus Himself said: "Now is the judgment of this world: now shall the prince of this world be cast out" (John 12:31).

But what about today, this desperate hour in which we live? I tell you, there is victory for the Christian now! "...greater is he that is in you, than he that is in the world" (1 John 4:4). Ephesians 6:10, 12 speaks to us about putting on the whole armor of God that we might stand against the wiles of the devil.

You may say that you see the desperate plight we are in, but you cannot find the answer for your own life. What can you do about it? You can lay hold of God in the Word of God as you have never done before, for a man who is soaked in the Word of God has always an answer ready for the devil in the moment of temptation. "Wherewithal shall a young man cleanse his way? By taking heed thereto according to thy word" (Psalm 119:9). However the Word of God is not magic. It all depends how you approach it. If you approach it to submit it to your intellectual criticism, then you will never know victory. But if you submit yourself to the criticism of the Book, then you will discover the power of God to defeat in you the power of the enemy.

More than that, you must not only soak yourself in His Word, but you must run to Him, the living Word, who is made unto us wisdom. This battle is not with flesh and blood, but with spiritual forces, and therefore it requires spiritual weapons, and "…the weapons of our warfare are not carnal…" (2 Corinthians 10:4). The sheep are never so safe as when they are near the shepherd; we are never so secure from the fiery darts of Satan as when we are near to Jesus. What does that mean? It means to walk according to His example: "…Christ also suffered for us, leaving us an example, that ye should follow his steps" (1 Peter 2:21). It means walking in the way He walked. It means living daily in His fellowship: "…if we walk in the light, as he is in the light, we have fellowship with one another…" (1 John 1:7). It means trusting always in His blood, for the blood of Jesus cleanses from all sin. Jesus said, "Blessed are the pure in heart, for they shall see God."

May I suggest to you that promise does not only mean one day in heaven when we shall see Him face to face, but it means that now, in the heat of the battle, in the tremendous intensity of the spiritual warfare in which we are engaged, in the light of world conditions that constantly challenge us, it is not only that we *will* see God in heaven, but we will see Him *now*. In the midst of the battle we are able to see not only God, but also the devil, and we are given the spiritual discernment to know which is which.

We live today in a world that is on fire. We see national and political corruption, and worst of all, a church that is lethargic, disunited, worldly, tripped up by the angel of light. What can we do before it is too late?

Shake off the shackles, break free from the fetters, snap the chains, and lay hold of God as we have never laid hold of Him before! The Lord wants a chance to answer the fire of hell with the fire of the Holy Ghost, and He will do this very thing for you, because it is the only hope, the only answer. You cannot answer fire by human reasoning or human intellect; you can answer fire with fire. Today, the Holy Ghost on fire in the lives of God's people is the only hope for fundamental Christianity.

I beg of you that you personally will give God the opportunity to answer the fire of the enemy with the fire of heaven, for then the power of Satan cannot prevail against you. Are you on the Lord's side in the battle? Go now into the very presence of Jesus our Lord, close to His wounded side, and say to Him, "Lord Jesus, please put on the armor for me, for I have no might and no power against all these who come against me, neither know I what to do, but my eyes are upon Thee." Like Gideon of old, He will clothe you with the armor of righteousness on the right hand and on the left, and you will go forth as a man who has gripped the Word of God and who has been gripped by the Spirit of God. Only as revival comes to individual hearts can disaster, in nation and in the church, be averted in our time.

CHAPTER TWENTY

COSTLY
COMPASSION

2 CORINTHIANS 11:15–33

Let us take time here to review some of Paul's statements which we have considered that emphasize the truth that blessing does come out of buffeting. First Paul says that he had the sentence of death in himself that he should not trust in himself, but in God which raiseth the dead (1:9). Then giving testimony to his own experience Paul said, I have been "persecuted, but not forsaken; cast down, but not destroyed; Always bearing about in the body the dying of the Lord Jesus, that the life also of Jesus might be made manifest in our body" (4:9–10). Then he writes, "…death worketh in us, but life in you" (v. 12).

Summing it all up Paul says, "…our light affliction, which is but for a moment, worketh for us a far more exceeding and eternal weight of glory" (4:17–18). He speaks of himself "As sorrowful, yet always rejoicing; as poor, yet making many rich…" (6:10). Then he says, "…without were fightings, within were fears. Nevertheless God…" (7:5). Finally, he states, "…the weapons of our warfare are not carnal, but mighty through God to the pulling down of strong holds" (10:4).

Blessing out of buffeting—this has been the great principle of Paul's life, the principle that made the man who practised it the greatest missionary that the church has ever known, and this has been the great principle of every life that has truly known God ever since. It is a principle, of course, which has found its more glorious expression in the Lord Jesus Himself, who was wounded for our transgressions

442 / Blessings Out of Buffetings

and bruised for our iniquities, who indeed was made sin for us. What buffeting, that we might be made the righteousness of God in Him! What blessing! And there is no spiritual blessing that is authentic which ever gets released from a child of God unless he has taken some of the buffeting. This is the principle of Christian living just because we are Christians.

Somehow in this chapter Paul seems to rise to a tremendous height of testimony, and excels himself as he recounts his experience as a servant of Jesus Christ. I know of no other place in the Bible where you could find this principle of blessing through buffeting more clearly outlined and taught than in these tremendous verses.

You will recall that there were those at Corinth who sought to undermine Paul's testimony, his influence, and his authority, who boasted of their own ancestry, their social position, their religious training, and for a moment in this chapter Paul meets them on their own ground, apologizing to heaven for doing so! "That which I speak, I speak it not after the Lord, but as it were foolishly, in this confidence of boasting" (v. 17). Again: "I speak as concerning reproach, as though we had been weak" (v. 21). "Howbeit whereinsoever any is bold, (I speak foolishly), I am bold also"; and: "Are they ministers of Christ? (I speak as a fool)..." (v. 23). For a moment he departs, as it were, from the direct command of the Spirit of God and meets these men on their own ground. If they try to rebut his authority, refuse to recognize his spirituality, and claim that because of their tradition and social standing and religious education they stood head and shoulders above the great apostle he says, in effect, "If that is your basis of evaluating a servant of Christ, then I can measure up with any of you. 'Are they Hebrews? So am I. Are they Israelites? So am I. Are they the seed of Abraham? So am I'" (v. 22).

Observe, however, that he forsakes such an attitude immediately and says, "If I must needs glory, I will glory of the things which concern my infirmities." The true test of discipleship, the mark of an authentic testimony, of a genuine saving experience of the grace of God is found in a totally different area from all of this.

After the Lord Jesus met Paul on the Damascus road, He spoke to Ananias concerning him and said, "...for he is a chosen vessel unto me, to bear my name before the Gentiles ... for I will shew him how great things he will do in my name's sake." No! "What great success he will have as a missionary." No! "How many people he will move toward

God," No! "What heights of fame and what a name he will make for himself." No! "I will shew him how great things he must suffer for my name's sake" (Acts 9:16).

Paul says, in effect, "You challenge my authority! You dare to stand upon the ground of your religious training, your social position, your racial prejudice; you boast of this and say that is the mark of authority. I say to you, if I would glory, I will glory in the things that concern my infirmities, for the only valid test of my worth as a man of God is that the very thing that Jesus said would happen to me has happened."

When God began a good work in your heart and life at the moment He first met you at Calvary, I doubt whether there has ever been such a spiritual moment in your whole life. I wonder if there has ever been a moment since that day when, maybe with tear-stained face and certainly with a broken heart (if the experience was genuine) you first met God and gazed upon those nail-pierced hands and upon that thorn-crowned brow and said, as Thomas said of old, "My Lord and my God!" There was nothing of carnality or worldliness about you then. There was not a care for anything, except that the burden of sin had been lifted at Calvary, the condemnation of guilt had gone, and new life had started. You were right with God and the time of the singing of the birds had come. Oh, that was a spiritual moment! He who has begun that good work began it by breaking your heart and revealing the great intention that He would perform that work until that day when you see your Lord face to face. And the only platform for the performance of God's work is the platform of suffering.

See now, therefore, the price Paul paid (vv. 23–28). It is amazing how we can read a list like this and neither think about it nor apply it personally. There are twenty-three experiences mentioned, and as we, with Paul, go through them, I pray the Holy Spirit may impress them upon your heart and mind.

You say you are minister of Christ? I speak as a fool. I am more than any of you. I have worked harder than any, I have taken more lashings than any, I have been in prison more often than any of you, I have been facing death more often too. In fact, nobody has experienced such trouble over sin but that I have become more involved because I am a Christian. There is no one who has suffered and been so persecuted as I have. I have had one hundred and ninety-five lashes on my bare back, which is the limit they could give me.

Paul continues. Contrary to all Roman justice, I have been beaten three times with rods. When I was in Derbe, I was stoned and left for dead. Three times (I have only made public one instance) I have been shipwrecked. Once I spent a night and a day on a raft. And have I traveled! In journeyings often, and always I have been in danger. I have been in danger on the seas; in danger of being robbed, especially when I took the offering from the churches up to Jerusalem. I have been in danger from my own countrymen, as well as from nationals of other countries. I have been in danger when I was in cities, and acutely so when I was in the wilderness on the mission field. I have been in perils everywhere, and perhaps the worst of all, I was in danger among people who called themselves Christians. That was the hardest thing to take.

Then I have been desperately tired, and I have had such pain, not all physical pain, but pain because of speaking with brethren who have lost out on the journey. It has been the exhaustion of spiritual counsel, it has been the pain in my own soul as I felt the pain in others, and as I watched people I loved so dearly fall apart spiritually. I have often been in watchings: there have been nights when I have not been able to sleep because of the burden. I have sometimes not had enough food or drink, but regardless of this I voluntarily went through times of fasting because I knew that the kind of situations I was dealing with and the kind of people I had to cope with would only be dealt with by prayer and fasting. So in spite of my own necessary privations I went through times of fasting, and sometimes I have been cold without clothes for my back.

Such is the price that Paul paid. How does that react upon you? Do you congratulate yourself that you have escaped it? One week of such living and we would be done, but Paul went through it for a lifetime and gloried in his infirmities.

Does this make you feel ashamed? Of course, I recognize that the law of this country would protect its citizens from much of this because of the religious freedom we enjoy, but I cannot let myself off on that account. Investigating a little further, I must ask myself, "Why is it that I have escaped, why have we all escaped this?" What was it that made Paul live as he did? I ask you therefore to notice the natural thought that comes here in the following verses, the pressure that Paul felt in his spirit. Why did he live like that? "Besides those things which are without, that which cometh upon me daily, the care of all the churches. Who is weak, and I am not weak? Who is offended, and I burn not?"

"...that which cometh upon me daily..." I have paraphrased twenty-three things that constantly hit this man from without, and I give you the one inclusive reason why any of them were allowed to touch him at all, for he could have escaped them all. Not one of them was necessary, and he could have avoided them all and lived in comfort and luxury—except for one thing. There was one thing internal in his heart that forced him to face all these twenty-three things that were external: "...that which cometh upon me daily..."

I could not possibly convey to you adequately in the English language the force of that statement. I tried to picture it in terms of being smothered under a blanket, or by being attacked and crushed by some great animal, for he could not have used a stronger word when he said, in effect, "That which bears me down, that which is upon me as an intolerable load, that which is a burden, that which is something that I never shake off day or night. It is with me always. I have no vacation from it ever. It is upon me daily. The care, the compassion, the concern of all the churches." And please note, not the churches in an indefinite, vague, universal world-wide sense, but Paul says, in effect, "Who is weak, and I do not feel for him; who is offended and it does not cause me to burn with anxiety on his behalf?"

This great man paid the price because he felt the pressure, and again I ask you lovingly in Jesus' name, how much of that do you know? I say it tenderly, and yet I say it firmly; we have escaped a great deal of the price of buffeting because we just do not care about other people. Although the law of the land would protect us from much of this, nevertheless, if we began really to live with no release and no vacation as those who care, as those who are pressed down under a burden which is intolerable, but for the grace of God, a burden cannot be shaken off—the burden of God's family everywhere, a burden that goes round the earth in concern for His blood-washed children—I say to you, if we lived as though we really cared and longed to rescue one soul from hell, the buffeting would begin at once. To our shame, we escape because we do not arouse ourselves to take up the fight, and we rarely launch a personal attack in the name of the Lord Jesus to rescue a sinner from his way. I am sorry to say it, but we just do not care, and therefore we never experience the pressure that Paul felt.

If you are being honest with the Lord as you hear Him speak, perhaps you are saying to yourself, "I know that is true, I don't really care, for I would not live as I do if I cared—then why don't I care? Why is it I have no compassion? Why is it my concern for the lost is so inadequate, and why do I rarely feel when I am under a burden or experience a real sense of concern? So often I exhibit that I don't care in my superficiality, in the way I behave when I am off-duty, in the things I do and in the places I attend. But *why* don't I care?"

"If I must needs glory, I will glory of the things which concern mine infirmities." What is the principle behind a statement like that? "I am going to glory," says Paul, in effect, "and boast only in the things in which God has made me weak, and in the infirmities which I suffer for His sake." What is the principle? I give it to you in three brief, simple statements. I give you the thought to pray over.

The first principle is that Paul had learned the value of a soul. "And unto the Jews I became as a Jew, that I might gain the Jews; to them that are under the law, as under the law, that I might gain them that are under the law; To them that are without law, as without law, (being not without law to God, but under the law to Christ) that I might gain them that are without law. To the weak became I as weak, that I might gain the weak: I am made all things to all men, that I might by all means save some" (1 Corinthians 9:20–22).

Have you ever asked God in prayer to show you what it means for a soul to go out into a Christless eternity, into hell? I do not believe God would ever show us that completely, because if He did we would go out of our minds. We would become deranged if we knew that the person with whom we are rubbing shoulders every day, he who lives next door to us, maybe even he in our own homes, if he knows nothing of the grace of God in Jesus Christ, that he is going to hell to be lost for all eternity. We rarely dare think on these things because of the horror of the truth.

There are only two alternatives here. If the souls of men and women deserve no more attention than we give them, then Paul was a lunatic. But if we are truly to value the worth of a soul by his labors for them, then God forgive us! How sinful we are to value so much worthless and material things—things that we possess and then one day leave behind—and care so little for the undying souls of our fellow men! The first principle behind Paul's statements, "…I glory in the things that concern my infirmities" is that he knew the value of a soul.

The second principle is that Paul knew the virtue of the gospel. Romans 1:16: "…I am not ashamed [I am proud] of the gospel of Christ;

for it is the power of God unto salvation to every one that believeth..."
In other words, I know that I have not simply *a* message to preach, but
I have *the* message, and it is the only message that works in human lives.
It delivers a man from the depths of his depravity, lifts him from the
dunghill, and sets him among the princes in heaven.

This is the only message that is adequate, and I am proud of it. I do
not apologize for it. I do not talk in uncertain terms, nor does the trumpet blow with an uncertain sound. I am sure and positive of it because
I have proved it in my own life. It has worked for me by transforming
and turning me completely inside out! Therefore I do not go to people
with any apology: I know the reality in my heart of the transforming
power of the gospel of Jesus Christ, that there is no other way and no
other answer. I know that for the lands where millions are without God
and without hope today, there is a balm in Gilead, and that the gospel is
God's final and only answer. Such was Paul's conviction.

When the Holy Spirit presses upon us the necessity for absolute commitment without reservation to Jesus Christ, no matter if people do say that
we are narrow and fanatical, then something within us reveals the need for
money and men for missions to get the task done in our generation, and
to evangelize to a finish to bring back the King of kings. But there is too
often another voice saying that it is too dangerous, too uncertain, doors are
closing, and surely it is better to leave these heathen people to their own
religions: God will not condemn them, for He is a loving heavenly Father!

Who would endure all that Paul endured if he had not known that
the eternal destiny of the human race was at stake in the acceptance or
rejection of his message? Who would have faced what he did if he had
not known with an absolute conviction that nothing could shake him,
that this message was totally adequate and it still is. He knew the value
of a soul, he knew the virtue of the gospel, and he also knew the third
principle, the victory of love.

If you asked Paul what inspired him to say, "...I will glory of the things
which concern mine infirmities," he would answer, "The love of Christ
constraineth me." From the buffetings in the life of this Pharisee who
became such a disciple, from the life of this man who revolutionized the
first century of the Christian faith and to whom we owe such a large section of the New Testament, from the life of this man who blazed a trail as
few others ever have, there flowed immeasurable blessing—but, I do not
preach Paul: I proclaim Paul's Savior, and would say that what he faced in

terms of buffeting was only a pale reflection of what the Savior faced to redeem our souls.

Open your Bible to Isaiah 53 and read it through again and again: "We did esteem him stricken, smitten of God, and afflicted. But he was wounded for our transgressions, he was bruised for our iniquities: the chastisement of our peace was upon him; and with his stripes we are healed. ... We have turned every one to his own way; and the LORD hath laid on him the iniquity of us all."

Oh, precious Lord, what buffeting He endured to save such wretches as we! Why did He endure it? Because He was moved with compassion. He paid the price because He saw the multitude as sheep without a shepherd, and as He went up the lonely road to Calvary He said, "...weep not for me, but weep for yourselves, and for your children," for He knew that eternal destiny depended upon their attitude to Himself. Ah, what buffeting, what burden! But oh, what blessing came out of His life! Let us say it to the Lord with stricken spirits and broken hearts, we escape the buffeting and we know so little of the burden, with the result that there is so little of the blessings.

The Holy Spirit is waiting to work through the person who is willing to take the buffeting because he has the burden, and out from buffeting comes the flow of Holy Spirit power. It is when the rock is smitten that the water gushes out.

I think of David Brainerd who, though in a cool dry wind, sweated and prayed, and hundreds of hard-hearted Indians were mowed down like grass under the conviction of the Holy Ghost. I think of Praying Hyde who shook a continent for the Lord. Does this put you out of the picture? I think of two dear old ladies aged eighty-one and eighty-two, who for two years prayed for hours a day in the Hebrides of Scotland until one day the fire of God fell and revival came.

In Revelation 21 there is the picture of the New Jerusalem coming down from God out of heaven prepared as a bride adorned for her husband. Here is God's purpose for His children, to prepare them to meet the heavenly Bridegroom, prepared through buffeting. Then what does God say? "...God shall wipe away all tears from their eyes; and there shall be no more death, neither sorrow, nor crying, neither shall there be any more pain: for the former things are passed away.

What does that mean? We have often read those verses in times of sadness and loneliness, when friends have been going through the valley of the shadow, and we have always found comfort in them. But I do not think that is what the Holy Spirit is saying. The bride is prepared, and how is she prepared? The Captain of our salvation was made perfect through suffering; He learned obedience through the things that He suffered, and one day God will wipe away all tears. What tears? The tears I have shed for a soul. Will there be any? The times I have wept over someone who has rejected Jesus. Have I ever wept? When I meet God face to face, will He find dry eyes, and no tears to wipe away because I have never really cared?

"And there shall be no more death..." I have had the sentence of death in me all my life, says Paul. So have you and so have I, if we have really cared. There will be no more buffeting, no more sorrow, no more crying, and no more pain. The former things are passed away.

Yes, there is coming a day, bless God, when the buffeting will be over, and the last tear over a lost soul will have been checked, the last sentence of death will have been concluded, and the last pain of anguish over people who care nothing for our Lord Jesus will have finished, and God shall wipe away all signs of sorrow and concern. Let us covet a compassion that costs, so that on that day He may have many tears to wipe away.

CHAPTER TWENTY-ONE

THE MINISTRY
OF THE THORN*

2 CORINTHIANS 12:1–10

The ministry of the thorn is a great subject: "...there was given to me a thorn in the flesh, the messenger of Satan to buffet me. ... For this thing I besought the Lord thrice, that it might depart from me. And he said unto me, My grace is sufficient for thee..." I would say at the very beginning that though we are considering something about which Paul has opened his heart to unveil as his own experience, we are really just considering a very faint reflection of the same experience that came to the Lord Jesus, Paul's Savior. Paul's thrice repeated urgent prayer is but an echo of One who prayed in a garden, "...Father, if it be possible, let this cup pass from me..." The answer which heaven gave to our Lord was the answer given to Paul. The cup was left, confronting Him, to drink to the last drop. The thorn remained for the rest of Paul's life. But that was not the only answer, for in the garden angels came to strengthen the Savior, and to the heart of the apostle came the word, "...My grace is sufficient for thee: for my strength is made perfect in weakness."

Therefore, as we consider this great word, the Lord Jesus stands, as it were, in the shadows as He did when He heard Paul's prayer and answered it so unexpectedly, so differently, and yet so gloriously, to test his reactions and to equip him for all his ministry. In the same way the

---

* Based upon a booklet entitled *The Discipline of Disappointment*, by the Rev. G. B. Duncan, and reproduced by the author's kind permission.

Lord stands in the shadows now to watch your reactions to a similar situation.

Perhaps you have looked into the face of a Christian who is always smiling, who never seems to have any worry, is always happy and radiant and, as you have thought about your own circumstances, you have said in your heart, "I wish I were he! He seems to have no problems. He doesn't have to take what I do." But perhaps you have lived long enough, as I have, to know that sometimes the most radiant face hides great pressures, and often the man who is being most blessed of God is being most buffeted by the devil. I am glad, therefore, that we can consider now what I have called "the ministry of the thorn."

I notice, in the first place, what I am sure Paul would have called, at least for a time, a very frustrating experience, for to quote his own words: "...There was given to me a thorn in the flesh, the messenger of Satan to buffet me ... For this thing, I besought the Lord thrice..." What a comfort it must have been for him to address his urgent petition to the One who Himself had faced this all the more completely in Gethsemane! Quite evidently, therefore, we have here the pressure of a very severe trial in Paul's life. It was not just a little thing; it was a very big thing. The word which is translated in our New Testament *thorn* is not the kind of thing you might get in your finger while gardening, which is very painful. Then you can very quickly pull it out. Actually it is a word which is used for a stake upon which people were impaled to be crucified. Paul's experience, therefore, was a very severe trial.

It would be sheer speculation to imagine what it could have been. It might have been something in his own personal character and life which was constantly reminding him of the sinfulness of the flesh which ultimately brought him to say, "I know that in me [that is, in the flesh] dwelleth no good thing." It might have been something in his environment or circumstances which seemed to be completely impossible for him to take any longer. It might have been some physical problem, and most people seem to think this was most likely. Some have suggested, and I think with a measure of authority, that Paul was suffering from partial blindness, if not total blindness. This is, of course, mere speculation, and what really matters is that when this thing hit him, he was absolutely convinced that it was the most restricting thing that had ever happened to him, and was inevitably going to affect and ultimately destroy his usefulness to the Lord.

Paul felt, therefore, that it must be dealt with, and the only way to deal with it was to remove it altogether. Paul went into the presence of God—not merely thrice, because that is simply the symbol of a persistent and consistent agony of heart—and said, in effect, "Lord, please take it away! It is the only thing to be done, for I just cannot live for You and serve You like this! O Lord, if only You would please remove this pressure! If only this opposition would cease; if only the pain and agony of this thorn would be removed, then I could do Thy will. If only…"

I wonder if you have been saying this to the Lord in the past weeks and months, or even longer? "If only I were stronger in body! If only I did not have to work next to that difficult person in my office! If only my husband were an out-and-out Christian! If only my wife were really dedicated to Jesus! If only my job were different! If only…"

Yes, but notice that in spite of Paul's tremendous prayer and in spite of his agony the pressure was maintained. Paul prayed about it, as I am sure you have often prayed, and in his estimation of the situation the only thing that God could do, if he was ever to be of any use to Him again, was to take this thing out of his life altogether, and set him free from it. "…I besought the Lord thrice," says Paul, with an intensity of desire and agony of soul, "Lord, remove this thing and cause it to depart!"

Is that how you and I have prayed? Do you share Paul's convictions concerning your own situation that the only adequate answer is that God must take the problem away, remove that person, or get you out of this situation and into another circumstance. You are so convinced that you have told God what He must do!

Observe carefully that the word is, "For this thing I besought the Lord thrice…" In other words, there came a time in Paul's experience when he ceased to pray about this particular matter. He besought the Lord, and then he stopped praying about it. The pressure went on and was maintained because God did not remove it, but Paul ceased praying, because as he prayed and pleaded, God gave to him a most revealing explanation. After Paul stopped praying, the Lord said to him, as the correct rendering of that little phrase would be, "For this thing I besought the Lord thrice that it might depart from me." And Paul goes on, in effect, "he has been saying unto me…"

I do not know how long this had been going on, certainly for fourteen years, because that is the period during which he speaks about the revelation which, as we shall see in a moment, is personally connected with this thought. But for all this time Paul had been praying, "Lord, take this thing away!" and for all that time the Lord had been trying to get through to him in vain.

Some of us are so busy telling God what He ought to do about our situation that we are incapable of hearing what He wants to do and say to us! We are so sure that the only thing to be done is to remove the problem altogether that we never give the Lord a moment to speak to our hearts about His alternative.

"I besought the Lord thrice, and when I stopped praying I heard Him say unto me..." Well, what did He say? First of all it is clear that the Lord made plain to the apostle Paul that there was a purpose in this. Did you notice that verse 7 begins and ends with exactly the same statement: "...lest I should be exalted above measure..."? In other words, Paul's estimation of what had happened to him was quite wrong. He had been sure that it was not merely useless but that it was a positive hindrance to him; but now he discovers that this has been right at the very heart of God in his life. "...lest I be exalted above measure..."—in other words, as long as this thing continues, it is impossible for him ever to be proud lest he be exalted above measure.

God had sent into this man's life something that came to him in a moment of spiritual ecstasy, in a time of wonderful revelation of the things of the Lord. At that very moment there came the pressure of the thorn to keep Paul humble. That is why many people suggest that when Paul said concerning himself that in speech he was contemptible and in bodily presence he was weak, these were his outward testimonies concerning this thorn. As people looked at him, there was no striking appearance, no big personality. Here was a man who, judged by every human basis of authority and power, was in a totally different area altogether, and the suggestion is that the reason for this was something that God had done to him, this thorn that had come into his life. For as long as the apostle Paul was conscious of the old nature within him, he could only call himself the chief of sinners.

Truly God knows best how to deal with a man like Paul. I would say it very reverently, but when the Lord calls a man into a place of spiritual opportunity, into any place of leadership, be it as a missionary, as a pastor, as an administrator in some sphere of Christian work, whatever it may be, the Lord cannot afford to take any risks with him. There is too much at stake. God wanted to be sure that Paul's usefulness would never be marred and that he would be kept available, usable, and humble. When God's purpose is accomplished in your life, whatever that purpose may be, I can think of no better way of expressing it than by likening it to a greasy pan that you have taken and scrubbed, turned upside down, wiped round and round, and placed clean on the shelf. When God does that, His purpose is fulfilled, and the thorn is put into a man's life to turn him upside down, to wipe him thoroughly, and to leave him in a place where he says that he knows that in him dwells no good thing, for the flesh profits nothing.

I dare not speculate about the thorn in your life, nor presume to guess what it may be, but I know that behind it there is this ultimate purpose of God doing this very thing. However, I want to show you from this passage that there was not only a purpose in the thorn, but a wonderful provision. "…Lest I should be exalted above measure" was the purpose. The provision, "…My grace is sufficient for thee," and then the explanation, "for my strength is made perfect in weakness."

Notice that the Lord did not say to him, "My grace will prove to be sufficient," nor "I will give you enough grace to get through." No! But He is saying, in effect, "Paul, as I put the pressure on and allow this thorn to remain, I want you to understand that at each moment now there is ample provision for your every need, for My grace is sufficient for thee."

Do you see the humor of this situation? God's grace: me. His grace sufficient for little me! How absurd to think that it could ever be any different! As if a little fish could swim in the ocean and fear lest it might drink it dry! The grace of our crucified, risen, exalted, triumphant Savior, the Lord of all glory, is surely sufficient for me! Do you not think it is rather modest of the Lord to say *sufficient*? It is such a contrast, is it not?

I saw a most striking billboard in the state of New Jersey some time ago, and all it said was, "Our products are satisfactory." That did me good. So often we read that products are the world's finest, or the world's greatest, or the world's best, but this advertisement told us all we need to know to invite us to buy.

"…My grace is sufficient…" Does that mean to say that in the midst of the pressure of the thorn we are only just going to have enough grace to see us through? Indeed it isn't! In the story of the feeding of the five thousand the common folk in the presence of Andrew said, "…Two

456 / B<small>LESSINGS</small> O<small>UT OF</small> B<small>UFFETINGS</small>

hundred pennyworth of bread is not sufficient for them. ..." Omnipotence said, "Bring the loaves and fishes and give them to me." Faith distributed them among the crowd. Experience gathered up twelve baskets that remained over and above. "...My grace is sufficient..."

Then comes the word of explanation: "...for my strength is made perfect in weakness." Would you please notice the contrast here? His strength (and the word is *dynamis*, dynamite) is made perfect in my weakness (and the word is *neurasthenia*). His power, my weakness, and the connecting link is the *made perfect*, which is the same word that the Lord Jesus used when He hung upon the cross and cried, "It is finished!" God's strength is completely made perfect in your weakness.

God does not work through those who think they are the pillars of the church. He works through weakness. There was a king in the Old Testament, Uzziah by name, of whom it was said, "...he was marvelously helped until he was strong..." but when weakness, personal insufficiency, and utter inability are consciously felt, realized, and known, then the power of God and His purpose for the thorn have been fulfilled.

When I see a young preacher begin to taste success, my heart trembles for him. When there is a Sunday school teacher beginning to see things happen, and where a Christian worker sees evidences of blessing, that is the moment to watch out. God works through weakness. I am reminded of the tremendous work Paul wrote of in his first letter to the church at Corinth, "...God hath chosen the foolish things of the world to confound the wise; and God hath chosen the weak things of the world to confound the things which are mighty; And base things of the world, and things which are despised, hath God chosen, yea, and things which are not, to bring to nought things that are: That no flesh should glory in his presence" (1 Corinthians 1:27–29).

Do you really think that the modern preparations for the education of young people for Christian work recognize that principle? God works through the man who has been wiped clean and turned inside out, his life emptied before the Lord until he is hopelessly weak, that no flesh might glory in His presence.

There is one other thing to say to make this picture complete, for there is not only a frustrating experience, then a revealing explanation for the thorn, but also the transforming estimate in Paul's life. Here is a wonderful double transformation: "...when I am weak, then am I strong..." Therefore I take pleasure in infirmities..." (v. 10). And "Most gladly therefore will I rather glory in my infirmities, that the power of Christ may rest upon me" (v. 9).

That word *rest* is interesting. When the Lord Jesus came, John says, He tabernacled among us and we beheld His glory, the glory as of the only begotten of the Father, full of grace and truth (John 1:14). He tabernacled, He dwelt among us—that is the word. "...Most gladly therefore will I rather glory in my infirmities, that the power of Christ may [tabernacle] upon me." This means that weakness was turned immediately into strength.

Would it not be a wonderful thing if in the place where you have been so weak, where there has been a breakdown in your faith, where there has been the impetuous demand to heaven to shift your circumstances or remove this or that burden from your life, if in the place where you have failed to glorify God, you could remain strong?

How did it happen to Paul? I think I know, though he does not really tell us. It seems that there was a very deep and real relationship in the thorn that God gave to Paul and the cross that God gave to our Savior. "...My strength is made perfect in weakness." This was the statement of the Lord to the apostle. Was that a far-off statement, a truth not related to the apostle's experience? Oh, no. He had only to think back a few years, to remember the coming of a little Baby; he had only to think about Gethsemane, about a mock trial, a cruel cross, a grave, and the death of One of whom he himself wrote: "He was crucified in weakness." Could anyone on earth be more meek than the Son of God to be hung on the cross, hung in our place that He might redeem us from our sins? As that point of absolute weakness was met by the mighty power of God as He raised Him from the dead, I wonder if the pressure of the thorn in Paul's life was a reminder of the power of the cross. Did it remind Paul that Jesus went down to the place of absolute weakness, and that God raised Him up to the throne? I wonder if at the very moment when Paul became aware of severest pressure, if he also became aware of the presence of God in Jesus Christ, who Himself had been weak but was raised up to the place of all power.

Herein lies a mystery, because Paul says, "...there was given to me a thorn in the flesh, the messenger of Satan to buffet me..." But I am sure of this, that in every thorn and in every pressure like this, God and the devil are both equally concerned. If God gives it, Satan seeks to distort it; if Satan gives it, then the Lord seeks to sanctify it. If the pressure stems from

458 / BLESSINGS OUT OF BUFFETINGS

heaven, Satan will seek to make it the opportunity to destroy it, whereas God sends it to prove us. It seems here that the very weapon which was the messenger of Satan, by which he was planning to overthrow the apostle, was seized out of his hands and turned into a weapon to overthrow him.

When Satan sent that thorn to buffet, his desire was that the old nature might express itself and be stimulated and roused into sinful action by it. The pressure continues, and Satan watches to see that it might be the means of rousing the self-life and the flesh into rebellion against the will of God. That is why it is called Satan's messenger. But when Satan sent that trial to buffet Paul, he found that all it did, in fact, was to drive Paul to a new depth of trust and obedience and faith in God; and the pressure of the thorn and the power of Calvary became completely bound up together so that Paul could say, "…when I am weak, then I am strong."

Unseen by you, the Lord Jesus watches His children, and He does not take the pressure off. He intends it to remain, all the rest of your life probably. He does not intend it to go. He watches your reactions, and so does Satan. The pressure is there in the mind of the devil that he might drive the self-life into action that will prove sinful. The Lord Jesus watches because He allows the pressure to continue in order that, in the severest moment of testing, it may drive you to His wounded side, and teach you that for overwhelming pressure there is adequate grace. Oh, would it not be wonderful if that experience could be yours today! Stop praying for the removal of the thorn, and understand the transforming power of the cross!

Lastly, there is the transformation of misery into happiness: "Most gladly therefore would I rather glory in my infirmities, that the power of Christ may rest upon me." I am so thankful, he says, for this thing that keeps me humble and dependent as God's trusting and believing child. I am so glad of it all, for if God does grant me blessing and success in any measure, it drives me constantly back to Him.

Are you a dear child of God for whom the sunshine has departed from your life recently? Do you want it back? Life has become so hard and drab, so dry and uninteresting. Ah, but there was nothing lovely about the cross and the crown of thorns that God gave to the Lord Jesus, and I am sure there is nothing lovely about the thorn that you have either. The cross seems so cruel and so dreadful. Your trial is all that, I am sure, almost too much to bear. But you notice Paul says, "…there was *given* to me…"—all the time I have been trying to thrust it away while the Lord has been handing it back to me, putting it on His hand and saying, "Take it, My child, this is from Me."

In Psalm 106:15 we read a tremendous statement: "…he gave them their request; but sent leanness into their soul." If you keep saying, "Lord, take the thorn away!" and you refuse to submit to the discipline of it, then maybe He will do that very thing and send leanness to your soul. God forbid!

An old saint of God once prayed, "Lord, when wilt Thou cease to strew my path with trials and thorns?" The Lord answered him, "My child, that is how I prove My friends." The saint replied, "Lord, perhaps that is why You have so few of them." Yes, that may be the very reason. How often we seek to get from under the pressure, out of the will of God, when all the time He is holding out His hand and saying, "Take this thorn from Me."

When I was small, I used to get Christmas presents from my parents. Some of them I liked, others I disliked. I liked electric trains, kites, a toboggan, and interesting things like these. But how I hated getting a pair of gloves—fancy a pair of gloves for a boy at Christmas! What an infliction! But these were the useful things, and the thorn in the mind of the Lord is the gift that is useful, that is necessary when it comes from Him. The Lord Jesus holds out His hand of love and says, "Here is the thorn, My child. Will you lift up your hand tremblingly, yet in faith and accept it?" Look up as Jesus did when He said, "Father, not my will but thine be done."

A Sunday school child asked her teacher why it was that when the Lord Jesus came three times to His disciples in the garden and said, "Watch and pray," the third time He did not say that; He just said, "Sleep on and take your rest." The teacher was quite baffled to know the answer, and then the little child said to her, "I think I know. It was because Jesus had seen the face of His Father, and He didn't need their help any more!"

I trust that you have now by faith looked into the face of your heavenly Father, and are saying, "Most gladly will I glory in my infirmities!" At that moment you will begin to rejoice in the ministry of the thorn, and to see God's glorious purpose for it, for while He is prodigal in His riches of grace, He does not send any affliction unnecessarily to those He loves.

CHAPTER TWENTY-TWO

GOD'S ULTIMATE AIM

2 CORINTHIANS 12:11–21

This is indeed a fascinating and challenging Epistle, for as we have reminded each other more than once in the course of studying it, in no other letter does Paul open his heart so completely as he does here, to reveal all that was involved to him in being a minister of the gospel or, if you like, a missionary. He tells us in this chapter, if you will allow me to paraphrase, that he almost feels he has made a fool of himself in boasting of all his experiences, but the Corinthian Christians have forced him into it! Instead of defending and standing by him, they had questioned the authority of his ministry. They had challenged the authenticity of what he had to say. They had even been questioning what right he had to speak to them as he did. "So," says Paul, in effect, "I have been forced to show you that though I am only a nobody, I am in fact not a little bit behind the very greatest of the apostles" (v. 11). To prove that he reminds them that they had seen in him a demonstration of the power of God given to all His true ministers in miracles, signs, and spiritual authority. It is interesting that the greatest evidence that Paul brought to the Corinthian church for the reality and genuineness of his life was his patience, and this they had seen with their own eyes.

Now he has just one last appeal to make to the church at Corinth which will succeed, perhaps, if nothing else has succeeded, in disarming their suspicion of him and winning their confidence. Again to paraphrase, "You must forgive me," he says, "if, because I have taken no money from you, I have made you feel inferior to other churches" (v. 13). Then, "But even though I have taken nothing from you, you thought I was being crafty, even though you questioned my motive and you thought I was taking you by guile. But did I make any profit out of Titus, who came to speak to you, or the brother I sent with him? They acted towards you in exactly the same spirit as I have done, and you want to know why I have behaved like this in my ministry, and why it is that I have acted toward you in this way. Let me tell you. I have done it to prove to you that I seek not yours but you. In other words, in all my life and ministry I have no extraneous motives. I will gladly spend and be spent for you. In my ministry there is no limit to my expendability, and no reward expected for my services" (v. 16).

So in perhaps what is the climax of the whole principle of this tremendous letter, Paul opens his heart completely, and we see laid bare before us the selflessness of a man of God, which is indeed a copy, a high standard, for all of God's servants for all time.

However, we have not come to magnify Paul, but to magnify Christ. Paul is only a faint shadow of the Lord Jesus; and if these qualities are found in his life, it is only because they were found completely in the life of Jesus Christ our Lord. My concern, therefore, is that you should see these tremendous statements with which Paul bares his heart to them: "...I seek not yours, but you ... I will very gladly spend and be spent for you; though the more abundantly I love you, the less I be loved." I trust that you will see those statements as God's goal for your life, as God's grace in your heart, as God's glory in your service.

Consider, first, God's great goal for your life. Our theme, you will recall, has been *Blessings Out of Buffetings*, and that is the principle which Paul has been revealing, the things which God has been doing with him in order that He might bring Paul to this place in his experience where he is completely selfless. This was God's goal—and it is God's goal for you and for me—so that Paul was able to say in relation to his ministry, "...I am ready to come to you. ..."

In all the buffetings through which you and I have passed in life—and who is there today who has not experienced some that are inexplicable—what is God aiming at? What has God been doing? What has He been trying to say to us? Though we have often been so slow to listen, what is His goal for my life and yours? Surely it is to enable us to say in relation to our service and in relation to Him, "I am ready to come to you." You are ready, not because of your academic qualifications, but because God has brought you through many shattering experiences in life to a place of utter selflessness. When He has brought you there, you can truly say in relation to your testimony, "I seek not yours but you." In other words, as Oswald Chambers puts it in a portion from *My Utmost for His Highest*: "When the Spirit of God has shed abroad the love of God in our hearts, we begin deliberately to identify ourselves with Jesus Christ's interests in other people, and Jesus Christ is interested in every kind of man there is. We have no right in Christian work to be guided by our affinities; this is one of the biggest tests of our relationship to Jesus Christ." Your interest in another individual is to be centered in what is Christ's interest in them.

"I desire nothing from you," says Paul, in effect, "I do not want your money, your things, or your gifts; I want you. I am ready to come to you; and I am ready because God has brought me to this place of selflessness. My only motive is to lay down my life like a rug at the feet of the Lord Jesus that you may walk upon it and do what you like with me, if only the will of God may be wrought out in your life. I have become all things to all men that by all means I might win some." So this great apostle, this tremendous Christian, has learned to live sacramentally as broken bread and poured out wine, and again quoting Oswald Chambers, "so that Jesus Christ can help Himself to my life at any moment for any purpose."

The goal of God has no extraneous motives, "...I seek not yours but you. ..." Being abandoned completely to the Lord Jesus He has no end of his own to serve the goal of God. Also, it has no limits to our expendability: "...very gladly [rather] I will spend and be spent for you. ..." In other words, in relation to your sphere of Christian testimony, your time, strength, interest, everything is absolutely at the disposal of others. "I will spend it all for you." Indeed, I will do it to such an extent that not only will I spend, but I will be spent as a candle which is lit and gives out light, but in order to give out the light it consumes itself in the interest of bringing light to others until there comes a moment when it splutters for the last time and is extinct. I will gladly spend and be spent for you like that.

Paul went so far as to say, writing to the church at Rome: "...I could wish myself accursed from Christ for my brethren..." (Romans 9:3). He would rather go to hell than see them lost. Extravagant and fanatical language? Oh, no! The buffeting of life, the sentence of death upon himself over and over again, the affliction through which he had passed, all these things demonstrate that this man was passionate and governed by one tremendous, moving power within his heart and life which enabled him to face another Christian and say, in effect, "I am just here in order that Christ's interests in your life might be fulfilled. I have no other concern than that."

No limits to expendability, no extraneous motives, and no reward except, says Paul, "...the more abundantly I love you, the less I be loved." In other words, I do not expect anything in return; I do not care what you think about me too much, whether you like me or not. I will spend and be spent, though the more abundantly I love you, the less I am loved in return. I will deprive myself of anything if only I can get you through to God.

There was no question in Paul's mind concerning salary. He does not ask, what about social security? What about furlough? What about climate? What if I don't get married? What if I go through life and face old age alone, what shall I do then? After all, you have to think about these things! No, there were no reservations in Paul's mind. He had learned the word of his Lord, "He that would be the greatest among you, let him be the servant of all."

God's goal in this man's life was accomplished and achieved because he found that through all the buffetings he was being brought to a place where he was absolutely selfless, and he could say, "I am ready." I would say to any young people who are planning on offering to a missionary society, for the home ministry, or perhaps to serve in some capacity in your church, and who may say, "I am ready to come to you"—are you?

"Oh, yes," you say, "because I have been to university or Bible college and I have my degree. Of course I am ready!"

Are you? I am sure that all of these things will stand you in good stead and usefulness, but if you dare to go to the mission field or into the ministry and you have some other motive, some extraneous desire, if you put some limit upon your expendability, and you are expecting some reward, you are not ready. For it is in a life which has been made so utterly selfless as this that the Lord Jesus sees of the travail of His soul and is satisfied.

Today, when people think about missionary service, they ask what provision is made for retirement and furlough, what percentage will be set aside for travel, what percentage will be available for them when they come home. They want to be sure they have all the equipment and necessities. Such, however, is not God's goal for their lives.

Observe now God's grace in your heart. I wonder how Paul had become so passionate and selfless. We have to admit that we have failed here and must hang our heads. Why was Paul like this? It was because one little drop from an infinite ocean of love had entered his heart, one little spark from a fire that had its source in the very heart of God had kindled a flame within him, one echo of the voice of Jesus Christ was heard by him: that was all.

I am suggesting to you that these words would never have been uttered by Paul if they had not first of all been the Savior's words, and He says to you, "I am ready to come to you: I am ready, because one day I stepped out of heaven to a manger and poverty. I am ready, because I lived a life that was utterly in obedience to My heavenly Father with no rival claim at all. I am ready to come to you because I triumphed in every place where you failed. I am ready because I went through the garden of Gethsemane, because I endured the buffeting, the spitting, the shame. I am ready because they took Me up a green hill outside a city wall and nailed Me to a cross, where I paid the price to the limit. I am ready because they laid Me in a tomb, but the third day I arose from the dead and ascended into heaven, and today I am seated at the right hand of My Father in the place of all power and authority. Because of all these things I am ready to come to you, but I seek not yours, but you. I am not after your talents or your gifts, or your service primarily. I can do nothing with any of these things until first of all I have you."

The heart of God is only satisfied when we give our whole selves to Him just as we are, so that He might lavish Himself upon us. "…I seek … you." I wish that word *you* would grip the heart of someone with all sorts of emotional and moral problems, tempted by sin and evil, beset by psychological problems and every problem under the sun. You say you have given Christ your service, your gifts, your talents, but you have never given Him *you*. Perhaps you have been too ashamed to give Him yourself. The wonderful marvel of the grace of God to your heart is that Jesus wants to have *you*, with all your problems, your failures and defeats, with everything that He knows about only too well, and about which He can do literally nothing until He has *you*. He does not want a part of you, while the tyrant of self is left undisturbed deep down on the throne of your life. He wants all of you, so that you may say, "…I live, yet not I, but Christ liveth in me …" That is God's goal for your life, and He will use a thousand experiences, buffetings, sadnesses, tragedies, disappointments, disillusionments, until there comes a moment when you answer His cry, "I seek not yours, but *you*"!

I am fearful for so many people who imagine they are serving the Lord when they have given Him their voice, or their talents or abilities, even their pocket books, but have never given themselves to Him. Not merely has the Lord no extraneous motives in relation to your life, but there is no limit to His expendability. He says, "...I will very gladly spend and be spent for you. ..." Hear Him say that to you today: "I want you for My instrument, My tool, to get My will done on earth as it is in heaven. I want you in order that you may be used to establish My rule in the hearts of other people. I will place all My resources at your disposal in order that this may be accomplished. I will most gladly spend and be spent for you."

If only He can get you, then it will be no more a vain effort to flog an idle Christian into His service and get him moving. It will be to discover that in being possessed by Christ you are empowered by Him, and that emptiness in your life will be filled up with a great moving tide. It was that principle that enabled Paul to say, "...I also labour, striving according to his working, which worketh in me mightily" (Colossians 1:29).

May the Word of God come to you like a sword from heaven as He says, "My child, I want not yours, but I want *you*. There is no limit to My expendability, and furthermore, I have no expectation of reward, though the more abundantly I love you, the less I be loved." No coldness of heart on our part, no lethargy, no indifference ever quenches the flame of love in the heart of Jesus Christ for His children. That is the grace of God, that He might be all that to you.

Finally, there is here the glory of God in your service. I doubt whether Paul could ever have said all that to the Corinthian church—or to anybody else for that matter. He could never have lived on this principle of expendability, he could never have satisfied the heart of God unless this was not merely the echo of what he had heard Jesus say to him, but his response in just those words to the Lord Jesus Himself.

Here is the heart of the whole matter. God's goal in your life is not only to get you living sacramentally with no extraneous motive, no limit to your availability, no expectation of reward (for He knows this is only possible when the Holy Spirit shows you this principle upon which Jesus is available for your life), but He waits for the day when He hears you say this very thing in answer to the grace of the Lord, "Lord Jesus, I am ready to come to You!"

Are you ready to come to Him today? Why? "Because, Lord Jesus, I seek not Yours, but You! It is not now the gift, but the Giver. It is not now the blessing, but the Blesser. It is not the joy, but it is You Yourself, Lord. I am not concerned about gifts, but I cannot live without You, and You have said to my heart, 'I do not want yours but I want you — and I am answering now.' Lord Jesus, I do not want Your gifts, I want You as a living, loving Savior who will step into my life and keep me day by day, sheltering me from all the attacks of the enemy, and dealing with this strange, wretched me, of which I am so sick."

Perhaps for the first time there is no extraneous motive, for you are not looking at the Word or in the face of Christ today because of something you can get out of Him. You are looking not for blessing only, something you can get from Jesus. Your heart is lonely, defeated, sad, beset with so many problems and difficulties, therefore you want only Jesus Himself.

Perhaps for the first time you have put no limits upon your expendability. You are willing to spend and be spent for Him, and you are not going to discuss terms any more with the Lord. For the first time you do not expect any reward for such devotion though, "…the more abundantly I love, the less I be loved." You may lose many friends who will not understand, perhaps some of them very dear friends, but you will not put any reservations there. Has the Lord ever heard you say these things to Him?

CHAPTER TWENTY-THREE

The Peril of Self-Deception

2 Corinthians 13:1–14

In our studies of 2 Corinthians we have purposely made no attempt to analyze it. As a matter of fact, in a very real sense this letter more than any other of Paul's defies analysis, because it is simply the outpouring of a man's heart, and that runs away from analysis. It is like the breaking up of a fountain. Whereas 1 Corinthians was an objective and practical letter, this one has been subjective and personal. First Corinthians was a deliberate approach to a subject; 2 Corinthians is a passionate appeal.

Our concern in studying it has been to catch all that we can of the fire that burned in Paul's heart, and to learn his spiritual secret. It was in the midst of so much buffeting that he became a channel of blessing. As we come to the close of the letter, I remind you of some background facts against which Paul makes this final appeal.

In the first place, Corinth was a city in Greece which was a Roman colony with a very mixed population: Jews, Greeks, Romans, Asiatics, Phoenicians, to mention a few. A great expositor of Scripture, Farrar, has called it the "Vanity Fair" of the Roman Empire. It was famous for its wisdom and its wealth. It was also famous for its luxury and its license. In a very real sense, Corinth in the first century has its equivalent in the twentieth century in New York, Chicago, London, or Paris, where you have great centers of population, areas of people from different kinds of situations and backgrounds.

The church at Corinth, as you would read in Acts 18, was established by Paul, and it was composed mainly of the poorer and more unlearned people in Corinth (1 Corinthians 1:26–29). It was not by accident that God had done this. It was the purpose of God, and He had chosen such people in order that through them might be demonstrated a principle of life in the midst of all the philosophy and learning and wisdom of Corinth, that no flesh might glory in His presence. These were the people who had received Paul's two letters.

The first letter to the church at Corinth gives an indication of the condition and the character of the church, but Paul's second letter was a tremendous revelation of the life and character of Paul himself. The first letter exposed the wounds of sin, but the second letter tells us what it cost a man of God when he set about trying to heal the wounds. That is the distinction.

There is one outstanding thing that you cannot escape if you read this letter through carefully: it is the tremendous change in the tone between the first nine chapters and the last four chapters. In the first nine chapters Paul is writing with a wonderful sense of warmth, comfort, thanksgiving, and a sort of conciliatory attitude; but in the last four chapters, he is sad and severe again. Many reasons are suggested for this, but I think the exact one would be that in this church, as in most churches anywhere, there is a majority party and a minority party.

Titus had brought the message of the condition of the church that gave Paul much gladness: "Nevertheless God, that comforteth those that are cast down, comforted us by the coming of Titus; And not by his coming only, but by the consolation wherewith he was comforted in you, when he told us your earnest desire, your mourning, your fervent mind toward me; so that I rejoiced the more. For though I made you sorry with a letter, I do not repent, though I did repent: for I perceive that the same epistle hath made you sorry, though it were but for a season. Now I rejoice, not that ye were made sorry, but that ye sorrowed to repentance:…" (2 Corinthians 7:6–9). And so Paul was made glad because the majority of the church at Corinth had been chastened by his first letter, had responded to his message, had truly repented and turned to the Lord.

But there were some who had not, and they were showing it by attacking Paul's ministry. "For if he that cometh preacheth another Jesus, whom we have not preached, or if ye receive another spirit, which ye have not received, or another gospel, which ye have not accepted, ye might well bear with him. For I suppose I was not a whit behind the very chiefest apostles" (2 Corinthians 11:4–5).

There was a minority group in the church, from which Paul had suffered severe buffeting, for they had never truly taken his message to their own hearts, and now they spent their time attacking him. It seems to me that the first nine chapters of this letter were written to the majority, and the last four were written to the minority who were accusing him.

Notice some of the things of which they were accusing him. They said that "...his bodily presence is weak, and his speech contemptible" (chapter 10:10). "Though I be rude in speech, yet not in knowledge" (chapter 11:6): they were accusing him of being rough and uncultured in his speech. They even accused him of being insane: "I say again, Let no man think me a fool; if otherwise, yet as a fool receive me, that I may boast myself a little" (chapter 11:16). They are accusing him of dishonesty: "But be it so, I did not burden you: nevertheless, being crafty, I caught you with guile" (chapter 12:16).

That is just a little of the buffeting this man of God had taken from the church at Corinth. He was accused of weakness, of roughness of speech, of insanity, of being contemptible in appearance, of being no apostle, and even of being dishonest.

Therefore we come now to consider his final appeal and vindication of his own ministry. His appeal was to those who would examine him, "Examine yourselves, whether ye be in the faith; prove your own selves." In verse 3 you see the context: "...ye seek a proof of Christ speaking in me,..." all right, examine yourselves whether you be in the faith. Consider his vindication of his own ministry: "For we also are weak in him, but we shall live with him by the power of God toward you" (v. 4).

I have taken time to say all that with a definite purpose, because I firmly believe that in this twentieth century counterpart of Corinth in which we live, we are in very serious danger of falling into the same trap and the same peril of self-deception which threatened disaster to the minority group in the church at Corinth. While we are very careful in criticizing and examining the viewpoint of others in theological and other matters, we very often fail to allow the searchlight of God's Word to probe our own hearts, and we are greatly in need of this same injunction, "Examine yourselves, whether ye be in the faith. ..."

Furthermore, this objective criticism, which we direct anywhere except to our own heart, is apt to give us a completely false idea of the real standard of Christian discipleship by which Paul vindicated his own ministry. You want the evidence of reality and authority in me, Paul says in effect; very well, we are weak in Christ, but we shall live with Him in the power of God toward you. All thought that would avoid any possibility of self-deception is in this phrase: "Know ye not your own selves, how that Jesus Christ is in you, except ye be reprobates?"

That is the standard: Jesus Christ is in you; and the vindication of his own ministry was in taking them back to the cross, when he reminds the Corinthian Christians that Jesus, though crucified in weakness, was raised by the power of God. Paul opened his heart to show them that through all the buffetings of his life, he had been made utterly weak, until he came to the point where he had no confidence in the flesh, for no flesh shall glory in the presence of God. He had accepted that principle, and therefore found that he had been raised up in the power of God. "…Most gladly therefore will I rather glory in my infirmities, that the power of Christ may rest upon me" (chapter 12:9).

We have this great appeal now for self-examination, in order that we might avoid the peril of self-deception and at the same time demonstrate the reality of our testimony. I realize that this is an unpopular subject, but I come to it with a deep conviction of its necessity, so I would elaborate upon the need for self-examination. In 1 Corinthians 11 Paul spoke about the Lord's table and preparing for the breaking of bread: "But let a man examine himself, and so let him eat of that bread, and drink of that cup … For if we would judge ourselves, we should not be judged" (vv. 28, 31).

Therefore before breaking bread together, and also at other times, it is appropriate that we spend time in what the Book calls self-examination, because I am sure that a great number of professing Christians are living in self-deception, assuming that because externally things are more or less all right with them in their lives, then everything else can be taken for granted. They have a sound doctrinal basis of faith, their lives are lived more or less righteously, they are not conscious that anything is particularly wrong, but as Paul says here, if Christ is not in you, then there is nothing in you whereby you will be approved of God.

I am concerned not only about outward conduct but inward life. The question I ask my own heart in the presence of God is, Am I in the faith?

Is Christ living in me? Is there any evidence of reality? How important that is!

A ship is very carefully examined before it is put out to sea, both before and after launching. After launching it goes through trials, and it has quite a period before it is entrusted with passengers and cargo. So Paul says, in effect, "Examine yourselves, but not only that, prove yourselves." That word *prove* is a stronger word still.

Some people's religion will stand a bit of examination, but when their religion comes into daily life, it fails to pass the test, it does not prove itself adequate. The objective test of matters of doctrine with which so many are satisfied these days is just inadequate. Now no one would give second place to me concerning the necessity for correctness of creed, for a sound, fundamental, scriptural approach to all matters in life; but I would say that an objective test which merely submits myself to a statement of creed is not adequate, because I am not saved by a statement of creed. I am saved by a step of commitment of my life to Jesus Christ as Lord. Therefore it behooves me to examine myself.

I remind you that the Puritans recognized the need of this, and made provision for it. They believed in being much alone with God and surveying their lives in His presence with an unsparing scrutiny. I was reading of the members of the Holy Club in Oxford in John Wesley's day, who examined themselves every Sunday on the love of God and the simplicity of their faith; on Monday, they examined themselves on their love toward their fellowmen, and submitted themselves to twenty-seven questions; and so on throughout the week. Here are some of the questions, which I use in my own life, at least once a week, and often every day.

> Am I consciously or unconsciously creating the impression that I am a better man than I really am? In other words, am I a hypocrite?
> Am I honest in all my acts or words, or do I exaggerate?
> Do I confidentially pass on to another what was told to me in confidence?
> Can I be trusted?
> Am I a slave to dress, friends, work, or habits?
> Am I self-conscious, self-pitying, or self-justifying?
> Did the Bible live to me today?
> Do I give it time to speak to me every day?

Am I enjoying prayer?

When did I last speak to somebody else with the object of trying to win that person for Christ?

Am I making contacts with other people and using them for the Master's glory?

Do I pray about the money I spend?

Do I get to bed in time and get up in time?

Do I disobey God in anything?

Do I insist upon doing something about which my conscience is uneasy?

Am I defeated in any part of my life: jealous, impure, critical, irritable, touchy, or distrustful?

How do I spend my spare time?

Am I proud?

Do I thank God that I am not as other people, especially as the Pharisees who despised the publican?

Is there anybody whom I fear, dislike, disown, criticize, hold resentment toward, or disregard? If so, what am I doing about it?

Do I grumble or complain constantly?

Is Christ real to me?

Do these questions find you out, and make you angry or resentful? They come straight to you from John Wesley and the Puritans of two hundred years ago. That kind of self-examination has gone right out of our Christian living. I use these tests in my own heart because I find them necessary, and those who are most neglectful to use them are the people who are always the most quick to criticize others. That was the trouble at Corinth. They criticized Paul and failed to examine themselves.

The great question for us to settle today is, Am I in the faith? Is Christ in me? Have I come to Him as a sinner and pleaded for His mercy through the blood of His cross? Am I living by faith in Him? Am I receiving from His fullness grace upon grace? Does my life prove it? As I have said before, an unholy life is merely the evidence of an unchanged heart, and an unchanged heart is the evidence of an unsaved soul. What value is there in the kind of grace which makes us no different from what we were before? None at all.

It would be a good thing if you were to keep a copy of these questions and use them personally in your own life. I think you would find prayer would be an uncomfortable thing until your heart was made tender. Someone will say to me, "This is too morbid! Surely as a Christian I must never look into myself, but I must look up." True! The statement is made, "For every look within, take ten long looks at Christ."

Let me say a further word about the secret of self-examination, lest you get me wrong. This is given to us in Psalm 139: 23–24, "Search me, O God, and know my heart: try me, and know my thoughts: And see if there be any wicked way in me…" In other words, this self-examination is not something that I can do myself, but something which only God can do, and to attempt it without the Holy Spirit's guiding and enabling is indeed to lead to a morbid introspection and ultimately to psychological help in care and treatment. This is what happens to so many people, simply because of morbid introspection, but this is totally different.

In the kind of thing I am talking to you about a man is not looking for sin, he is looking for Jesus. He is not looking for evil—he does not have to look far for that for he knows that in the flesh dwelleth no good thing—but he is searching within his heart for evidences of indwelling Holy Spirit life. Ah, there are tokens within that Christ is in him by His Spirit as a living power, and because He is there, He is dealing with all these things.

To examine yourself, in fact, is to submit to the examination and scrutiny of Jesus Christ the Lord—and this is never to fix attention on sin but on Christ—and to ask Him to reveal that in you which grieves His Spirit; to ask Him to give you grace that it might be put away and cleansed in His precious blood. It is to search within your heart for the sense of His peace, His forgiveness, His cleansing, His presence. When these qualities are lacking and you cannot find them, you ask Him to point out where you have gone wrong, where the cloud has come between yourself and your Savior, and to show the way to you so that fellowship might be restored.

It is self-examination that keeps the heart tender. It is self-examination which keeps the will submissive. It is self-examination which keeps the mind open to the leading of the Spirit of God. Spurgeon once said about another preacher, who was known for his freshness and life, his power and authority, "Do you know, that man lives so near the gate of heaven that he hears a great many things that we don't get to hear because we don't live near enough." May I say that is exactly what self-examination does. It takes the chill away from your soul, it takes the hardness away from your heart, it takes the shadows away from your life, it sets the prisoner free.

Have you submitted yourself in the presence of God to self-examination lately? That is how to come to the Lord's table; before you ever come into the house of God early in the morning, set your heart open before God and ask Him to search your heart. Have you done that recently? That is how revival breaks out in church. That is how it broke out in Ruanda, and how it has been maintained all through the years. There must be an openness in my dealings with Him and in my dealings with fellow-Christians; that is the secret of self-examination.

What is the standard of this self-examination? What is our goal in this? Paul goes right back to the cross to prove the reality of his apostleship. "...Though he was crucified through weakness, yet he liveth by the power of God. For we also are weak in him, but we shall live with him by the power of God toward you" (v. 4). Here is the apostle vindicating his own apostleship, testifying to the reality of his own witness and his own Christian life; here he is summing up all that it has meant to him to seek to heal the wounds. He goes back to Calvary. That is where you want to be.

Paul says concerning the Lord Jesus, "...He was crucified through weakness..." Ah, yes indeed, and such was the extremity of His weakness that He died under it. He made no use of His divine strength at all. He gave Himself over to His enemies to be crucified and slain and His crucifixion was the greatest display of weakness that this world has ever witnessed. Yet He was raised again from the dead by the power of God. Here is the principle: in the absolute extremity of the weakness of our Savior, power came to Him from another quarter altogether.

So Paul says the ultimate standard of reality is at Calvary, at the place of human weakness, of utter submission, the place where that is all met by the mighty power of God. That was the standard and reality of Paul's testimony. It seemed he had been overcome by his enemies, and had been powerless in their hands, yet in that weakness he too revealed the power of God, "For we also are weak in him, but we shall live with him by the power of God toward you." This ties up with the first chapter of his first letter, in which Paul reminds the Corinthian church that there were not many mighty and not many wise called. But you see, no flesh is to glory in His presence. This is the principle of the Christian life, the reality and evidence of it: "But of him are ye in Christ Jesus, who of God is made unto us wisdom, and righteousness, and sanctification, and redemption" (1 Corinthians 1:30).

Paul has told the story of buffeting to the Corinthian church and to no one else. He did not tell it to Luke (if he had, Luke would have recorded it in the Acts of the Apostles), but he opened his heart to the people who challenged his authority at every point, to prove to them that in submission to all the buffeting he has demonstrated that the Spirit of God was in him, and because that was so, He had raised Paul up, and was working mightily through him. Just as in that human body Jesus became so weak and suffered and was buffeted to be raised by the power of God, so Paul in submission to all the buffeting has found exactly the same experience.

Examine yourselves, whether you be in the faith. Here is the ultimate standard, the plumbline for every one of us. How have you reacted in your immediate circle of witness? What happens when you have been buffeted? Is the procedure and growth of your Christian life marked by a progressively increasing sense of weakness in yourself, so emptied of every trace of self-esteem and self-confidence that you find yourself being raised up by the power of God? Do you seek to be a blessing in your area? Do you seek to heal the wounds in some circle of Christian witness, on a mission field, in a Sunday school, in a church, somewhere in your immediate situation?

The Christian, if he is real, will always seek to heal the wounds, but as he does so he discovers that they are healed by the acceptance of the buffetings to such a point that he is brought right back to the cross where he is able at last to know that the words of Galatians 2:20 are not a theory but are real: "I am crucified with Christ: nevertheless, I live; yet not I, but Christ liveth in me: and the life which I now live in the flesh I live by the faith of the Son of God, who loved me, and gave himself for me."

Examine yourselves. Prove yourselves. "Know ye not your own selves that Jesus Christ is in you, except ye be reprobate?" And if He is in you, then His strength is being perfected when you come to that place where, in yourself, you are utterly weak. That is the whole principle of First and Second Corinthians. That is the reason why Paul wrote to demonstrate this great principle of Christian life, so that the church for all its history

478 / B<small>LESSINGS</small> O<small>UT OF</small> B<small>UFFETINGS</small>

might know that it is "not by might, nor by power, but by my Spirit"; so the church may answer all the philosophy in any generation, all the wealth and all the wisdom, all the luxury and all the license. We may combat these things not on that level, but by apparently being knocked down to a point of weakness only to discover that we are raised up by the power of God to demonstrate His indwelling life. Is that your experience? May God help us to submit ourselves to self-examination in the power of His Spirit.

Also by Alan Redpath...

VICTORIOUS CHRISTIAN LIVING
ISBN: 978-1-59751-022-6
Retail: $12.99

Studies in the Book of Joshua

The emphasis in the book of Joshua is to move us beyond conversion into the land of the promise of *Victorious Christian Living*.

VICTORIOUS CHRISTIAN SERVICE
ISBN: 978-1-59751-009-7
Retail: $12.99

Studies in the Book of Nehemiah

As we join Nehemiah in his journey to reconstruct the walls of Jerusalem, we will learn lessons that will compel us as God's people to *Victorious Christian Service*.

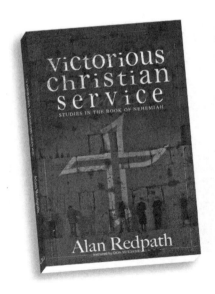

Retail orders, contact:
The Word for Today
www.twft.com
800-272-9673

Wholesale orders, contact:
Calvary Distribution
www.calvaryd.org
800-444-7664